COMPENDIUM OF LAWS
UNDER THE NIGERIAN LEGAL SYSTEM

First Edition

Published by

MAIYATI CHAMBERS

Edited by
ABUBAKAR SADIQ OGWUCHE
with a foreword by **Justice M.B. Belgore**

Printed and bound in Great Britain by
Creative Print and Design (Wales), Ebbw Vale
ISBN 9-7805661-71

Abubakar Sadiq Ogwuche

Maiyati Chambers
(Solicitors & Advocates)

310A Badagry Road, Dolphin Estate, P.O. Box 54209, Ikoyi, Lagos, Nigeria

Tel/Fax: 01-2691359

E-mail: maiyati@infoweb.abs.net

Foreword

I have witnessed the agonising experiences of persons who deal with case laws. Some have had to wade in vain, through a great number of cases, piles of law reports and textbooks in search of authorities to support a simple submission. This Compendium of Laws lessens such a problem. The Compendium with some of the leading cases on various branches of law is a good pointer to where details of these authorities can be located.

The Compendium is a thorough work as a result of much research, and it is recommended to law lecturers, legal practitioners, students and persons associated with the law as a quick reference point.

I praise the authors of the Compendium for great effort put forward. They deserve our recognition by making this Compendium a handy companion.

Justice M.B. Belgore

Former Chief Judge
Federal High Court,
31 Cameron Road,
Ikoyi, Lagos, Nigeria.

Preface

The main object of *Compendium of Laws* is to provide legal practitioners, judges, law lecturers, law students and persons associated with the law easy and quick access to case laws. It is also intended to be a readily available means of acquiring legal knowledge by members of the public with respect to their legal rights and duties in a democratic society.

It is important to note that the aim of this work is to espouse important principles of law derived from and based upon sound, current and established authorities. It did not, neither does it intend to, create new laws. The principles in this Compendium are thus abstractions from decided cases encompassing all branches of Nigerian Law. In addition, it contains well established principles derived from decided cases in other legal jurisdictions. It is hoped that these foreign principles will be considered as persuasive authorities in situations where there are no established Nigerian authorities.

The Compendium is a product of experienced legal practitioners and academicians whose combined intellectual labour power gave this work its peculiar feature. Thus, it is a product of a highly dedicated and innovative team. Due credit must be given to the individual members of the team namely, *Abubakar Sadiq Ogwuche, Olujimi Adeoye Osho* and *Chika Nwego Nnoli*.

We have attempted to state the laws as they were as at 31st December 2001. We are conscious of the fact that in a work covering so much ground, errors may be found. We shall be grateful to be informed of such errors and any other useful observation. The errors and observation, if any, will be given due attention in subsequent editions.

It is important at this point to express profound gratitude to our Secretary, *Stella Nneka Eboh*, without whose invaluable assistance we could not have hoped to produce this text.

Special thanks also go to *General Aliyu Mohammed (rtd)* of the *Presidency, Abuja* and *Mrs Gwen Fairer-Smith* of *Argen Limited, London* for their unflinching support and assistance.

PROFESSOR AMECHI UCHEGBU
Department of International Law & Jurisprudence,
Faculty of Law, University of Lagos, Akoka, Lagos, Nigeria.

 # Acknowledgment

W e are indebted to, among others, the following authors whose Law Reports, Journals and Books, we found very helpful and made use of in the course of this work.

Chief Fawehinmi, Gani: *Nigerian Weekly Law Reports (N.W.L.R.)*

Babatunde, Layi Esq.: *Judgments of the Supreme Court of Nigeria*

Falana, Femi Esq.: *Weekly Law Reports (W.L.R.)*

Dan-Musa, M.A. Esq.: *Islamic Law Reports (I.L.R.)*

Nemieboka, I.A. Esq.: *The Nigerian Independent Law Reports (N.I.L.R.) 1996*

Jimoh, A.A. Esq.: *Modern Practice Journal of Finance and Investment, Vol. 4 No. 3, July 2000*

Ojo, A.: *Constitutional Law and Military Rule in Nigeria, 1987*

Kodilinye and Aluko: *The Nigerian Law of Torts (2nd ed. 1999)*

Aguda, T.A.: *The Criminal Law and Procedure of the Southern States of Nigeria (3rd ed. 1982)*

Etikerentse, G.: *Nigerian Petroleum Law, 1985*

Akanki, E.O.: *Essays on Company Law, 1992*

Sagay, I.E.: *Nigerian Law of Contract (2nd ed. 2000)*

Smith, I.O.: *Nigerian Law of Secured Credit, 2001*

Harris, D.J.: *Cases and Materials on International Law (5th ed. 1998)*

Oppenheim: *Oppenheim's International Law (9th ed. 1992, Vol. 1)*

Brown, E.D.: *The International Law of the Sea, 1994: Vols. 1 & II*

Maclean, R.: *Public International Law Textbook (15th ed. 1993)*

Schwazenberger, G.: *International Law Volume II: The Law of Armed Conflict (1968)*

Ivamy Hardy, E.R.: *General Principles of Insurance Law (5th ed. 1986)*

Holden, J.M.: *The Law and Practice of Banking (5th ed. Vol. I. 1991)*

Davies, M.: *Textbook on Medical Law (2nd ed. 1998)*

Northey, J.F.: *Introduction to Company Law (4th ed. 1987)*

Tapper, C.: *Computer Law* (4th ed. 1989)

The Right Honourable, Lord Hailsham of St. Marylebone: *Halsbury's Laws of England* (4th ed. 1973-1987)

Ministry of Defence, United Kingdom: *Manual of Military Law* Part 1 (12th ed. 1996)

Federal Ministry of Justice of Nigeria: *Laws of the Federation of Nigeria* (LFN) 1990

Nigerian Army: Terms and Conditions of Service Nigerian Army Officers, 1984

The co-operation of the Nigerian court registrars are also hereby acknowledged.

Contents

CHAPTERS

I.   Action

II.   Administrative Law

III.   Admiralty Law

 # Table of Cases

Abubakar v. Manulu (1998) 10 NWLR (Pt. 568) 41 CA (p.350)

Abuja v. Bizi (1989) 5 NWLR (Pt. 119) 120 CA (p.234)

Aburime v. N.P.A. (1978) 4 SC 11 (p.350)

Abusomwan v. Aiwerioba (1996) 4 NWLR (Pt. 441) 130 SC (p.37)

Abusomwan v. Mercantile Bank Ltd. (1987) 3 NWLR (Pt. 60) 196 SC (p.425)

Achille Lauro Incident (1988) 82 A.J.I.L. 269 (p.339)

Achimugu v. Minister, F.C.T. (1998) 11 NWLR (Pt. 574) 467 CA (p.241)

Acka v. Akure (1987) 1 NWLR (Pt. 47) 74 CA (p.418)

ACME Builders Ltd v. Kaduna State Water Board (1999)
    2 NWLR (Pt. 590) 288 SC (pp.115,328)

Adah v. Adah (2001) 14 WRN 74 CA (p.35)

Adaka v. Anekwe (1997) 11 NWLR (Pt. 529) 417 CA (p.82)

Adams v. Cape Industrial Plc (1988) The Times, June 23 (p.57)

Adams v. Ibadan District Council (1961) WRNLR 67 (p.179)

Adams v. Lindsell (1818) 1 B & Ald 681 (p.299)

Adamu v. Bashiru (1997) 10 NWLR (Pt. 523) 81 CA (p.204)

Adamu v. Gwadabawa (1999) 3 NWLR (Pt. 594) 256 CA (p.107)

Adeagbo v. Williams (1998) 2 NWLR (Pt. 536) 120 CA (p.259)

Adebileje v. NEPA (1998) 12 NWLR (Pt. 577) 219 CA (p.72)

Adebisi v. Odukoya (1997) 11 NWLR (Pt. 527) 83 CA (p.160,343)

Adebo v. Saki Estates Ltd. (1999) 7 NWLR (Pt. 612) 525 SC (p.250)

Adediran v. Interland Transport Ltd (1991) 9 NWLR (Pt. 214) 155 SC (pp.424,425)

Adedoyin v. Sonuga (1999) 13 NWLR (Pt. 635) 355 CA (pp.215,399)

Adefulu v. Okulaja (1998) 5 NWLR (Pt. 550) 435 SC (p.344)

Adegboyega v. Awe (1993) 3 NWLR (Pt. 280) 224 CA (p.376)

Adegoroye v Adegoroye (1996) 2 NWLR (Pt. 433) 712 CA (p.143)

Adelaja v. Alade (1999) 6 NWLR (Pt. 608) 544 SC (p.251)

Adelaja v. Fanoiki (1990) 2 NWLR (Pt. 131) 137 SC (pp.44,422)

Adele v. State (1995) 2 NWLR (Pt. 377) 269 SC (p.107)

Adeniji v. Starcola (Nigeria) Ltd (Suit No. M/135/70 of 18/1/71
    High Court of Lagos Judgment) (p.55)

Adeniji-Adele v. Ogbe (1998) 9 NWLR (Pt. 567) 650 CA (pp.77,81)

Adenuga v. Ilesanmi Press (1991) 5 NWLR (Pt. 189) 82 CA (p.67)

Adenuga v. Odumeru (2001) 10 WRN 104 SC (pp.77,155)

Adeosun v. Jibesin (2001) 14 WRN 106 CA (pp.1,7)

Adeoye v. State (1999) 6 NWLR (Pt. 605) 74 SC (pp.90,96)

Adepetu v. State (1998) 9 NWLR (Pt. 565) 185 SC (p.124)

Adepoju v. Oke (1999) 3 NWLR (Pt. 594) 154 SC (pp.253,255)

Aderonke Bakery Ltd v. M/S .D. Onyejekwe Ltd (1999) 2 NWLR (Pt. 590) 228 CA (p.219)

Adesanoye v. Akinwale (1997) 3 NWLR (Pt. 496) 664 CA (p.254)

Adesanya v. Aderonmu (2000) 6 SC (Pt. II) 18 (pp.166,249,257)

Adesanya v. Otuewu (1993) 1 NWLR (Pt. 270) 414 SC (p.316)

Adesokan v. Adegorolu (1997) 3 NWLR (Pt. 493) 261 SC(pp.1,4)

Adewunmi v. Plastex Ltd. (1986) 3 NWLR (Pt. 32) 767 SC (p.342)

Adewusi v. Popoola (1998) 12 NWLR (Pt. 579) 579 CA (p.349)

Adeyemi v. State (1991) 6 NWLR (Pt. 195) 1 SC (p.105)

Adeyemo v. Ida (1998) 4 NWLR (Pt. 546) 504 CA (pp.120,259)

- C -

Eastwood v. Henyon (1840) 11 A & E 438 (p.302)

Ebba v. Ogodo (2000) 6 SC (Pt. I) 133 (p.134)

Ebimotureh v. Inekembagha (1998) 3 NWLR (Pt. 543) 548 CA (p.258)

Eboade v. Atomesin (1997) 5 NWLR (Pt. 506) 490 SC (p.346)

Ebohon v. A-G, Edo State (1997) 5 NWLR (Pt. 505) 298 SC (p.246)

Ebongo v. Uwemedimo (1995) 8 NWLR (Pt. 411) 22 CA (pp.4,5,14)

Ebute v. State (1994) 8 NWLR (Pt. 360) 66 CA (p.91)

Echi v. Nnamani (2000) 5 SC 62 (p.250)

Ecobank (Nig.) Plc v. Gateway Hotels (Nig.) Ltd. (1999) 11 NWLR (Pt. 627) 397 CA
(p.10)

Edamine v. State (1996) 3 NWLR (Pt. 438) 530 SC (p.83)

Edet v. Chief of Air Staff (1994) 2 NWLR (Pt. 324) 41 CA (pp.16,367)

Edet v. Essien (1932) 11 NLR 47 (p.109)

Edgington v. Fitzmaurice (1885) 29 Ch D 459 (p.319)

Edhigere v. State (1996) 8 NWLR (Pt. 464) 1 SC (p.94)

Edokpolo & Co. Ltd v. Ohenhen (1994) 7 NWLR (Pt. 358) 511 SC (p.126)

Edokpolor & Co. Ltd v. Bendel Insurance Co. Ltd. (1997) 2 NWLR (Pt. 486) 131 SC (p.181)

Edokpolor & Co. Ltd v. Sem-Edo Wire Ind. Ltd (1984) 7 SC 119 (p.64)

Edonkumoh v. Mutu (1999) 9 NWLR (Pt. 620) 633 CA (p.347)

Edun v. Odan Community (1980) 9-11 SC 103 (p.353)

Edun v. Provost, Lagos State College of Education (LACOED) (1998) 13 NWLR
(Pt. 580) 52 CA (p.281)

Effia v. State (1998) 2 NWLR (Pt. 537) 275 CA (p.123)

Effiong v. State (1998) 8 NWLR (Pt. 562) 362 SC (pp.92,93,129,131)

Egbe v. Adefarasin (1987) 1 NWLR (Pt. 47) 1 SC (pp.342,330,418)

Egboghonome v. State (1993) 7 NWLR (Pt. 306) 383 SC (pp.92,127,355)

Egbue v. Araka (1996) 1 NILR 139 CA (p.118)

Egbuonu v. Borno Radio Television Corporation (1997) 12 NWLR
(Pt. 531) 29 SC (p.245)

Egolum v. Obasanjo (1999) 7 NWLR (Pt. 611) 423 CA (p.10)

Egwu v. Eke (1999) 3 NWLR (Pt. 594) 189 CA (p.4)

Ehidimhen v. Musa (2000) 4 SC (Pt II) 166 (pp.70,227,377,378,379)

Eholor v. Idahosa (1992) 2 NWLR (Pt. 223) 323 CA (p.424)

Ehot v. State (1993) 4 NWLR (Pt. 290) 644 SC (pp.50,51)

Eichmann Case (1962) 36 I.L.R. 5 (p.193)

Ejekam v. Devon Ind. Ltd (1998) 1 NWLR (Pt. 534) 417 CA (p.58)

Ejelikwu v. State (1993) 7 NWLR (Pt. 307) 554 SC (p.106)

Ejikeme v. Amaechi (1998) 3 NWLR (Pt. 542) 456 CA (pp.4,59)

Ejikeme v. Okonkwo (1994) 8 NWLR (Pt. 362) 266 SC (p.263)

Ejitagha v. Psychiatric Hospital Management Board (1995) 2 NWLR
(Pt. 376) 189 CA (pp.240,241)

Ejiwunmi v. Costain (W.A) Plc (1998) 12 NWLR (Pt. 576) 149 CA (pp.39,265)

Ekennia v. Nkpakara (1997) 5 NWLR (Pt. 504) 152 SC (p.255)

Ekpechi v. Owhonda (1998) 3 NWLR (Pt. 543) 618 CA (p.250)

Ekpenga v. Ozogula II (1962) 1 SCNLR 423 (p.110)

Ekpeogu v. Ashaka Cement Co. Plc (1997) 6 NWLR (Pt. 508) 280 CA (p.242)

Ekrebe v. Efeizomor II (1993) 7 NWLR (Pt. 307) 588 CA (p.177)

Falomo v. Banigbe (1998) 7 NWLR (Pt. 559) 679 SC (pp.162,164,342)

Faloughi v. Faloughi (1995) 3 NWLR (Pt. 384) 434 (pp.301,302)

Fareast Mercantile Co. Ltd v. Boothia Maritime Inc. (1998) 5 NWLR (Pt. 551) 620 CA (p.31)

Fasakin v. Fasakin (1994) 4 NWLR (Pt. 340) 597 CA (p.66)

Fasikun II v. Oluronke II (1999) 2 NWLR (Pt. 589) 1 SC (pp.21,255,356)

Fasonu v. Fawehinmi (1997) 3 NWLR (Pt. 492) 182 CA (p.268)

Fawehinmi v. Akilu (1990) 1 NWLR (Pt. 127) 450 CA (p.400)

Fawehinmi v. N.B.A. (No. 1) (1989) 2 NWLR (Pt.105) 494 SC (pp.166,342,345)

Fawehinmi v. N.B.A (No. 2) (1989) 2 NWLR (Pt. 105) 558 SC (pp.53,118,120)

Fayehun v. Fadoju (2000) 4 SC (Part I) 48 (p.261)

Federal Minister of Internal Affairs v. Shugaba Darman (1982) 3 NCLR 915 (p.148)

Fesco (Nig.) Ltd v. N.R. & C.P.Co. Ltd (1998) 11 NWLR (Pt. 573) 227 CA (p.393)

Finnih v. Imade (1992) 1 NWLR (Pt. 219) 511 SC (p.376)

Finunion Ltd v. M.V. Briz (1997) 10 NWLR (Pt. 523) 95 CA (p.28)

First Bank of Nigeria Plc v. Mamman (Nig.) Ltd (2001) 3 WRN 58 CA (p.411)

Fisher v. Bell (1960) 3 All ER 73 (p.296)

Fisheries Jurisdiction Case: UK v. Iceland (Jurisdiction) (1973) I.C.J. Rep. p.3 (p.192)

Fisheries Jurisdiction (Merits) Cases: (United Kingdom v. Iceland); (Federal Republic of Germany v. Iceland) (1974) I.C.J. Rep.pp. 3 &175 (p.335)

FMBN v. NDIC (1999) 2 NWLR (Pt. 591) 333 SC (p.403)

Folarin v. State (1995) 1 NWLR (Pt. 371) 313 CA (p.83)

Folbod Invest. Ltd v. Alpha Merchant Bank Ltd (1996) 10 NWLR (Pt. 478) 344 CA (p.38)

Foley v. Hill and Others (1848) 2 HLC 28 (p.404)

Foss v. Harbottle (1843) 2 Hare 461 (p.59)

Foster v. Makinnon (1869) L.R. 4 (p.312)

Framo (Nig.) Ltd v. Daodu (1993) 3 NWLR (Pt. 281) 372 CA (p.128)

Franchal Nigeria Ltd v. Nigeria Arab Bank Ltd (2000) 6 SC (Pt. I) 1 (pp.397,398)

Francis v. Municipal Councillors of Kuala Lumpur (1962) 2 All ER 633 (p.244)

Franus v. Union Territory of Delhi, AIR 1981 SCC 7 (p.147)

Fraser v. Balfour (1918) 34 T.L.R 502 (p.366)

Fraser v. Hamilton (1917) 3 T.L.R 431 (p.366)

Fumudoh v. Aboro (1991) 9 NWLR (Pt. 214) 210 CA (p.46)

- G -

G.M.C. (UK) Ltd v. Medicair W/A Ltd (1998) 2 NWLR (Pt. 536) 86 CA (p.159)

G.S. & F.C. Ltd v. Obiekezie (1997) 10 NWLR (Pt. 526) 577 CA (p.408)

Gadzama v. Rims Merchant Bank Ltd (1997) 4 NWLR (Pt. 498) 234 CA (pp.64,65,69,298)

Galadima v. Tambai (2000) 6 SC (Part I) 196 (pp.230,231,232)

Galland Steamship Corporation Claim (1924) 7 R.I.A.A. p.73 (p.291,292)

Gallie v. Lee (1969) 2 Ch. 31 (p.312)

Galloway v. Galloway (1914) 30 TLR 531 (p.318)

- L -

L'Estrange v. Graucob (1934) 2 K.B. 394 (p.312)

L.S.D.P.C. v. Adold/Stamm Int. Ltd (1994) 7 NWLR (Pt. 358) 545 SC (pp.119,127)

Laban-kowa v. Alkali (1999) 9 NWLR (Pt. 620) 601 CA (pp.54,259)

Ladimeji v. Salami (1998) 5 NWLR (Pt. 548) 1 SC (pp.134,135)

Ladipo v. Aminike Invest. Co. Ltd (1998) 4 NWLR (Pt. 546) 496 CA (p.401)

Lado v. State (1999) 9 NWLR (Pt. 619) 369 SC (pp.100,102)

Lagricom Co. Ltd v. U.B.N. Ltd (1996) 4 NWLR (Pt. 441) 185 CA (p.50)

Laguro v. Toku (1992) 2 NWLR (Pt. 223) 278 SC (pp.49,378,380)

Laker Airways v. Department of Trade (1977) Q.B. 643 (p.23)

Lamurde v. Adamawa State J.S.C (1999) 12 NWLR (Pt. 629) 86 CA (pp.216,346)

Lauwers Import-Export v. Jozebson Industries Ltd. (1988) 3 NWLR (Pt. 83) 429 SC (p.342)

Law Union and Rock Ins. v. Onuoha (1998) 6 NWLR (Pt. 555) 576 CA (p.173)

Lawal v. Ejidike (1997) 2 NWLR (Pt. 487) 319 CA (pp.257,259,355)

Lawal-Osula v. Lawal-Osula (1993) 2 NWLR (Pt. 274) 158 CA (pp.137,139,140)

Lawal-Osula v. Lawal-Osula (1995) 3 NWLR (Pt. 382) 128 SC (p.80)

Lawal-Osula v. Lawal-Osula (1996) 1 NILR 22 SC (pp.110,112)

Lawson v. Ajibulu (1997) 6 NWLR (Pt. 507) 14 SC (p.158)

Layanju v. Araoye (1959) 4 F.S.C. 154 (p.24)

Leaf v. International Galleries (1950) 2 KB 86 (p.319)

Legality of the Threat or Use of Nuclear Weapons Case. ICJ Advisory Opinion (1997) 35 I.L.M. 809 & 1343 (p.286)

Lekwot v. Judicial Tribunal (1997) 8 NWLR (Pt. 515) 22 SC (p.20)

Leontaritis v. Nigerian Textile Mills Ltd (1967) N.C.L.R. 114 (p.316)

Leventis Motors Ltd v. Nunieh (1999) 13 NWLR (Pt. 634) 235 CA (p.311)

Leventis Tech. Ltd v. Petrojessica Ent. Ltd (1999) 6 NWLR (Pt. 605) 45 SC (p.29)

Lewis v. Bankole (1908) 1 NLR 81 (p.110)

Leyland (Nig.) Ltd v. Dizengoff (1990) 2 NWLR (Pt. 134) 610 CA (pp.307,308)

Leyland Shipping Co. Ltd v. Norwich Union Fire Insurance Society Ltd (1918-19) All ER Rep 443 (p.176)

LIAMCO v. Libya Case (1981) 20 I.L.M. 1 (p.194)

Liberty Ins. Co. Ltd v. John (1996) 1 NWLR (Pt. 423) 192 CA (pp.171,172,173)

Libya v. Malta (1985) I.C.J. Rep.p.35 (p.335)

Liesbosch Dredger v. SS Edision (1933) AC 448 (p.177)

Liman v. Mohammed (1999) 9 NWLR (Pt. 617) 116 SC (p.221)

Lindgreen v. L & P Estates Ltd (1968) Ch. 572 (p.61)

Lion of Africa Insurance Co. Ltd v. Esan (1999) 8 NWLR (Pt. 614) 197 CA (p.6)

Livingstone v. Rawyards Coal Co. (1880) AC 25 (p.176)

Lloyd's Bank Ltd v. Bundy (1975) Q.B. 326 (pp.317,318)

London General Omnibus Co. Ltd v. Holloway (1911-13) All ER Rep 518 (p.174)

London Joint Stock Bank Ltd v. Macmillian and Arthur (1918) AC 777 (p.407)

Long-John v. Blakk (1998) 6 NWLR (Pt. 555) 524 SC (pp.126,349)

Looker v. Law Union and Rock Insurance Co. Ltd (1927) 137 LT 648 (p.175)

Lotus Case: France v. Turkey (1927) P.C.I.J. Rep.Series A No. 10 (p.186)

Louisiana v. Mississippi (1931) United States Supreme Court Judgment (p.185)

Lovable Corp v. Honeywell Inc. 431 F. 2d 668 (5thCir, 1970) 677 (p.333)

Lucena v. Craufurd (1806) 2 BOS & PNR 269 (p.173)

Lydney and Wig pool Iron Ore Co. v. Bird (1886) 3 Ch D 85(p.56)

- M -

M. v. Secretary of State for the Home Department (1995) Times 7 November (Court of Appeal: Millett and Ward LJJ) (p.191)

M. Ibrahim Abba v. Mrs. Margret A. Mohammed & Anor (1975) N.N.L.R. 208, High Court of North-Central State. Suit No. NCH/26/74 (p.427)

M.I.A. & Sons Ltd. v. F.H.A. (1991) 8 NWLR (Pt. 209) 295 CA (P.134)

M.O. Kanu, Sons & Co. v. F.B.N. Plc (1998) 11 NWLR (Pt. 572) 116 CA (p.54)

Maal Case: Netherlands v. Venezuela (1903) RIAA, 10 p.730 (p.197)

Macaulay v. Omiyale (1997) 4 NWLR (Pt. 497) 94 CA (p.278)

Macaura v. Northern Assurance Co. Ltd (1925) All ER Rep 51 (p.174)

Mackonochie v. Lord Penzance (1881) 6 A.C. 443 (p.26)

Mad Zimbamuto v. Lardner-Burke (1969) 1 AC 645 (p.76)

Madu v. Okeke (1998) 5 NWLR (Pt. 548) 159 CA (p.345)

Madu v. Ononuju (1986) 3 NWLR (Pt. 26) 23 CA (p.8)

Madu v. State (1997) 1 NWLR (Pt. 482) 386 SC (pp.89,93)

Maduagwu v Maduagwu (1991) 8 NWLR (Pt. 212) 684 CA (p.138)

Madubuonwu v. Nnalue (1999) 11 NWLR (Pt. 628) 673 SC (p.251)

Maduekwe v. Okoroafor (1992) 9 NWLR (Pt. 263) 69 CA (p.120)

Madukolu v. Nkemdilim (1962) 1 All NLR 587 SC (p.232)

Magaji v. Matari (2000) 5 SC 46 (pp.204,232,234)

Maigoro v. Garba (2001) 2 WRN 1 SC (p.40)

Mainagge v. Gwamna (1997) 11 NWLR (Pt. 528) 191 CA (p.125)

Majekodunmi v. National Bank of Nigeria (1978) 3 SC 119 (pp.296,306)

Major General George Innih (rtd) & Ors v. Ferado Agro and Consortium Ltd (1990) 5 NWLR (Pt. 152) 604 CA (p.298)

Major Ladejobi v. A.-G., Federation (1982) 3 N.C.L.R 563 (p.365)

Makinde v. Akinwale (2000) 1 SC 89 (pp.254,268,375)

Makinde v. Ojeyinka (1997) 4 NWLR (Pt. 497) 80 CA (p.232)

Malgit v. Dachen (1998) 5 NWLR (Pt. 550) 384 CA (p.127)

Management Enterprises Ltd. v. Otusanya (1987) 2 NWLR (Pt. 55) 179 SC (pp.427,428)

Maneka Ghandi v. Union of India (1978) 1 SCC 248 (Indian Supreme Court Judgment) (p.147)

Mangai v. State (1993) 3 NWLR (Pt. 279) 108 CA (p.88)

Manu v. Muhammad (1997) 11 NWLR (Pt. 528) 323 CA (p.207)

Marais (D.F) v. General Officer Commanding the Lines of Communication and Attorney General of Cape Colony (1902) AC 109 (p.366)

Marina Nominees Ltd v. Federal Board of Inland Revenue (1986) 2 NWLR (Pt. 20) 48 (p.53)

Martins v. State (1997) 1 NWLR (Pt. 481) 355 CA (pp.83, 84)

Massey Case: US v. Mexico (1927) 4 R.I.A.A. 155 (p.192)

Mavronmmatis Palestine Concessions Case (Jurisdiction): Greece v. United Kingdom (1924) P.C.I.J. Rep.Series A No. 2 p.12 (p.194)

Mazin Eng. Ltd v. Tower Aluminium (1993) 5 NWLR (Pt. 295) 526 SC (pp.309,323)

- N -

N.A.B. Ltd. v. Comex Ltd (1999) 6 NWLR (Pt. 608) 648 CA (p.345)
N.A.B. Ltd. v. Felly Keme (Nig.) Ltd. (1995) 4 NWLR (Pt. 387) 100 CA (p.425)
N.B.C. Plc V Borgundu (1999) 2 NWLR (Pt. 591) 408 CA (pp.115,425,426, 427,428)
N.B.C. Plc v. Ogundele (1997) 9 NWLR (Pt. 521) 446 CA (p.389)
N.B.N. Ltd v. S.C.D.C. Co. Ltd (1998) 5 NWLR (Pt. 548) 144 CA (p.113)
N.B.N. Ltd v. T.A.S.A. Ltd (1996) 8 NWLR (Pt. 468) 511 CA (pp.43,239)
N.D.I.C. v. F.M.B (1997) 2 NWLR (Pt. 490) 735 CA (pp.69,234)
N.D.I.C. v. F.M.B. Ltd. (1997) 4 NWLR (Pt. 501) 519 SC (p.69)
N.E.W. Ltd v. Denap Ltd (1997) 10 NWLR (Pt.525) 481 CA (p.280)
N.H.R.I v. Ayoade (1997) 11 NWLR (Pt. 530) 541 SC (p.281)
N.I.D.B. v. De Easy Life Electronics (1999) 4 NWLR (Pt. 597) 8 CA (pp.121,223)
N.I.D.B. v. Fembo (Nig.) Ltd (1997) 2 NWLR (Pt. 489) 543 CA (pp.60,347)
N.I.D.B. v. Limani (Nig.) Enterp.Ltd (1998) 10 NWLR (Pt. 568) 97 CA (p.217)
N.I.M.B Ltd. v. Narindex Trust Ltd. (1998) 13 NWLR (Pt.582) 404 CA (p.12)
N.M.B. Plc. v. Onabolu (1999) 12 NWLR (Pt. 630) 302 CA (p.123)
N.N.P.C. v. Elumah (1997) 3 NWLR (Pt. 492) 195 CA (p.232)
N.N.S.C. v. Sabana Ltd (1988) 2 NWLR (Pt. 74) 23 SC (p.346)
N.T.B. Lawson v. Kevin Mahor & Anor (1975) N.N.L.R. 154, High Court of North-Central State. Suit No. NCH/45/75 (p.416)
Na-Bature v. Mahuta (1992) 9 NWLR (Pt. 263) 85 CA (p.129)
Nabisco Inc. v. Allied Biscuits Co. Ltd (1998) 10 NWLR (Pt. 568) 16 SC (p.66)
Naim Molvan v. Att.-Gen. for Palestine [The Asya] (1948) A.C. 351 (p.337)
Nalon v. Metropolitan Police Commissioner (No. 2) (1979) 2 AER 620 (p.331)
Nalsa & Team Associates v. N.N.P.C. (1991) 8 NWLR (Pt. 212) 652 SC (p.46)
Nalsa and Team Ass. v. N.N.P.C. (1996) 3 NWLR (Pt. 439) 621 SC (p.396)
Namibia Case ICJ AO (1971) (p.202)
Nance v. British Columbia Railway Co. Ltd (1915) A.C. 601 (p.179)
Nasiru v. Abubakar (1997) 4 NWLR (Pt. 497) 32 CA   (p.253)
Nasiru v. State (1999) 2 NWLR (Pt. 589) 87 SC (pp.74, 90,114)
National Carriers Ltd v. Pannalpina (Northern) Ltd (1981) A.C. 675; (1981) 1 All ER 161 (p.324)
National Salt Company of Nigeria Ltd v. Innis-Palmer (1992) 1 NWLR (Pt. 218) 422 CA (p.274)
Ndaeye v. Ogunnaya (1997) 1 SC 11 (p.308)
Ndigwe v. Ibekendu (1998) 7 NWLR (Pt. 558) 486 CA   (pp.222,224)
Ndigwe v. Nwude (1999) 11 NWLR (Pt. 626) 314 SC (p.13)
NDLEA v. Okorodudu (1997) 3 NWLR (Pt. 492) 221 CA (p.79)
Nebo v. F.C.D.A. (1998) 11 NWLR (Pt. 574) 480 CA (p.349)
Neer Claim: United States v. Mexico (1926) 4 R.I.A.A. 60 (p.197)
Nelson v. Ebanga (1998) 8 NWLR (Pt. 563) 701 CA (p.278)
NEPA v. Alli (1992) 8 NWLR (Pt. 259) 279 SC (p.427)
New Zealand v. France, I.C.J Report, 1974, p.457 (p.337)
Newsholme Bros v. Road Transport and General Insurance Co. Ltd (1929) All ER Rep 442 (p.172)
Ngbdobe v. Dubrare (1997) 11 NWLR (Pt. 529) 382 CA (p.209)
Ngwu V. Ozougwu (2001) 4 WRN 26 SC (p.343)

Nicaragua Case (Merits) (Nicaragua v. United State) I.C.J. Reports 1986, p.14 (pp.283,284,285)

Nig. Soc. Ins. T.F.M.B v. Adebiyi (1999) 13 NWLR (Pt. 633) 16 CA (pp.75,151)

Niger Chemists Ltd v. Nigeria Chemists Ltd (1961) 1 All NLR 171 (p.157)

Niger Insurance v. Abed Brothers (1976) 7 SC 35 (p.307)

Nigerbras Shipping Line Ltd v. Aluminium Extrusion Industries (1994) 4 NWLR (Pt. 341) 733 CA (p.31)

Nigerian Bank for Commerce & Industry Ltd v. Europa Traders (U.K) Ltd (1990) 6 NWLR (Pt. 154) 36 CA (p.56)

Nigerian Wire Ind. Plc v. European Trade & Finance Plc (1997) 6 NWLR (Pt. 510) 632 CA (p.63)

Nikolic and Matric (Trial) ILR 108 (1998) 21 (p.369)

Ningi v. F.B.N Plc. (1996) 3 NWLR (Pt. 435) 220 CA (p.416)

Nishizawa Ltd v. Jethwani (2001) 8 WRN 153 SC (p.381)

Nissan v. Attorney-General (1970) A.C. 179 (p.23)

NITEL Plc. v. Rockonoh Prop.Co. Ltd. (1995) 2 NWLR (Pt. 378) 473 CA (p.422)

NITEL v. Oshodin (1999) 8 NWLR (Pt. 616) 528 CA (p.310)

Njiokwuemeni v. The State (2001) 14 WRN 96 CA (p.101)

Njoku v. C.O.P.(1999) 10 NWLR (Pt. 622) 192 CA (p.103)

Njoku v. Dikibo (1998) 1 NWLR (Pt. 534) 496 CA (p.119)

Nkado v. Obiano (1997) 5 NWLR (Pt. 503) 31 SC (pp.249,377)

Nkpuma v. State (1995) 9 NWLR (Pt. 421) 505 SC (pp.43,45)

Nkume v. The Regt. Trustees of the Diocese of Aba (1998) 10 NWLR (Pt. 570) 514 CA (p.255)

Nkwo v. Iboe (1998) 7 NWLR (Pt. 558) 354 SC (pp.117,249)

Nnabo v. State (1994) 8 NWLR (Pt. 361) 173 SC (p.102)

Nnadika v. Ejire (1994) 1 NWLR (Pt. 320) 295 CA (p.25)

Nnamdi Azikiwe University (N.A.U.) v. Nwafor (1999) 1 NWLR (Pt. 585) 116 CA (p.20)

NNPC v. Fawehinmi (1998) 7 NWLR (Pt. 559) 598 CA (p.74)

Nnubia v. A-G Rivers State (1999) 3 NWLR (Pt. 593) 82 CA (pp.3,121,259)

Nocton v. Ashburton (1914) A.C. 932 (p.321)

Nokoprise Int. Co. Ltd v. Dobest Trading Corporation (1997) 9 NWLR (Pt. 520) 334 CA (pp.229,230)

Normandy v. Ind. Coope & Co. Ltd (1908) 1 Ch. 84 (p.64)

North Ocean Shipping Co. Ltd v. Hyundai Construction Co. Ltd (1979) Q.B. 705 (p.317)

North Sea Continental Shelf Cases (1969) I.C.J. Rep.p.3 (pp.199,201)

Northern Assurance Co. Ltd v. Idugboe (1966) 2 All N.L.R. 88 SC (p.172)

Nottebohm Case: Liechtenstein v. Guatemala (1955) I.C.J. Rep.p.4 (p.187)

Nsirim v. Nsirim (1990) 3 NWLR (Pt. 138) 285 SC (pp.43,415)

Nuclear Test Case: Australia v. France; New Zealand v. France (1974) ICJ Report pp.253,457 (p.198)

NV Scheep v. "S. Araz" (2001) 4 WRN 105 SC (pp.3,225,353)

Nwaeze v. State (1996) 2 NWLR (Pt. 428) 1 SC (pp.36,94,97,99)

Nwaibe v. State (1996) 9 NWLR (Pt. 472) 343 CA (p.52)

Nwakonobi v. Udeorah (1991) 9 NWLR (Pt. 213) 85 CA (p.159)

Nwambe v. State (1995) 3 NWLR (Pt. 384) 385 SC (pp.93,341)

Nwangwa v Ubani (1997) 10 NWLR (Pt. 526) 559 CA (pp.138,142)

Nwanji v. Coastal Services (Nig.) Ltd (1999) 11 NWLR (Pt. 628) 641 CA (p.123)

Odogwu v Odogwu (1992) 2 NWLR (Pt. 225) 539 SC (pp.77,79,144)
Oduba v. Houtmangracht (1997) 6 NWLR (Pt. 508) 185 SC (pp.227,385)
Odukwe v. Ogunbiyi (1998) 8 NWLR (Pt. 561) 339 SC (p.261)
Oduneye v. The State (2001) 13 WRN 88 SC (pp.83,84,130)
Odunmodi v. Mohammed (1973) NCLR 452 (p.60)
Odunsi v. Abeke (1999) 12 NWLR (Pt. 632) 601 CA (p.399)
Odunsi v. U.N.M.I.C. (1998) 2 NWLR (Pt. 536) 95 CA (pp.224,349)
Oduntan v. Akibu (2000) 7 SC (Part II) 106 (p.1,22)
Oduntan v. Gen. Oil Ltd (1995) 4 NWLR (Pt. 387) 1 SC (p.46)
Odunukwe v. Ofomata (1999) 6 NWLR (Pt. 607) 416 CA (p.252)
Oduola v. Nabham (1981) N.S.C.C. Vol. 12 p.180 (p.254)
Odusoga v. Ricketts (1997) 7 NWLR (Pt. 511) 1 SC (p.258)
Odutola v. Kayode (1994) 2 NWLR (Pt. 324) 1 SC (p.344)
Odutola v. Lawal (2001) 11 WRN 34 CA (p.155)
Offiong v. African Development Corporation Ltd (1964) 2 All N.L.R. 75,
    High Court of Lagos (p.302)
Offor v. State (1999) 12 NWLR (Pt. 632) 608 CA (p.347,394)
Ofondu v. Niweigha (1993) 2 NWLR (Pt. 275) 253 SC (p.376)
Oforlete v. The State (2000) 7 SC (Part I) 80 (pp.85,97,101,124)
Ogana II v. Awulor (1997) 9 NWLR (Pt. 522) 668 CA (p.9)
Ogbole v. Onah (1990) 1 NWLR (Pt. 126) 357 CA (p.139)
Ogbonda v. Eke (1998) 10 NWLR (Pt. 568) 73 CA (pp.385,386)
Ogbonna v. A.-G., Imo State (1992) 1 NWLR (Pt. 220) 647 SC (pp.2,385,386)
Ogiale v. Shell Pet. Dev. Co. (Nig.) Ltd (1997) 1 NWLR (Pt. 480) 148 CA
    (p.128)
Ogidi v. Egba (1999) 10 NWLR (Pt. 621) 42 SC (p.118)
Ogigie v. Obiyan (1997) 10 NWLR (Pt. 524) 179 SC (p.277)
Ogiugo v. Ogiugo (2001) 1 WRN 131 SC (pp.2,219)
Ogoja L.G. v. Offoboche (1996) 7 NWLR (Pt. 458) 48 CA (pp.47,376)
Ogualaji v. A.-G., Rivers State (1997) 6 NWLR (Pt. 508) 209 SC (p.18)
Oguchi v. F.M.B. (Nig.) Ltd (1990) 6 NWLR (Pt. 156) 330 CA (p.263)
Oguejiofor v. Osaka (2000) 3 SC 1 (p.261)
Ogugu v. State (1994) 9 NWLR (Pt. 366) 1 SC (p.107)
Ogun v. Akinyelu (1999) 10 NWLR (Pt. 624) 671 CA (p.269)
Ogundare v. Ogunlowo (1997) 6 NWLR (Pt. 509) 360 SC (p.110)
Ogundele v. Fasu (1999) 12 NWLR (Pt. 632) 662 SC (p.132)
Ogundana v. Araba & Anor (1978) 11 NSCC 334 (p.263)
Ogunmokun v. Mil. Adm., Osun State (1999) 3 NWLR (Pt. 594) 261 CA
    (pp.3,4)
Ogunremi v. Dada (1962) 2 SCNLR 417 (p.36)
Ogunsola v. NICON (1996) 1 NWLR (Pt. 423) 126 SC (p.44,46)
Oguntayo v. Adebutu (1997) 12 NWLR (Pt. 531) 83 CA (pp.61,64)
Ogunye v. State (1999) 5 NWLR (Pt. 604) 548 SC (p.89)
Oguonzee v. State (1998) 5 NWLR (Pt. 551) 521 SC (p.129)
Ogwuegbu v. Agomuo (1999) 7 NWLR (Pt. 609) 144 CA (p.217)
Ogwuru v. Co-op.Bank of Eastern (Nig.) Ltd (1994) 8 NWLR (Pt. 365) 685
    CA (p.29)
Ohiaeri v. Akabueze (1992) 2 NWLR (Pt. 221) 1 SC (p.376)
Ohuka v. State (No. 2) (1988) 4 NWLR (Pt. 86) 36 SC (p.132)
Ohuta v. Okigbo (1995) 4 NWLR (Pt. 389) 352 CA (p.348)
Oilfield Supply Centre Ltd. v. Johnson (1987) 2 NWLR (Pt. 58) 625 SC (p.68)
Ojelade v. Soroye (1998) 5 NWLR (Pt. 549) 284 CA (p.116)

Ojeme v. Punch (Nig.) Ltd. (1996) 1 NWLR (Pt. 427) 701 CA (p.416)
Ojibah v. Ojibah (1991) 5 NWLR (Pt. 191) 296 SC (p.111)
Ojo v. Anibire (1999) 11 NWLR (Pt. 628) 630 CA (p.251)
Ojo v. Azama (2001) 12 WRN 1 SC (p.252)
Ojo v. Philips (1993) 5 NWLR (Pt. 296) 751 CA (p.381)
Ojokolobo v. Alamu (1991) 1 NWLR (Pt. 165) 1 CA (p.130)
Ojokolobo v. Alamu (1998) 9 NWLR (Pt. 565) 226 SC (pp.122,252)
Ojomo v. Ibrahim (1999) 12 NWLR (Pt. 631) 415 CA (p.255)
Ojukwu v. Gov., Lagos State (1986) 3 NWLR (Pt. 26) 39 SC (p.80)
Okafor v. A-G., Anambra State (1991) 6 NWLR (Pt. 200) 659 SC (p.392)
Okafor v. Asoh (1999) 3 NWLR (Pt. 593) 35 CA (pp.3,75,115,149)
Okafor v. Igwilo (1997) 11 NWLR (Pt. 527) 36 CA (pp.70,301)
Okafor v. Nnodi (1963) 1 All NLR 373 (p.177)
Okafor v. Nwude (2001) 3 WRN 105 SC (p.13)
Okechukwu v. Okechukwu (1989) 3 NWLR (Pt. 108) 234 CA (p.160)
Okechukwu v. Onuorah (2000) 12 SC (Part II) 104 (pp.270,271,307)
Okefi v. Ogu (1996) 2 NWLR (Pt. 432) 603 CA (p.168)
Okegbe v. Chikere (2000) 7 SC (Part 1) 106 (pp.220,225,268,346)
Okeke v. A-G., Anambra State (1997) 9 NWLR (Pt. 519) 123 CA (p.78)
Okeke v. Oche (1994) 2 NWLR (Pt. 329) 688 CA (p.327)
Okeke v. Oruh (1999) 6 NWLR (Pt. 606) 175 SC (p.121)
Okelola v. Boyle (1998) 2 NWLR (Pt. 539) 533 SC (pp.42,116)
Okene v. Orianwo (1998) 9 NWLR (Pt. 566) 408 CA (pp.109,110,115)
Okenwa v. Mil. Gov., Imo State (1997) 6 NWLR (Pt. 507) 136 CA
    (pp.18,21,112)
Okere v. Nlem (1992) 4 NWLR (Pt. 234) 132 SC (p.48)
Okereke v. State (1998) 3 NWLR (Pt. 540) 75 CA (p.124)
Oko v. Igweshi (1997) 4 NWLR (Pt. 497) 48 CA (p.226)
Okoebor v. Police Council (1998) 9 NWLR (Pt. 566) 534 CA (p.246)
Okoli v. Ojiakor (1997) 1 NWLR (Pt. 479) 48 CA (p.9)
Okolo v. U.B.N. Ltd (1998) 2 NWLR (Pt. 539) 618 CA (pp.343,411)
Okon v. Administrator-General, Cross-River (1992) 6 NWLR (Pt. 248) 473
    CA   (p.140)
Okon v. State (1995) 1 NWLR (Pt. 372) 382 SC (pp.46,90,344)
Okongwu v. N.N.P.C (1989) 4 NWLR (Pt. 115) 296 SC (p.328)
Okonkwo v. C.C.B. (Nig.) Plc (1997) 6 NWLR (Pt. 507) 48 CA (p.386)
Okonkwo v. M.D.P.D.T (1999) 9 NWLR (Pt. 617) 1 CA (pp.18,419,426)
Okonkwo v. Ogbogu (1996) 5 NWLR (Pt. 449) 420 SC (pp.45,389,419,420)
Okonkwo v. Okonkwo (1998) 10 NWLR (Pt. 571) 554 SC (p.261)
Okonkwo v. State (1998) 8 NWLR (Pt. 561) 210 CA (pp.84,102,129)
Okoro v. State (1993) 3 NWLR (Pt. 282) 425 CA (pp.95,89)
Okoro v. State (1998) 14 NWLR (Pt. 584) 181 SC (pp.92,93,129)
Okoromaka v. Odiri (1995) 7 NWLR (Pt. 408) 411 CA (pp.3,376,382)
Okoronkwo v. Chukweke (1992) 1 NWLR (Pt. 216) 175 CA (p.130)
Okosi v. State (1989) 1 NWLR (Pt. 100) 642 SC (p.344)
Okosun v. Katsina and Another (1976) 8 CCHCJ 2225 (p.179)
Okotete v. Electricity Corporation of Nigeria (Unreported) High Court of
    Midwest, Warri, May 29, 1970 (p.309)
Okoya v. Santilli (1990) 2 NWLR (Pt. 131) 172 SC (pp.57,165)
Okoya v. Santilli (1994) 4 NWLR (Pt.338) 256 SC (p.65)
Okoye v. Dumez (Nig.) Ltd (1983) 1 NWLR 783 (p.264)
Okoye v. Dumez Nig. Ltd. (1985) 1 NWLR (Pt. 4) 783 SC (p.119)

Onashile v. Idowu & Ors (1969) All NLR (Pt. 2) 313 (p.262)
Ondo State University v. Folayan (1994) 7 NWLR (Pt. 334) 1 SC (p.330)
Onifade v. Olayiwola (1990) 7 NWLR (Pt. 161) 130 SC (p.40,43)
Ononuju v. A.-G., Anambra State (1998) 11 NWLR (Pt. 573) 304 CA (p.281)
Ononuju v. Ononuju (1991) 5 NWLR (Pt. 192) 479 CA (pp.144,143)
Onowhosa v. Odiuzou (1999) 1 NWLR (Pt. 586) 173 SC (p.132)
Onuh v. C.O.P.(1994) 1 NWLR (Pt. 323) 671 CA (p.105)
Onuoha v. State (1998) 5 NWLR (Pt. 548) 118 CA (p.114,130)
Onuzulike v. Commissioner for Special Duties, Anambra State (1990) 7
    NWLR (Pt. 161) 252 CA (p.159)
Onwu v. Nka (1996) 7 NWLR (Pt. 458) 1 SC (p.388,389)
Onwualu v. Mokwe (1999) 1 NWLR (Pt. 585) 146 CA (p.348)
Onwuchekwa v. C.C.B. (Nig.) Ltd. (1999) 5 NWLR (Pt. 603) 409 CA (p.217)
Onwugbufor v. Okoye (1996) 1 NWLR (Pt. 424) 252 SC (pp.45,116)
Onwuka v. Omogui (1992) 3 NWLR (Pt. 230) 393 SC (p.375)
Onyeachimba v. State (1998) 8 NWLR (Pt. 563) 587 CA (p.98)
Onyegbu v. State (1995) 4 NWLR (Pt. 391) 510 SC (p.101)
Onyejekwe v. Onyejekwe (1999) 3 NWLR (Pt. 596) 482 SC (p.117)
Onyeke v. Harriclem (Nig.) Ltd (1998) 7 NWLR (Pt. 556) 64 CA (pp.344,345)
Onyekwulunne v. Ndulue (1997) 7 NWLR (Pt. 512) 250 CA (p.166)
Onyenucheya v. Mil. Adm., Imo State (1997) 1 NWLR (Pt.482) 429 CA
    (p.230)
Onyesoh v. Nnebedun (1992) 3 NWLR (Pt. 229) 315 SC (pp.163,164)
Opara v. D.S. (Nig.) Ltd (1995) 4 NWLR (Pt. 390) 440 CA (pp.38,270,271)
Opara v. Ihejirika (1990) 6 NWLR (Pt. 156) 291 CA (pp.161,162)
Opara v. State (1998) 2 NWLR (Pt. 536) 108 CA (pp.85,98)
Oparaji v. Ohanu (1999) 9 NWLR (Pt. 618) 290 SC (p.123)
Ordia v. Piedmont (Nig.) Ltd (1995) 2 NWLR (Pt. 379) 516 SC (p.424)
Oredoyin v. Arowolo (1989) 4 NWLR (Pt. 114) 172 SC (p.35)
Orient Bank (Nig.) Plc v. Bilante Int'l Ltd (1997) 8 NWLR (Pt. 515) 37 CA
    (pp.295,296,299)
Oriental Airlines Ltd v. Air VIA Ltd (1998) 12 NWLR (Pt. 577) 271 CA (p.69)
Orinoco Steamship Company (1903) 1 R.T.A.A. p.102-103 (p.291)
Orizu v. Uzoegwu (1999) 6 NWLR (Pt. 605) 32 CA (p.344)
Orji v. Zaria Ind. Ltd (1992) 1 NWLR (Pt. 216) 124 SC (pp.161,163)
Orubon v. Gbondu (1999) 11 NWLR (Pt. 628) 661 CA (p.251)
Oruche v. C.O.P (1997) 4 NWLR (Pt. 497) 1 SC (pp.48,226)
Oruobu v. Anekwe (1997) 5 NWLR (Pt. 506) 618 CA (pp.20,73)
Osafile v. Odi (1994) 2 NWLR (Pt. 325) 125 SC (p.382)
Osakwe v. Nigerian Paper Mill Ltd (1998) 10 NWLR (Pt. 568) 1 SC (p.244)
Osazuwa v. Ojo (1999) 13 NWLR (Pt. 634) 286 CA (p.278)
Oshin & Oshin Ltd v. Livestock Feed Ltd (1997) 2 NWLR (Pt. 486) 162 CA
    (p.328)
Osho v. Ape (1998) 8 NWLR (Pt. 562) 492 SC (p.257)
Osho v. Foreign Finance Corporation (1991) 4 NWLR (Pt. 184) 157 SC
    (pp.270,271)
Oshoboja v. Dada (1999) 12 NWLR (Pt. 629) 102 CA (p.269)
Oshodi v. Eyifunmi (2000) 7 SC (Part II) 145 (pp.135,375,383,384)
Oshunrinde v. Akande (1996) 6 NWLR (Pt. 455) 383 SC (p.345)
Osibamowo v. Osibamowo (1991) 3 NWLR (Pt. 177) 85 CA (pp.144,145)
Osolu v. Osolu (1998) 1 NWLR (Pt. 535) 532 CA (pp.109,110,132)
Osondu v. Boneh (2000) 3 SC 42 (p.239)

Partridge v. Crittenden (1968) All ER 421 (p.297)
Paton v. British Pregnancy Advisory Service Trustees (1979) QB 276 (p.359)
Pavex International Co. (Nig.) Ltd v. I.B.W.A (2000) 4 SC (Pt. II) 196 (pp.52, 218,397)
Paye v. Gaji (1996) 5 NWLR (Pt. 450) 589 CA (p.330)
Peace Treaties Case (I.C.J. AO 1949) (p.200)
Pearce v. Brooks (1866) LR 1 Ex 213 (p.315)
Peek v. Gurney (1837) L.R. 6 H.L. 377 (p.320)
Pelfaco Ltd. v.W.A.O.S Ltd. (1997) 10 NWLR (Pt.524) 222 CA (pp.12, 356)
Peter E. Venture (Nig.) Ltd v. Gazasonner Ind. Ltd (1998) 6 NWLR (Pt. 555) 619 CA (pp.4,67)
Peters v. State (1992) 9 NWLR (Pt. 265) 323 SC (p.38)
Pever v. Adaa (1998) 3 NWLR (Pt. 540) 129 CA (p.257)
Pharmaceutical Society of Great Britain v. Boots Cash Chemists (1953) 1 QB 401 (p.297)
Pharmatek Industrial Ltd v. Trade Bank (Nig.) Plc (1997) 7 NWLR (Pt. 514) 639 CA (p.68)
Phoenix Motors Ltd v. National Provident Fund Management Board (1993) 1 NWLR (Pt. 272) 718 CA (p.237)
Photo Production Ltd v. Securicor Ltd.(1980) AC 827 (p.313)
Pincent v. State (1997) 1 NWLR (Pt. 480) 234 CA (pp.84, 87)
Planche v. Colburn (1831) 8 Bing. 14 (p.322)
Popoola v. Adeyemo (1992) 8 NWLR (Pt. 257) 1 SC (pp.40,51)
Powell v. Powell (1900) 1 Ch. 243 (p.317)
Preist v. Last (1903) 2 K.B. 148 (p.309)
Prendergast v. Sam and Dee Ltd (1988) The Times, 24 March 1988 (p.362)
Price and Co. v. The Union Lighterance Co. (1904) I.B.B. 412 (p.313)
Princewill v. State (1994) 6 NWLR (Pt. 353) 703 SC (p.100)
Progress Bank (Nig.) Ltd. V. Ugonna (Nig.) Ltd. (1996) 3 NWLR (Pt. 435) 202 CA (p.425)
Prosecutor v. Tadic (Jurisdiction) I.L.R. 105 (1997) 419 (pp.284,285)
Prospect Textile Mills v. I.C.I. Plc England, (1996) 6 NWLR (Pt. 457) 668 CA (p.302)
Provincial Council, Ogun State University v. Makinde (1991) 2 NWLR (Pt. 175) 613 CA (p.8)
Prudential Insurance Co. v. IRC (1904) 2 KB 658 (p.173)
Psychiatric Hospital Management Board (P.H.M.B) v. Ejitagha (2000) 6 SC (Part II) 1 (p.24)
Psychiatric Hospital Management Board (PHMB) v. Edosa (2001) 12 WRN 183 SC (p.238)
Public Finance Securities Ltd v. Jefia (1998) 3 NWLR (Pt. 543) 602 CA (pp.54,61,63)

- Q -
Queen v. Adaroh (1999) 1 NWLR (Pt. 586) 330 CA (pp.163,164)
Queen v. Uche (1994) 6 NWLR (Pt. 350) 329 CA (p.422)

- R -
R Baby M (1988) 537 A 2d 1227 (USA) (p.359)
R v. Adams (1957) Crim LR 365 (p.364)
R v. Anderson (1868) 11 Cox's Criminal Cases, 198, Court of Criminal Appeal (p.336)

- S -

- T -

Torvald Klaveness A/S v. Arni Maritime Corpn, The Gregos (1994) Times, 28 October (p.33)
Total (Nig.) Plc. v. Efakpokire (1998) 5 NWLR (Pt. 549) 307 CA (p.156)
Touche v. Metropolitan Railway Warehousing Co. (1871) 6 Ch App 671 (p.56)
Tournier v. National Provincial and Union Bank of England (1924) 1 KB 461 (pp.405,406)
Trans Nab Ltd v. Joseph (1997) 5 NWLR (Pt. 504) 176 CA (pp.222,226)
Trenco (Nigeria) Ltd v. African Real Estate Ltd (1978) 1 L.R.N. 146 (pp.53,60)
Trendtex Trading Corp.v. Central Bank of Nigeria (1977) Q.B. 527 (p.189)
Trial Smelter Arbitration: United States v. Canada (1938 and 1941) 3 R.I.A.A. 1905 (p.193)
Tsakiroglou & Co. v. Noblee Thorh G.m.b.h. (1962) A.C. 93 (p.324)
Tukur v. Government of Taraba State (1997) 6 NWLR (Pt. 510) 549 SC (pp.112,233)
Tukur v. Govt. of Gongola State (1988) 1 NWLR (Pt. 68) 39 SC (p.341)
Tukur v. Govt., Gongola State (1996) 5 NWLR (Pt.447) 186 CA (p.47)
Turner v. M.G.M. Pictures Ltd (1950) 1 All E.R. 449 (p.419)
Twaddle v. Atkinson (1861) 1 B & S 393 (pp.300,305)
Twycoss v. Grant (1877) 2 CPD 469 (p.55)
Tyum v. Atavti (1996) 8 NWLR (Pt. 469) 675 CA (p.376)

- U -

U-2 Incident of May 1960 (p.193)
U.A.C (Nig.) Ltd v. Fasheyitan (1998) 11 NWLR (Pt. 573) 179 SC (p.49)
U.B.A Ltd v. Achoru (1990)6 NWLR (Pt. 156) 254 SC (pp.425,426,427)
U.B.A. Ltd v. Michael O'Abimbolu & Co. (1995) 9 NWLR (Pt. 419) 371 CA (p.3)
U.B.A. Plc v. Ekene Dili Chukwu (Nig.) Ltd. (1999) 12 NWLR (Pt. 629) 128 CA (p.409)
U.B.N. Ltd v. Ayoola (1998) 11 NWLR (Pt. 573) 338 CA (p.410)
U.B.N. Ltd v. Ogboh (1995) 2 NWLR (Pt. 380) 647 SC (pp.238,243,244)
U.B.N. Ltd v. Oki (1999) 8 NWLR (Pt. 614) 244 CA (p.412)
U.B.N. Ltd v. Okwara (1998) 1 NWLR (Pt. 532) 118 CA (p.412)
U.B.N. Ltd v. Osezuah (1997) 2 NWLR (Pt. 485) 28 CA (p.412)
U.B.N. Ltd v. Salami (1998) 3 NWLR (Pt. 543) 538 CA (p.410)
U.B.N. Ltd v. Tropic Foods Ltd (1992) 3 NWLR (Pt. 228) 231 CA (p.158)
U.B.N. Ltd. v. Odusote Bookstores Ltd (1995) 9 NWLR (Pt. 421) 558 SC (p.46)
U.B.N. Plc v. Adjarho (1997) 6 NWLR (Pt. 507) 112 CA (p.227)
U.B.N. Plc. v. Eskol Paints (Nig.) Ltd (1997) 8 NWLR (Pt. 515) 157 CA (p.413)
U.B.N. Plc v. Jase Motors (Nig.) Ltd (1997) 7 NWLR (Pt. 513) 387 CA (pp.57, 59)
U.B.N. Plc v. Olori Motors Co. Ltd (1998) 5 NWLR (Pt. 551) 652 CA (p.398)
U.B.N. Plc v. Scpok (Nig.) Ltd (1998) 12 NW LR (Pt. 578) 439 CA (pp.126,382,409)
U.B.N. Plc v. Sparkling Breweries Ltd (1997) 5 NWLR (Pt. 505) 344 CA (p.411)
U.B.N. v. Ozigi (1994) 3 NWLR (Pt. 333) 385 SC (p.121)
U.N.I.C. v. U.C.I.C. Ltd (1999) 3 NWLR (Pt. 593) 17 CA (pp.119,174)

Waziri v. Waziri (1998) 1 NWLR (Pt. 533) 322 CA (p.206)
Weide & Co. (Nig.) Ltd v. Weide & Co. Hamburg (1992) 6 NWLR (Pt. 249) 627 CA (p.50)
Wema Bank Nigeria Ltd v. Odulaja (2000) 3 SC 83 (p.391)
Wema Bank Plc v. Balogun (1999) 7 NWLR (Pt. 610) 242 CA (pp.221,398)
Wema Bank v. Adebowale (2001) 4 WRN 1 CA (p.161)
Westac v. Sokoto State Government (S.S.G) (2001) 1 WRN 113 CA (p.322)
Western Nigerian Finance Corporation v. West Coast Builders Ltd (1971) 1 U.I.L.R. 93 (p.324)
Whaley Bridge Calico Printing Co. v. Green (1889) 5 QBD 109 (p.55)
White v. Molley (1899) 2 Q.B. 34 at 39 (p.24)
Whitehouse v. Jordan (1981) 1 WLR 246 (p.363)
Wildenhus's Case 120 U.S. 1 (1887) US Supreme Court (p.336)
Williams v. Bayley (1866) L.R. 1 H.L. 200 (pp.316,317)
Williams v. Daily Times (1990) 1 NWLR (Pt. 124) 1 SC (p.37)
Williams v. Hope Rising Voluntary Funds Society (1982) 2 SC 145 (p.349)
Williams v. Majekodunmi (1962) 1 AII NLR 413 SC (p.148)
Willoughby v. International Merchants Bank (Nig.) Ltd (1987) 1 NWLR (Pt. 48) 105 (p.353)
Wilson v. Oshin (2000) 6 SC (Part III) 1 (pp.126, 133,356)
Wilson v. Pringle (1986) 2 All E.R. 440 CA (p.419)
Wilson v. United Countries Bank Ltd (1920) AC 102 (p.409)
Wisher v. Essey Area Health Authority (1988) AC 1074 (p.363)
Woods v. Martins Bank Ltd and Another (1959) 1 QB 55 (p.403)
WR & PC Ltd v. Onwo (1999) 12 NWLR (Pt. 630) 312 CA (pp.11,242,385)
Wright v. Carter (1903) 1 Ch. 27 (p.317)
Wuyep v. Wuyep (1997) 10 NWLR (Pt. 523) 154 CA (p.232)

- Y -
Ya'u v. Dikwa (2001) 5 WRN 40 CA (p.389)
Yakubu v. Gov., Kogi State (1995) 8 NWLR (Pt. 414) 386 SC (p.10)
Yakubu v. Gov., Kogi State (1997) 7 NWLR (Pt. 511) 66 CA (p.19)
Yare v. Nunku (1995) 5 NWLR (Pt. 394) 129 SC (p.7)
Yaro v. Arewa Construction Ltd (1998) 7 NWLR (Pt. 558) 368 SC (p.400)
Yeager v. Iran (U.S. v. Iran) (1987) 17 Iran-U.S.C.T.R. 92 (p.192)
Yeboah v. Boateng (1963) 1 G.L.R. 182 (p.421)
Yepremian v. Scarborough General Hospital (1980) 110 DLR (3d) 513 (Canadian case) (p.361)
Yisau v. Wema Bank (2001) 11 WRN 91 CA (p.423)
Yongbish v. Bulus (1997) 2 NWLR (Pt. 489) 621 CA (p.137)
Youmans Claim: United States v. Mexico (1926) 4 R.I.A.A. 110 (p.192)
Younis v. Chidiak (1970) All N.L.R. 188 SC (p.301)
Yusuf v. Co-op.Bank Ltd (1994) 7 NWLR (Pt. 359) 676 SC (p.2)
Yusuf v. Matthew (1999) 13 NWLR (Pt. 633) 30 CA (pp.250,257)
Yusuf v. Mobolaji (1999) 12 NWLR (Pt. 631) 374 CA (p.311)
Yusuf v. Oyetunde (1998) 12 NWLR (Pt. 579) 483 SC (pp.114,377)
Yusuf v. U.B.N. Ltd (1996) 6 NWLR (Pt. 457) 632 SC (p.421)

 Table of Statutes

Nigerian Legislation

List of Abbreviations

AC:	Appeal Cases
A 2D:	Atlantic Reporter, Second Series (USA)
AJIL	American Journal of International Law
All ER:	All England Reports
ALJR:	Australian Law Journal Reports
All NLR:	All Nigeria Law Reports
BMLR:	British Medical Law Reports
B & S:	Best and Smith's Reports, Queen's Bench
Bing:	Bingham's Reports, Common Pleas
Bos & PNR:	Bosanquet and Puller's New Reports, Common Pleas
Brooklyn:	Brooklyn Journal of International Law
Burr:	Burrow's Reports, King's Bench
Camp:	Campbell's Reports
CCC:	Cox Criminal Cases
CCHCJ:	Selected Judgment of the High Court of Lagos State
ChD:	Law Reports, Chancery Division
CLT:	Canadian Law Times
Cmd:	Command Paper (United Kingdom), 1919-56
Cr App R.:	Cohen's Criminal Appeal Reports
Cri. LR:	Criminal Law Reports
Crim. LR:	Criminal Law Review
DLR (2nd, 3rd & 4th):	Dominion Law Reports, Second, Third, and Fourth Series (Canada)
East:	East's Reports, King's Bench
ECSLR:	Law Reports of East Central States
EHRR:	European Human Rights Reports
Fam:	Law Reports, Family Division
FLR:	Family Law Reports
FSC:	Selected Judgment of the Federal Supreme Court
F Supp.:	Federal Supplement (USA)
FSR:	Fleet Street Reports
F 2d:	Federal Reporter, Second Series (USA)
GLR:	Ghana Law Reports
Harv. ILJ:	Harvard International Law Journal
HCLJ:	High Court of Lagos State Judgment
HLC:	Judgments of the House of Lords
HMSO:	Her (His) Majesty's Stationery Office
HR:	Hare Reports
ICJ Rep:	International Court of Justice Reports
ICLQ:	International and Comparative Law Quarterly
ILM:	International Legal Materials

ILR:	Islamic Law Reports or International Law Reports
Imm AR:	Immigration Appeal Reports
Iran-USCTR:	Iran-U.S. Claims Tribunal Reports
KB:	King's Bench
LT:	Law Times
LJ:	Law Journal
LJ EX:	Law Journal, Exchequer
LJKB:	Law Journal, King's Bench
LJQB:	Law Journal, Queen's Bench
LR Eq.:	Law Reports Equity
LR Ex:	Law Reports, Exchequer
Lloyd's Rep:	Lloyd's List Law Reports
LLR:	Law Reports of High Court of Lagos State
LRN:	Law Reports of Nigeria
MWSJ:	Selected Judgment of the High Court of Mid-Western State
MAT:	Mixed Arbitral Tribunals
Med. LR:	Medical Law Reports
Moore Int. Arb:	International Arbitrations
NCLR:	Nigerian Constitutional Law Report
NMLR:	Nigerian Monthly Law Report
NLR:	Nigerian Law Report
NRNLR:	Northern Region of Nigeria Law Report
NNLR:	Northern Nigeria Law Reports
NSCC:	Nigerian Supreme Court Cases
NWLR:	Nigerian Weekly Law Reports
NZLR:	New Zealand Law Reports
OR(2nd):	Ontario Reports, Second Series
PCIJ:	Permanent Court of International Justice
QBD:	Queen's Bench Division
RIAA:	Reports of International Arbitral Award
SACLR:	South African Constitutional Law Report
SC:	Judgment of the Supreme Court of Nigeria or Court of Session Cases (Scotland)
SCC:	Indian Supreme Court Judgment
SCNLR:	Supreme Court of Nigeria Law Reports
SLRN:	Sharia Law Reports of Nigeria
TAUNT:	Taunton's Reports Common Pleas
TLR:	Times Law Reports
UILR:	University of Ife Law Reports
US Rep:	U.S Reports
Ves Sen:	Vesey Sen's Reports
WACA:	West African Court of Appeal
WCR:	War Crimes Reports
WLR:	Weekly Law Reports
WRN:	Weekly Reports of Nigeria
WRNLR:	Western Region of Nigeria Law Reports
Yale JIL:	Yale Journal of International Law

I
Action

1.1 Cause of Action

1. A cause of action is the entire set of circumstances giving rise to an enforceable claim. It is the fact or combination of facts, which gives rise to a right to sue and it consists of two elements, viz, the wrongful act of the defendant, which gives the plaintiff his cause of complaint; and the consequent damage.

> - *Adesokan v. Adegorolu (1997) 3 NWLR (Pt. 493) 261 SC*
> - *Ajayi v. Mil. Adm., Ondo State (1997) 5 NWLR (Pt. 504) 237 SC*
> - *Rhein Mass Und See GMBH v. Rivway Lines Ltd. (1998) 5 NWLR (Pt. 549) 265 SC*
> - *Emiator v. Nigerian Army (1999) 12 NWLR (Pt. 631) 362 SC*
> - *Agbanelo v. Union Bank of Nigeria Ltd (2000) 4 SC (Pt. 1) 233*
> - *Oduntan v. Akibu (2000) 7 SC (Part II) 106*
> - *Messrs NV Scheep v. The M.V. "S.Araz" (2000) 12 SC (Part I) 164*

2. A cause of action arises on the date of the event whereby the cause of action becomes complete so that the aggrieved party can begin and maintain his action.

> - *Shell Pet. Dev. Co. (Nig.) Ltd. v. Farah (1995) 3 NWLR (Pt. 382) 148 at 154 CA*
> - *Alese v. Aladetuyi (1995) 6 NWLR (Pt. 403) 527 CA*
> - *Adeosun v. Jibesin (2001) 14 WRN 106 CA*

3. For a plaintiff to succeed in an action instituted in a particular capacity, he must establish that capacity in which the suit is instituted.

> - *Agbabiaka v. Saibu (1998) 10 NWLR (Pt. 571) 534 SC*

4. A cause of action in *rem* commenced by a party who subsequently dies survives the party if continued by his surviving heir. Section 15(1) of the Administration of Estates

Law, Cap. 2 Laws of Bendel State, 1976 considered.

- *Ogiugo v. Ogiugo (2001) 1 WRN 131 SC*

5. A cause of action in trespass to land survives death of the original party to the action, since trespass to land involves an injury to the estate of a deceased person.

- *Erinfolabi v. Oke (1995) 5 NWLR (Pt. 395) 296 at 299 CA*

6. A counter-claim is for all intents and purposes, a separate, independent and distinct action and a counter-claimant, like all other plaintiffs, must prove his claim against the person being counter-claimed before he can obtain judgment on the counter-claim.

- *Ogbonna v. A.-G., Imo State (1992) 1 NWLR (Pt. 220) 647 SC*
- *Obmiami Brick & Stone (Nig.) Ltd v. A.C.B. Ltd (1992) 3 NWLR (Pt. 229) 260 SC*
- *Dabup v. Kolo (1993) 9 NWLR (Pt. 317) 254 SC*
- *Jeric (Nig.) Ltd v. U.B.N. Plc (2000) 12 SC (Pt. II) 133*

7. A declaratory relief is an independent cause of action and it is a discretionary remedy.

- *Dantata v. Mohammed (2000) 5 SC 1*

8. A reasonable cause of action is a cause of action with a chance of success.

- *Combined Trade Ltd v. All States Trust Bank Ltd (1998) 12 NWLR (Pt. 576) 56 CA*
- *Dantata v. Mohammed (2000) 5 SC 1*

9. Where there is a failure to disclose reasonable cause of action against a party, the court is obliged to strike out the case against the party.

- *Abubakar v. Falola (1997) 11 NWLR (Pt. 530) 638 CA*

10. A cause of action differs from a right of action. A cause of action constitutes a set of facts or fact which gives a person a right to claim a judicial redress where he is wronged. A right of action, on the other hand, entitles him to maintain an action on the wrong alleged with a view to getting a judicial redress.

- *Yusuf v. Co-op. Bank Ltd (1994) 7 NWLR (Pt. 359) 676 SC*

- *U.B.A. Ltd v. Michael O'Abimbolu & Co. (1995) 9 NWLR (Pt. 419) 371 CA*

11. Security for damages, interest and/or cost is not a cause of action that can ground a claim, unless otherwise specifically provided by statute.

- *NV Scheep v. "S. Araz" (2001) 4 WRN 105 SC*

12. An issue is a disputed point or question to which parties to an action have narrowed their several allegations and upon which they are desirous of obtaining decision of the court either on question of law, or question of fact.

- *Jumbo v. Bryanko Int. Ltd (1995) 6 NWLR (Pt. 403) 545 CA*
- *Okoromaka v. Odiri (1995) 7 NWLR (Pt. 408) 411 CA*

13. Issues joined in a suit are, as a rule, identified or determined from the pleadings of the parties. Therefore, issues are joined on pleadings and not on plans.

- *Ikoku v. Ekeukwu (1995) 7 NWLR (Pt. 410) 637 SC*

1.2 Locus Standi

1. *Locus standi* **or standing to sue is the legal right of a party to an action to be heard in litigation before a court of law or tribunal. A person is said to have** *locus standi* **if he has shown sufficient interest in the action and that his civil rights and obligations have been or are in danger of being infringed.**

- *Olagunju v. Yahaya (1998) 3 NWLR (Pt. 542) 501 CA*
- *Okafor v. Asoh (1999) 3 NWLR (Pt. 593) 35 CA*
- *Nnubia v. A.G., Rivers State (1999) 3 NWLR (Pt. 593) 82 CA*
- *Ogunmokun v. Mil. Adm, Osun State (1999) 3 NWLR (Pt. 594) 261 CA*
- *Ibrahim v. INEC (1999) 8 NWLR (Pt. 614) 334 CA*
- *Guda v. Kitta (1999) 12 NWLR (Pt. 629) 21 CA*

2. For a person to bring an action in respect of any subject matter, such a person must show that he has a legal right or special

interest in that subject matter.

> - *Akinnubi v. Akinnubi (1997) 2 NWLR (Pt. 486) 144 SC*
> - *Attahiru v. Bagudu (1998) 3 NWLR (Pt. 543) 656 CA*

3. It is a well established principle of law that a defendant who challenges *in limine* the *locus standi* of a plaintiff is deemed to accept as correct all the averments contained in the plaintiff's statement of claim.

> - *Adesokan v. Adegorolu (1997) 3 NWLR (Pt. 493) 261 SC*

4. *Locus standi* and jurisdiction are interwoven, in the sense that *locus standi* goes to affect the jurisdiction of the court before which an action is brought. Thus, where there is no *locus standi* to file an action in the first place, the court cannot properly assume jurisdiction to entertain the action.

> - *Waziri v. Danboyi (1999) 4 NWLR (Pt. 598) 239 CA*

5. Where a plaintiff has no *locus standi* to bring a suit, the suit becomes incompetent and the court lacks the jurisdiction to entertain it.

> - *Ejikeme v. Amaechi (1998) 3 NWLR (Pt. 542) 456 CA*
> - *Ogunmokun v. Mil. Adm., Osun State (1999) 3 NWLR (Pt. 594) 261 CA*
> - *Ayoola v. Baruwa (1999) 11 NWLR (Pt. 628) 595 CA*

6. The proper order that a court should make where a petitioner lacks *locus standi* in an election petition, is an order of dismissal.

> - *Egwu v. Eke (1999) 3 NWLR (Pt. 594) 189 CA*

7. The issue of *locus standi* could be raised after the plaintiff has duly filed his pleadings, by a motion and / or in a statement of defence.

> - *Ebongo v. Uwemedimo (1995) 8 NWLR (Pt. 411) 22 CA*
> - *Peter E. Venture (Nig.) Ltd. v. Gazasonner Ind. Ltd. (1998) 6 NWLR (Pt. 555) 619 CA*

8. The burden is on the plaintiff to prove that he has the *locus standi* to commence an action and failure to discharge the burden, the action must fail.

> - *Contract Resources (Nig.) Ltd. v. Wende (1998) 5 NWLR (Pt. 549) 243 CA*

- *Ezechigbo v. Gov., Anambra State (1999) 9 NWLR (Pt. 619) 386 CA*

9. A party to a suit does not have the *locus standi* to raise the issue of non-joinder of other parties, since the issue of non-joinder of parties can only be raised by the parties themselves who were left out of the action if indeed they have interest in the matter.

- *Mil. Gov., Ondo State v. Ajayi (1998) 3 NWLR (Pt. 540) 27 CA*

10. A plaintiff can only seek redress in a court of law if he has interest which the law regards as sufficient. The term "sufficient interest" could however be determined in the light of the facts and circumstances of each case.

- *Guda v. Kitta (1999) 12 NWLR (Pt. 629) 21 CA*
- *In Re: Obianwu (1999) 12 NWLR (Pt. 629) 78 CA*

11. It is the statement of claim or evidence adduced and not the writ of summons that must be gleaned to find out whether or not a litigant has *locus standi* to sue.

- *Ebongo v. Uwemedimo (1995) 8 NWLR (Pt. 411) 22 CA*
- *Douglas v. Shell Petroleum Dev. Co. Ltd. (1999) 2 NWLR (Pt. 591) 466 CA*
- *Ezechigbo v. Gov., Anambra State (1999) 9 NWLR (Pt. 619) 386 CA*

12. It is not sufficient in a chieftaincy suit for the plaintiff to merely say he is a descendant of a chieftaincy line; he has to state further that he has an interest in the chieftaincy title and must demonstrate how his interest arose.

- *Amusa Momoh v. Jimoh Olotu (1970) 1 All NLR 117 SC*
- *Obala of Otan-Aiyegbaju v. Adesina (1999) 2 NWLR (Pt. 590) 163 SC*

13. *Locus standi* or legal capacity to institute proceedings in a court of law is not dependent on the success or merits of a case; it is a condition precedent to a determination of a case on the merits.

- *Owodunni v. Registered Trustees of C.C.C (2000) 6 SC (Part III) 60*

14. The words "Mr. & Mrs." combined do not create a legal term as such to confer on a married couple a legal right and capacity to sue and be sued. In law, they are two separate people and either of them can only be sued in his or her own name.

> - *Lion of Africa Insurance Co. Ltd v. Esan (1999) 8 NWLR (Pt. 614) 197 at 199 CA*

1.3 Limitation of Action

1. Time begins to run for the purposes of the limitation law from the date the cause of action accrues.

> - *British Airways Plc. v. Akinyosoye (1995) 1 NWLR (Pt. 374) 722 at 724 CA*
> - *Shell Pet. Dev. Co. (Nig.) Ltd. v. Farah (1995) 3 NWLR (Pt. 382) 148 at 156 CA*
> - *Jallco Ltd v. Owoniboys Tech. Serv. Ltd (1995) 4 NWLR (Pt. 391) 534 at 538 SC*

2. By virtue of Section 8(1)(a) of the Limitation Law Cap 70 Laws of Lagos State, all actions founded on simple contract must not be brought after the expiration of six years from the date on which the cause of action accrued.

> - *British Airways Plc. v. Akinyosoye (1995) 1 NWLR (Pt. 374) 722 CA*

3. A reference in an enactment to a period of days shall be construed, where the period is reckoned from a particular event, as excluding the day in which the event occurred. Section 15(2) of the Interpretation Act Cap 192, Laws of the Federation, 1990 considered.

> - *Balewa v. Muazu (1999) 5 NWLR (Pt. 604) 636 CA*

4. The law does not prohibit parties to a dispute from engaging in negotiation for the purpose of settling the dispute. Except where as a result there is what can be reasonably regarded as a settlement of the dispute or an admission of liability on the part of the defendant, the limitation time continues to run.

> - *Shell Pet. Dev. Co. (Nig.) Ltd. V. Farah (1995) 3 NWLR*

(Pt. 382) 148 at 156 CA

5. The right for damages in international carriage of goods by air shall be extinguished if an action is not brought within two years, reckoned from the date of arrival at the destination, or from the date on which the carriage stopped. Article 29(1) of the Warsaw Convention considered.

> - *Ibidapo v. Lufthansa Airlines (1997) 4 N.W.L.R (Pt. 498) 124 SC*

6. A public officer can avail himself of the protection afforded by Section 2 of the Public Officers (Protection) Law, while discharging his duties as such, if the action against him is not instituted within three months next after the act, neglect or default complained of, or in the case of a continuing damage or injury, within three months next after the ceasing thereof.

> - *Yare v. Nunku (1995) 5 NWLR (Pt. 394) 129 SC*

7. Where a person affected by an arbitration award wishes to have it set aside, he must do so by way of an application to the court within three months from the date of the award. Section 29(1) of the Arbitration and Conciliation Act, 1988 considered.

> - *Araka v. Ejeagwu (2001) 5 WRN 1 SC*

8. It is trite that a legal right to enforce an action is not perpetual right, but a right generally limited by statute. Therefore, a cause of action is statute barred if legal proceedings cannot be commenced in respect of same because the period laid down by the Limitation Law or Act had elapsed.

> - *Adeosun v. Jibesin (2001) 14 WRN 106 CA*

9. Where a cause of action is based on fraud or the right of action is concealed by fraud, the limitation period does not commence until the fraud is or could reasonably have been discovered or in the case of disability of a plaintiff either from infancy or unsoundness of mind, the period of limitation is also extended.

> - *Nwosu v. Offor (1997) 2 NWLR (Pt. 487) 274 at 276 SC*

10. Where the limitation of time is imposed in a statute, decree or edict, unless the said statute, decree or edict makes provision for extension of time, the courts cannot extend the time.

- *Akinnuoye v. Military Administrator, Ondo State (1997) 1 NWLR (Pt. 483) 564 at 566 to 567 CA*

1.4 Demurrer

1. In a demurrer proceeding, the defendant admits every allegation of fact as contained in the statement of claim and says in spite of that no cause of action exists.

- *IAL 361 Inc. v. Mobil Oil (Nig.) Plc. (1999) 5 NWLR (Pt. 601) 9 CA*

2. In a demurrer proceeding, any procedure adopted which involves the taking or assessing of evidence, whether documentary or oral will be outside the procedure for demurrer and accordingly will be irregular.

- *Brawal Shipping (Nigeria) Ltd. v. F.I. Onwadike Co. Ltd. (2000) 6 SC (Part II) 133*

3. Under the various High Court (Civil Procedure) Rules of Lagos, Ogun and Oyo States, proceedings by way of demurrer have been expressly abolished. Thus, a defendant wishing to challenge the competence of a suit by a preliminary objection on a point of law is entitled to file his statement of defence and raise the point of law therein.

- *Madu v. Ononuju (1986) 3 NWLR (Pt. 26) 23 CA*
- *Provincial Council, Ogun State University v. Makinde (1991) 2 NWLR (Pt. 175) 613 CA*
- *Akinade v. N.A.S.U. (1999) 2 NWLR (Pt. 592) 570 CA*

1.5 Parties

1. The plaintiff has a duty to bring before a court all parties whose presence are crucial to the resolution of the case and failure to so do, the action is liable to be struck out.

- *Adisa v. Oyinwola (2000) 6 SC (Part II) 47*

2. A necessary party to a case is a person whose presence is necessary for the effectual and complete adjudication of the questions involved in the cause or matter.

- *O.K. Contact-Point Ltd v. Progress Bank Plc (1999) 5 NWLR (Pt. 604) 631 CA*
- *B.O.N. Ltd v. Saleh (1999) 9 NWLR (Pt. 618) 331 CA*

3. Where a necessary party is not joined in a case, the court or tribunal lacks jurisdiction to entertain the case.

- *Amuda v. Ajobo (1995) 7 NWLR (Pt. 406) 170 CA*
- *Tafida v. Bafarawa (1999) 4 NWLR (Pt. 597) 70 CA*
- *Kaliel v. Aliero (1999) 4 NWLR (Pt. 597) 139 CA*
- *Bashir v. Audu (1999) 5 NWLR (Pt. 603) 433 CA*
- *Santa Fe Drilling (Nig.) Ltd. v. Awala (1999) 6 NWLR (Pt. 608) 623 CA*
- *Ayoola v. Baruwa (1999) 11 NWLR (Pt. 628) 595 CA*

4. Where a plaintiff fails to join the persons against whom he is seeking a relief, the action in respect thereof would be struck out on the ground that it is improperly constituted.

- *Ayorinde v. Oni (2000) 2 SC 33*

5. Dead men are no longer legal persons in the eyes of the law as they have laid down their legal personality with their lives at death. Being destitute of rights or interests, they can neither sue nor be sued.

- *C.C.B. (Nig.) Plc v. O'Silvawax Int'l Ltd (1999) 7 NWLR (Pt. 609) 97 CA*

6. A party interested or an interested party in the subject matter of a suit can seek to be joined either at the trial or in the appellate court. In either case, he has to show an interest in the result of the litigation.

- *Okoli v. Ojiakor (1997) 1 NWLR (Pt. 479) 48 CA*
- *Ogana II v. Awulor (1997) 9 NWLR (Pt. 522) 668 CA*
- *Dagazau v. Borkir Int'l Co. Ltd. (1999) 7 NWLR (Pt. 610) 293 CA*

7. By virtue of Section 50(2) of Decree No. 6 of 1999, where a petitioner in an election petition makes complaints against any

electoral official or any other person who took part in the conduct of the election, such a person should be joined in the petition as a necessary party.

- *Egolum v. Obasanjo (1999) 7 NWLR (Pt. 611) 423 CA*
- *Bashir v. Audu (1999) 5 NWLR (Pt. 603) 433 CA*

8. For a person to be joined as a party in an action, it must be shown that the person is entitled to some share/interest in the subject matter; or lays claim to such share/interest; or is likely to be affected by the result of the action; or is a necessary party; and/ or it is just and convenient to join him.

- *Yakubu v. Gov., Kogi State (1995) 8 NWLR (Pt. 414) 386 SC*
- *Umar v. Onikata (1999) 3 NWLR (Pt. 596) 558 CA*
- *Ecobank (Nig.) Plc v. Gateway Hotels (Nig.) Ltd. (1999) 11 NWLR (Pt. 627) 397 CA*
- *Guda v. Kitta (1999) 12 NWLR (Pt. 629) 21 CA*

9. For an insurance company to be sued or be joined in a suit, a notice of intention to sue must have been served on the company at least one clear month before the institution of the suit or joinder of the insurance company. Section 58(1) and (2) of the Insurance Decree No. 58 of 1991 considered.

- *IAL 361 Inc v. Mobil Oil (Nig.) Plc (1999) 5 NWLR (Pt. 601) 9 CA*

10. A person carrying on business in a name (business name) or style other than his own name may be sued in such name or style as if it were a firm's name.

- *Fabno Ind. Ltd. v. United Distillers Plc (1999) 5 NWLR (Pt. 602) 314 CA*

11. Where a court orders joinder of a person who was not originally a party to the proceedings, the court must further order that the writ of summons and statement of claim be amended pursuant to the order of joinder and served on all parties.

- *Uchendu v. Ogboni (1999) 5 NWLR (Pt. 603) 337 SC*

12. A statutory provision on joinder cannot be watered down

by merely calling as a witness a person who should have been joined as a party.

- *Asikpo v. Ekene (1999) 5 NWLR (Pt. 604) 578 CA*

13. An application for alteration of parties should be made before judgment in a suit.

- *Kaduna Textile Ltd. v. Obi (1999) 10 NWLR (Pt.621) 138 CA*

14. It is a settled principle of law that non-joinder or misjoinder of parties will not be fatal to an action and no proceedings shall be rendered null and void for lack of competence or jurisdiction simply because a plaintiff joins a party who ought not to have been joined.

- *C.R.S.N. Corp. v. Oni (1995) 1 NWLR (Pt. 371) 270 SC*
- *WR & PC Ltd.v.Onwo (1999)12 NWLR (Pt.630) 312 CA*

15. A person who is not a party before the court and has not sought and obtained the leave of court before deposing to affidavit to his own benefit is just a busy body and the court ought not to look at his affidavit at all.

- *Aniekan v. Aniekan (1999) 12 NWLR (Pt. 631) 491 CA*

16. By virtue of Paragraph 48(1) Schedule 6 to the State Government (Basic Constitutional and Transitional Provisions) Decree No. 3 of 1999, where an election petition complains of the conduct of an Electoral Officer, Returning officer or any other official of the Electoral Commission, he shall for all purposes be deemed a respondent and joined in the election petition as a necessary party.

- *Doma v. Adamu (1999) 4 NWLR (Pt.598) 311 at 313 CA*

17. A party is joined in a suit on the date the application for his joinder is granted. It is also on that date that the action is commenced against the person joined.

- *Omeh v. Okoro (1999) 8 NWLR (Pt.615) 356 CA*

18. Children or infants, cannot sue as plaintiffs in an action under the rules of court, they can only do so through or by their "next friend", for instance, their mother.

- *Akinnubi v. Akinnubi (1997) 2 NWLR (Pt.486) 144 SC*

19. Parties need not appear in court if they are properly represented nor do they need to personally give evidence at trial so long as the available evidence is sufficient to prove or sustain their case.

- *Igyuse v. Ocholi (1997) 2 NWLR (Pt. 487) 352 CA*

20. Orders of court in an action are not binding on non-parties to the action.

- *Pelfaco Ltd. v.W.A.O.S Ltd. (1997) 10 NWLR (Pt.524) 222 CA*

21. The grant or refusal of joinder of party is exercised at the discretion of the court. Such judicial discretion must be exercised judicially and judiciously.

- *CMI Trading Serv. Ltd . v. Yuriy (1998) 11 NWLR (Pt. 573) 284 CA*

22. A privy is a person whose title is derived from and who claims through a party.

- *Bright Motors Ltd. v. Honda Motor Co. Ltd (1998) 12 NWLR (Pt. 577) 230 CA*

23. Where a cause of action survives the death of a party, such action is not abated by death. If both sole or surviving plaintiff and defendant die and the cause of action survives, the facts of the death of both parties will not cause the suit to abate for an order could be made for the action to continue in the names of the legal representatives of both parties.

- *Bintumi v. Fantami (1998) 13 NWLR (Pt.581) 264 CA*

24. It is wrong for a court to unilaterally take a decision to strike out the name of a party to a suit without any application from any of the parties or indeed the party himself.

- *N.I.M.B Ltd. v. Narindex Trust Ltd. (1998) 13 NWLR (Pt.582) 404 CA*

1.6 Representative Action

1. A representative is a person authorised to act or speak for another or others. Thus, the party wishing to sue or defend in a representative capacity must obtain the authorisation to sue or defend from the person or persons he wishes to represent.

- *Okukuje v. Akwido (2001) 10 WRN 1 SC*

2. The burden is on the party seeking to sue in a representative capacity to prove his authority.

- *Adukwu v. Comm. for Works, Enugu State (1997) 2 NWLR (Pt. 489) 588 CA*

3. It is not in all cases that the court will hold that a party has no authority to sue in a representative capacity where there is no formal authorisation by way of document. The court adopts a flexible attitude, based on the facts and circumstances of each case.

- *Adukwu v. Comm. for Works, Enugu State (1997) 2 NWLR (Pt. 489) 588 CA*

4. A representative plaintiff enjoys an unfettered powers as *dominus litis* until judgment. He can discontinue, compromise, submit to dismissal and other things as he decides during the course of the proceedings.

- *Ndigwe v. Nwude (1999) 11 NWLR (Pt. 626) 314 SC*

5. Where a representative party falls out with the represented persons and withdraws from a suit for any reason, the court has power to add or substitute any person represented though unnamed in the representative action and brings him in as at the date of the original action.

- *Okafor v. Nwude (2001) 3 WRN 105 SC*

6. For an action to lie in a representative capacity, there must be a common interest; a common grievance; and the relief claimed must be beneficial to all.

- *Idise v. Williams Int'l Ltd (1995) 1 NWLR (Pt. 370) 142 SC*

7. All members of a family are bound by a decision of a court in

an action instituted for and on behalf of the family.

   - *Balogun v. Adejobi (1995) 2 NWLR (Pt. 376) 131 SC*
   - *Ude v. Ojechemi (1995) 8 NWLR (Pt. 412) 152 SC*

8. The death of a named representative party in an action does not terminate the action where an application is made by any represented person to be substituted with the dead named representative party.

   - *Ebongo v. Uwemedimo (1995) 8 NWLR (Pt. 411) 22 CA*

1.7 Pre-Action Notice

1. The purpose of serving pre-action notice on a party is that such party is not taken by surprise and to allow the party to have adequate time to prepare to deal with the claim against it.

   - *Captain E.C.C. Amadi v. N.N.P.C. (2000) 6 SC (Part. I) 66*

2. An applicant in a certiorari proceedings does not have to comply with the requirement of issuing a pre-action notice on a public officer.

   - *Ezenwa v. Bestway Elect. Manuf. Co. Ltd. (1999) 8 NWLR (Pt. 613) 61 CA*

3. A statute which prescribes conditions for commencement of an action against certain bodies or persons does not constitute a denial of the right of access to the court by anyone wishing to do so and is not unconstitutional or inconsistent with Section 6(6)(b) of the 1979 Constitution of Nigeria.

   - *Anambra State Govt. v. Nwankwo (1995) 9 NWLR (Pt. 418) 245 CA*

4. Any action commenced without issuing a pre-action notice where it is statutorily provided for is incompetent.

   - *Umukoro v. N.P.A. (1997) 4 NWLR (Pt. 502) 656 SC*

 # II
Administrative Law

2.1 Supremacy of the Constitution

1. The Constitution is the supreme law and its provisions shall have binding force on all authorities and persons throughout Nigeria and any law that is inconsistent with its provisions shall to the extent of the inconsistency be void. Consequently, the law, which purports to limit the jurisdiction of the courts in hearing and determining civil rights, is contrary to the provisions of the Constitution and is therefore null and void.

   - *Doherty v. Balewa (1963) 1 WLR 949*

2. The law, which provides that court processes cannot be served within the legislative chambers or its precincts while the legislature is in session, is void.

   - *Tony Momoh v. Senate of the National Assembly and Others (1981) 1 NCLR 21*

3. The age-long principle of law that the courts have no power to question the validity of an Act of Parliament is very much alive and valid. The function of the court is to construe and apply the enactment of Parliament. However, the legislative supremacy may be subjected to constitutional limitations. A statute passed by the legislature of Sri Lanka, setting up a bribery tribunal was declared invalid by the court, as it had not been passed by the special procedure required by the Constitution.

   - *Bribery Commission v. Ranasinghe (1965) A.C. 172*
   - *R. v. Jordan (1967) Crim. L.R. 483*

2.2 Separation of Powers

1. The doctrine of separation of powers is predicated on the proposition that the organs of government can be classified into

the Executive, the Legislative and the Judiciary, and that no one of these should exercise the functions of the other. The Presidential System entrenched in the 1979 Constitution of Nigeria deliberately separated and balanced powers among the Legislative, the Executive and the Judiciary. It is therefore, not the function of the legislative arm of Government to interpret the Constitution or law it made. This will amount to usurpation of judicial powers and therefore void. Where the Legislature or the Executive is in doubt, it has a duty to refer the interpretation of laws to the courts.

- *Samuel L. Ekeocha v. The Civil Service Commission, Imo State (1981) 1 NCLR 155*

2. The law is that a court of law has no power to interfere in any matter within the internal affairs of the other arms of Government, that is, the Executive and the Legislature. Each organ is to that extent independent within its own domain and no one organ has any supervisory powers or control over the conduct of the affairs of the other unless there has been a violation of any of the provisions of the Constitution.

- *Senator B.C. Okwu v. Senator Wayas and Others (1981) 2 NCLR 522*

2.3 Administration of Justice

1. It is a rule of natural justice that if a person is accused of misconduct, such a person must be confronted with the result of whatever investigation was conducted or if charged, be allowed to defend himself or offer an explanation.

- *Edet v. Chief of Air Staff (1994) 2 NWLR (Pt. 324) 41 CA*

2. Whenever any body or persons having legal authority to determine questions affecting the rights of subjects and having the duty to act judicially, act in excess of their legal authority, they are subject to the controlling jurisdiction of the courts.

- *R. v. Electricity Commissions Ex Parte London, Electricity Joint Committee Co. Ltd (1924) 1 K.B. 171*

3. The law is that those who are called upon to deprive other persons of their personal liberty in the discharge of what they

consider to be their duty, must strictly and scrupulously observe the forms and rules of law.

- *Singh v. Delhi (1942) 16 Supreme Court of India Journal 326*

4. A man may be disqualified from sitting in a judicial capacity on one of two grounds. First, if he has a direct pecuniary interest in the subject matter. Second, if he is biased in favour of one side or against the other.

- *Metropolitan Properties Co. v. Lannon (1969) 1 Q.B. 577*

5. Conduct of examinations and assessment of the work of students by examiners are not subject to judicial review.

- *Thorne v. University of London (1966) 2 Q.B. 237*

6. The law is that no action can be maintained against a judge for anything said or done by him in the exercise of his jurisdiction. The words, which he speaks, are protected by an absolute privilege. The orders, which he gives, and the sentences, which he imposes, cannot be made the subject of civil proceedings against him. The remedy of the party aggrieved is to appeal to a Court of Appeal or to apply for Habeas Corpus or a Writ of Certiorari or take some steps to reverse his ruling. However, if the judge has accepted bribes or being in the least degree corrupt, or has perverted the cause of justice, an action can be maintained against him in criminal courts.

- *Sirros v. Moore (1975) Q.B. 118*

7. An administrative panel is not bound to follow the practice and procedure of a court of law but it is bound to observe and comply with the principles of natural justice. In implementing the recommendation of a panel of inquiry, it is imperative to observe the rules of natural justice because the recommendation per se does not affect the civil rights of a person but acting upon such recommendation does.

- *Tionsha v. Judicial Service Committee Benue State (1997) 6 NWLR (Pt. 508) 307 at 311 CA*

8. The determination of the guilt or innocence of any person accused of committing a crime is within the exclusive jurisdiction of a court of law constituted in the manner

prescribed under the 1979 Constitution of the Federal Republic of Nigeria. It follows, therefore, that no other tribunal, investigating panel or committee is competent to "try", and to find a person accused of the commission of a criminal offence, guilty or innocent.

- *Mil. Gov., Imo State v. Nwauwa (1997) 2 NWLR (Pt. 490) 675 SC*

- *Anyebe v. Adesiyun (1997) 5 NWLR (Pt. 505) 403 CA*

- *Okonkwo v. M.D.P.D.T (1999) 9 NWLR (Pt. 617) 1 CA*

- *UniAgric v. Jack (2001) 3 WRN 83 CA*

9. Where the law prescribes a particular method of exercising a statutory power, such power must be exercised accordingly and no other method is permissible.

- *Ogualaji v. A.-G., Rivers State (1997) 6 NWLR (Pt. 508) 209 SC*

10. Generally, a statutory disciplinary power cannot be delegated but where the same statute expressly authorises delegation, it becomes possible and valid.

- *Moronkeji v. Osun State Poly (1998) 11 NWLR (Pt. 572) 145 CA*

- *Bamgboye v. University of Ilorin (1999) 10 NWLR (Pt. 622) 290 SC*

11. Public officers are under a duty to exercise their powers within the precinct of an enabling law or statute.

- *Okenwa v. Mil. Gov., Imo State (1997) 6 NWLR (Pt. 507) 136 CA*

- *Republic Bank Ltd v. C.B.N. (1998) 13 NWLR (Pt. 581) 306 CA*

12. A statute, which gives power to a person, may also expressly authorise that person to delegate such powers. In such cases, delegation is valid. Sections 9(c) and 18 of the Polytechnic, Iree, Osun State Law, 1992 considered.

- *Moronkeji v. Osun State Poly (1998) 11 NWLR (Pt. 572 145 CA)*

13. Where a student is alleged to have committed a crime, the

determination of his guilt or otherwise is not an internal affair of the University.

> - *Garba v. University of Maiduguri (1986) 1 NWLR (Pt. 18) 550 SC*
> - *University of Calabar v. Esiaga (1997) 4 NWLR (Pt. 502) 719 at 724-726 CA*

14. Where, however, a student is alleged to have committed a crime, the question whether or not such a student should continue to retain his status or be suspended or dismissed is an internal affair of the University. In fact, the University can still exercise its power of suspension or dismissal of a student adjudged by a court of law not guilty of the offence charged. This power shall be exercised within the law establishing the University.

> - *University of Calabar v. Esiaga (1997) 4 NWLR (Pt. 502) 719 at 724-726 CA*

15. Where a student is alleged to have committed a crime and thereby suspended, there is need for the authority of the institution of higher learning to withhold the suspension and allow the student to continue with his studies until found guilty in the court of law. It will amount to travesty of justice if the student is kept out of the institution and he eventually succeeds in court.

> - *University of Abuja v. Ibietan (1998) 3 NWLR (Pt. 542) 387 at 393 CA*

16. *Audi alteram partem* means no man should be condemned unheard. Where a person's rights and obligations are affected, there is a duty on the relevant authority to accord him the opportunity to be heard before taking any adverse decision against him.

> - *Ceekay Traders Ltd. v. General Motors Co. Ltd (1992) 2 NWLR (Pt. 222) 132 SC*
> - *Yakubu v. Gov., Kogi State (1997) 7 NWLR (Pt. 511) 66 at 72 CA*
> - *C.O.P. v. Iheabe (1998) 11 NWLR (Pt. 575) 666 at 669 CA*

17. Where a party seeks to set aside the proceedings or judgment

of a tribunal, he has a duty to exhibit such proceedings or judgment before the court. This is because no court would make an order setting aside or nullifying proceedings or judgment on which it has never set its eyes upon. Thus, failure to exhibit such proceedings or judgment is a serious error that may amount to abuse of court process.

> - *Lekwot v. Judicial Tribunal (1997) 8 NWLR (Pt. 515) 22 SC*

18. The right of access to approach the courts for redress against any legislative act or law is guaranteed by section 4(8) of the 1979 Constitution. Thus, the courts have a supervisory jurisdiction over the exercise of legislative powers by the legislature. However, this power does not affect the ouster clause preserved under section 6(6) (d) of the said Constitution in respect of laws made between 15 January, 1966 and 30 September, 1979.

> - *Oruobu v. Anekwe (1997) 5 NWLR (Pt. 506) 618 CA*

19. A secret society or association is a body that is not solely a cultural or religious body. It uses secret signs and symbols. It holds meetings in secret. Its members are under oath or obligation to promote the interest of its members under all circumstances without due regards to merit, fair play or justice.

> - *Reg. Trustees of Amorc v. Awoniyi (1994) 7 NWLR (Pt. 355) 154 SC*

20. The admission offered by the Joint Admission and Matriculation Board (JAMB) to candidates is provisional in nature. Certain conditions must be fulfilled before a candidate can obtain final admission. These conditions include, a valid qualification by virtue of crediting relevant subjects required to pursue the desired discipline in the university.

> - *Onagoruwa v. JAMB (2001) 12 WRN 123 at 125 CA*

21. Cheating in examination (copying and exchanging answer scripts) constitutes an offence under section 392 of the Criminal Code, Cap. 36, Laws of Anambra State. Consequently, any person accused of examination malpractice must be arraigned and tried in a court of law where he is entitled to a fair hearing.

> - *Nnamdi Azikiwe University (N.A.U.) v. Nwafor (1999) 1*

NWLR (Pt. 585) 116 CA

22. An allegation of bias made against a judge on the ground that she seeks to interpret an instrument signed by her spouse in his administrative capacity as a Governor is remote and cannot, without more, sustain an allegation of bias.

- Adio v. A.-G., Oyo State (2000) 5 SC 82 at 117

23. The conditions precedent to the withdrawal of a chief's recognition are that, there must be an allegation of grave misconduct against the chief; the Commissioner for Chieftaincy Affairs must investigate the allegation and if satisfied that the allegation has been proved against the chief, or that the chief has ceased to enjoy popular support of his communities, the Commissioner may advise the Governor to withdraw the chief's recognition. Sections 9 and 14 of the Chieftaincy Law of Imo State 1978 considered.

- Okenwa v. Mil. Gov., Imo State (1997) 6 NWLR (Pt. 507) 136 CA

24. Section 5 of the Local Government and Community Boundaries Settlement Law of Oyo State 1978 provides that only the State Executive Council can refer the settlement of boundary disputes to the Boundary Settlement Commission. Therefore, the State High Court has no jurisdiction to transfer suit to that Commission.

- Fasikun II v. Oluronke II (1999) 2 NWLR (Pt. 589) 1 at 6 SC

25. The police have a duty to investigate and where substantial facts are found, institute criminal prosecution against any person involved in fraud.

- Societe Generale Bank (Nig.) Ltd v. Afekoro (1999) 11 NWLR (Pt. 628) 521 at 526 SC

26. Where a junior police officer is to face an orderly room trial, he shall first be informed through a memorandum of charges of the offences alleged against him. Witnesses are to be called to testify against him and he shall be at liberty to defend himself. Sections 379(1) - 403 of the Nigeria Police Regulations, Cap 359 Laws of the Federation of Nigeria, 1990 considered.

- Agha v. I.G.P. (1997) 10 NWLR (Pt. 524) 317 CA

27. There is need to comply with the provisions of the constitution of an incorporated body where they are clear and unambiguous.

- *Owodunni v. Registered Trustees of C.C.C. (2000) 6 SC (Part III) 60*

28. A void act cannot be validated by subsequent approval and anything based on a void act is bad and incurably bad. Once it is void *ab initio*, it remains void.

- *Oduntan v. Akibu (2000) 7 SC (Part II) 106 at 141-142*

29. For the purposes of section 38(1)(f) of Decree No. 3 of 1999, a public officer of a State is a staff of either the civil service of the State or a staff of a Commission, Corporations or Authorities of the State. A part-time Chairman of a limited liability company, in which the State holds a controlling share, cannot be regarded as a public officer of the State.

- *Doukplolagha v. Alamieyesigha (1999) 6 NWLR (Pt. 607) 502 at 505 CA*

30. There are two ways of removing public officers in Nigeria, namely: through the normal civil service method or through the procedure under Decree No. 17 of 1984, which gives the Head of State arbitrary powers to remove public officers.

- *Shitta-Bey v. A-G, Federation (1998) 10 NWLR (Pt. 570) 392 SC*

31. The Minister of Internal Affairs is the only person conferred with the right to issue a passport and withdraw or cancel a passport already issued. However, the exercise of this power by the Minister is not arbitrary. He is under a duty to give reasons for the withdrawal.

- *Director, SSS v. Agbakoba (1999) 3 NWLR (Pt. 595) 314 at 321-332 SC*

32. The State Security Service (SSS) not being servants of the Federal Minister of Internal Affairs cannot seize a citizen's passport. Where they do, the seizure does not only amount to unwarranted interference but also illegal.

- *Director, SSS v. Agbakoba (1999) 3 NWLR (Pt. 595) 314 at 333 SC*

2.4 Judicial Control of Public Authorities

1. The court does not interfere with the proper exercise of the discretion by the executive. However, it can intervene if the discretion is exercised improperly or mistakenly.

> - *Laker Airways v. Department of Trade (1977) Q.B. 643*

2. Prerogative is a discretionary power to be exercised by the executive for the public good. It follows, therefore, that its exercise can be examined by the courts just as any other discretionary power, which is vested in the executive.

> - *Burmah Oil Case (1965) A.C. 75*
> - *Nissan v. Attorney-General (1970) A.C. 179*
> - *Laker Airways v. Department of Trade (1977) Q.B. 643*

3. The courts have the authority and, indeed, the duty to correct a misuse of power by a Minister or his department. Thus, when a Minister is given discretion and he exercises it for reasons, which are bad in law, the court can interfere so as to get him back on the right course.

> - *Padfield v. Minister of Agriculture, Fisheries and Food (1968) A.C. 997*
> - *Congrave v. Home Office (1976) Q.B. 629*

4. The rule of law is that whenever questions of national security are being considered by any court for any purposes, it is not what the Crown thinks to be necessary or expedient that counts. What counts is what is necessary or expedient in fact and in law. This is so, because, the servants of the Crown, like other men animated by the highest motives are capable of formulating a policy *ad hoc* so as to prevent the citizen from doing something that the Crown does not want him to do. It is the duty of the courts to be alert to prevent abuse of executive prerogatives.

> - *Chandler v. Director of Public Prosecutions (1964) A.C. 763*

5. It is a well established principle of law that a Governor of a State can only act in pursuance of the powers given to him by

law. Consequently, no member of the executive can interfere with the ownership of property of a citizen except on condition that he can support the legality of his action before a court of justice.

- *Eshugbayi Eleko v. Officer Administering the Government of Nigeria (1931) A.C. 662; (1931) All ER 44*

6. Where a statutory tribunal purports to exceed the jurisdiction conferred on it by the legislature, the court has power to intervene and prevent such excesses. Also where the tribunal while acting within jurisdiction, decides a point of law wrongly, the court has power to declare such decision a nullity.

- *Udosen v. NECON (1997) 5 NWLR (Pt. 506) 570 CA*

7. A minister's policy speech cannot supersede the law.

- *Psychiatric Hospital Management Board (P.H.M.B) v. Ejitagha (2000) 6 SC (Part II) 1*

8. A by-law is not bad for the simple reason that it deals with something that is not dealt with by the general law. But it must not alter the general law, by making that lawful which the general law makes unlawful; or that unlawful which the general law makes lawful.

- *White v. Molley (1899) 2 Q.B. 34 at 39*

2.5 Prerogative Orders

1. An order of *mandamus* is a device for securing judicial enforcement of public duties. It is discretionary in nature and as such, a court exercises its discretion in deciding whether or not to grant it. For *mandamus* to apply, there must be an imperative public duty and not a discretionary power to act; the applicant must have requested for the performance of the duty and this must have been refused; the applicant must have a substantial personal interest in the performance of the duty concerned and the court to which the application for *mandamus* is made must itself have jurisdiction to grant it.

- *Layanju v. Araoye (1959) 4 F.S.C. 154*
- *Banjo & Ors v. Abeokuta Urban District Council (1965)*

NMLR 295

2. *Certiorari* is a prerogative order which enables a court of record to call upon an inferior court, tribunal or a body entrusted with the performance of a judicial or quasi-judicial functions to certify the record upon which the inferior court, administrative tribunal or body based its decision.

- *Arzika v. Governor, Northern Nigeria (1961) All NLR 379*
- *Okupe v. Fed. Board of Inland Revenue (1974) 4 SC 93*

3. The writs of *certiorari* and *prohibition* may be issued where any body of persons having legal authority to determine questions affecting the rights of citizens, and having the duty to act judicially, act in excess of its legal authority.

- *Nwoboshi v. State (1998) 10 NWLR (Pt. 568) 131 CA*

4. It is not every procedural error made by any body that would justify the issuance of a writ of *certiorari*. The omission or failure to comply with the enabling law must be of such a nature that would go to the root of the entire action of the body.

- *Nwoboshi v. State (1998) 10 NWLR (Pt. 568) 131 CA*

5. Where the judgment of an inferior court is found to have been given without jurisdiction or in excess of jurisdiction or there is an error on the face of the record of the court or a breach of observance of natural justice regarding fair hearing, the order of *certiorari* will be granted to quash such a judgment.

- *Unitex Ltd v. Yabuku (1998) 13 NWLR (Pt. 581) 334 CA*
- *Ezenwa v. Bestway Elect. Manuf. Co. Ltd. (1999) 8 NWLR (Pt. 613) 61 at 67 CA*

6. Where an order for leave to apply for an order of *certiorari* to quash a proceeding for lack of jurisdiction is given, such order for leave operates as a stay of that proceeding until the application for *certiorari* is disposed of.

- *Nnadika v. Ejire (1994) 1 NWLR (Pt. 320) 295 CA*

7. A writ of prohibition is a judicial writ, issued out of a court of superior jurisdiction and directed to an inferior court for the purpose of preventing the inferior court from usurping a jurisdiction with which it is not legally vested. In other words, it is issued to compel courts entrusted with judicial duties to keep within the limits of their jurisdiction.

> - *Mackonochie v. Lord Penzance (1881) 6 A.C. 443*

8. An order of prohibition will lie against a criminal prosecution where an accused is charged with an offence not known to law.

> - *Ekwuazi v. D.P.P. Lagos State (1999) 3 NWLR (Pt. 593) 31 CA*

9. The order of *habeas corpus* is applicable as a remedy in the High Court in all cases of wrongful deprivation of personal liberty as guaranteed by the 1979 Constitution of the Federal Republic of Nigeria.

> - *Agbaje v. Commissioner of Police (Suit No. CAW/81/69 of 27th August, 1969, Court of Appeal, West) (unreported)*

10. Any proceedings arising from an application by way of *habeas corpus* which procedure is for committal for contempt, is quasi-criminal.

> - *Comptroller, Nig. Prison Serv., Ikoyi v. Adekanye (1999) 5 NWLR (Pt. 602) 167 at 171 CA*

11. An action by a writ of *quo warranto* arises when a person exercises an office of State recognised by law but alleges that he had no authority to do so. The aim of the action is to make such a person show by what authority he exercised that office.

> - *Obioha v. Mil. Adm., Imo State (1998) 10 NWLR (Pt. 569) 205 CA*

III
Admiralty Law

3.1 Jurisdiction

1. The jurisdiction of the Federal High Court in admiralty matters is prescribed in sections 1, 2 and 3 of the Admiralty Jurisdiction Decree No. 59 of 1991.

> - *Tigris International Corp v. Ege Shipping & Trading Ind. Inc. (1999) 6 NWLR (Pt. 608) 701 CA*

2. Although the law confers on the Federal High Court admiralty jurisdiction, the jurisdiction cannot be invoked for the sole purpose of obtaining security for the satisfaction of an award that might be made in foreign arbitration proceedings.

> - *Messrs. NV Scheep v. The MV "S. Araz" (2000) 12 SC (Pt. 1) 164*

3. There is a distinction between an action "*in rem*" and an action "*in personam*". An action in personam is an action brought against a person requiring him to do or not to do a particular thing or take or not to take a particular course of action or inaction. Actions for damages in tort or for breach of contract are clearly directed against a person and are, therefore, action *in personam*. On the other hand, an action *in rem* is one which is directed against a ship alleged to have been the instrument of wrongdoing in a case where it is sought to enforce a maritime or statutory lien or in a possessory action against the ship whose possession is claimed. Thus, an action *in rem* properly commenced before a competent court of jurisdiction shall enable the plaintiff to arrest a ship or other property and to have it detained, until his claim has been adjudicated upon or until security by bail has been given for the amount or for the value of the property.

> - *Rhein Mass Und See GMBH v. Rivway Lines Ltd (1998) 5 NWLR (Pt. 549) 265 SC*

4. The Federal High Court has the power to order the detention of a ship or property. Where a ship or other property is under arrest in a proceedings and the court is satisfied that a bail bond

for an amount equal to the amount claimed or the value of the ship or property, whichever is less, has been filed in the proceedings, the Registrar may, on written application by the relevant person, release from arrest the ship or property. Order 21, Rule 1 of the Federal High Court (Civil Procedure) Rules 1976 and Order 1, Rule 1(b) of the Admiralty Jurisdiction Procedure Rules 1993 considered.

> - *Finunion Ltd v. M.V. Briz (1997) 10 NWLR (Pt. 523) 95 CA*

5. By virtue of Order 1 Rule 3 of the Admiralty Jurisdiction Procedure Rules, 1993, the Federal High Court can by order reduce or increase the amount of bail bond in respect of which bail has been given to ensure fairness between parties.

> - *Finunion Ltd v. M.V. Briz (1997) 10 NWLR (Pt. 523) 95 CA*

3.2 Carriage of Goods by Sea

1. A charter-party contract is a contract for the affreightment of goods between the ship owner and the shipper or charterer for a particular voyage or for a specific period of time.

> - *Awolaja v. Seatrade Groningen B.V. (1993) 3 NWLR (Pt. 280) 209 CA*

2. A carrier and the ship shall be discharged from all liabilities in respect of loss or damage in a contract of carriage of goods by sea, unless action is brought within one year after delivery of the goods or the date when the goods should have been delivered. Article 3 Rule 6 of the Carriage of Goods by Sea Act, 1990 considered.

> - *Balogun v. Panalpina W.T. (Nig.) Ltd (1999) 1 NWLR (Pt. 585) 66 at 68 CA*

3. Under the contract of carriage of goods by sea, the law requires that notice of loss or damage and the general nature of such loss or damage be given in writing to the carrier or his agent at the port of discharge or at the time of the removal of the goods into the custody of the person entitled to delivery thereof. If

the loss or damage is not very apparent, the notice shall be given within three days of the delivery. In the absence of the aforesaid notice, the removal of the goods into the custody of the person entitled to delivery shall be *prima facie* evidence of the delivery by the carrier of the goods as described in the bill of lading. Similarly, the notice in writing need not be given if the state of the goods has at the time of their receipt been subjected to a just survey or inspection.

> *- Leventis Tech. Ltd v. Petrojessica Ent. Ltd (1999) 6 NWLR (Pt. 605) 45 SC*

3.3 *Bill of Lading*

1. A bill of lading is a document in writing normally issued upon the goods being received for shipment, or traditionally upon shipment and signed by the representative or agent of the owner of the ship carrying the goods.

> *- Awolaja v. Seatrade Groningen B.V. (1993) 3 NWLR (Pt. 280) 209 CA*

2. A bill of lading serves three functions. First, it constitutes a receipt for the goods, which have been received for shipment. Secondly, it constitutes a contract for the carriage of the goods and delivery thereof, as it contains the terms and conditions of the carriage. Lastly, it is evidence that the holder of the bill of lading has the property in the goods, that is, it is a document of title.

> *- Awolaja v. Seatrade Groningen B.V. (1993) 3 NWLR (Pt. 280) 209 CA*
>
> *- Ogwuru v. Co-op. Bank of Eastern (Nig.) Ltd (1994) 8 NWLR (Pt. 365) 685 CA*

3. Where there is a dispute between a ship owner and a cargo owner as to the goods delivered in a contract of carriage of goods by sea, the statement about the goods contained in the bill of lading becomes very important.

> *- Comet Shipping v. Babbit (2001) 13 W.R.N. 114 CA*

4. Every bill of lading in the hands of a consignee or endorsee

for valuable consideration representing goods to have been shipped on board a vessel, is conclusive proof of that shipment as against the master or other person who signed the bill of lading.

- Comet Shipping v. Babbit (2001) 13 W.R.N. 114 CA

5. The law is that only those who are parties to a bill of lading are bound by the terms of the bill.

- Comet Shipping v. Babbit (2001) 13 WRN 114 CA

6. A ship owner who is not a party to the contract contained in a bill of lading is not entitled to invoke the exclusive jurisdiction clause contained in the contract against the cargo owners.

- The Muhkutai (1996) Times, 26 April

7. A ship owner is not entitled to deliver cargo in the absence of an original bill of lading, except where in lieu thereof, there is an agreement requiring a letter of indemnity or bank guarantee, or if he is reasonably satisfied that the person seeking possession of the goods is entitled to do so, and the whereabouts of the bill of lading is reasonably explained. Delivery, in the absence of the aforesaid conditions, shall enable the person entitled to possession to recover damages for financial loss and damage.

- Sucre Export SA v. Northern Shipping Ltd (The Sormousky 3068) 1994, Times, 13 May

8. The mere presentation of shipping documents is not conclusive evidence to prove that the goods imported or contained therein had actually arrived in the country of destination.

- Bello v. Farmers Supply Co. Ltd (1998) 10 NWLR (Pt. 568) 64 CA

9. It is not every consignee or endorsee of a bill of lading that has the right to sue on the bill of lading. The right to sue is vested only on a consignee or endorsee to whom the property in the goods mentioned therein shall pass upon or by reason of such consignment or endorsement. Therefore, a court of law cannot simply rely on an endorsement on a bill of lading, without more, in coming to a decision as to who may sue on it. The court is duty-bound to go beyond the mere formal endorsement to determine the legal and factual aspects as to

whether the property mentioned in the bill of lading was actually transferred. Thus, the only way to prove whether property has passed is by evidence.

- *Nigerbras Shipping Line Ltd v. Aluminium Extrusion Industries (1994) 4 NWLR (Pt. 341) 733 CA*

- *Fareast Mercantile Co. Ltd v. Boothia Maritime Inc. (1998) 5 NWLR (Pt. 551) 620 CA*

- *Brawal Shipping (Nig.) Ltd v. F.I Onwadike Co. Ltd (2000) 6 SC (Part II) 133*

10. One major consideration in determining whether property in a bill of lading has passed to a consignee or endorsee is to establish whether or not he gave value for the bill of lading to the person who got it from the consignors of the cargo. Thus, a *prima facie* right of action is established by proving that the endorsee gave value for the bill of lading to the person who got it from the consignors of the cargo.

- *Nigerbras Shipping Line Ltd v. Aluminium Extrusion Industries (1994) 4 NWLR (Pt. 341) 733 CA*

- *Fareast Mercantile Co. Ltd v. Boothia Maritime Inc. (1998) 5 NWLR (Pt. 551) 620 CA*

- *Brawal Shipping (Nig.) Ltd v. F.I Onwadike Co. Ltd (2000) 6 SC (Part II) 133*

3.4 Safety of Ship

1. A ship owner is required to exercise due diligence in ensuring that his vessel is seaworthy before and at the time of a voyage. The duty to ensure that a vessel is seaworthy takes precedence over any right to claim relief where a shipper's cargo is of an inflammable, explosive or dangerous nature.

- *Mediterranean Freight Services Ltd v. BP Oil International Ltd, The Fiona (1994) Times, 27 July CA*

2. A ship owner, charterer or manager is duty bound to take all reasonable steps to ensure that the vessel is operated in a safe manner. Thus, to secure conviction, the prosecution must prove beyond reasonable doubt that the accused owner, charterer or

manager has himself failed to take all reasonable steps to ensure that the ship was operated in a safe manner.

   - *Seaboard Offshore Ltd v. Secretary of State for Transport (1994) 2 All ER 99*

3. In a war situation, a ship owner has a right and even a duty to delay in obeying the charterer's instructions in order to check the source and validity of such instruction even though there may be no immediate physical threat to the cargo or ship.

   - *Kuwait Petroleum Corpn. v. I & D Oil Carriers Ltd, The Houda (1994) Independent, 17 August*

3.5 Claims

1. A cargo owner who renders salvage services as a volunteer to a ship carrying his cargo is, in certain circumstances, entitled to claim salvage against the ship.

   - *The Sava Star (1995) 2 Lloyd's Rep 134*

2. Salvage is defined as a compensation allowed to persons by whose assistance a ship or its cargo has been saved in whole or in part from impending danger, or recovered from actual loss in cases of shipwreck, derelict or recapture.

   - *The Oceanic Grandeur (1872) 2 Lloyd's Report 496 (High Court of Australia)*

3. At common law, to claim salvage, the services rendered to the property in peril have to be voluntary, that is, without any pre-existing contractual or other legal duty. Consequently, voluntariness of the services rendered is a prerequisite to a salvage award.

   - *The Oceanic Grandeur (1872) 2 Lloyd's Report 496 (High Court of Australia)*
   - *The National Defender (1970) 1 Lloyd's Report 40 (U.S. District Court)*

4. "Success" is an essential ingredient in a claim for salvage. Consequently, a person rendering salvage services voluntarily, is not entitled to any remuneration unless he saves the property

in whole or in part. In other words, no remuneration is due if the services rendered have no beneficial effect. Article 2 of the Brussels Convention on Salvage, 1910 considered.

  - *The Tojo Maru (1972) A.C. 242, 293*

5. In an action for loss of containers containing goods/packages at sea, the carrier cannot limit his liability by reference to the number of containers. The packages enumerated in the bill of lading as packed in such containers shall be regarded as the "unit" for the purpose of the limitation of liability.

  - *Gurara v. Nigerian National Shipping Line Ltd (1996) Times, 6 March*

6. A charter party is under a duty not to give invalid voyage orders especially after the charter period has expired. Where he does, it will repudiate the contract in every respect and the owner of the ship is entitled to damages.

  - *Torvald Klaveness A/S v. Arni Maritime Corpn, The Gregos (1994) Times, 28 October*

# IV
Appeal

4.1 Nature of Appeal

1. An appeal is an invitation to a higher court to review the decision of a lower court in order to find out whether, on proper consideration of the facts placed before it and the applicable law, the lower court arrived at a correct decision.

  - *Oredoyin v. Arowolo (1989) 4 NWLR (Pt. 114) 172 SC*

2. An appeal is generally regarded as a continuation of an original suit rather than as an inception of a new action. An appeal should be a complaint against the decision of a trial court. Thus, in the absence of such a decision on a point, there cannot possibly be an appeal against what has not been decided against a party.

  - *Oredoyin v. Arowolo (1989) 4 NWLR (Pt. 114) 172 SC*
  - *Babalola v. State (1989) 4 NWLR (Pt. 115) 264 SC*
  - *Jumbo v. Bryanko Int. Ltd (1995) 6 NWLR (Pt. 403) 545 at 547 CA*

3. The filing of a notice of appeal is a necessary prerequisite for the hearing of an appeal. A notice of appeal may also be amended at any time.

  - *Okpala v. Ibeme (1989) 2 NWLR (Pt. 102) 208 SC*

4. For a notice of appeal to be valid, such notice of appeal must set forth concisely and under distinct heads, the grounds upon which an appellant intends to rely at the hearing of the appeal without any argument or narrative and shall be numbered consecutively. Order 8 rule 2(3) of the Supreme Court Rules, 1985 (as amended) considered.

  - *Adah v. Adah (2001) 14 WRN 74 CA*

5. It is trite law that both the leave to appeal and the notice of appeal must be filed within three months as prescribed by section 31(2) of the Supreme Court Act 1960.

  - *Owoniboys v. John Holt (2001) 1 WRN 162 SC*

6. An appeal is entered when the court below transmits the record of appeal to the appellate court and the appellate court, indeed receives the record of appeal.

   - *Ogunremi v. Dada (1962) 2 SCNLR 417*
   - *Ezeokafor v. Ezeilo (1999) 9 NWLR (Pt. 619) 513 at 517 SC*

7. An appeal is usually against the *ratio decidendi* of the judgment of a lower court and not in respect of *obiter dicta* made by the court in the course of the said judgment, except in cases where the *obiter dicta* is so clearly linked with the *ratio decidendi* as to be deemed to have radically influenced the *ratio decidendi*.

   - *Saude v. Abdullahi (1989) 4 NWLR (Pt. 116) 387 SC*
   - *Okpeji v. Minister of Agriculture (1997) 9 NWLR (Pt. 522) 693 CA*

8. It is not every error in a case that will result in an appeal being allowed. It is only when the error is substantial, in that it has occasioned a miscarriage of justice that an appellate court is bound to interfere.

   - *Nwaeze v. State (1996) 2 NWLR (Pt. 428) 1 SC*

9. A party, who fails to object to the admissibility of evidence at the trial court, is at liberty to challenge the admissibility of such evidence on appeal.

   Ipinlaiye II v. Olukotun (1996) 6 NWLR (Pt. 453) 148 SC

10. Where a party on appeal is absent and not represented at the hearing of the appeal but has filed his brief of argument, the party will be taken to have argued the appeal in terms of the brief filed. Order 6 Rule 8(6) of the Supreme Court Rules, 1985 (as amended) considered.

   - *Jiddun v. Abuna (2000) 10-11 SC 19 at 28*
   - *Igago v. The State (2001) 3 WRN 153 SC*

11. The fact that an appeal is against concurrent findings of fact does not, without more, make it an abuse of the process of the court. There is no law, which says that the concurrent findings of fact of the High Court and Court of Appeal cannot be set aside or reversed by the Supreme Court.

   - *Dieli v. Iwuno (1996) 4 NWLR (Pt. 445) 622 SC*

12. It is trite that the Supreme Court will not interfere with the findings of fact made by both the High Court and the Court of Appeal where there is sufficient evidence in support of such findings and where there is no substantial error apparent on the record of proceedings, such as miscarriage of justice or violation of some principle of law or procedure.

- *Ezeonwu v. Onyechi (1996) 3 NWLR (Pt. 438) 499 SC*
- *Shittu v. Egbeyemi (1996) 6 NWLR (Pt. 457) 650 SC*
- *Babuga v. State (1996) 7 NWLR (Pt. 460) 279 SC*

13. An appellate court will make an order for retrial of a case, where the retrial will not lead to a miscarriage of justice, or where the court, exercising its appellate jurisdictions, cannot adequately do justice to the case, or where from the circumstances of the case, it is just to make such an order.

- *Abusomwan v. Aiwerioba (1996) 4 NWLR (Pt. 441) 130 SC*

14. In considering an application to relist an appeal earlier struck out for absence of the appellant, the appellate court must consider and examine the following factors, viz: the reasons for the failure by the applicant to appear when the appeal came up for hearing; whether there has been delay in making the application; whether the respondent would be prejudiced or embarrassed by the relisting order; and, whether it is in the interest of justice to grant the application so as to hear the substantive case.

- *Dangardi v. Jibril (1997) 4 NWLR (Pt. 501) 590 CA*

15. It is settled that the Supreme Court has no jurisdiction to re-enter an appeal dismissed under the provisions of Order 6 Rule 3(2) of its 1985 Rules (as amended), for want of prosecution. Under such circumstance, the dismissal is final.

- *Chime v. Ude (1996) 7 NWLR (Pt. 461) 379 SC*

4.2 Cross-Appeal

1. A cross-appeal is an appeal by a respondent to a main appeal.

- *Williams v. Daily Times (1990) 1 NWLR (Pt. 124) 1 SC*

- Opara v. D.S. (Nig.) Ltd (1995) 4 NWLR (Pt. 390) 440 CA

2. A cross-appeal is akin to a counter-claim which is distinct from the main action. In like manner, a cross-appeal is distinct from an appeal.

- Opara v. D.S. (Nig.) Ltd (1995) 4 NWLR (Pt. 390) 440 CA

4.3 Grounds of Appeal

1. A ground of appeal is consisted of the error of law or fact alleged by an appellant as the defect in a judgment appealed against and relied upon to set the judgment aside.

- Metal Const. (W.A.) Ltd v. Migliore (1990) 1 NWLR (Pt. 126) 299 SC

2. Grounds of appeal are the reasons for considering a decision of court wrong. Thus, the purpose of the grounds is to isolate and accentuate, for attack, the basis of the reasoning of the decision being challenged.

- Saraki v. Kotoye (1992) 9 NWLR (Pt. 264) 156 SC

3. Like pleadings, parties are bound by their grounds of appeal and are not at liberty to argue grounds, which are not related to the judgment appealed against.

- Saraki v. Kotoye (1992) 9 NWLR (Pt. 264) 156 SC

4. A ground of appeal must be couched in such a way as to attack the judgment of a court on the issue decided by it.

- F.B.N. Plc v. May Med Clinics (1996) 9 NWLR (Pt. 471) 195 CA

- Folbod Invest. Ltd v. Alpha Merchant Bank Ltd (1996) 10 NWLR (Pt. 478) 344 at 351 CA

5. Grounds of appeal filed and argued should address themselves to and consider the facts of each particular case.

- Peters v. State (1992) 9 NWLR (Pt. 265) 323 SC

6. The term "omnibus ground of appeal" implies that the judgment of a trial court cannot be supported by the weight of the evidence adduced by the successful party or that the

inference drawn or conclusion reached by the trial court based on the accepted evidence cannot be justified. It also implies that there is no acceptable evidence to support the findings of the trial court or that the judgment given in favour of a successful party is against the totality of the evidence adduced before the trial court.

> - *Sha v. Kwan (2000) 5 S.C. 178*

7. An omnibus ground of appeal in civil cases is one, which states that the judgment of a trial court is unwarranted, unreasonable and cannot be supported having regard to the weight of evidence adduced.

> - *Isiekwe v. State (1999) 9 NWLR (Pt. 617) 43 CA*

8. The omnibus ground of appeal, in criminal cases, should be couched to read that the decision is unwarranted, unreasonable and cannot be supported having regard to the evidence adduced.

> - *Isiekwe v. State (1999) 9 NWLR (Pt. 617) 43 CA*

9. The mere fact that an appellant describes a ground of appeal as of law would not necessarily render it to be so.

> - *Ejiwunmi v. Costain (W.A) Plc (1998) 12 NWLR (Pt. 576) 149 CA*

10. It is not the label given to a particular ground of appeal by counsel that determines whether it is of law, of mixed law and fact or of fact *simpliciter*. Although, the line of distinction between a ground of law and mixed law and fact is very thin, that does not convert a ground of mixed law and fact to one of law simply because counsel labels it as such.

> - *In Re: Otuedon (1995) 4 NWLR (Pt. 392) 655 SC*
> - *Obatoyinbo v. Oshatoba (1996) 5 NWLR (Pt. 450) 531 SC*
> - *Yusuf v. U.B.A. Ltd (1996) 6 NWLR (Pt. 457) 632 SC*

11. In determining whether a ground of appeal raises a question of law alone or of facts or of mixed law and facts, the court is required to examine thoroughly the ground of appeal together with its particulars, in order to see whether the ground reveals a misunderstanding of the law by the lower court, or a misapplication of the law to the facts already proved or admitted, in which case it would be a question of law. Where however,

the ground is such that would require questioning the evaluation of facts by the lower court before the application of the law, that would amount to question of mixed law and fact. Ground of appeal, which raises facts, which needed to be determined either way, is a ground of fact.

- *Onifade v. Olayiwola (1990) 7 NWLR (Pt. 161) 130 SC*
- *Olanrewaju v. Ogunleye (1997) 2 NWLR (Pt. 485) 12 SC*
- *Shanu v. Afribank (Nig.) Plc (2000) 10-11 SC 1*
- *Maigoro v. Garba (2001) 2 WRN 1 at 4 SC*

12. It is generally accepted that where a ground of appeal is based on an allegation of errors deduced from a conclusion on undisputed facts, it is a ground of law. Where, on the other hand, the error of law is founded on disputed facts calling into question the correctness of the facts determined, then it is a question of mixed law and fact.

- *A.C.B. Plc v. Obmiami Brick & Stone (1993) 5 NWLR (Pt. 294) 399 SC*
- *Ajayi v. Omorogbe (1993) 6 NWLR (Pt. 301) 512 SC*

13. A ground of appeal is one of facts where the ground of appeal is based on a conclusion of a court, which is founded on evaluation of or inference from facts.

- *Ajayi v. Omorogbe (1993) 6 NWLR (Pt. 301) 512 SC*

14. It is trite law that where a ground of appeal raises questions of mixed law and fact, leave of court is required to argue it. Therefore, failure by an appellant to obtain the necessary leave will make the ground incompetent and liable to be struck out.

- *Popoola v. Adeyemo (1992) 8 NWLR (Pt. 257) 1 SC*
- *Abidoye v. Alawode (2001) 13 WRN 71 SC*

15. For a ground of appeal to be competent, it should not allege both misdirection and an error in law at the same time. By their very nature, one ground of appeal cannot be the two. Therefore, a ground of appeal, which alleges both errors in law and in fact is incompetent and should be struck out. Order 3 Rule 2(2) of the Court of Appeal Rules, 1981 (as amended) considered.

- *Elendu v. Ekwoaba (1995) 3 NWLR (Pt. 386) 704 CA*

> - *Rotimi v. Faforiji (1999) 6 NWLR (Pt. 606) 305 at 312 CA*
> - *Chuke v. F.H.A. (1999) 10 NWLR (Pt. 624) 574 at 576 CA*

16. A misdirection occurs when a judge misconceives the issues before him whether of fact or of law, or summarises the evidence inadequately or incorrectly for one side or the other, or makes mistake in the law applicable to the issues in the case. The judge may commit misdirection either by a positive act or by non-direction. However, where his error relates to his findings, it cannot properly be called a misdirection but, rather, an error in law.

> - *Elendu v. Ekwoaba (1995) 3 NWLR (Pt. 386) 704 CA*
> - *Rotimi v. Faforiji (1999) 6 NWLR (Pt. 606) 305 at 312 CA*

17. An appellant, filing a ground of appeal alleging a misdirection or error in law, must supply the particulars of error he is relying on. Such particulars must be clearly stated and must be specific so as to give sufficient notice to the respondent to enable him prepare his reply brief.

> - *Chuke v. F.H.A. (1999) 10 NWLR (Pt. 624) 574 CA*

18. Order 8 Rule 2(2) of the Supreme Court Rules, 1985 enjoins the use of particulars only for misdirections or errors in law. Therefore, grounds of fact do not require particulars. Likewise, where it is clear that the particulars would relate to the substantive complaint, setting out the particulars of the alleged misdirection would not arise.

> - *Bamgboye v. University of Ilorin (1999) 10 NWLR (Pt. 622) 290 at 313 SC*

19. Although by its very nature, the categories of errors in law are not closed, the following may be classified and recognised as errors of law. First, where a court took into account wrong criteria or applied wrong standard of proof or gave wrong weight to relevant factors in reaching its conclusion. Secondly, issues raised on legal interpretation of deeds and documents, words or phrases and inferences drawn therefrom are grounds of law. Thirdly, where a ground deals merely with a matter of inference, even if it were an inference of fact, which is already proved, a ground framed on it is a ground of law.

Fourthly, where a court states the law on a point wrongly. Fifthly, where the complaint is that there was no evidence or admissible evidence upon which a finding or decision was based. Lastly, where there is a misunderstanding of the law or a misapplication of the law by a trial court, to facts already proved or admitted.

- *Comex Ltd v. N.A.B. Ltd (1997) 3 NWLR (Pt. 496) 643 SC*
- *Bamgboye v. University of Ilorin (1999) 10 NWLR (Pt. 622) 290 at 312 SC*

20. An appellate court can only hear and decide on issues raised on the grounds of appeal filed before it. Thus, an issue not covered by the grounds of appeal is incompetent and is liable to be struck out.

- *Alli v. Alesinloye (2000) 4 SC (Part I) 111 at 140*

21. A ground of appeal on which no issue for determination is formulated is deemed abandoned by the appellate court and it is liable to be struck out.

- *Abodunrin v. Arabe (1995) 5 NWLR (Pt. 393) 77 at 83 CA*
- *Morakinyo v. Adesoyero (1995) 7 NWLR (Pt. 409) 602 at 609 CA*

22. It is the law that where a ground of appeal cannot be fixed and circumscribed within a particular issue in controversy in the judgment challenged, such a ground of appeal cannot justifiably be regarded as related to the decision. Therefore, if an issue which was neither considered nor determined by the lower court forms the basis of an appeal in grounds of appeal, such grounds of appeal are incompetent and therefore liable to be struck out.

- *Saraki v. Kotoye (1992) 9 NWLR (Pt. 264) 156 at 162 SC*
- *Bakule v. Tanerewa (Nig.) Ltd (1995) 2 NWLR (Pt. 380) 728 at 733 CA*

23. It is trite that arguments on issues not predicated on any grounds of appeal will be discountenanced, since an appeal will only be determined on issues arising out of the ground of appeal.

- *Okelola v. Boyle (1998) 2 NWLR (Pt. 539) 533 SC*

24. The striking out of incompetent grounds of appeal does not amount to a dismissal of the case on merit. When incompetent grounds are struck out, the affected party can still bring a notice

of motion to amend.

> - *Obala of Otan-Aiyegbaju v. Adesina (1999) 2 NWLR (Pt. 590) 163 at 166 SC*

25. An appellant wishing to file new or additional grounds of appeal must seek and obtain leave of the court to file and argue them. Likewise, where new issues are involved in the new grounds, special leave of court must be obtained to argue them.

> - *Nkpuma v. State (1995) 9 NWLR (Pt. 421) 505 SC*

26. An application to amend grounds of appeal by filing additional grounds will be granted where the proposed grounds *prima facie* raise substantial points of law.

> - *Jessica Trading Co. Ltd v. Bendel Ins. Co. Ltd (1993) 1 NWLR (Pt. 271) 538 SC*

27. A preliminary objection to the competence of a ground of appeal should be by motion on notice before the hearing of the appeal, so that arguments on it can be heard by the court. Although notice of objection may be given in a brief, it does not dispense with the need for the respondent to move the court at the oral hearing for the relief prayed for.

> - *Nsirim v. Nsirim (1990) 3 NWLR (Pt. 138) 285 SC*
> - *N.B.N. Ltd v. T.A.S.A. Ltd (1996) 8 NWLR (Pt. 468) 511 CA*

4.4 Issues on Appeal

1. An issue for determination is a combination of facts and circumstances. It includes the law on a particular point which, when decided one way or the other, affects the fate of an appeal.

> - *Onifade v. Olayiwola (1990) 7 NWLR (Pt. 161) 130 SC*

2. Issues for determination in an appeal should be formulated in general practical terms and tailored to the real questions in controversy in a case. Such issues should not contain any argument.

> - *Nwosu v. Imo State Environmental Sanitation Authority (1990) 2 NWLR (Pt. 135) 688 SC*

3. Issue for determination formulated in a brief must be based on the grounds of appeal filed by the parties. If the issues are not related to any ground of appeal, then they become irrelevant and go to no issue. Consequently, any argument in the brief in support of such issues will be discountenanced by the court.

- *Adelaja v. Fanoiki (1990) 2 NWLR (Pt. 131) 137 SC*
- *Momodu v. Momoh (1991) 1 NWLR (Pt. 169) 608 SC*
- *J.C. Ltd v. Ezenwa (1996) 4 NWLR (Pt. 443) 391 at 399 SC*
- *Shitta-Bey v. A.-G., Federation (1998) 10 NWLR (Pt. 570) 392 SC*
- *Dalori v. Sadikwu (1998) 12 NWLR (Pt. 576) 112 at 116 CA*
- *Amadi v. NNPC (2000) 6 SC (Pt. 1) 66 at 72*

4. Any issue formulated for determination by the respondent in an appeal must relate to the grounds of appeal filed by the appellant. However, for the respondent to validly raise any issue not related to the grounds of appeal filed by the appellant, he must file a cross appeal or file a respondent's notice.

- *Momodu v. Momoh (1991) 1 NWLR (Pt. 169) 608 SC*

5. It is not permissible for an appellant to formulate and argue in his brief, an issue for determination predicated on proposed grounds of appeal which has not been filed at the time of filing his brief.

- *Unegbu v. Woli (1997) 2 NWLR (Pt. 486) 194 at 197 CA*

6. It is a settled principle that arguments are to be canvassed on the basis of issues formulated and not on the ground of appeal.

- *Aja v. Okoro (1991) 7 NWLR (Pt. 203) 260 SC*
- *Adeyeri II v. Atanda (1995) 5 NWLR (Pt. 397) 512 at 518 SC*
- *Ogunsola v. NICON (1996) 1 NWLR (Pt. 423) 126 SC*
- *Koya v. U.B.A. Ltd (1997) 1 NWLR (Pt. 481) 251 at 253 SC*
- *Amadi v. N.N.P.C. (2000) 6 S.C (Pt. 1) 66*

7. It is trite law that issues for determination on appeal must be based on the decision of the court against which the appeal is made. However, an issue challenging the jurisdiction of a trial

court, can be raised on appeal even in the Supreme Court, for the first time.

- *Ifabiyi v. Adeniyi (2000) 5 SC 31 at 42*
- *Durwode v. The State (2001) 7 WRN 50 SC*

8. It is the law that where an issue for determination is predicated on an incompetent or defective ground of appeal, such issue becomes unarguable.

- *Nkpuma v. State (1995) 9 NWLR (Pt. 421) 505 at 507 SC*

9. It is also settled that where the issues postulated by parties on appeal, are inappropriate or inadequate having regard to the grounds of appeal filed, the court should, without any hesitation, attempt to identify the appropriate issues in the circumstances of the case. Care must, however, be taken to ensure that the issue(s) formulated by the court does not or do not raise new issues not contemplated by the grounds of appeal and not canvassed by the parties except it is an issue on jurisdiction.

- *Ifabiyi v. Adeniyi (2000) 5 SC 31 at 42*

10. Where there is sufficient material before an appellate court in respect of an issue which a trial court had failed to treat or advert its mind to, such issue, shall be resolved by the appellate court. An order of retrial will therefore not be necessary in such a case.

- *The State v. Godfrey Ajie (2000) 7 SC (Part 1) 24 at 30*

11. As a general rule, an appellant will not be allowed to raise on appeal a question which was not raised, tried and considered in the court below unless the question involves substantial points of law, whether substantive or procedural, and it is clear that no further evidence can be adduced which will affect the decision on them.

- *Bankole v. Pelu (1991) 8 NWLR (Pt. 211) 523 SC*
- *Onwugbufor v. Okoye (1996) 1 NWLR (Pt. 424) 252 SC*
- *Okonkwo v. Ogbogu (1996) 5 NWLR (Pt. 449) 420 SC*
- *Yusuf v. U.B.N. Ltd. (1996) 6 NWLR (Pt. 457) 632 SC*
- *Koya v. U.B.A. Ltd (1997) 1 NWLR (Pt. 481) 251 SC*

12. Generally, leave of court is required to raise new issues on appeal. However, leave of court is not needed to raise fresh issues for the first time at the Supreme Court where the issues are based

on errors in a decision of the Court of Appeal.

> - *Ogunsola v. NICON (1996) 1 NWLR (Pt. 423) 126 SC*

13. By virtue of section 213(1) of the 1979 Constitution, the Supreme Court receives and entertains an appeal from the Court of Appeal and not from the High Court. Consequently, any ground of appeal challenging the judgment of a High Court in the Supreme Court is incompetent.

> - *Okon v. State (1995) 1 NWLR (Pt. 372) 382 at 385 SC*
> - *Oduntan v. Gen. Oil Ltd (1995) 4 NWLR (Pt. 387) 1 at 8 SC*

14. Like a statement of claim, which supersedes the writ of summons, the issues formulated for determination in an appeal take the place of the grounds of appeal. Therefore, a consideration of the issues on appeal is equivalent to a consideration of the grounds of appeal.

> - *Momodu v. Momoh (1991) 1 NWLR (Pt. 169) 608 SC*
> - *U.B.N. Ltd. v. Odusote Bookstores Ltd (1995) 9 NWLR (Pt. 421) 558 at 563 SC*

4.5 Leave to Appeal

1. By virtue of section 221 of the 1979 Constitution and section 15 of the Court of Appeal Act, 1976, as amended, the word "leave" means permission. Therefore, an appellant is bound, where necessary, to seek the formal permission of the court before setting in motion an appeal process.

> - *Fumudoh v. Aboro (1991) 9 NWLR (Pt. 214) 210 CA*

2. Leave of court, where it is required, is a condition precedent to the exercise of the right to appeal. Thus, failure to obtain leave where it is required will render any appeal filed incompetent as no jurisdiction can be conferred on the appellate court.

> - *Nalsa & Team Associates v. N.N.P.C. (1991) 8 NWLR (Pt. 212) 652 SC*
> - *Ayansina v. Co-op. Bank Ltd (1994) 5 NWLR (Pt. 347) 742 CA*

- *Shaka v. Salisu (1996) 2 NWLR (Pt. 428)22 CA*
- *F.B.N. Plc v. Bukar (1997) 1 NWLR (Pt. 483) 625 CA*

3. An appeal from the Court of Appeal to the Supreme Court on grounds other than of law alone is incompetent and invalid unless leave of either the Court of Appeal or the Supreme Court is first sought and obtained.

- *Nyambi v. Osadim (1997) 2 NWLR (Pt. 485) 1 SC*
- *Olanrewaju v. Ogunleye (1997) 2 NWLR (Pt. 485) 12 SC*

4. Where an appeal is against an interlocutory decision of a court and it raises a question of facts or mixed law and facts, leave of court is required. However, an appeal is as of right and requires no leave of court, where the decision appealed against is either interlocutory or final provided the ground of appeal involves a question of law alone.

- *Ayansina v. Co-op. Bank Ltd (1994) 5 NWLR (Pt. 347) 742 CA*

5. The test for the determination of the question whether a decision of a court is final or interlocutory, is whether the decision finally disposes the right of the parties to the suit. It is a final decision if it finally disposes the right of the parties. However, if the decision does not, then the ruling remains an interlocutory decision.

- *Ogoja L.G. v. Offoboche (1996) 7 NWLR (Pt. 458) 48 CA*

6. A party aggrieved by an interlocutory decision of a court may bring an appeal against it within 14 days of giving the decision.

- *Tukur v. Govt., Gongola State (1996) 5 NWLR (Pt. 447) 186 CA*

7. Where the statutory period in which to exercise a right of appeal has expired, the court cannot entertain an application for leave to appeal, unless the application contains a prayer for extension of time within which the appellant may seek leave to appeal and also a prayer for extension of time within which to file such appeal.

- *Iroegbu v. Okwordu (1990) 6 NWLR (Pt. 159) 643 SC*

8. Where a party, seeking leave of court to appeal as an interested party fails to do so within the prescribed time, he must apply to

the court for three reliefs, namely: extension of time within which to seek leave to appeal; leave to appeal; and enlargement of time within which to file the appeal.

> - *In Re: Madaki (1996) 7 NWLR (Pt. 459) 153 SC*
> - *Owena Bank (Nig.) Plc v. N.S.E Ltd (1997) 8 NWLR (Pt. 515) 1 at 5 SC*
> - *C.C.B. (Nig.) Ltd v. Ogwuru (1993) 3 NWLR (Pt. 284) 630 SC*

9. For an application for extension of time to appeal to succeed, the applicant must show to the court that the delay in bringing the application is neither wilful nor inordinate; that there are good and substantial reasons for failure to appeal within the prescribed period; and that there are grounds which *prima facie* show good cause why the appeal should be heard.

> - *Okere v. Nlem (1992) 4 NWLR (Pt. 234) 132 SC*
> - *C.C.B. (Nig.) Ltd v. Ogwuru (1993) 3 NWLR (Pt. 284) 630 SC*
> - *S.B.N Plc. v. Abdulkadir (1996) 4 NWLR (Pt.443) 460 CA*

10. In an application for extension of time to appeal, it is not enough for the applicant to merely state that he did not receive a certified copy of the judgment appealed against on time. The applicant must further state the date when he made an application for the certified copy of the judgment and a copy of the letter for such application must be attached to the affidavit in support of the application for extension of time to appeal.

> - *Ikenna v. Bosah (1997) 3 NWLR (Pt. 495) 503 SC*
> - *Oruche v. C.O.P (1997) 4 NWLR (Pt. 497) 1 SC*

11. In an application for extension of time to appeal, counsel's error of judgment, if reasonable, is an acceptable ground for delay to apply for leave to appeal.

> - *Shanu v. Afribank (Nig.) Plc (2000) 10-11 SC 1 at 11-12*

12. In an application for extension of time to appeal, pardonable inadvertence of counsel is acceptable as a good and substantial reason for failure to appeal within time.

> - *Doherty v. Doherty (1964) 1 All NLR 299*
> - *Bowaye v. Adediwura (1976) 6 SC 143*

13. An appellate court has the power to grant leave to amend a writ of summons and, or a pleading if such application for amendment is made for the purpose of enabling the court to determine the real question in controversy between the parties or correcting any defect or error in the proceedings.

> - *Laguro v. Toku (1992) 2 NWLR (Pt. 223) 278 SC*
>
> - *Jessica Trading Co. Ltd v. Bendel Ins. Co. Ltd (1993) 1 NWLR (Pt. 271) 538 SC*
>
> - *Asolo v. Asolo (1996) 2 NWLR (Pt. 431) 480 CA*
>
> - *Diko v. Ibadan South West L.G. (1997) 2 NWLR (Pt. 486) 235 CA*

14. By virtue of section 220(2)(c) of the 1979 Constitution, an appeal against a consent judgment can only be made with the leave of the High Court or of the Court of Appeal.

> - *J.C. Ltd v. Ezenwa (1996) 4 NWLR (Pt. 443) 391 at 398 SC*

15. Where there is a consent order, neither the parties in the case nor the court could reverse or resile from the consent order except where the consent was obtained by fraud or gross mistake of law. Therefore, any party wishing to challenge the consent order on appeal must obtain the leave of the appellate court to do so.

> - *I.M.B (Nig.) Ltd v. Dabiri (1998) 1 NWLR (Pt. 533) 284 CA*

4.6 Brief of Argument

1. A brief of argument is a succinct statement of the propositions of law or fact or both, which a party or his counsel wishes to establish at the appeal together with reasons and authorities to sustain them.

> - *Emodi v. Kwentoh (1996) 2 NWLR (Pt. 433) 656 at 660 SC*
>
> - *U.A.C (Nig.) Ltd v. Fasheyitan (1998) 11 NWLR (Pt. 573) 179 SC*

2. The purpose of brief writing in the appeal courts is to assist the administration of justice by making the work of both counsel

and the court easier once the matter has reached the oral hearing stage. It is to promote justice, so that both counsel and the court may not embark on a wild goose chase, chasing a futile course.

- *Ehot v. State (1993) 4 NWLR (Pt. 290) 644 SC*

3. It is well settled that a good brief of argument should be brief and concise, containing concise statement of the facts of a case, which are material to the consideration of the questions presented for determination by the court. It should also contain a direct, concise and succinct statement of the argument in the appeal.

- *Shell Pet. Dev. Co. (Nig.) Ltd v. F.B.I.R. (1996) 8 NWLR (Pt. 466) 256 SC*

4. Although a defective, faulty and inelegantly written brief may attract the attention and comment of an appellate court, an appellate court will not and cannot dismiss an appeal of an appellant merely on the ground that his brief of argument is defective, unless the defect, fault or inelegance of the brief affects the merits of the appeal.

- *Weide & Co. (Nig.) Ltd v. Weide & Co. Hamburg (1992) 6 NWLR (Pt. 249) 627 CA*

5. The time within which an appellant ought to file his brief of argument starts to run from the date of service on him of the Registrar's notice that the record of appeal has been compiled, and not from the date any of the parties decides to collect the record.

- *Consortium M.C. v. N.E.P.A. (1992) 6 NWLR (Pt. 246) 132 SC*
- *Ajayi v. Omorogbe (1993) 6 NWLR (Pt. 301) 512 SC*

6. Where a respondent to an appeal fails to file his brief of argument, he will be deemed to have admitted the truth of everything stated in the appellant's brief in so far as such is borne out by the records.

- *Lagricom Co. Ltd v. U.B.N. Ltd (1996) 4 NWLR (Pt. 441) 185 CA*

7. Although the filing of a reply brief by an appellant is not mandatory, where a respondent's brief raises issues or points of law not covered in the appellant's brief, an appellant ought to

file a reply brief. Where an appellant fails to file a reply brief in the circumstances described above, but merely relies on or adopts his brief at the hearing of the appeal, without an oral reply, it may amount to a concession of the points of law or issues raised in the respondent's brief.

- *Popoola v. Adeyemo (1992) 8 NWLR (Pt. 257) 1 SC*
- *Shuaibu v. Maihodu (1993) 3 NWLR (Pt. 284) 748 CA*

8. A supplementary brief of argument cannot be filed by a party to an appeal except with the leave of the appellate court.

- *Okpala v. Ibeme (1989) 2 NWLR (Pt. 102) 208 SC*
- *Ehot v. State (1993) 4 NWLR (Pt. 290) 644 SC*

9. The Court of Appeal has the discretionary power to grant an application for amendment of brief of argument. Such discretion must however, be exercised judicially, and on good and substantial grounds.

- *Bob-Manuel v. Briggs (1995) 7 NWLR (Pt. 409) 537 CA*

10. Since the introduction of brief writing in the appellate courts, oral arguments play a secondary role in an appeal. Save with the leave of the Court of Appeal, no argument will be heard on behalf of any party for whom no brief has been filed and in respect of a point not covered by the brief. Also, where briefs have been filed, but counsel for the parties fail to appear on the date fixed for hearing, the appeal shall be treated as having been duly argued. Order 6 Rules 9(d)(e) & 10 of the Court of Appeal Rules, 1981, (as amended) considered.

- *Bob-Manuel v. Briggs (1995) 7 NWLR (Pt. 409) 537 CA*

11. Save in a substantive appeal or in applications for leave to appeal and for the enlargement of time to appeal, no brief of argument is required in the Supreme Court. Order 6 Rules 1-10 and Order 10 of the Supreme Court Rules, 1985, considered.

- *Obioha v. Ibero (1994) 1 NWLR (Pt. 322) 503 SC*

4.7 Record of Appeal

1. The Court of Appeal has the power to look at anything

contained in the record of an appeal before it, in order to enable it arrive at a just decision of the appeal.

- *Chevron (Nig.) Ltd. v. Onwugbelu (1996) 3 NWLR (Pt. 437) 404 CA*

2. It is the duty of an appellate court to consider and give necessary appraisal to all the pieces of evidence forming part of the record before it.

- *Pavex International Co. (Nig.) Ltd v. I.B.W.A (2000) 4 SC (Pt. II) 196*

3. An appellant has a duty to ensure the accuracy of the record of appeal forwarded to the appellate court. Similarly, the appellant must also ensure that the record of appeal reaches the Appellate Court on time.

- *Ajayi v. Omorogbe (1993) 6 NWLR (Pt. 301) 512 SC*

4. The law is quite clear that once an appellant has deposited the money for making up and forwarding the record of appeal, he has performed his duty. Therefore, if any portion of the record of proceedings is missing, it is the fault of the Registrar of the High Court.

- *Akaide v. State (1996) 8 NWLR (Pt. 468) 525 CA*

5. An appellate court has inherent powers to amend the record of a trial court so as to comply with the facts proved before the court and the decision given by it. The powers are exercised to correct obvious accidental slips and omissions apparent on the record and also to enable the pleadings conform to the evidence on record.

- *Jessica Trading Co. Ltd v. Bendel Ins. Co. Ltd (1993) 1 NWLR (Pt. 271) 538 SC*
- *Asolo v. Asolo (1996) 2 NWLR (Pt. 431) 480 CA*

6. The proper order to make in a murder charge where the record of appeal is incomplete is to order a retrial of the case *de novo*. Therefore, to discharge an accused because of incomplete record of appeal in a murder charge, will occasion a miscarriage of justice.

- *Nwaibe v. State (1996) 9 NWLR (Pt. 472) 343 at 345 CA*

V
Company Law

5.1 Incorporation and Legal Personality of a Company

1. There is a clear distinction between unincorporated and incorporated associations. An unincorporated association does not legally exist and must of necessity act through its appointed representative. On the other hand, an association that has been incorporated has legal personality. It can sue and be sued in its corporate name. It has the capacity to enter into any agreement in its corporate name.

> - *Anyaegbunam v. Osaka (2000) 3 SC 1*

2. To be able to prove in law the corporate status of a body or company, one must produce a certificate of incorporation in respect of the body or the company. The certificate is also evidence that the company came into existence on the date of incorporation.

> - *Jubilee Cotton Mills v. Lewis (1924) AC 950*
> - *Fawehinmi v. N.B.A (No. 2) (1989) 2 NWLR (Pt. 105) 558 at 632 SC*
> - *A.C.B. Plc v. Emostrade Ltd (1998) 2 NWLR (Pt. 536) 19 at 25 CA*

3. An incorporated company is a creature of law clothed with independent legal personality from the moment of incorporation, distinct and separate from those who laboured to give birth to it.

> - *Salomon v. Salomon & Co. Ltd (1897) AC 22 at 51*
> - *Trenco Nigeria Ltd v. African Real Estate Ltd (1978) 1 L.R.N. 146 at 153*
> - *Marina Nominees Ltd v. Federal Board of Inland Revenue (1986) 2 NWLR (Pt. 20) 48 at 61*

4. Notwithstanding the principle that an incorporated company has a separate personality and its entity is distinct from its members, the court has the power to lift the veil of incorporation under certain circumstances, for instance, where the company is involved in fraud, crime or fraudulent trading activities or where it is used to evade a contractual or other legal obligation.

> - *Public Finance Securities Ltd v. Jefia (1998) 3 NWLR (Pt. 543) 602 at 604 CA*

5. A Company can ratify a pre-incorporation contract after its incorporation and thereby making the company bound by it and entitling it to the benefit thereof. Sections 72(1), 625(1)(a) - (d), 626(a)-(c) and 651(2) of the Companies and Allied Matters Act, 1990 considered.

> - *Kelner v. Baxter (1866-67) L.R.C.P. 174*
> - *S.G.F v. S.G.B (Nig.) Ltd (1997) 4 NWLR (Pt. 497) 8 at 12 & 13 SC*
> - *A.C.B. Plc v. Emostrade Ltd (1998) 2 NWLR (Pt. 536) 19 at 23 CA*

6. The fact that an incorporated company's name does not end with "limited" does not raise any reasonable presumption that it is not a juristic person who can sue and be sued.

> - *Bank of Baroda v. Iyalabani Ltd (1998) 2 NWLR (Pt. 539) 600 CA*

7. A body corporate is a juristic person. It has legal personality and it can be an occupier of premises. The word "occupier" includes any number of persons and a body corporate.

> - *Laban-kowa v. Alkali (1999) 9 NWLR (Pt. 620) 601 CA*

8. A holding company and its subsidiaries are each distinct and separate legal person. Each owns its own assets and property separately.

> - *M.O. Kanu, Sons & Co. v. F.B.N. Plc (1998) 11 NWLR (Pt. 572) 116 at 121 CA*

9. A subsidiary company is not an agent of the parent company, rather, it is an entirely different entity.

> - *Musa v. Ehidiamhen (1994) 3 NWLR (Pt. 334) 554 CA*

10. A Company may be liable in crime to the same extent as a natural person. Thus, a company could be prosecuted for a common law offence of conspiracy to defraud even though *mens*

rea is an essential element of the offence. Section 65 of the Companies and Allied Matters Act, 1990 considered.

- *Bolton (Engineering) Co. Ltd v. Graham & Sons (1957) 1 Q.B. 159*
- *D.P.P. v. Kent and Sussex Contractors Ltd (1944) AC 146*
- *R v. L.C.R. Havlage Ltd (1944) K.B. 551*

5.2 Promoters

1. A promoter is one who undertakes to form a company with reference to a given project and sets it going, and who takes the necessary steps to accomplish that purpose. It includes those who undertake to take part in raising the capital for it. However, solicitors and accountants when acting in their professional capacity are not promoters. Section 61 of the Companies and Allied Matters Act (CAMA), 1990 considered.

- *Twycoss v. Grant (1877) 2 CPD 469*
- *Adeniji v. Starcola (Nigeria) Ltd (Suit No. M/135/70 of 18/ 1/71 High Court of Lagos Judgment)*

2. Usually, to ascertain who are the promoters of a company, it is useful to determine the following, namely: who started the idea of forming the company for the purpose in question; who decided what was to be included in the memorandum and articles of association and in the prospectus; who undertook the liability for the costs of preparing those documents; who sought out the persons who ultimately became the first directors, and induced them to undertake the offices; who procured the subscription of the capital; and, who benefited by the formation of the company.

- *Whaley Bridge Calico Printing Co. v. Green (1889) 5 QBD 109*

3. A promoter stands in a fiduciary position to the company. Thus, a promoter owes a primary duty to disclose to the company any profit made by him in the process of promoting the company. Also, where a promoter acquires any property or information in circumstances in which it is his duty as a fiduciary to acquire it on behalf of the company, he shall account

to the company for such property and for any profit which he may have made from the use of such property or information. Section 62(1), (2) of the Companies and Allied Matters Act 1990 considered.

- *Lydney and Wig pool Iron Ore Co. v. Bird (1886) 3 Ch D 85, 94*

- *Erlanger v. New Sambrero Phosphate Co. (1878) 3 App Cas. 1218, 1236*

4. A promoter must make full disclosure of his dealings to the company. Thus, where he fails to make full disclosure, the company can rescind the contract.

- *Gluckstein v. Barnes (1990) AC 240*

5. A promoter is entitled to adequate remuneration, which may take a number of forms, for instance, he may be paid a fee or he may, in lieu of payment of remuneration and expenses, take shares of the company which are credited as fully paid up or be given shares to be paid for within a specified time.

- *Touche v. Metropolitan Railway Warehousing Co. (1871) 6 Ch App 671, 676*

- *Omnium Electric Palaces Ltd. v. Baines (1914) 1 Ch 332*

5.3 Nationality

1. The law of the country in which a company is incorporated determines its nationality. Thus, a company incorporated in Nigeria is a Nigerian company.

- *Jenson v. Driefontein Consolidated Mines Ltd (1902) A.C. 484*

2. A foreign company or corporation duly registered according to the laws of a foreign State recognised by Nigeria may sue or be sued in Nigeria in its name or in the name of its agent. This is in accordance with the provision of Section 60(1) of Companies and Allied Matters Act, 1990 and the common law.

- *Nigerian Bank for Commerce & Industry Ltd v. Europa Traders (U.K) Ltd (1990) 6 NWLR (Pt. 154) 36-41 CA*

- *Ishola v. Societe Generale Bank (Nig.) Ltd (1997) 2 NWLR (Pt. 488) 405 SC*

- *U.B.N. Plc v. Jase Motors (Nig.) Ltd (1997) 7 NWLR (Pt. 513) 387 CA*

- *Watanmal (Singapore) v. Liz Olofin & Co. (1998) 1 NWLR (Pt. 533) 311 CA*

- *Ritz & Co. KG v. Techno Ltd (1999) 4 NWLR (Pt. 598) 298 CA*

- *Saeby v. Olaogun (2001) 11 WRN 179 SC*

3. The place where the registered office of a company is situated is its domicile. Unlike the domicile of an individual, the domicile of a company remains the same throughout its life.

- *Gasque v. Commissioner for Inland Revenue (1940) 2 KB 80*

4. The fact that a company has a wholly owned subsidiary in a foreign country does not make the parent company amenable to the jurisdiction of that foreign country.

- *Adams v. Cape Industrial Plc (1988) The Times, June 23*

5.4 Ultra Vires

1. The term "*ultra vires*" means acts, which are outside the scope of the objects of the company set forth in the object clause of its memorandum of association. Thus, any act performed outside the company's objects is *ultra vires*, that is, the act is beyond the powers of the company and is, therefore, void and creates no legal rights against the company. Also, the company cannot claim on it.

- *Ashbury Railways Carriage and Iron Co. Ltd v. Riche (1875) L.R. 7 H.L*

- *Re Jon Beauforte (London) Ltd (1953) CL 137*

- *Continental Chemists Ltd v. Ifeakandu (1966) 1 All N.L.R 1*

2. It is *ultra vires* for a company to conduct its affairs outside the prescriptions of its memorandum and articles of association.

- *Okoya v. Santilli (1990) 2 NWLR (Pt. 131) 172 SC*

3. The doctrine of *ultra vires* has two basic defects. First, it unduly restricts the right of a company to change or engage in activities, which it finds profitable. Secondly, it caused great hardship to creditors who lent money to the company on *ultra vires* transaction.

- *Ashbury Railways Carriage and Iron Co. Ltd v. Riche (1875) L.R. 7 H.L*

- *Beauforte (Jon) (London) Ltd, Re, Applications of Grainger Smith & Co. (Builders) Ltd, John Wright & Son (Veneers) Ltd and Lowell Baldwin Ltd (1953) Ch. 131*

4. The adverse effect of the doctrine of *ultra vires* has now being whittled down by the abolition of the doctrine in many jurisdictions. In Nigeria, the doctrine has been abolished by virtue of sections 38(1) and 39(3) of the Companies and Allied Matters Act, 1990, in relation to a third party. However, in relation to the company itself and its members, the doctrine is still much alive by virtue of sections 39 and 40 of the Act.

- *Bell Houses Ltd v. City Walls Properties Ltd (1966) 2 QB 207*

5.5 *Instituting an Action by or Against a Company*

1. Only the Board of directors of a company in a general meeting can authorise the institution of an action on behalf of the company. However, a Director who enjoys the confidence of the Board can in certain appropriate or emergency and situational circumstances commence an action in the name of the company with the intent that such action would be ratified. A Company Secretary cannot defend or sue without the authority of the company. Sections 279(3), 298 and 299 of CAMA Act 1990 considered.

- *Ejekam v. Devon Ind. Ltd (1998) 1 NWLR (Pt. 534) 417 CA*

2. The service of court process on a company may be effected through its branch office within jurisdiction and not necessarily in its head office.

- *Palm Beach Insurance v. Bruhns (1997) 9 NWLR (Pt. 519) 80 CA*

3. By virtue of Section 78 of CAMA 1990, court processes are to be served on a company in the manner provided by the rules of the court. All other documents are to be served on the company by leaving such documents at or sending same by post to the registered office or head office of the company.

> - *Texaco (Nig.) Plc v. Lukoko (1997) 6 NWLR (Pt. 510) 651 CA*
>
> - *Ranco Trading Co. Ltd. v. U.B.N. Ltd (1998) 4 NWLR (Pt. 547) 566 at 568-569 CA*

4. A Company is a legal person or a juristic person. It is not a natural person. It can only act through its agents or servants. Therefore, any of its agents or servants can testify or give evidence before a court or tribunal to establish any transaction entered into by the company.

> - *Ishola v. Societe Generale Bank (Nig.) Ltd (1997) 2 NWLR (Pt. 488) 405 SC*
>
> - *U.B.N. Plc v. Jase Motors (Nig.) Ltd (1997) 7 NWLR (Pt. 513) 387 CA*

5. The rule of law established in the case of *Foss v. Harbottle* is to the effect that where there is a wrong done to a company or in an action to recover money or damages due to a company, it is only the company itself and not an individual or minority shareholder that can sue or take action to redress, recover, ratify the wrong or irregular conduct. However, there are exceptions to the rule. One of such exceptions is that a minority shareholder can take action or sue where there is a fraud or where the majority of shareholders are attempting directly or indirectly to appropriate to themselves money, property, or advantages which belong to the company.

> - *Foss v. Harbottle (1843) 2 Hare 461*
> - *Gombe v. P.W. (Nig.) Ltd (1995) 6 NWLR (Pt. 402) 402 SC*
> - *Ejikeme v. Amaechi (1998) 3 NWLR (Pt. 542) 456 CA*
> - *Daily Times (Nig.) Plc v. Akindiji (1998) 13 NWLR (Pt. 580) 22 at 27 CA*

6. The rule of law laid down in the case of *Royal British Bank v. Turguand* known as the *Turguand Rule* is to the effect that a person who transacts with a company in reliance on public documents, and such transactions are consistent with the public

documents is entitled to assume that all matters of internal management of the company had been complied with. If the company's internal management had not been complied with, that fact cannot prejudice the rights of a person who had acted in reliance on the public document. There are, however, exceptions to the rule which include suspicious circumstances which put the outsider on inquiry; where the party seeking to enforce the contract knows of the internal irregularity of the company and where the document relied upon by the person dealing with the company was forged.

- *Royal British Bank v. Turquand (1856) 6 E & B 327*
- *Metalimpex v. A.G. Leventis & Co. (Nig.) Ltd (1976) 2 SC 91*
- *Trenco (Nigeria) Ltd v. African Real Estate Ltd (1978) 1 L.R.N. 146*

5.6 Membership of a Company

1. A person may become a member of a company by subscribing to the memorandum of association of the company or by agreeing in writing to become a member of the company, that is, by allotment of shares. Section 79 of CAMA 1990 considered.

- *Starcola (Nig.) Ltd v. Adeniji (1972) 1 SC 202*
- *Odunmodi v. Mohammed (1973) NCLR 452 at 460*

2. A registered company has a separate and distinct legal entity from its members. It is neither an agent of its members nor a trustee for them. Also, members of a company are not liable in law, in any shape or form for the acts of a company, except to the extent and in the manner provided by law.

- *N.I.D.B. v. Fembo (Nig.) Ltd (1997) 2 NWLR (Pt. 489) 543 at 547 CA*

5.7 Directors, Secretaries and Agents of a Company

1. A director of a company is a person appointed or elected according to law and authorised to manage or direct the affairs

of the company.

> - *Olufosoye v. Fakorede (1993) 1 NWLR (Pt. 272) 747 CA*
> - *Iwuchukwu v. Nwizu (1994) 7 NWLR (Pt. 357) 379 SC*

2. A registered company has separate and distinct entity from its directors or other natural persons who act on behalf of the company.

> - *Royal Petroleum Company Ltd v. First Bank of Nigeria Ltd (1997) 6 NWLR (Pt. 510) 584 at 589 CA*

3. Directors of a company are bound to exercise the powers conferred upon them *bona fide* and to consider the interest of the company as paramount. This duty of honesty and good faith in the exercise of their powers is in fact the primary duty of directors.

> - *Re Smith & Fawcett Ltd (1942) Ch. 304*
>
> - *Artra Industries (Nig.) Ltd v. N.B.C.I. (1998) 4 NWLR (Pt. 546) 357 SC*

4. It is an established general rule of law that in so far as a director is bound by fiduciary duties, these duties are owed to the company only. Thus, they are not owed to other companies or body corporate with which the company is associated, for example, its holding company or subsidiary.

> - *Bell v. Lever Bros Ltd (1932) AC 161*
>
> - *Lindgreen v. L & P Estates Ltd (1968) Ch. 572*

5. Where a company borrows money for a specific project and the money is not applied for that purpose but for some other fraudulent purposes, every director or officer of the company is liable to the person or organisation from whom they borrowed the money. Section 290 of CAMA 1990 considered.

> - *Public Finance Securities Ltd v. Jefia (1998) 3 NWLR (Pt. 543) 602 at 604 CA*

6. A director of a company upon his own personal security may borrow money from a bank and lend the money to his company. In so doing, he must act *bona fide* in the interest of the company.

> - *Oguntayo v. Adebutu (1997) 12 NWLR (Pt. 531) 83 at 86 CA*

7. Directors, Managing Directors or Managers are, in the eyes of the law, the directing mind and the will of the company. The state of mind of this special class of employees is, indeed, the state of mind of the company because they control what the company does and what it does not do.

    - Delta Steel (Nig.) Ltd v. A.C.T. Incor. (1999) 4 NWLR (Pt. 597) 53 CA

8. Directors must exercise ordinary care and skill, and where they possess special knowledge or experience they must use it in the interest and the affairs of the company.

    - Re Brazillian Rubber Plantation and Estates Ltd (1911) 1 Ch. 425

9. A director will not be held liable for negligence unless he is guilty of gross or culpable negligence in a business sense.

    - Re City Equitable Fire Insurance Co. Ltd (1925) Ch. 407

10. In some circumstances, directors will be expected to seek specialist advice and will be held liable for loss occasioned by their failure to do so.

    - Re Duomatic Ltd (1969) 2 Ch. 365

11. A director is not entitled to keep profits which he makes by reason of opportunities acquired as a result of his position unless these profits are disclosed to and approved by the company.

    - Regal (Hastings) Ltd v. Gulliver (1942) 1 All ER 378

12. A director will be liable to account to the company where he has made profits by using information which has come to him whilst he is a director or which he has acquired in the course of his duties, and which is of concern to the company.

    - Industrial Development Consultants Ltd v. Cooley (1972) 2 All ER 162, (1972) 1 WLR 443

13. Section 343(1) of the Companies and Allied Matters Act, 1990 provides that a company's balance sheet and every copy of it which is laid before the company in general meeting or delivered to the commission shall be signed on behalf of the board by two of the directors of the company. Also, subsection (4) of Section 343 provides that the balance sheet and the profit and loss account annexed to it shall be approved by the board of

directors and signed on their behalf by two directors authorized to do so. A company's financial statement made in compliance with the aforesaid law is valid for all intents and purposes, until the contrary is shown.

> - *Nigerian Wire Ind. Plc v. European Trade & Finance Plc (1997) 6 NWLR (Pt. 510) 632 at 640 CA*

14. A company secretary is an officer of the company with extensive duties and responsibilities. He is not a mere clerk. He regularly makes representation on behalf of the company and enters into contracts on its behalf. He can sign contracts of administrative nature, such as employment of staff. Sections 295 and 296 of CAMA considered.

> - *Panorama Developments (Guildford) Ltd v. Fidelis Furnishing Fabrics Ltd (1971) 2 Q.B. 711*

15. A company secretary is protected by section 296 of the Companies and Allied Matters Act, 1990 regardless of the fact that he holds a dual position in the company as the company secretary/legal adviser.

> - *Daily Times (Nig.) Plc v. Akindiji (1998) 13 NWLR (Pt. 580) 22 at 25 CA*

16. The Chairman, Managing Director or any other officer of a company may be liable for constructive fraud where he induces a person through his assurance and warranty to deposit funds with his company and subsequently fails to repay such funds because of a decline in business fortunes. Section 290 of the Companies and Allied Matters Act, 1990 considered.

> - *Public Finance Securities Ltd v. Jefia (1998) 3 NWLR (Pt. 543) 602 CA*

17. The principle of law generally known as "vicarious liability" is to the effect that a master is liable for any wrong even if it is criminal offence or a tortious act committed by his servant while acting in the course of his employment. However, to succeed against a master, the plaintiff must first of all establish the liability of the wrongdoer, and prove that the wrongdoer is a servant of the master and that the wrongdoer acted in the course of his employment with the master.

> - *Ifeanyi Chukwu (Osondu) Co. Ltd v. Soleh Boneh (Nig.) Ltd (2000) 3 SC 42 at 48*

5.8 Meetings and Proceedings

1. No business shall be transacted at any general meeting unless a quorum is formed when the meeting proceeds to business.

   - *Re Hartley Bairo Ltd (1955) Ch. 143*

2. In conducting annual general meeting of a limited liability company and indeed, any other meeting, members must be given adequate notice both of the meeting and of the substance of the matter, which the meeting is to consider. Notice must disclose facts upon which the members can exercise an informed business judgment.

   - *Baillie v. Oriental Telephone and Electric Co. Ltd (1915) 1 Ch. 503*
   - *Normandy v. Ind. Coope & Co. Ltd (1908) 1 Ch. 84*

3. Inaccuracies or a breach of procedure in recording the minutes of meetings, or the like, will not necessarily invalidate the minutes book of a company.

   - *Oguntayo v. Adebutu (1997) 12 NWLR (Pt. 531) 83 at 88 CA*

5.9 Shares

1. The authority to allot shares is vested in the company, which may delegate it to the directors subject to any conditions or directions that may be imposed by the articles, or from time to time by the company in general meeting. Section 124 of CAMA 1990 considered.

   - *Edokpolor & Co. Ltd v. Sem-Edo Wire Ind. Ltd (1984) 7 SC 119*

2. A shareholder who has sold all his shares in a company has no more right under section 114 of the Companies and Allied Matters Act, 1990 to attend any general meeting of the company and vote at such a meeting.

   - *Gadzama v. Rims Merchant Bank Ltd (1997) 4 NWLR (Pt. 498) 234 CA*

3. A trustee of shares in a company in whose name the shares are registered is still regarded the registered legal owner of the shares while the beneficial owners are the beneficiaries. This is because a trust relationship is generally equitable in nature.

- *Kotoye v. Saraki (1994) 7 NWLR (Pt. 357) 414 SC*

4. The principles governing contract of sale of shares of a company are similar to those, which apply to other contracts save that sale must conform to the provisions of the articles of the company. A contract to sell shares may be made in writing or orally.

- *Gadzama v. Rims Merchant Bank Ltd (1997) 4 NWLR (Pt. 498) 234 at 237 CA*

5. The law is that shares in a company are in the nature of personal estate and are transferable in the manner provided by the articles of association.

- *Okoya v. Santilli (1994) 4 NWLR (Pt. 338) 256 SC*

6. Transfer of shares becomes effective in law when the name of the transferee is entered in the register of members in respect of the transferred shares. Section 152(2) of the Companies and Allied Matters Act, 1990 considered.

- *Jethwani v. Nigeria Wire Ind. Plc (1999) 5 NWLR (Pt. 602) 326 CA*

7. The consent or permission or approval of the Minister of Finance is essential for the valid transfer of security when the business transaction involves or affects someone resident outside the shores of Nigeria. Section 10(1) of the Exchange Control Act Cap. 113 Laws of the Federation of Nigeria, 1990 considered.

- *Jethwani v. Nigeria Wire Ind. (1999) 5 NWLR (Pt. 602) 326 CA*

8. The Securities and Exchange Commission is empowered to suspend the registration of any person's security for a period of twelve calendar months or obtain the approval of the Minister of Finance in order to revoke the registration of a person's securities. Section 24(1) of the Securities and Exchange Commission Act Cap. 406 Laws of the Federation of Nigeria 1990

considered.

> - *Owena Bank (Nig.) Plc v. N.S.E. Ltd (1997) 8 NWLR (Pt. 515) 1 SC*

9. Dividend is the payment made out of profits to a shareholder of a company from time to time.

> - *Kotoye v. Saraki (1994) 7 NWLR (Pt. 357) 414 SC*

10. A debenture is a document, which either creates or acknowledges a debt.

> - *Fasakin v. Fasakin (1994) 4 NWLR (Pt. 340) 597 CA*

5.10 Trade Names and Marks, Copyrights, Patents and Designs

1. The court has power and jurisdiction to stop a person or a company from using a trade name which is similar to that being used by an existing company if the name is likely to deceive or cause confusion between the two companies and is likely to lead customers to conclude that the other business is connected in some way with the existing company's business.

> - *Motor Manufacturers and Traders Society Ltd v. Motor Manufacturers and Traders Mutual Insurance Co. Ltd (1925) ALL E.R 616*
> - *Daily-Need Pharm. Ind.v. Daily-Needs Ind. (1997) 3 NWLR (Pt. 491) 99 CA*

2. It is trite that a party, opposing an application for the registration of a trademark, must file a notice of opposition, stating the grounds of his opposition. The applicant, if he wishes to maintain his application, must then file a counter-statement. The parties thereafter file evidence in turn, the opposing party first.

> - *Nabisco Inc. v. Allied Biscuits Co. Ltd (1998) 10 NWLR (Pt. 568) 16 at 18 & 19 SC*

3. Copyright, in the case of a literary work is the right to control, in Nigeria, the reproduction of the literary work in any material

form, and the communication and broadcasting of it to the public, subject to the exceptions specified in schedule 2 of the Copyright Act, Cap. 68 Laws of the Federation of Nigeria, 1990.

> - *Adenuga v. Ilesanmi Press (1991) 5 NWLR (Pt. 189) 82 CA*

4. Reproduction, under the copyright law, is defined as the making of one or more copies of a literary, musical or artistic work, cinematographic film or sound recording. Section 1(1) of the Copyright Act, Cap. 68 Laws of the Federation of Nigeria, 1990.

> - *Adenuga v. Ilesanmi Press (1991) 5 NWLR (Pt. 189) 82 CA*

5. Copyright, according to section 14(1) of the Copyright Act, 1990, would be infringed by any person who, without the licence of the owner of the copyright, did or caused any other person to do an act, the doing of which is controlled by copyright.

> - *Adenuga v. Ilesanmi Press (1991) 5 NWLR (Pt. 189) 82 CA*

6. By the provision of section 19(1) of the Patents and Designs Act, Cap. 344, Laws of the Federation of Nigeria, 1990, the registration of an industrial design confers upon the registered owner the right to preclude any other person from producing and or marketing the design.

> - *Peter E. Venture (Nig.) Ltd v. Gazasonner Ind. Ltd (1998) 6 NWLR (Pt. 555) 619 CA*

5.11 Receivers and Managers

1. A receiver is an impartial person appointed by the court to manage, collect and receive, pending the proceedings, rent, issues and profits of land or personal estate which does not seem reasonable to the court that either party to the proceedings should collect or receive.

> - *Uwakwe v. Odogwu (1989) 5 NWLR (Pt. 123) 562 SC*
> - *Abbas v. Ajoge (1996) 4 NWLR (Pt. 444) 596 CA*

2. A receiver, when appointed by a court, is not an agent of either party to the litigation. He is, rather, an officer of court. When appointed over land or real property, he *de jure* takes over possession and his appointment operates as a general injunction against all the parties to the litigation.

- *Uwakwe v. Odogwu (1989) 5 NWLR (Pt. 123) 562 SC*

3. The Federal High Court has the power to appoint a receiver and or a manager. Section 13 of the Federal High Court Act Cap. 134 Laws of the Federation of Nigeria, 1990; Order 22 rule 1 of the Federal High Court (Civil Procedure) Rules, 2000 and Section 389(1) of the Companies and Allied Matters Act, 1990 considered.

- *Intermarket (Nig.) Ltd v. Aderounmu (1998) 12 NWLR (Pt. 576) 131 at 135 CA*

4. The legal effect of appointing a receiver/manager to manage an existing registered company is that the company's right to deal with its assets is suspended. The receiver/manager would act as agent of the company for the purposes of dealing with assets in receivership. Thus, it is only the receiver/manager who on behalf of the company, can bring action or be sued. However, the company does not lose its legal personality or its title to the goods in receivership.

- *Intercontractors Nig. Ltd v. N.P.F.M.B. (1988) 1 NSCC 759*
- *Pharmatek Industrial Ltd v. Trade Bank (Nig.) Plc (1997) 7 NWLR (Pt. 514) 639 at 642 CA*

5.12 Winding Up

1. An application to the court for the winding up of a company shall be by petition presented either by the company, a creditor, the official receiver, a contributory, a trustee in bankruptcy to or a personal representative of a creditor or contributory, the Corporate Affairs Commission, a receiver if authorised by the instrument under which he was appointed. Section 410(1) of the Companies and Allied Matters Act, 1990 considered.

- *Oilfield Supply Centre Ltd. v. Johnson (1987) 2 NWLR (Pt. 58) 625 SC*

- *Gadzama v. Rims Merchant Bank Ltd. (1997) 4 NWLR (Pt. 498) 234 CA*

2. The object of advertisement of a petition for winding up of a company is to put creditors of the company on notice of the petition while the object of proceedings for winding up of a company is to terminate the life of the company. Therefore, an order made in respect of one cannot be validly substituted for the other.

- *Ezenwa v. J.C. Ltd (1994) 7 NWLR (Pt. 356) 292 CA*

3. A court is empowered to wind up a company if the company is unable to pay its debt. However, the petitioner must establish before the court that there is an existing debt; the debt is due, and the company is unable to pay the debt after formal demand thereof. Sections 408(d) and 409(a) of the Companies and Allied Matters Act, 1990 considered.

- *Oriental Airlines Ltd v. Air VIA Ltd (1998) 12 NWLR (Pt. 577) 271 CA*

4. A liquidator who has been appointed in accordance with the provisions of section 422(9) of the Companies and Allied Matters Act, 1990 is empowered to take over the powers of the directors of the company.

- *N.D.I.C. v. F.M.B. Ltd (1997) 4 NWLR (Pt. 501) 519 SC*

5. A provisional liquidator has the same powers as a liquidator. Thus, upon the appointment of a provisional liquidator, the directors cannot exercise any of their powers unless the court grants them the leave to do so. Sections 422(9) and 423 of the Companies and Allied Matters Act, 1990 considered.

- *N.D.I.C. v. F.M.B. Ltd (1997) 4 NWLR (Pt. 501) 519 SC*

6. The execution of goods and chartels of a company in liquidation is deemed to be completed by seizure and sale; and an attachment of a debt is deemed to be completed by receipt of the debt, and an execution against land is deemed to be completed by seizure; and, in the case of an equitable interest, by the appointment of a receiver. Section 500(2) of the Companies and Allied Matters Act, 1990 considered.

- *F.M.B.N. v. N.D.I.C. (1999) 2 NWLR (Pt. 591) 333 at 342 SC*

7. The law applicable to sharing of assets of a company wound up is to the effect that the liabilities of the company must first of all be identified and settled. Subsequently, the court can then order the sharing of the remaining assets (if any) among the parties entitled thereto.

- *Okafor v. Igwilo (1997) 11 NWLR (Pt. 527) 36 at 39 CA*

8. A company fully wound up and dissolved loses its legal entity and cannot be one and the same company as before.

- *Ehidimhen v. Musa (2000) 4 SC (Part II) 166 at 184*

5.13 Partnership

1. The prerequisite of a partnership relationship is that the person or partners are carrying on business in common.

- *Omidiora v. Ademiluyi (1997) 6 NWLR (Pt. 508) 294 at 295 CA*

2. Any two or more persons claiming or alleged to be liable as partners may sue or be sued in the name of the firm in which they claim to be partners.

- *Fabno Ind. Ltd v. United Distillers Plc (1999) 5 NWLR (Pt. 602) 314 CA*

3. Any unincorporated business enterprise, whether of single or multiple ownership within the jurisdiction of the appropriate court may be sued as defendants in their business names.

- *Fabno Ind. Ltd v. United Distillers Plc (1999) 5 NWLR (Pt. 602) 314 at 316 CA*

VI
Constitutional Law

1. The Constitution is the basic law of the land. It is superior to all other laws. Statutory provisions cannot therefore render constitutional provisions nugatory.

    - Adisa v. Oyinwola (2000) 6 SC (Part II) 47 at 92

2. Immunity granted to the President or Vice President, Governor or Deputy Governor under Section 267 of the 1979 Constitution does not apply to his official capacity or where he is only a nominal party in a civil or criminal proceeding. The immunity is to protect such a person from the harassment of his person while in office for his action done in his private capacity before or during his tenure in office.

    - Abacha v. Fawehinmi (2000) 4 SC (Part II) 1

3. The right to fair hearing is one of the fundamental human rights provided for under Section 33 of the 1979 Constitution. This right cannot be waived or statutorily taken away.

    - Chigbu v. Tonimas (Nig.) Ltd (1999) 3 NWLR (Pt. 593) 115 CA

    - Bamgboye v. University of Ilorin (1999) 10 NWLR (Pt. 622) 290 at 305 SC

    - Awoniyi v. The Registered Trustees of the Rosicrucian Order, Amorc (Nigeria) (2000) 6 SC (Part I) 103

    - Araka v. Ejeagwu (2001) 5 WRN 1 SC

4. Where there is a breach of the principle of fair hearing, any decision arrived at would be cut down notwithstanding that the conclusion would not have been any different if the principle had been adhered to.

    - Mika'ilu v. State (2001) 5 WRN 74 at 80 CA

5. To lay allegation of bias against a judge, the person levying it must be armed with all the materials required to support his allegation.

    - Ajibola v. Popoola (1997) 4 NWLR (Pt. 498) 206 CA

- *Okpanachi v. Comm. For Works (1997) 6 NWLR (Pt. 509) 482 at 484-486 CA*
- *Adio v. A-G Oyo State (2000) 5 SC 82*

6. Civil Service Rules were made pursuant to powers conferred by virtue of the Constitution. The Rules therefore have constitutional force.

- *Busari v. Edo State C.S.C. (1999) 4 NWLR (Pt. 599) 365 at 368 CA*

7. By the provisions of Section 37(1) of Decree No. 3 of 1999, it is only when a Governor-elect dies that the Deputy Governor elect could be sworn in as Governor. The Decree does not cover when the Governor elect abandons his mandate.

- *P.D.P. v. I.N.E.C (1999) 11 NWLR (Pt. 626) 200 SC*

8. In a Military Regime, Decrees are the Supreme Law of the land and other laws including the Constitution are regarded as inferior.

- *A-G Fed. V. Guardian Newspapers Ltd. (1999) 9 NWLR (Pt. 618) 187 at 193-196 SC*

9. By virtue of Section 25(11) of the 1979 Constitution, right of address by counsel is given before judgment. When this is not given, any decision arrived at amounts to breach of fair hearing rendering the proceedings null and void.

- *Ihom v. Gaji (1997) 6 NWLR (Pt. 509) 526 at 527-528 SC*

10. By virtue of item 13 of Part II (Concurrent Legislative List) of the 1979 Constitution, the National Assembly is empowered to make laws with respect to electricity, establishment of electric power stations, the generation and transmission of electricity in or to any part of the Federation and from one state to another state.

- *Adebileje v. NEPA (1998) 12 NWLR (Pt. 577) 219 CA*

11. The Federal High Court has exclusive jurisdiction to entertain matters relating to the administrative or the management and control of the Federal Government or any of its agencies pursuant to Section 230 (1) (q) of the Constitution (Suspension and Modification) Decree No. 107 of 1993.

- *Adebileje v. NEPA (1998) 12 NWLR (Pt. 577) 219 at 222-224 CA*

12. Whenever the issue of *locus standi* is raised, there is need to give it priority over other issues.

- *Gbadamosi v. Dairo (2001) 11 WRN 129 at 138 CA*

13. The State High Court has unlimited jurisdiction to entertain any matter by virtue of section 236(1) of the 1979 Constitution. This jurisdiction is limited by the combined provisions of section 7 of the Federal High Court Act and section 230 of the Constitution (Suspension and Modification) Decree 107 of 1993 which confer exclusive jurisdiction on the Federal High Court in relation to certain matters affecting the revenue of the Federal Government. These provisions validly limit the unlimited jurisdiction conferred on the State High Court constitutionally. Any state law, which purports to take away the unlimited jurisdiction of the State High Court, is void.

- *Okulate v. Awosanya (2000) 1 SC 107 at 114*

14. Giving effect to the doctrine of separation of powers, the Constitution vests the power of adjudication on the judiciary under Section 6 of the 1979 Constitution. Section 6 (6) (b) concerns itself with the delimitation of the separation of powers between the judiciary and the other arms of government.

- *Amadi v. NNPC (2000) 6 SC (Part I) 66 at 94-95*

15. The Constitution being the Supreme Law of the land prevails over other statutes including the African Charter on Human and Peoples' Rights (Ratification and Enforcement) Act, Cap. 10 LFN, 1990.

- *Abacha v. Fawehinmi (2000) 4 SC (Part II) 1*

16. Powers vested in the Attorney General of the Federation under section 160(1) of the 1979 Constitution cannot be delegated to lawyers outside his department.

- *Comptroller, Nig. Prison Serv., Ikoyi v. Adekanye (1999) 5 NWLR (Pt. 602) 167 CA*

17. In fundamental rights proceedings, the principal claim must border on infringement of fundamental rights of an individual. An action based principally on dismissal of employee cannot be brought under Fundamental Rights (Enforcement Procedure) Rules, 1979.

- *Egbuonu v. B.R.T.C (1997) 12 NWLR (Pt. 531) 29 at 31 SC*

18. By Section 220(1) and (2) of the 1979 Constitution, appeal against consent judgment shall lie to the Court of Appeal only by leave of a High Court or the Court of Appeal.

- *Enigbokan v. Baruwa (1998) 8 NWLR (Pt. 560) 96 CA*

19. Under the Constitution, the Local Government Councils are vested with the power to compile the valuation list for the purpose of assessing rates on private properties vide Section 7(5) of the 1979 Constitution. Therefore, a state will act *ultra vires* if it purports to interfere with the power exercisable by the Local Government Council.

- *Knight Frank & Rutley (Nig.) v. A-G Kano State (1998) 7 NWLR (Pt. 556) 1 SC*

20. Whenever the court is interpreting any provisions of the Constitution, it is duty-bound to construe such provisions as not to defeat the obvious ends of the Constitution.

- *Braithwaite v. G.D.M (1998) 7 NWLR (Pt. 557) 307 CA*

21. Pre-action notice does not interfere with a person's right of access to court. The idea is to give the other party adequate notice to enable him prepare his answer to a case made against him.

- *NNPC v. Fawehinmi (1998) 7 NWLR (Pt. 559) 598 CA*

22. An accused person has a right to remain silent in his own trial if he chooses. However, a court can comment or draw unfavourable inferences against an accused who fails to testify having regard to the evidence adduced by prosecution against him. This does not infringe on the right granted by Section 33(11) of the 1979 Constitution.

- *Nasiru v. State (1999) 2 NWLR (Pt. 589) 87 at 92 SC*

23. Every citizen has a right of access to court for legal redress.

- *Ihenacho v. Uzochukwu (1997) 2 NWLR (Pt. 487) 257 at 262 SC*
- *Amadi v. NNPC (2000) 6 SC (Part I) 66 at 96-97*

24. The right to life guaranteed by the provisions of section 30(1) of the 1979 Constitution is qualified. Death penalty is a recognised form of punishment under the Nigerian Constitution.

However, for it to be constitutional, it must be in execution of the sentence of a court of law in a criminal offence of which the accused has been found guilty in Nigeria.

  - Kalu v. State (1998) 13 NWLR (Pt. 583) 531 at 537-561 SC

25. Wrongful termination of employment does not fall under the types of rights protected by chapter 4 of the 1979 Constitution.

  - Nig. Soc. Ins. T.F.M.B v. Adebiyi (1999) 13 NWLR (Pt. 633) 16 CA

26. Section 37 of the 1979 Constitution guarantees every Nigerian Citizen the fundamental right to peaceful assembly and freedom of association. However, this right is not absolute but restrictive. A person proposing to join an association must therefore show how that association would protect his interest.

  - Akaniwon v. Nsirim (1997) 9 NWLR (Pt. 520) 255 CA

  - Okafor v. Asoh (1999) 3 NWLR (Pt. 593) 35 CA

  - Sea Trucks (Nig.) Ltd v. Pyne (1999) 6 NWLR (Pt. 607) 514 CA

27. The fundamental rights to freedom of movement and ownership of property are guaranteed under Section 38(1) of the 1979 Constitution. These rights are not absolute. By Sections 38 (2) (a) and 41(1) of the 1979 Constitution, any act done pursuant to any justifiable law which imposes restriction of movement on a person suspected of having committed a crime is valid. Also where the government, compulsorily acquires a property like land, for a public purpose, such acquisition is valid provided there is adequate compensation made to the owner of such land.

  - Director, SSS v. Agbakoba (1999) 3 NWLR (Pt. 595) 314 SC

  - Ikem v. Nwogwugwu (1999) 13 NWLR (Pt. 633) 140 at 142 CA

28. The right to movement is guaranteed under section 38(1) of the 1979 Constitution. In exercising this right, a person is entitled to hold a passport in accordance with the Passport (Miscellaneous Provisions) Act. There are instances however, where the Minister of Internal Affairs can exercise his powers under section 5 of the Passport (Miscellaneous Provisions) Act and withdraw a citizen's

passport.

> - *Director, SSS v. Agbakoba (1999) 3 NWLR (Pt. 595) 314 SC*

29. A person is presumed innocent until proved guilty. This presumption is guaranteed under Section 33(5) of the 1979 Constitution. There is a proviso to this section to the effect that its provision does not invalidate any law, which imposes on a person the burden of proving any facts.

> - *Anaekwe v. C.O.P (1996) 3 NWLR (Pt. 436) 320 CA*
> - *Ifejirika v. State (1999) 3 NWLR (Pt. 593) 59 CA*

30. Although the Constitution provides generally for the right to bail, the pre-trial freedom is restricted particularly in capital offences.

> - *Anaekwe v. C.O.P. (1996) 3 NWLR (Pt. 436) 320 CA*

31. There is no distinction between 'pardon' and 'full pardon' under the Nigerian law. Both mean the same thing.

> *Falae v. Obasanjo (No. 2) (1999) 4 NWLR (Pt. 599) 476 CA*

32. To deliver a judgment in a judge's chambers is unconstitutional.

> - *Uviasu v. Uviasu (1973) 11 SC 315*

33. Acts of an illegal regime or a secessionist regime which fail are *ipso facto* illegal, particularly when such acts are in furtherance of the prosecution and sustenance of the regime. The situation could be different in respect of acts, which promote peace and good order amongst citizens.

> - *Okwuosa v. Okwuosa (1974) 4 SC 13*
> - *Eleh v. Anyadike (1999) 5 NWLR (Pt. 603) 454 CA*

34. Where there is a successful coup d'etat, the norms of the old order are regarded as devoid of validity. Accordingly, the pre-existing laws do not continue to apply but the illegal regime could make laws, which are necessary and consistent with the pre-existing law.

> - *Ugandan v. Commissioner of Prisons; Ex parte Matovu 1966, Judgment No. GD/CIV/23/66 of September 9, 1966 Govt Blue Bk 1968 SA 284 Appeal 1310*
> - *Mad Zimbamuto v. Lardner-Burke (1969) 1 AC 645*

VII
Contempt of Court

7.1 *Meaning and Nature of Contempt*

1. Contempt of court is an act calculated to interfere with the administration of justice.

> - *Ezeji v. Ike (1996) 1 NILR 173 CA*
> - *Globestar Eng. (Nig.) Ltd v. Malle Holdings Ltd (1999) 10 NWLR (Pt. 622) 270 CA*

2. The judicial powers constitutionally vested in Nigerian courts include all the inherent powers and sanctions of courts of law. These involve the powers to regulate its proceedings, punish for contempt and regulate the exercise of its discretion.

> - *Odogwu v. Odogwu (1992) 2 NWLR (Pt. 225) 539 SC*

3. In a pending suit, where there is no subsisting interlocutory order made against a party, such a party cannot be cited for contempt based on alleged breach of an anticipated order of the court in the same suit.

> - *Adenuga v. Odumeru (2001) 10 WRN 104 SC*

4. Contempts are classified into two, civil and criminal. A civil contempt basically comprises the failure to comply with an order of court, while criminal contempt consists of words or acts which obstruct or tend to obstruct or interfere with the administration of justice. The rules of contempt are concerned to uphold effective administration of justice.

> - *Mobil Oil (Nig.) Ltd v. Assan (1995) 8 NWLR (Pt. 412) 129 SC*
> - *C.O.P. v. Omanukwue (1999) 2 NWLR (Pt. 590) 190 CA*
> - *Adeniji-Adele v. Ogbe (1998) 9 NWLR (Pt. 569) 650 CA*

5. The standard of proof of disobedience of court order is not

---

just on balance of probabilities but the standard prescribed in a criminal trial, because the disobedience of court order by a contemnor is punished as if it is a criminal act. Thus, the proof must be beyond reasonable doubt.

- *Okeke v. A-G., Anambra State (1997) 9 NWLR (Pt. 519) 123 CA*

6. Failure of a party to a case to obey an order of court is not in itself a bar to the party's right to be heard by the court. The court has a discretion whether or not to hear him on some further application by him in the same suit in the interest of justice.

- *Mobil Oil (Nig.) Ltd v. Assan (1995) 8 NWLR (Pt. 412) 129 SC*
- *Globestar Eng. (Nig.) Ltd v. Malle Holdings Ltd (1999) 10 NWLR (Pt. 622) 270 CA*

7. Where a party is appealing against a matter in which he had suffered a defeat and asked for a stay of execution pending the determination of the appeal, he would not be liable in contempt merely because he had not obeyed the order which he is appealing against or which he wants stayed pending the appeal.

- *Mobil Oil (Nig.) Ltd v. Assan (1995) 8 NWLR (Pt. 412) 129 SC*

8. Failure of a party to pay costs does not by itself amount to contempt. A mere order for costs is enforceable in the ordinary way by execution like a money judgment.

- *Shugaba v. U.B.N. Plc (1999) 11 NWLR (Pt. 627) 459 SC*

9. Contempt *infacie curiae*, otherwise known as contempt in the face of the court can be tried summarily. This procedure requires observation of certain requirements, which include, asking the alleged contemnor to go into the dock, stating his offence specifically, and distinctly to him and asking him to show cause from the dock why he should not be committed for contempt. Where contempt is committed outside the court (*ex facie curiae*) the proper procedure of apprehension, charge and prosecution must be applied and followed. In such a situation, the case should and must be tried by another judge.

- *Dibia v. Igwe (1998) 9 NWLR (Pt. 564) 78 CA*

10. An alleged contemnor must not be put in the witness box, for putting him in the witness box is tantamount to compelling him to give evidence. This clearly offends and is against the provisions of section 33(1) of the 1979 Constitution of the Federal Republic of Nigeria, which states that no person who is being tried for a criminal offence shall be compelled to give evidence at the trial.

> - *Dibia v. Igwe (1998) 9 NWLR (Pt. 564) 78 CA*

11. A person who has committed a civil contempt by disobeying a court order may be subject to the rule that a party in contempt cannot be heard or take proceedings in the same cause until he has purged his contempt. But it is a step, which the court will take only when the contempt itself impedes the course of justice, and there is no other effective means of securing its compliance.

> - *Odogwu v. Odogwu (1992) 2 NWLR (Pt. 225) 539 SC*
> - *F.A.T.B. v. Ezegbu (1992) 9 NWLR (Pt. 264) 132 SC*
> - *Mobil Oil (Nig.) Ltd v. Assan (1995) 8 NWLR (Pt. 412) 129 SC*
> - *Doma v. Ogiri (1997) 1 NWLR (Pt. 481) 322 CA*

12. There are exceptions to the rule that a party in contempt cannot be heard. These exceptions are namely: where the party is seeking for leave to appeal against the order of which he is in contempt; or where he intends to show that, because of procedural irregularities in making the order, it ought not to be sustained; or where the party is challenging the order on the ground of lack of jurisdiction; or where all that the contemnor is asking for is to be heard in respect of matters of defence, and that a person against whom a committal order has not been made cannot be a contemnor.

> - *F.A.T.B. v. Ezegbu (1992) 9 NWLR (Pt. 264) 132 SC*
> - *Mobil Oil (Nig.) Ltd v. Assan (1995) 8 NWLR (Pt. 412) 129 SC*
> - *Doma v. Ogiri (1997) 1 NWLR (Pt. 481) 322 CA*
> - *NDLEA v. Okorodudu (1997) 3 NWLR (Pt. 492) 221 CA*

13. The court has summary powers to punish for contempt. This power should be used sparingly. The power to punish is not

retained for the personal aggrandisement of a judge. The powers are created, maintained and retained for the purpose of preserving the honour and dignity of the court and so the judge holds the power on behalf of the court. Judges should not display undue degree of sensitiveness about this matter of contempt and should act with restraint on such occasion.

- *Dibia v. Igwe (1998) 9 NWLR (Pt. 564) 78 CA*

14. A person who is in contempt of a subsisting court order is not entitled to be granted court's discretion to enable him continue with the breach.

- *Lawal-Osula v. Lawal-Osula (1995) 3 NWLR (Pt. 382) 128 SC*
- *Doma v. Ogiri (1997) 1 NWLR (Pt. 481) 322 CA*
- *Shugaba v. U.B.N. Plc. (1999) 11 NWLR (Pt. 627) 459 SC*

15. A party who openly flouts the order of a court of law is in contempt of that court and has no right to seek a further remedy in that court.

- *Owena Bank (Nig.) Plc v. Olatunji (1999) 13 NWLR (Pt. 634) 218 CA*

16. The courts regard contempt by the executive arm of government as lawlessness, which is tantamount to a deliberate violation of the Constitution. If any one should be wary of orders of courts, it is the authorities; for they, more than any one else, need the application of the rule of law in order to govern properly and effectively.

- *Ojukwu v. Gov., Lagos State (1986) 3 NWLR (Pt. 26) 39 SC*
- *Doma v. Ogiri (1998) 3 NWLR (Pt. 541) 246 CA*

7.2 Committal Proceedings

1. As committal proceedings touch on deprivation of freedom and liberty of the person, the service and procedure thereof are applied strictly and any departure from strict application of the

rules vitiates the proceedings. Similarly, contempt of court being a deliberate disobedience of a court order involves *mens rea* and being also quasi-criminal, the standard of proof is the standard required in a criminal matter, which is proof beyond reasonable doubt.

> *- Ezeji v. Ike (1997) 2 NWLR (Pt. 486) 206 CA*

2. Failure to serve forms 48 and 49 in contempt proceedings vitiates the entire application. As committal proceedings for contempt affect the freedom and liberty of the contemnor, the law and procedure are strictly applied and any slightest wrongful step taken shall vitiate the entire proceedings.

> *- Oyeyinka v. Osague (1994) 2 NWLR (Pt. 328) 617 CA*
> *- Ezeji v. Ike (1997) 2 NWLR (Pt. 486) 206 CA*
> *- Adeniji-Adele v. Ogbe (1998) 9 NWLR (Pt. 567) 650 CA*

3. It is trite law that a committal for contempt must specify a period not longer than the period provided by the Criminal Code of the State concerned within which the contemnor shall purge himself of the contempt. This is because, by virtue of section 33(8) of the 1979 Constitution, no penalty shall be imposed for any criminal offence heavier than the penalty in force at the time the offence was committed.

> *- Oyeyinka v. Osague (1994) 2 NWLR (Pt. 328) 617 CA*
> *- Ezeji v. Ike (1997) 2 NWLR (Pt. 486) 206 CA*

4. In certain situations, leave to appeal can be sought by an applicant against an order of which he is in contempt. A contemnor may also be heard where he intends to show that because of procedural irregularities in making the order, it ought not to be sustained or where he is challenging the order on ground of lack of jurisdiction.

> *- Mobil Oil (Nig.) v. Assan (1995) 8 NWLR (Pt. 412) 129 SC*

5. In a representative action, there is no legislation that requires that leave of court must be obtained before the initiation of committal proceedings against persons who under Nigerian law and procedure are parties to the suit and are fully aware of any

court order made against them but have persistently disobeyed the order.

- *Adaka v. Anekwe (1997) 11 NWLR (Pt. 529) 417 CA*

VIII
Criminal Law and Procedure

8.1 Offences

1. The two elements of a crime are *actus reus* and *mens rea*. The *actus reus* is the physical act while the *mens rea* is the intention to commit the act.

- *Folarin v. State (1995) 1 NWLR (Pt. 371) 313 CA*
- *Edamine v. State (1996) 3 NWLR (Pt. 438) 530 SC*
- *Abogede v. State (1996) 5 NWLR (Pt. 448) 270 SC*
- *Idowu v. State (2000) 7 SC (Part II) 50*

2. By virtue of schedule 3 of Decree No. 105 of 1979 which repealed section 6 of Decree No. 47 of 1970, armed robbery matters shall be triable in the High Court of the State concerned.

- *Eyisi v. The State (2000) 12 SC (Pt. 1) 24*

3. To secure conviction on armed robbery, the prosecution is expected to establish beyond reasonable doubt that there has been an act of stealing by the use of threat or violence and the threat must be immediately before or after the stealing and the purpose must be to obtain or retain the stolen property.

- *Martins v. State (1997) 1 NWLR (Pt. 481) 355 CA*

4. At common law, conspiracy means an agreement of two or more persons to do an act, which constitute an offence, to agree to do.

- *The State v. Haruna (1972) 8-9 SC 174*

5. Conspiracy consists not merely in the intention of two or more persons but rather in the agreement of two or more persons to do an unlawful act, or to do a lawful act, by unlawful means.

- *Oduneye v. The State (2001) 13 WRN 88 SC*

6. The offence of conspiracy is not defined in the Criminal or Penal Code. Therefore, direct positive evidence of the plot between the co-conspirators is hardly capable of proof. The

courts tackle the offence of conspiracy as a matter of inference to be deduced from certain criminal acts or inactions of the parties concerned.

  - *Oduneye v. The State (2001) 13 WRN 88 SC*

7. The ingredients of the offence of joint act under section 79 of the Penal Code are that there must be a common intention to commit the crime in question and the criminal act must be shown to have been committed by several persons in pursuance of their common goal.

  - *Pincent v. State (1997) 1 NWLR (Pt. 480) 234 CA*

8. In a charge of receiving stolen property, apart from proving that goods were stolen, it is necessary for the prosecution to prove that the accused actually received the stolen goods. It must be established that the accused either physically received the goods or that the goods were in the possession of a person over whom the accused had control.

  - *Martins v. State (1997) 1 NWLR (Pt. 481) 355 CA*
  - *Unuigboje v. State (2001) 11 WRN 170 CA*

9. An accomplice is one who is guilty of complicity in a crime charged either by being present and aiding or abetting in it; or having advised and encouraged it, though absent from the place where it was committed. An accomplice includes the perpetrators and accessory of the offence charged.

  - *Okonkwo v. State (1998) 8 NWLR (Pt. 561) 210 CA*

10. The law under the Penal Code is that once an abettor is found to be present at the commission of the offence he abetted, he automatically becomes a principal offender and it is mandatory on the trial court to convict him of the main offence and not its abetment.

  - *Abu Peter & Anor v. The State (1977) N.N.L.R. 81 CA*

11. In a criminal trial, a court has the power to convict a person charged with a particular offence, of an attempt to commit that offence although he was not separately charged with the offence of attempt. This power is exercisable even without amending the original charge. Section 219 Criminal Procedure Code considered.

  - *Sanni v. State (1993) 4 NWLR (Pt. 285) 99 CA*

12. A court can convict for the offence of assault occasioning bodily harm contrary to the provisions of section 355 of the Criminal Code where there has been no sensible defence made out on behalf of an accused in the face of unchallenged and uncontroverted evidence by the prosecution witness.

- *Oforlete v. The State (2000) 7 SC (Part I) 80 at 88*

13. If a man fires his gun without being sure of the degree of safety, he is criminally negligent and if he should injure someone, he must be found guilty for doing so.

- *The State v. Bello Ayinde (1976) N.N.L.R. 38, High Court of Kwara State. Suit No. KWS/6C/76*

14. There is a clear duty on any person discharging a firearm to ensure that he will not thereby endanger any other person. A shooter must, before firing his gun, ensure that the bullets projected would come to rest within a distance which he can see clearly and that the space through which the bullets would travel is occupied by no one who might be injured by them.

- *The State v. Bello Ayinde (1976) N.N.L.R. 38, High Court of Kwara State. Suit No. KWS/6C/76*

15. Criminal responsibility is personal and cannot be transferred. There is no law that says that the sin of a son be visited on the mother simply because of that relationship.

- *A.C.B. v. Okonkwo (1997) 1 NWLR (Pt. 480) 194 CA*

16. *Coup d'etat* is a treasonable offence but only when it fails. If it succeeds, the *status quo* changes, that is, the Constitution is suspended and the Decree of the military regime becomes the grund norm.

- *Enahoro v. The Queen (1965) 1 All NLR 126*
- *Abacha v. Fawehinmi (2000) 4 SC (Pt. II) 1 at 119*

17. The offence of dangerous driving can be determined and proved, where, for instance, there is evidence that the driver of a vehicle left his own side of the road and hit another vehicle on the other side of the road.

- *Opara v. State (1998) 2 NWLR (Pt. 536) 108 CA*

18. Traditionally, contempts are classified as being either criminal or civil. A civil contempt basically comprises the failure to comply with an order of court. While criminal contempt relates to conduct in relation to particular proceedings in a court of law which tends to undermine that system, or to inhibit citizens from availing themselves of it for the settlement of their disputes.

- *C.O.P. v. Omanukwe (1999) 2 NWLR (Pt. 590) 190 CA*
- *Globestar Eng. (Nig.) Ltd v. Malle Holdings Ltd (1999) 10 NWLR (Pt. 622) 270 CA*

19. Seducing another person's wife is a sinful act and not a criminal act. The husband has no moral, societal or legal right to kill the seducer.

- *Biruwa v. State (1992) 1 NWLR (Pt. 220) 633 SC*

20. It is an offence for a person to hold himself out as a traditional ruler where the incumbent has neither died nor been deposed.

- *State v. Okechukwu (1994) 9 NWLR (Pt. 368) 273 SC*

21. Unlawful carnal knowledge is the sexual connection which takes place otherwise than between husband and wife. Generally, it follows necessarily that a husband cannot be guilty of rape of his wife.

- *R v. Miller (1954) 2 All E.R. 529*

22. Sexual intercourse between a husband and wife cannot amount to rape until a *decree absolute* or possibly a *decree nisi* of divorce has been made. Where an injunction has been granted against the husband, any sexual intercourse thereafter will be unlawful and will amount to rape, unless consented to by the wife.

- *R v. Clarke (1949) 2 All E.R. 448*

23. A separation order with a provision that the wife will no longer be obliged to co-habit with the husband has the effect of rendering sexual intercourse between spouses unlawful unless consented to by the wife.

- *R v. Clarke (1949) 2 All E.R. 448*

24. Mere commencement of proceedings for an injunction or for divorce would not make intercourse between husband and wife unlawful.

- *R v. Clarke (1949) 2 All E.R. 448*
- *R v. Miller (1954) 2 All E.R. 529*

25. A husband is not entitled to use force or violence in exercising his right to intercourse. Where he does, he may be guilty of wounding occasioning grievous harm or assault, according to the circumstances.

- *R v. Miller (1954) 2 All E.R. 529*

8.2 Charges

1. The word "charge" as used in sections 162-165 of the Criminal Procedure Law has two separate and distinct meanings. It is sometimes used in the sense of an accusation of an offence, the equivalent of a count in an Information; while it is also used in the sense of a "charge sheet", a whole document that may contain one or more counts of accusation or statement of offence.

- *Attah v. State (1993) 7 NWLR (Pt. 305) 257 SC*

2. "Holding charge" is unknown to Nigerian Law and an accused person detained thereunder is entitled to be released on bail within a reasonable time before trial especially where the offence is not a capital offence.

- *Enwere v. C.O.P. (1993) 6 NWLR (Pt. 299) 333 CA*

3. Section 208(1) of the Criminal Procedure Code gives the court the discretion to alter, add or frame a new charge at any time before judgment is pronounced. In allowing this, the court is not limited to the facts as alleged in the Information. However, the court is required to read and explain the new charge to the accused and record a fresh plea for the accused. It is also trite law that where there is an amendment to a charge, there shall be a fresh plea, after which the accused has a right to be allowed to recall witnesses.

- *Attah v. State (1993) 7 NWLR (Pt. 305) 257 SC*
- *Pincent v. State (1997) 1 NWLR (Pt. 480) 234 CA*

4. Section 164(1) of the Criminal Procedure Law renders an amendment of a charge retrospective to the date of the filing of the charge. It is settled law that where a charge of a single count is altered or amended, it is mandatory for the court to take a fresh plea of the accused and it is imperative on the accused to

plead to the amended charge. This procedure is fundamental and failure to comply with this procedure renders the conviction based on the amended count invalid.

- *Attah v. State (1993) 7 NWLR (Pt. 305) 257 SC*

5. A defective charge could, in appropriate cases, be cured, as defect in a charge which does not render it bad in law cannot nullify a conviction so long as an offence known to law is disclosed in the charge and the accused is not misled thereby.

- *Essien v. C.O.P. (1996) 5 NWLR (Pt. 449) 489 CA*

6. Where a charge is defective, for the defence to succeed on an objection to the charge as defective, the defence must show he is prejudiced by the charge. Where an accused is not embarrassed or prejudiced by the defective charge, an objection to the charge will not be sustained.

- *Mangai v. State (1993) 3 NWLR (Pt. 279) 108 CA*

7. Where there is an effective and sufficient charge of a substantive offence, the addition of a charge of conspiracy is undesirable because it adds nothing to the charge.

- *Ibrahim v. State (1995) 3 NWLR (Pt. 381) 35 CA*

8. A charge against a surety for refusing to produce an accused is not known to Nigerian law. Thus, it is unconstitutional by virtue of section 33(12) of the 1979 Constitution.

- *Ekwuazi v. D.P.P. (1999) 3 NWLR (Pt. 593) 31 CA*

9. A First Information Report (F.I.R.) is an information contained in a special form, drafted by the police authority alleging that a particular individual(s) has/have committed a criminal offence which is punishable by law. It is the commonest form of initiating a criminal proceeding in the Magistrate's Courts of a given territorial jurisdiction.

- *Abbas v. C.O.P. (1998) 12 NWLR (Pt. 577) 308 CA*

10. The proceedings in a summary trial are not a nullity merely because the Magistrate who read the particulars of the offence under section 156 of the Criminal Procedure Code was different from the one who heard the evidence.

- *Dominic Anule v. Commissioner of Police (1977) N.N.L.R 76 CA*

8.3 Arraignment

1. A valid arraignment entails that an accused person charged with a criminal offence shall be placed before the court unfettered unless the court shall see cause to order otherwise. The charge shall be read over and explained to the accused in a language he understands and he shall plead instantly to the charge.

- *Aladu v. State (1998) 8 NWLR (Pt. 563) 618 CA*
- *Okoro v. State (1998) 14 NWLR (Pt. 584) 181 SC*
- *Idemudia v. State (1999) 7 NWLR (Pt. 610) 202 SC*
- *Ajile v. State (1999) 9 NWLR (Pt. 619) 503 CA*
- *Durwode v. The State (2001) 7 WRN 50 SC*

2. For an arraignment to be valid in law it is not necessary to read the charge to the accused person in his language if he understands English Language which is the language of the court. It is also not mandatory for the judge to record that the charge has been read over and explained to the accused. Once the trial court is satisfied that the accused understood the nature of the charge framed against him, failure to record does not amount to miscarriage of justice and would not invalidate the arraignment.

- *Ogunye v. State (1999) 5 NWLR (Pt. 604) 548 SC*
- *Durwode v. State (2000) 12 SC (Pt. I) 1 at 6*

3. Criminal trial commences once an accused person has been arraigned before a judge and the charge is read over and explained to him.

- *State v. Ajayi (1996) 1 NWLR (Pt. 423) 169 at 174 CA*

4. The right of an accused to an interpreter in criminal trials is mandatory and failure to accord the accused person this right amounts to a clear violation of his constitutional right and, a denial of his right to fair hearing. But where the accused understands the language of the court, an interpreter is not necessary and it is the duty of the accused to inform the court that he does not understand the language used.

- *Madu v. State (1997) 1 NWLR (Pt. 482) 386 SC*

5. By virtue of section 210 of the Criminal Procedure Act, every

accused person shall, subject to the provisions of section 100 and of subsection (2) of section 223, be present in court during the whole of his trial unless he misconducts himself by so interrupting the proceedings or otherwise as to render their continuance in his presence impracticable

- *Asakitikpi v. State (1993) 5 NWLR (Pt. 296) 641 SC*
- *Adeoye v. State (1999) 6 NWLR (Pt. 605) 74 SC*

6. The court can comment on failure of an accused to testify at his trial. The court can even draw unfavourable inferences against such an accused having regard to the evidence adduced by the prosecution. This does not amount to infringement of the accused person's right to remain silent during his trial.

- *Nasiru v. State (1999) 2 NWLR (Pt. 589) 87 SC*

7. Where a person is accused of and charged with a capital offence, and is not defended by a legal practitioner, the court, by virtue of section 352 of the Criminal Procedure Act, is enjoined and indeed bound to assign a legal practitioner for his defence.

- *Okon v. State (1995) 1 NWLR (Pt. 372) 382 SC*

8. The Attorney General may exercise his powers to institute, undertake, take over, continue and discontinue criminal proceedings in person or may delegate them to officers of his department. Thus, by express delegation, a donee of the Attorney General's power, for instance, the Director of Public Prosecution, could prefer an information in his own name.

- *Ibrahim v. State (1986) 1 NWLR (Pt. 18) 650 SC*

8.4 Plea

1. It has been a long standing practice in Nigeria that a man's plea of guilty to a murder charge is not accepted not only because of the nature of the offence but principally because the only sentence allowed by law is death by hanging.

- *Chukwu v. State (1994) 3 NWLR (Pt. 335) 640 SC*

2. Before convicting on a plea of guilty, the court must do the

following: explain the charge to the accused and record the manner in which it is explained; record the replies of the accused as nearly as possible in the words uttered by him; explain the ingredient of the offence to the accused and record his reply; and show that it satisfied itself that the accused has clearly understood the meaning of the charge in all its details and essentials and also the effect of the plea.

- *Sule Maidoki v. Commissioner of Police (1975) N.N.L.R. 142 CA*

3. Where there are more than one accused person in a criminal trial, their pleas must be individually and separately taken.

- *Eyisi v. The State (2000) 12 SC (Part I) 24 at 33*

8.5 Bail

1. An accused person who has not been tried and convicted by a competent court is entitled to bail as a matter of right unless there are special circumstances that prevent the court from granting it.

- *Eyu v. State (1988) 2 NWLR (Pt. 78) 602 CA*
- *Enwere v. C.O.P (1993) 6 NWLR (Pt. 299) 333 CA*

2. It is a general principle of law that in murder cases, bail is not granted except by a Judge of the High Court. In such cases, bail is granted at the discretion of the Judge and not as a matter of course.

- *Oladele v. State (1993) 1 NWLR (Pt. 269) 294 SC*
- *Okpe v. State (1994) 5 NWLR (Pt. 345) 490 CA*
- *Anaekwe v. C.O.P. (1996) 3 NWLR (Pt. 436) 320 CA*

3. Where an accused voluntarily submits to arrest, his application for bail ought to receive favourable consideration.

- *Ebute v. State (1994) 8 NWLR (Pt. 360) 66 CA*

4. Under the Criminal Procedure Act, and the Federal High Court Act or any other part of our criminal law, which is entirely statutory, there is no prescribed procedure to be followed in respect of an application for bail. Normally, application for bail

is made from the Bar and the prosecution in turn also states its objection. The court determines the application upon the informed statements made before it, not on oath. However, an application for bail under section 123 of the Criminal Procedure Act is by summons but this arises where a Magistrate court initially refused bail.

> - *Abiola v. Federal Republic of Nigeria (1995) 1 NWLR (Pt. 370) 155 CA*

5. A convict whose appeal is pending in a higher court has a right to apply for bail by virtue of section 29(1) Court of Appeal Act, 1976. However, the grant of bail by the Court of Appeal is discretionary.

> - *Mohammed v. Olawunmi (1993) 4 NWLR (Pt. 287) 254 SC*

6. Where the prosecution merely parades to the court the word "murder" without tying it with the offence, a court of law is bound to grant bail. Thus, a situation where there is no material before the court to show that the accused is facing a charge of murder, including proof of evidence, such a situation certainly qualifies as a special circumstance in which the court can grant bail.

> - *Anaekwe v. C.O.P. (1996) 3 NWLR (Pt. 436) 320 CA*

8.6 Witness

1. The inconsistency rule is to the effect that where a witness's statement to the police contradicts his evidence in court, the court should regard him as an unreliable witness and discountenance both his statement to the police and his testimony in court.

> - *Egboghonome v. State (1993) 7 NWLR (Pt. 306) 383 SC*
> - *Emoga v. State (1997) 1 NWLR (Pt. 483) 615 CA*

2. A tainted witness is a witness who might have his own purpose to serve by giving evidence.

> - *Effiong v. State (1998) 8 NWLR (Pt. 562) 362 SC*
> - *Okoro v. State (1998) 14 NWLR (Pt. 584) 181 SC*

3. The evidence of a single witness, if believed by the court, can establish a criminal case even if it is a murder charge.

  - *Effiong v. State (1998) 8 NWLR (Pt. 562) 362 SC*

4. It is trite that failure to interpret the evidence of particular witnesses to an accused does not render the whole trial null and void. It is only the testimony of witnesses whose evidence was established not to have been interpreted as required by law that needs to be expunged from the records of the court.

  - *Madu v. State (1997) 1 NWLR (Pt. 482) 386 SC*

5. By virtue of section 161(2) of the Evidence Act, a wife or husband of an accused person can only be a competent and compellable witness in a charge against him upon his own application. However, the accused must first prove that his marriage to his wife was monogamous before he can enjoy this privilege. Thus, section 2(1) of the Evidence Act restricts this benefit to spouses of a monogamous marriage.

  - *Okoro v. State (1998) 14 NWLR (Pt. 584) 181 SC*

8.7 Corroboration

1. Corroboration is a confirmation of a witness's evidence by independent testimony. Thus, corroborative evidence is one, which shows or tends to show not merely that the crime has been committed but that it was committed by the accused.

  - *Nwambe v. State (1995) 3 NWLR (Pt. 384) 385 SC*

2. It is settled law that to ground a conviction based on the unsworn testimony of a child, such unsworn evidence of the child must be corroborated.

  - *Sambo v. State (1993) 6 NWLR (Pt. 300) 399 SC*

3. It is the law that before the prosecution can secure conviction for the offence of rape, the evidence of the *prosecutrix* (the victim of the rape) must be corroborated in some material particular that sexual intercourse did take place and that it was without her consent.

  - *Sambo v. State (1993) 6 NWLR (Pt. 300) 399 SC*

8.8 Identification Parade

1. It is not in every case that identification parade is necessary. Where the prosecution witness has knowledge of the accused person, identification parade is not necessary.

> - *Aladu v. State (1998) 8 NWLR (Pt. 563) 618 CA*
> - *Igbi v. State (2000) 2 SC 67*

2. Identification parade is not the only way of establishing the identification of an accused person in relation to the offence charged. Where the witness has ample opportunity to identify the accused, a parade is not necessary. Recognition of an accused may be more reliable than identification.

> - *Eyisi v. The State (2001) 8 WRN 1 at 9 & 10 SC*

8.9 Confession

1. By virtue of section 27(1) of the Evidence Act, a confession is an admission made at any time by a person charged with a crime stating or suggesting by inference that he committed that crime.

> - *Gira v. State (1996) 4 NWLR (Pt. 443) 375 SC*

2. A free and voluntary confession of guilt whether judicial or extra-judicial, if it is direct and positive and properly established is sufficient proof of guilt and is enough to sustain a conviction, so long as the court is satisfied with the truth of such a confession.

> - *Edhigere v. State (1996) 8 NWLR (Pt. 464) 1 SC*
> - *Ihuebeka v. The State (2000) 4 SC (Pt. 1) 203*
> - *Idowu v. The State (2000) 7 SC (Pt. II) 50*
> - *Alarape v. State (2001) 14 WRN 1 SC*

3. A free and voluntary confession, which is direct and positive and properly proved is sufficient to sustain a conviction without any corroborative evidence so long as the court is satisfied with its truth. There is however a duty on the court to test the truth of a confession by examining it in the light of the other credible evidence before the court.

> - *Nwaeze v. State (1996) 2 NWLR (Pt. 428) 1 SC*

- Akinmoju v. The State (2000) 4 SC (Part I) 64

4. If a confessional statement is involuntarily made, it would not be admitted, and if it is admitted without a trial within a trial, it should be expunged as inadmissible. When such a statement that provides corroboration for other related pieces of evidence, is expunged from the record, there will be no pivot upon which the other corroborated evidence can stand, and thus, placing any reliance on such evidence would be unsafe and lead to a miscarriage of justice.

- Ekure v. State (1999) 13 NWLR (Pt. 635) 456 CA

5. Where a confessional statement is retracted, a trial within a trial is held to ascertain the truth of the statement. If the confession is found to be true, voluntary, direct and positive, it is admissible in law. Retraction thereof is immaterial.

- Nwosu v. State (1998) 8 NWLR (Pt. 562) 433 CA
- Idowu v. The State (2000) 7 SC (Part II) 50
- Ihuebeka v. The State (2000) 4 SC (Part I) 203

6. The requirement of trial within trial is not applicable where the objection to the admissibility of a confessional statement is that the statement was not read to the accused before he signed it or that he never made the statement at all.

- Okoro v. State (1993) 3 NWLR (Pt. 282) 425 CA

8.10 Burden of Proof

1. The standard of proof in a criminal trial is proof beyond reasonable doubt. This means that it is not enough for the prosecution to suspect a person of having committed a criminal offence. There must be evidence, which identified the person accused with the offence, and that it was his act, which caused the offence.

- Abadom v. State (1997) 1 NWLR (Pt. 479) 1 CA
- Akinyemi v. State (1999) 6 NWLR (Pt. 607) 449 CA
- Aigbadion v. State (2000) 4 SC (Pt. I) 1 at 15

2. The burden of proof in a criminal case is on the prosecution

to prove the guilt of the accused beyond reasonable doubt. If the accused gives an account which is consistent with his innocence and could be true, and is not proved to be untrue, he is entitled to be acquitted. This is because in such circumstances there must be a doubt with regard to his guilt.

> - *Christopher Okolo v. Commissioner of Police (1977) N.N.L.R. 1 CA*

3. In a criminal trial, the burden of proof lies, throughout, upon the prosecution to establish the guilt of the accused beyond reasonable doubt and it never shifts. Even where an accused in his statement to the police admitted committing the offence, the prosecution is not relieved of the burden. Failure to discharge this burden renders the benefit of doubt in favour of the accused.

> - *Ifejirika v. State (1999) 3 NWLR (Pt. 593) 59 CA*

4. The consequences of presumption of innocence in favour of an accused person is that the burden placed on the prosecution to prove the guilt of the accused beyond reasonable doubt must be satisfied. If not, a slightest doubt raised by the accused shall lead the court to resolve the doubt in favour of the accused

> - *Ifejirika v. State (1999) 3 NWLR (Pt. 593) 59 CA*

5. Before making a retrial order in a criminal case, an appellate court must be satisfied of the following, viz: that there has been an error in law or an irregularity in procedure of such character that on the one hand, the trial was not rendered a nullity and on the other hand the appellate court is unable to say that there has been no miscarriage of justice; that leaving aside the error or irregularity, the evidence taken as a whole discloses a substantial case against the appellant; that there are no special circumstances as would render it oppressive to put the appellant on trial a second time; that the offence(s) the appellant was convicted of or the consequences to the appellant or any other person are not merely trivial; and that to refuse an order of a retrial would occasion a greater miscarriage of justice than to grant it.

> - *Adeoye v. State (1999) 6 NWLR (Pt. 605) 74 SC*

6. Circumstantial evidence is sufficient to ground conviction only where the inferences drawn from the whole history of the

case point strongly to the commission of the crime by the accused.

- *Nwaeze v. State (1996) 2 NWLR (Pt. 428) 1 SC*
- *Akinmoju v. The State (2000) 4 SC (Part I) 64*
- *Durwode v. The State (2000) 12 SC (Part I) 1*

7. Suspicion, however strong, cannot take the place of legal proof. Indeed, it is no evidence. Items of evidence raising suspicion, which put together, do not have the quality of being corroborative evidence, cannot ground a conviction.

- *The State v. Ogbubunjo (2001) 13 WRN 1 SC*

8. By the provisions of section 42(1) of the Evidence Act, it is not mandatory for a medical officer who performed an autopsy on a deceased to be present in court in order to give evidence during trial. Production by either party of a certificate signed by the medical officer may be taken as sufficient evidence of the facts. However, the court has power to summon the medical officer *suo motu* or on the application of either party if it deems it necessary in the interest of justice. All the same, the identity of the corpse examined by the medical doctor must be satisfactorily established.

- *Isiekwe v. State (1999) 9 NWLR (Pt. 617) 43 CA*

9. Ascertainment of death is not within the exclusive preserve of medical experts. However, unlike an expert, an adult may not know the real cause of death but he can appreciate that a person is dead.

- *Akinyemi v. State (1999) 6 NWLR (Pt. 607) 449 CA*

10. It is not in all cases that medical evidence in proof of cause of death is necessary. A court can in the absence of a medical report properly infer the cause of death from the evidence and circumstances of the case.

- *Igago v. State (1999) 6 NWLR (Pt. 608) 581 CA*
- *Oforlete v. The State (2000) 7 SC (Part 1) 80 at 86*

11. In rape offences, for a conviction of murder to be sustained, there must be another or other unlawful act(s) done outside the very act of ravishment, which would likely cause death. If the very act of ravishment *simpliciter* causes death, there normally

will be no conviction for murder but manslaughter.

- Idowu v. The State (2000) 7 SC (Part II) 50

12. In murder cases, the prosecution must prove beyond reasonable doubt that the deceased has died; that the death resulted from the act of the accused; and the act of the accused was intentional with knowledge that death or grievous bodily harm was its probable consequence.

- Akinyemi v. State (1999) 6 NWLR (Pt. 607) 449 CA
- Idowu v. The State (2000) 7 SC (Part II) 50
- Durwode v. The State (2000) 12 SC (Part I) 1 at 16
- The State v. Ogbubunjo (2001) 13 WRN 1 SC

13. The degree of negligence required to support a charge of manslaughter in accident cases, must amount to gross or criminal negligence, utter recklessness in disregard for the lives and safety of other road users.

- Opara v. State (1998) 2 NWLR (Pt. 536) 108 CA

14. For the offence of unlawful wounding, the prosecution must prove any of a number of intents including an intention to maim, to disfigure, to disable; to do some other grievous harm or to resist or prevent the lawful arrest or detention of any person.

- Onyeachimba v. State (1998) 8 NWLR (Pt. 563) 587 CA

15. One of the ways of proving forgery is through scientific means, which is by employing a handwriting analyst as an expert witness. However, where the accused admits signing a document and his witness claims to have written the document, there is no compelling need to call expert witness. Moreso, when it is clear that the document was written by the accused.

- Abadom v. State (1997) 1 NWLR (Pt. 479) 1 CA

16. The onus of proof of the defence of insanity lies on the defence who pleads it and the defence can successfully be pleaded by adducing evidence to establish that the accused person lacks the capacity to understand what he is doing; the capacity to control his actions and, the capacity to know that he should not do the act or make the omission. Section 28 of the Criminal Code Law of Ondo State, Cap. 30, 1978 considered.

- Oladele v. State (1993) 1 NWLR (Pt. 269) 294 SC

17. The burden of establishing a defence on the ground of insanity rests on the accused person and the burden shall be deemed to be discharged if the court is satisfied by evidence including evidence by prosecution that such fact exist.

   - *Uluebeka v. State (1998) 12 NWLR (579) 567 CA*

18. An accused person should not be convicted simply because the court regards him as a liar. Despite lies told by the accused, the court still has a duty to examine the totality of the evidence carefully to see if his guilt has been proved beyond reasonable doubt.

   - *Agunbiade v. State (1999) 4 NWLR (Pt. 599) 391 CA*

19. It is not every trifling inconsistency in the evidence of the prosecution witnesses that is fatal to its case. It is only when such inconsistencies or contradictions are substantial and fundamental to the main issues in question before the court and thus necessarily create some doubt in the mind of the trial court that an accused is entitled to benefit therefrom.

   - *Theophilus v. State (1996) 1 NWLR (Pt. 423) 139 SC*
   - *Chukwu v. State (1996) 7 NWLR (Pt. 463) 686 SC*

20. The right of the prosecution to call witnesses required to prove its case is not a mere privilege but a prerogative. Accordingly, the prosecution is not bound to call a host of witnesses. All the prosecution needs to do is to call enough material witnesses to prove its case and, in so doing, it has discretion in the matter. Even one credible witness, if believed, is enough.

   - *Theophilus v. State (1996) 1 NWLR (Pt. 423) 139 SC*
   - *Nwaeze v. State (1996) 2 NWLR (Pt. 428) 1 SC*

21. It is the duty of the prosecution to place before the court all available relevant evidence. This does not mean, of course, that a host of witnesses must be called upon the same point, but it does mean that if there is vital point in issue and there is one witness whose evidence would settle it one way or the other, that witness ought to be called.

   - *F.O. Raphael v. Commissioner of Police (1971) N.N.L.R. 16 CA*

22. It is the duty of the prosecution to lay before the court all

relevant evidence in their possession in order to assist the court to arrive at a just decision of a case.

   - *Ibrahim Abdul-Rahaman v. Commissioner of Police (1971) N.N.L.R. 24 CA*

23. A relation of the victim of a crime can testify for the prosecution, moreso where he/she is also a victim of the crime committed.

   - *Hausa v. State (1994) 6 NWLR (Pt. 350) 281 SC*

24. Where there is positive evidence as to the death of the deceased named in a charge, whose body could not be discovered, the accused may still be convicted of murder based on his confessional statement or other circumstantial evidence which conclusively points to the fact that the accused caused the death.

   - *Princewill v. State (1994) 6 NWLR (Pt. 353) 703 SC*
   - *Babuga v. State (1996) 7 NWLR (Pt. 460) 279 SC*

25. The doctrine of *res gestae* means "things done". It is mainly concerned with the admissibility of statements made contemporaneously with the occurrence of some act or event into which the court is inquiring.

   - *Akpan v. State (1994) 8 NWLR (Pt. 361) 226 CA*

26. The declaration of a dying person is admitted in evidence under section 33(a) of the Evidence Act, only where there is positive evidence, which must be strictly proved, that the deceased was in danger of approaching death or in fear of death.

   - *Akpan v. State (1994) 8 NWLR (Pt. 361) 226 CA*

8.11 Defences

1. A court is under a duty to consider any defence open to an accused or raised by an accused before convicting on a particular charge.

   - *Ifejirika v. State (1999) 3 NWLR (Pt. 593) 59 CA*
   - *Lado v. State (1999) 9 NWLR (Pt. 619) 369 SC*
   - *Ihuebeka v. The State (2000) 4 SC (Part I) 203 at 231*

- *Oforlete v. The State (2000) 7 SC (Part I) 80 at 85*
- *Arabi v. The State (2001) 12 WRN 158 CA*

2. Where statements tending to establish some defences for an accused have been tendered, there is need for the accused to testify in court to buttress the contents of the statements.

- *Akinyemi v. State (1999) 6 NWLR (Pt. 607) 449 CA*

3. Where an accused makes a statement to the police before trial indicating that he will rely on a defence of alibi, it is for the State to have that statement investigated before the trial and, where appropriate to use the results of that investigation to rebut the defence of alibi.

- *Christopher Okolo v. Commissioner of Police (1977) N.N.L.R. 1 CA*

4. The word "*alibi*" means "elsewhere". Where the defence is raised by an accused, the prosecution has to verify or disprove it. The standard of proof required to establish the defence of alibi is on balance of probabilities and it is only where an accused has adduced evidence in support of his alibi and the police fail to investigate it that it could be construed against the prosecution.

- *Ifejirika v. State (1999) 3 NWLR (Pt. 593) 59 CA*
- *Isiekwe v. State (1999) 9 NWLR (Pt. 617) 43 CA*

5. The burden is on the prosecution to disprove a defence of alibi.

- *Christopher Okolo v. Commissioner of Police (1977) N.N.L.R. 1 CA*

6. The law relating to alibi is that an accused person who wishes to raise alibi must raise it at the earliest opportunity to enable the police to investigate it. The accused must offer evidence as to where he was at the time of the crime and with whom he was at the material time.

- *Onyegbu v. State (1995) 4 NWLR (Pt. 391) 510 SC*
- *Ifejirika v. State (1999) 3 NWLR (Pt. 593) 59 CA*
- *Isiekwe v. State (1999) 9 NWLR (Pt. 617) 43 CA*
- *Eyisi v. The State (2000) 12 SC (Part I) 24*
- *Njiokwuemeni v. The State (2001) 14 WRN 96 CA*

7. Provocation means some act or series of acts done by a deceased to an accused which could cause in any reasonable person, and actually does cause in the accused, a sudden and temporary loss of self control, rendering him so subject to passion as to make him for the moment not master of his mind. However, the retaliation must not be disproportionate to the provocation offered.

- *Lado v. State (1999) 9 NWLR (Pt. 619) 369 SC*
- *Ihuebeka v. The State (2000) 4 SC (Pt. 1) 203*

8. The defence of provocation may, in certain circumstances, be available to a husband who kills a man caught in sexual act with his wife under his roof. It would be manslaughter and not murder. However, where the husband has knowledge of the unfaithfulness and sexual immorality of his wife with another man and she has indeed deserted him, the defence of provocation will not be available to him.

- *Biruwa v. State (1992) 1 NWLR (Pt. 220) 633 SC*

9. An accident is the result of an unwilled act, and means an event without the fault of the person alleged to have caused it. The court applies an objective test where this defence is raised.

- *Igago v. The State (2001) 3 WRN 153 SC*

10. Self defence is an absolute and complete defence in that in ordinary language, the law would excuse a killing if the killer had reasonable grounds for believing that his own life was in danger and that he had to kill in order to preserve it. The court applies an objective test and the onus is on the prosecution to disprove an accused person's plea of self-defence and not on the accused person to establish this defence.

- *Okonkwo v. State (1998) 8 NWLR (Pt. 561) 210 CA*
- *Ahmed v. State (1999) 7 NWLR (Pt. 612) 641 SC*
- *Arabi v. The State (2001) 12 WRN 158 CA*

11. A defence founded on witchcraft or superstitious belief cannot afford a legal defence under the Criminal Code.

- *Nnabo v. State (1994) 8 NWLR (Pt. 361) 173 SC*

12. There is no principle of criminal law, which permits a person to commit a crime or to kill because he is on official duty.

Therefore, there is nothing to justify the innovative importation of the doctrine of "action in the course of employment" which is invoked in actions in tort into the realm of criminal law.

- *Ibe v. State (1993) 7 NWLR (Pt. 304) 185 CA*

13. Ignorance of the law does not afford any excuse for any act or omission which otherwise constitutes an offence unless knowledge of the law by the offender is expressly declared to be an element of the offence.

- *State v. Okechukwu (1994) 9 NWLR (Pt. 368) 273 SC*

8.12 No Case Submission

1. A no case submission can be appropriately made and upheld when there has been no evidence to prove an essential element in the alleged offence charged or when evidence adduced on the essential elements have been so discredited as a result of cross examination or is so manifestly unreliable that no reasonable tribunal could safely convict on it. A mere discharge of an accused does not amount to an acquittal. The accused could be charged again in relation to the same offence.

- *Ubanatu v. C.O.P. (2000) 1 SC 31*

2. A ruling of no case submission is a decision within the meaning of section 277(1) of the 1979 Constitution that can be appealed against notwithstanding the fact that the accused has not exercised the option to either enter his defence or rest his case on the prosecution.

- *Ajisefini v. D.P.P (1998) 8 NWLR (Pt. 562) 447 CA*
- *Njoku v. C.O.P. (1999) 10 NWLR (Pt. 622) 192 CA*

3. If an accused person rests his case on that of the prosecution, the trial court is constrained to determine the case only on evidence of prosecution. In such a case, the accused stands or falls with the case of the prosecution.

- *Akinyemi v. State (1999) 6 NWLR (Pt. 607) 449 CA*

4. Where a no case submission is wrongly overruled, and an accused withdraws from further participation in the

proceedings, he cannot be convicted on subsequent incriminating evidence.

- *Mumuni & Ors. v. The State (1975) 6 SC 79*

8.13 Nolle Prosequi

1. The State and the Federal Attorneys General have the power to discontinue at any stage before judgment is delivered, any criminal proceedings instituted or undertaken by them, or any other authority or person, by entering a *nolle prosequi*. It is trite that the power cannot be exercised by the Solicitor General or any officer of his department in the absence of an incumbent Attorney General.

- *Attorney General of Kaduna State v. Hassan (1985) 2 NWLR (Pt. 8) 483 SC*

2. The power of *nolle prosequi* can be exercised in person by an incumbent Attorney General or through officers of his department. However, a state counsel exercising the power of *nolle prosequi* vested in and delegated by the Attorney General can do so only in writing and not orally.

- *State v. Chukwurah & Ors (1964) NMLR 64*

3. The requirements that an Attorney General exercising the power of *nolle prosequi*, must have regard to public interest, the interests of justice and the need to prevent abuse of legal process as contained in sections 191(3) and 160(3) of the 1979 Constitution, are subjective and non justiciable. Thus, the power of *nolle prosequi* vested in the Attorney General is absolute and unfettered.

- *The State v. S.O. Ilori (1983) 1 SCNLR 94*

4. A person aggrieved by the exercise of the Attorney General's power of *nolle prosequi* can institute a civil suit against the Attorney General seeking the court's declaration that the Attorney General entered the *nolle prosequi mala fides*.

- *The State v. S.O. Ilori (1983) 1 SCNLR 94 at 111*

5. A *nolle prosequi* entered in criminal proceedings by the Attorney General in person or on his behalf by officers of his

department terminates the criminal proceedings. Thus, a *nolle prosequi* operates as a mere discharge and not as an acquittal. Section 73(1) of the Criminal Procedure Act and section 253(3) of the Criminal Procedure Code construed.

- *The State v. S.O. Ilori (1983) 1 SCNLR 94 at 115*
- *Clarke & Anor v. Attorney General of Lagos State (1986) 1 QLRN 119*

6. The only mode by which a criminal prosecution initiated against an accused person can be stopped is through the filing of a *nolle prosequi* by the Attorney General.

- *Onuh v. C.O.P. (1994) 1 NWLR (Pt. 323) 671 CA*

8.14 Conviction and Sentencing

1. A conviction is an act of a court of competent jurisdiction adjudging a person to be guilty of a punishable offence. It is nonetheless, a conviction even where the ensuing penalty is not imprisonment nor fine but the finding of sureties for good behaviour. Furthermore, there cannot be a sentence without a conviction. Once a conviction is set aside, any sentence passed has no leg to stand on.

- *Mohammed v. Olawunmi (1993) 4 NWLR (Pt. 287) 254 SC*

2. An accused cannot be convicted of a lesser offence unless the following conditions are satisfied, namely: the elements in the offence charged and those in the lesser offence for which the accused is convicted are the same; the evidence adduced and the facts found must be insufficient for conviction in respect of the offence charged, but however support the lesser offence in respect of which the accused was convicted; the lesser offence for which the accused was convicted is usually not charged; and that the accused must be tried on the more serious offence.

- *Ibrahim v. State (1991) 4 NWLR (Pt. 186) 399 SC*
- *Adeyemi v. State (1991) 6 NWLR (Pt. 195) 1 SC*
- *Kada v. State (1991) 8 NWLR (Pt. 208) 134 SC*

3. The ingredients of a crime alleged must be proved beyond reasonable doubt before a conviction can be sustained. Mere motive or suspicion however strong cannot amount to such circumstantial evidence as to prove the commission of the offence.

- *Anazodo v. Audu (1999) 4 NWLR (Pt. 600) 530 CA*

4. It is desirable that a trial judge should record the conviction and sentence of each accused person separately. However, where this is done collectively and the accused persons were not misled by the collective conviction and sentence, it amounts to a procedural slip and not necessarily a miscarriage of justice. Therefore, it will be manifestly unjust to upset the judgment of the trial court on the basis of the slip.

- *Eyisi v. The State (2001) 8 WRN 1 SC*

5. It is trite that where there is a pronouncement of a valid verdict, then the omission to pronounce a sentence after conviction per se cannot retrospectively affect the validity of properly conducted proceedings.

- *Ejelikwu v. State (1993) 7 NWLR (Pt. 307) 554 SC*

6. Death penalty and its method of execution is lawful and valid in Nigeria as it is sanctioned by both sections 30(1) and 31(1)(a) of the Constitution of Nigeria, 1979. It is good law and its purpose is to serve as deterrence in a mundane society where heartless and dangerous citizens abound in plenty.

- *Okoro v. State (1998) 14 NWLR (Pt. 584) 181 SC*
- *Akinyemi v. State (1999) 6 NWLR (Pt. 607) 449 CA*

7. The position of the law is that where a statute or section of the law creating an offence expressly prescribes that there is no option of fine, the court cannot impose fine. Where, however, the statute is silent, even if it only mentions imprisonment and is silent on the fine, the courts have a discretion to impose a fine in lieu of imprisonment. What a court must never do is to pass any sentence in excess of that provided by the law. In sentencing an accused person, the court must exercise its discretion judicially and judiciously. It is however desirable that in exercising its discretion over sentence, a trial court should state in its judgment the factors that influence its decision.

- Iortim v. State (1997) 2 NWLR (Pt. 490) 711 CA

- Apamadari v. State (1997) 3 NWLR (Pt. 493) 289 CA

8. An indictment is the result of a finding of guilt of committal of a crime. A person who has not committed a crime cannot be indicted.

- Adamu v. Gwadabawa (1999) 3 NWLR (Pt. 594) 256 CA

9. It is trite law that if an accused person is discharged and acquitted, the court should equally discharge and acquit a co-accused where the evidence against them have been totally discredited and rejected, and found to be lacking in probative value.

- Adele v. State (1995) 2 NWLR (Pt. 377) 269 SC

10. There is a difference between the discharge of an accused person and his acquittal. An accused person who is discharged of an offence may still be charged for the same offence because in the eyes of the law he had not received a full trial on the merits of the case. On the other hand, an accused person who is discharged and acquitted cannot be subsequently charged for the same offence. The benefit under section 33(9) of the 1979 Constitution and the common law defences of *autrefois acquit* and *autrefois convict* are available to him.

- Gbadamosi v. State (1991) 6 NWLR (Pt. 196) 182 CA

11. There is no known rule of law or practice, which says that cost must be awarded against the State where it failed to prove its case in a criminal prosecution.

- State v. Okechukwu (1994) 9 NWLR (Pt. 368) 273 SC

12. Since capital punishment is part of the Nigerian law, persons charged with capital offences and indeed all criminal cases are entitled to trial and appeal without delay. The Executive and Judicial Authorities must accept responsibility of ensuring that execution follows as swiftly as practicable after sentence, allowing reasonable time to appeal and consideration of reprieve.

- Ogugu v. State (1994) 9 NWLR (Pt. 366) 1 SC

IX
Customary Law

1. Customary law is a mirror of accepted usage. In other words, a particular customary law must be in existence at the relevant time and it must be recognised and adhered to by the community.

- *Owonyin v. Omotosho (1961) 1 AII NLR 304 at 309*
- *Bello v. Gov., Kogi State (1997) 9 NWLR (Pt. 521) 496 CA*
- *Osolu v. Osolu (1998) 1 NWLR (Pt. 535) 532 CA*
- *Okene v. Orianwo (1998) 9 NWLR (Pt. 566) 408 CA*

2. Customary law is initially a question of fact and it remains so until the rule in question is of such notoriety and has been so frequently followed by the courts that judicial notice would be taken of it.

- *Giwa v. Erinmilokun (1961) 1 SCNLR 337*
- *Osolu v. Osolu (1998) 1 NWLR (Pt. 535) 532 CA*

3. It is the assent of the native community that gives a custom its validity. Therefore, a valid custom, whether barbarous or mild, must be shown to be recognised by the native community whose conduct it is supposed to regulate.

- *Eshugbayi Eleko v. Government of Nigeria (1931) A.C. 662 at 673*
- *Bello v. Gov., Kogi State (1997) 9 NWLR (Pt. 521) 496 CA*

4. The courts have the power to administer a particular customary law in so far as it is not repugnant to natural justice, equity and good conscience.

- *Edet v. Essien (1932) 11 NLR 47*
- *Dawodu v. Danmole (1962) 1 WLR 1053*

5. The Bini customary law of inheritance that provides that the eldest son is entitled to inherit the house in which his father lived and died, that is "*Igiogbe*", is not incompatible with natural

justice, equity and good conscience.

- *Lawal-Osula v. Lawal-Osula (1996) 1 NILR 22 at 26 SC*

6. A particular customary law of succession to a chieftaincy can validly be challenged on the ground that such customary law is repugnant to natural justice and good conscience. Section 13(1) of the Oyo State High Court Law considered.

- *Ogundare v. Ogunlowo (1997) 6 NWLR (Pt. 509) 360 SC*

7. The Ishan custom, whereby a childless woman can marry another woman to bear issues for her is regarded as being repugnant to natural justice, equity and good conscience and therefore unenforceable.

- *Odigie v. Aika Suit No. 4/24A/79 Unreported Judgment of Honourable Justice Ohiwerei of Ubiaja Judicial Division, former Bendel State of Nigeria, delivered on Tuesday 23rd day of March, 1982*

8. The rules of native law and custom are very flexible and adaptable to changing social conditions and altered circumstances.

- *Lewis v. Bankole (1908) 1 NLR 81*
- *Bello v. Gov., Kogi State (1997) 9 NWLR (Pt. 521) 496 CA*
- *Okene v. Orianwo (1998) 9 NWLR (Pt. 566) 408 CA*

9. The courts are required to enforce the existing native law and custom.

- *Lewis v. Bankole (1908) 1 NLR 81*
- *Bello v. Gov., Kogi State (1997) 9 NWLR (Pt. 521) 496 CA*

10. It is settled that native law and custom must be strictly proved. Although, the quality of evidence required to prove a custom has nothing to do with multiplicity of witnesses, it is however, not enough that one who asserts the existence of a custom should be the only witness.

- *Ekpenga v. Ozogula II (1962) 1 SCNLR 423*
- *Osolu v. Osolu (1998) 1 NWLR (Pt. 535) 532 CA*
- *Okene v. Orianwo (1998) 9 NWLR (Pt. 566) 408 CA*

11. Where two parties to a dispute voluntarily submit their

matter in controversy to arbitration according to customary law and agreed expressly or by implication that the decision of the arbitrators would be accepted as final and binding, then once the arbitrators have reached a decision, none of the parties can subsequently back out of such a decision.

- *Ojibah v. Ojibah (1991) 5 NWLR (Pt. 191) 296 SC*
- *Igwego v. Ezeugo (1992) 6 NWLR (Pt. 249) 561 SC*

12. It is trite law that no person shall be convicted of a criminal offence, unless that offence is stated and the penalty therefor prescribed in a written law.

- *Aoko v. Fagbemi (1961) 1 AII NLR 40*

13. Where a person, subject to native law or custom marries under the Marriage Act and dies intestate, the applicable law for the distribution of his estate would be the Marriage Act and not the Administration of Estates Law or Customary Law. This is because his intestacy is governed and regulated by English Law.

- *Salubi v. Nwariaku (1997) 5 NWLR (Pt. 505) 442 at 447 CA*

14. Where persons who are not kingmakers participated in an election for the selection of a traditional ruler, the election is null and void.

- *Aliyu v. Ibrahim (1997) 2 NWLR (Pt. 489) 571 CA*

15. Once the State Government withdraws the certificate of recognition issued to a traditional ruler, the moment the withdrawal of recognition is communicated to the traditional ruler, he ceases to be a ruler and all incidents appurtenant to the traditional rulership automatically terminate as they relate to him.

- *Military Governor, Anambra State v. Ezemuokwe (1997) 3 NWLR (Pt. 494) 374 SC*

16. Where it is found that a contestant for a chieftaincy title does not belong to any ruling house for the chieftaincy, such contestant has no right to be recommended for appointment to the stool.

- *Amuda v. Adelodun (1997) 5 NWLR (Pt. 506) 480 at 482 SC*

17. In an action for the enforcement of Fundamental Human Rights, a condition precedent to the exercise of the court's jurisdiction is that the enforcement of fundamental right or the securing of the enforcement thereof should be the main claim and not an accessory claim. Where the main or principal claim is not enforcement or securing the enforcement of a fundamental right, the jurisdiction of the court cannot be properly exercised, as it will be incompetent. An action raising chieftaincy questions as main or principal claims cannot, therefore, be instituted under the Fundamental Rights (Enforcement Procedure) Rules, 1979.

- *Tukur v. Government of Taraba State (1997) 6 NWLR (Pt. 510) 549 SC*

18. There are two main conditions for withdrawal of recognition of a chief in Imo State. These are proven grave misconduct and lack of popular support from the members of his communities. Sections 9 and 14 of the Chieftaincy Law No.22 of 1978, Imo State considered.

- *Okenwa v. Mil. Gov., Imo State (1997) 6 NWLR (Pt. 507) 136 CA*

19. The grant of Letters of Administration is not totally inconsistent with the rights of inheritance under native law and custom.

- *George v. Sonekan (1997) 3 NWLR (Pt. 495) 618 at 620 CA*

20. The Benin native law and custom requires that a hereditary chief who died *testate* or *intestate* be buried in a house where he lived and died, that is "Igiogbe". After the first burial, all his property are held by the eldest son in trust up to such a time when he can perform the second burial. After performing the second burial, the eldest son is entitled to inherit the "*Igiogbe*" and the other items of the estate are, subsequently, shared amongst his children. The "*Igiogbe*" cannot be taken away from the eldest son who succeeds him to the title or office.

- *Lawal-Osula v. Lawal-Osula (1996) 1 NILR 22 at 26 SC*

X
Evidence

10.1 Burden of Proof

1. The phrase "burden of proof" has three meanings, namely: the persuasive burden, that is, the burden of proof as a matter of law and pleading; the evidential burden and; the burden of establishing the admissibility of evidence.

> - *Kala v. Potiskum (1998) 3 NWLR (Pt. 540) 1 SC*
> - *Igbi v. State (2000) 2 SC 67*

2. By virtue of section 137 of the Evidence Act, in civil cases, the burden of proof is on the party who asserts a fact to prove same, for he who asserts must prove. The standard of proof required is on a preponderance of evidence and balance of probabilities.

> - *Daodu v. N.N.P.C (1998) 2 NWLR (Pt. 538) 355 SC*
> - *Kala v. Potiskum (1998) 3 NWLR (Pt. 540) 1 SC*
> - *N.B.N. Ltd v. S.C.D.C. Co. Ltd (1998) 5 NWLR (Pt. 548) 144 CA*
> - *Braimah v. Abasi (1998) 13 NWLR (Pt. 581) 167 SC*
> - *Alhaji Otaru & Sons Ltd. v. Idris (1999) 6 NWLR (Pt. 606) 330 SC*
> - *Itauma v. Akpe-Ime (2000) 7 SC (Pt. II) 24*

3. In a criminal trial, the onus lies throughout upon the prosecution to establish the guilt of the accused beyond reasonable doubt by virtue of section 138 of the Evidence Act. The burden does not shift on the accused who in law is under no obligation to prove his innocence. Even where an accused in his statement to the police admitted committing the offence, the prosecution is not relieved of that burden.

> - *Akinfe v. State (1988) 3 NWLR (Pt. 85) 729 SC*
> - *Aigbadion v. The State (2000) 4 SC (Pt. 1) 1 at 15 & 16*

4. The case against an accused person must be proved beyond reasonable doubt. Any doubt in the prosecution's case must be resolved in favour of the accused.

> - *Baruwa v. State (1996) 7 NWLR (Pt. 460) 302 CA*
> - *Onuoha v. State (1998) 5 NWLR (Pt. 548) 118 CA*

5. Although the burden of proving a charge against an accused is upon the prosecution, where, however, the prosecution has adduced evidence, which shows that the accused is guilty of the offence charged, the burden of proving that he is innocent shifts to the accused by virtue of sections 138(3), 139, 141 and 143 of the Evidence Act.

> - *Nasiru v. State (1999) 2 NWLR (Pt. 589) 87 at 89 SC*

6. A party is only entitled to judgment if a trial court believes and accepts his evidence and if such evidence supports his case. The mere fact that the court rejected the evidence of a defendant does not entitle the plaintiff to judgment.

> - *Bello v. Aruwa (1999) 8 NWLR (Pt. 615) 454 CA*

7. It is trite law that what is admitted does not require further proof by evidence, whether oral or documentary.

> - *Olagunyi v. Oyeniran (1996) 6 NWLR (Pt. 453) 127 SC*
> - *Akpan v. Umoh (1999) 11 NWLR (Pt. 627) 349 SC*
> - *Agbanelo v. Union Bank of Nigeria Ltd (2000) 4 SC (Pt. 1) 233*

8. An admission of fact by a party against his interest is admissible in evidence and need no further proof.

> - *Awote v. Owodunni (No. 2) (1987) 2 NWLR (Pt. 57) 367 SC*
> - *Iso v. Eno (1999) 2 NWLR (Pt. 590) 204 CA*
> - *Atanze v. Attah (1999) 3 NWLR (Pt. 596) 647 CA*

9. The issue of age should be proved either scientifically or by production of documents like a birth certificate.

> - *Juli v. Mohammed (1999) 4 NWLR (Pt. 600) 682 CA*

10. An averment in the pleadings, on which no evidence is called in proof of, is deemed to have been abandoned.

> - *Yusuf v. Oyetunde (1998) 12 NWLR (Pt. 579) 483 SC*

11. Although in proper cases, unchallenged oral evidence of a

party establishing his claim has been held to be sufficient proof; where, however, the evidence is self-defeating and unacceptable, the court is not obliged to act on it.

> - *Artra Industries (Nig.) Ltd. v. N.B.C.I. (1998) 4 NWLR (Pt. 546) 357 SC*

12. Since consolidated suits remain separate and retain their identities, the burden of proof lies on the plaintiff in each suit. Each plaintiff must discharge his onus.

> - *Okene v. Orianwo (1998) 9 NWLR (Pt. 566) 408 CA*
> - *Sawuta v. Ngah (1998) 13 NWLR (Pt. 580) 39 CA*

13. Although the rule is that a party may not be allowed to lead evidence outside his pleadings, a plaintiff will be entitled to lead evidence on a point raised in the defendant's pleadings.

> - *Dokubo v. Omoni (1999) 8 NWLR (Pt. 616) 647 SC*

14. Where a plaintiff's competence to sue is challenged, the burden of proof is on him to show that he has some justiciable interest, which may be affected by the action or that he will suffer injury or damage as a result of the action.

> - *Okafor v. Asoh (1999) 3 NWLR (Pt. 593) 35 CA*
> - *Owodunni v. Registered Trustees of C.C.C. (2000) 6 SC (Pt. III) 60*

15. In an action for negligence, as in every other action, the burden of proof falls upon the plaintiff alleging it. It is proved on a preponderance of probabilities. The person alleging negligence has the onus to give the particulars of negligence and lead evidence in support thereof.

> - *N.B.C. Plc. v. Borgundu (1999) 2 NWLR (Pt. 591) 408 CA*

16. In an action for breach of contract, anticipated profits must be established by evidence, hence the burden is on the plaintiff who asserts it. He must discharge that burden before the defendant can be called upon to show that the anticipated profits were probable.

> - *Acme Builders Ltd. v. K.S.W.B. (1999) 2 NWLR (Pt. 590) 288 SC*

17. It is settled law that there are five different ways of proving title to land, namely: by traditional evidence; by documents of title; by various acts of ownership, numerous and positive and extending over a length of time as to warrant the inference of ownership; by acts of long enjoyment and possession of the land; and by proof of possession of connected or adjacent land in circumstances rendering it probable that the owner of such connected or adjacent land would, in addition, be the owner of the land in dispute.

- *Idundun v. Okumagba (1976) 9-10 SC 227*
- *Atanda v. Ajani (1989) 3 NWLR (Pt. 111) 511 SC*
- *Onwugbufor v. Okoye (1996) 1 NWLR (Pt. 424) 252 SC*

18. A party claiming declaration of title to land needs not prove all the five recognised ways of establishing title to land, for him to succeed. Each of the five ways is independent of the others to prove title in a land case. Therefore, the establishment of one out of the five ways is sufficient to grant ownership.

- *Nwosu v. Udeaja (1990) 1 NWLR (Pt. 125) 188 SC*
- *Onwugbufor v. Okoye (1996) 1 NWLR (Pt. 424) 252 SC*
- *Ezekwesili v. Onwuagbu (1998) 3 NWLR (Pt. 541) 217 CA*
- *Ojelade v. Soroye (1998) 5 NWLR (Pt. 549) 284 CA*

19. In proving the contents of a Will prepared by a legal practitioner, it is not enough to show that the Will was prepared by the legal practitioner. It must be shown further that the testator knew the contents of the instrument and that the contents complied with his instructions to the legal practitioner who prepared it.

- *Okelola v. Boyle (1998) 2 NWLR (Pt. 539) 533 SC*

20. In interpleader proceedings, the burden is generally on the claimant as the plaintiff, to establish his title to the property in dispute, or where his claim is not absolute title, he must prove the precise interest or title he claims. However, where the claimant is in possession of the property in issue at the time of its attachment, the judgment creditor shall be deemed a plaintiff and that the burden of proof shall be on him.

- *Kala v. Potiskum (1998) 3 NWLR (Pt. 540) 1 SC*
- *Olatunde v. O.A.U. (1998) 5 NWLR (Pt. 549) 178 SC*

21. Customary law, by virtue of section 14 of the Evidence Act, is entirely a matter of evidence to be decided on the facts presented before the court and must therefore be proved in any particular case unless it is of such notoriety and has been so frequently followed by the courts that judicial notice thereof would be taken without evidence required in proof. The onus is on the party who relies on customary law to establish the same.

> *- Agbabiaka v. Saibu (1998) 10 NWLR (Pt. 571) 534 SC*
>
> *- Onyejekwe v. Onyejekwe (1999) 3 NWLR (Pt. 596) 482 SC*

22. In a declaratory action, the onus of proof lies on the plaintiff and he must succeed on the strength of his own case and not on the weakness of the defence except where the case for the defence supports the plaintiff's case.

> *- Abasi v. Onido (1998) 5 NWLR (Pt. 548) 89 CA*
>
> *- Nkwo v. Iboe (1998) 7 NWLR (Pt. 558) 354 SC*
>
> *- Uche v. Eke (1998) 9 NWLR (Pt. 564) 24 SC*

23. Special damages must be specifically pleaded and strictly proved.

> *- Abdullahi v. Raji (1998) 1 NWLR (Pt. 534) 481 CA*
>
> *- Nze v. Unakalamba (1998) 2 NWLR (Pt. 537) 308 CA*
>
> *- Alhaji Otaru & Sons Ltd v. Idris (1999) 6 NWLR (Pt. 606) 330 SC*

24. The term "strict proof" required in proof of special damages means no more than that the evidence must show the same particularity as is necessary for its pleading. It should therefore normally consist of evidence of particular losses which are exactly known or accurately measured before the trial.

> *- Abdullahi v. Raji (1998) 1 NWLR (Pt. 534) 481 CA*

10.2 Admissibility

1. Ordinarily, admissibility of evidence is governed by section 6 of the Evidence Act. Once a piece of evidence is relevant, it is

admissible in evidence, irrespective of how it was obtained.

> - *Fawehinmi v. N.B.A. (No. 2) (1989) 2 NWLR (Pt. 105) 558 SC*
> - *B.O.N. v. Saleh (1999) 9 NWLR (Pt. 618) 331 CA*

2. There is a distinction between admissibility of a document and the weight to be attached to it. A document may be admissible in law but when put through the crucible of evaluation and ascription of probative value thereto, it may be found to be a worthless document.

> - *I.M.B. (Nig.) Ltd v. Dabiri (1998) 1 NWLR (Pt. 533) 284 CA*
> - *Buraimoh v. Karimu (1999) 9 NWLR (Pt. 618) 310 CA*

3. Where a piece of evidence which is inadmissible at all in law is wrongly admitted in evidence, the proper thing for the trial court to do is to discountenance it completely when writing its judgment.

> - *Hyppolite v. Agharevba (1998) 11 NWLR (Pt. 575) 598 CA*

4. Where inadmissible evidence is admitted without objection at the trial, failure to object to its admissibility at the trial will not prevent its inadmissibility from being raised and determined on appeal.

> - *Ogidi v. Egba (1999) 10 NWLR (Pt. 621) 42 SC*

5. Under section 97(2) of the Evidence Act, as far as a public document is concerned, the secondary evidence admissible is a certified copy of the document and no other kind of secondary evidence.

> - *Egbue v. Araka (1996) 1 NILR 139 CA*

6. A certified document is a copy of the original document signed and certified as true by the officer in whose custody the original document is entrusted, and it is admitted upon the credit of such officer without examining the original document.

> - *Egbue v. Araka (1996) 1 NILR 139 CA*

7. The photocopy of a certified true copy of a public document needs no further certification under section 111(1) of the

Evidence Act. Thus, photocopies of public documents endorsed as originals are admissible in evidence as original, being photographic reproduction of written matters.

> - *I.M.B. (Nig.) Ltd. v. Dabiri (1998) 1 NWLR (Pt. 533) 284 CA*

8. It is trite law that evidence acquired by a witness in the course of his employment is not only relevant but also admissible.

> - *Kate Enterprises Ltd v. Daewoo Nigeria Limited (1985) 2 NWLR (Pt. 5) 116 SC*
> - *Comet Shipping v. Babbit (2001) 13 WRN 114 CA*

9. Unpleaded documents, depending on the nature of the claim, may be admissible in evidence where the unpleaded documents constitute evidence by which material facts are to be proved.

> - *Ifeadi v. Atedze (1998) 13 NWLR (Pt. 581) 205 CA*

10. Documentary evidence can be admitted in court proceedings through any witness by consent or without objection, notwithstanding that their makers were available and not called as witnesses.

> - *U.N.I.C. v. U.C.I.C. Ltd (1999) 3 NWLR (Pt. 593) 17 CA*

11. It is settled law that evidence of a witness taken in earlier proceedings is not admissible in a later trial except for the purpose of discrediting such a witness in cross-examination and except where the provision of section 34(1) of the Evidence Act applies.

> - *L.S.D.P.C. v. Adold/Stamm Int. Ltd (1994) 7 NWLR (Pt. 358) 545 SC*
> - *Njoku v. Dikibo (1998) 1 NWLR (Pt. 534) 496 CA*
> - *Alakija v. Abdulai (1998) 6 NWLR (Pt. 552) 1 SC*

12. An unregistered registrable instrument is admissible as evidence of payment of purchase price. However, it is not admissible in evidence to prove or establish title, as it is not a valid document capable of transfering any title or estate. Such an instrument, coupled with the purchaser being in possession may give rise to an equitable interest.

> - *Okoye v. Dumez Nig. Ltd. (1985) 1 NWLR (Pt. 4) 783 SC*
> - *Obijuru v. Ozims (1985) 2 NWLR (Pt. 6) 167 SC*

- Tewogbade v. Obadina (1994) 4 NWLR (Pt. 338) 326 SC
- Alaya v. Akinduro (1998) 4 NWLR (Pt. 545) 311 CA
- Adeyemo v. Ida (1998) 4 NWLR (Pt. 546) 504 CA

13. A person who clogs the attempt of another to register a registrable instrument by entering a caution at the Lands Registry cannot subsequently, in an action based on the instrument, object to the admissibility of the said instrument in evidence on the ground of non-registration.

- Ajibade v. Pedro (1992) 5 NWLR (Pt. 241) 257 SC

14. For tape-recorded speech (audio or video) to be admissible in evidence, it must not only be pleaded, but also, a proper foundation must be laid for the source of the recorded speech and explanation must be made on how it was obtained.

- Maduekwe v. Okoroafor (1992) 9 NWLR (Pt. 263) 69 CA

15. Offers of compromise made expressly or impliedly "without prejudice" are not admissible in evidence against a party as admissions, for the law protects any negotiations *bona fide* entered into for the settlement of disputes.

- Fawehinmi v. N.B.A. (No. 2) (1989) 2 NWLR (Pt. 105) 558 SC

16. Hearsay evidence is an evidence which does not derive its value solely from the credit given to the witness himself, but which rests also, in part, on the veracity and competence of some other person. Thus, where a third party relates a story to another as proof of the contents of a statement, such story is hearsay.

- Judicial Service Committee v. Omo (1990) 6 NWLR (Pt. 157) 407 CA

17. Evidence of a statement made to a witness by a person who is not himself called as a witness may or may not be hearsay. It is hearsay and inadmissible when the object of the evidence is to establish the truth of what is contained in the statement. It is not hearsay and admissible when it is proposed to establish by evidence not the truth of the statement but the fact that it was said.

- Kala v. Potiskum (1998) 3 NWLR (Pt. 540) 1 SC

18. Where the only eyewitness to a crime is the accused alone,

whatever any other witness would testify to as to the unlawful act is hearsay, not circumstantial evidence.

- *Ahmed v. State (1999) 7 NWLR (Pt. 612) 641 SC*

19. Generally, hearsay evidence is not admissible.

- *Agoda v. Enamuotor (1999) 8 NWLR (Pt. 615) 407 CA*

20. Documentary evidence need not be specifically pleaded so long as facts and not evidence by which such a document is covered is pleaded.

- *Okeke v. Oruh (1999) 6 NWLR (Pt. 606) 175 SC*

21. By virtue of section 132(1) of the Evidence Act, oral evidence of the content of a document that has been reduced into writing is not only inadmissible but also oral testimony cannot be used to state the content of such document.

- *Nnubia v. A-G, Rivers State (1999) 3 NWLR (Pt. 593) 82 CA*

22. Under section 131(2) of the Evidence Act, oral evidence of a transaction is not excluded by the fact that a documentary memorandum of it was made if such memorandum was not intended to have legal effect as a contract, grant or disposition of property.

- *Tidex (Nig.) Ltd v. Maskew (1998) 3 NWLR (Pt. 542) 404 CA*

23. The general rule is that where parties have embodied the terms of their agreement or contract in a written document, extrinsic evidence is not admissible to add to, vary, subtract from or contradict the terms of the written instrument. Section 131(1) of the Evidence Act considered.

- *U.B.N. v. Ozigi (1994) 3 NWLR (Pt. 333) 385 SC*
- *N.I.D.B. v. De-Easy Life Electronics (1999) 4 NWLR (Pt. 597) 8 CA*
- *Koiki v. Magnusson (1999) 8 NWLR (Pt. 615) 492 SC*
- *Inwelegbu v. Ezeani (1999) 12 NWLR (Pt. 630) 266 CA*
- *B.O.N. Ltd v. Akintoye (1999) 12 NWLR (Pt. 631) 392 CA*

24. Evaluation of relevant and material evidence before court

and the ascription of probative value to such evidence are the primary functions of the trial court, which saw, heard and assessed the witnesses while they testified. Where the trial court unquestionably evaluates the evidence and justifiably appraises the facts, it is not the business of the appellate court to substitute its own views for the views of the trial court.

- *Bashaya v. State (1998) 5 NWLR (Pt. 550) 351 SC*
- *Ojokolobo v. Alamu (1998) 9 NWLR (Pt. 565) 226 SC*
- *Sha v. Kwan (2000) 5 SC 178*
- *State v. Ajie (2000) 7 SC (Pt. I) 24*

25. By virtue of section 45 of the Evidence Act, oral evidence of tradition or traditional history in respect of title to or interest in family or communal land is relevant and therefore admissible in proof of title or interest to such land.

Alli v. Alesinloye (2000) 4 SC (Pt. 1) 111

26. Although, evidence of tradition may be more easily established if it comes from members of the family or community concerned, such traditional evidence may still be admissible in land matters by virtue of section 45 of the Evidence Act, where it emanates from any other credible and reliable witness other than members of the said family or community.

- *Alli v. Alesinloye (2000) 4 SC (Pt. 1) 111*

27. It is settled law that where there is a conflict in the evidence of traditional histories, their cogency is to be determined by resort to acts or facts in recent times in so far as they lead the court to ascertain which of the histories is more probable. In such a case, the demeanour of witnesses is of little guide to the truth of the matter.

- *Igbojimadu v. Ibeabuchi (1998) 1 NWLR (Pt. 533) 179 CA*
- *Abasi v. Onido (1998) 5 NWLR (Pt. 548) 89 CA*
- *Ibenye v. Agwu (1998) 11 NWLR (Pt. 574) 372 SC*
- *Alli v. Alesinloye (2000) 4 SC (Pt. 1) 111*

28. It is trite law that a document, which is marked "rejected" when tendered in evidence, cannot subsequently be tendered and admitted in evidence as an exhibit in the case.

- *Ita v. Ekpenyong (2001) 9 WRN 147 CA*

29. By virtue of section 97(1)(b) and (c) of the Evidence Act, secondary evidence may be given of the existence, condition, or content of a document in the following cases, namely: when the existence, condition or contents of the original have been proved to be admitted in writing by the person against whom it is proved or by his representative in interest; and, when the original has been destroyed or lost, and in the latter case all possible search has been made for it.

> - *Nwanji v. Coastal Services (Nig.) Ltd (1999) 11 NWLR (Pt. 628) 641 CA*

30. Where the original document sought to be tendered in evidence is, in the possession or power of a party against whom the document is sought to be proved, secondary evidence of the document shall not be tendered unless a notice to produce the document has been issued to the party in possession of such document. Section 98 of the Evidence Act and Order 29 Rule 8 of the High Court of Lagos State (Civil Procedure) Rules, 1994 considered.

> - *N.M.B. Plc. v. Onabolu (1999) 12 NWLR (Pt. 630) 302 CA*

31. A trial court must not rely on a document not tendered as an exhibit before it except where its content has been rendered admissible in law, such as where after sufficient foundation has been laid, secondary evidence thereof is admitted in evidence.

> - *Oparaji v. Ohanu (1999) 9 NWLR (Pt. 618) 290 SC*

32. As a general rule, evidence led on facts not pleaded go to no issue.

> - *Alao v. A.C.B. Ltd (1998) 3 NWLR (Pt. 542) 339 SC*
> - *Babalola v. Ogun State Polytechnic (1998) 5 NWLR (Pt. 550) 483 CA*
> - *Akawu v. Mai-Unguwa (1998) 5 NWLR (Pt. 551) 665 CA*
> - *Anyanwu v. Iwuchukwu (2001) 7 WRN 104 SC*

33. The court needs to be circumspect and cautious in relying on and assigning probative value to the evidence of prosecution witnesses who are related to a deceased in a murder case.

> - *Ubochi v. State (1993) 8 NWLR (Pt. 314) 697 CA*
> - *Effia v. State (1998) 2 NWLR (Pt. 537) 275 CA*

34. Where an evidence is uncontroverted, unchallenged and credible, it should be accepted.

- *Contract Resources (Nig.) Ltd. v. Wende (1998) 5 NWLR (Pt. 549) 243 CA*

- *Tokimi v. Fagite (1999) 10 NWLR (Pt. 624) 590 CA*

- *Ifeanyi Chukwu Osondu Co. Ltd v. Akhigbe (1999) 11 NWLR (Pt. 625) 1 SC*

- *Olohunde v. Adeyoju (2000) 6 SC (Part III) 118*

- *Oforlete v. State (2000) 7 SC (Part I) 80*

- *Omo v. Judicial Service Committee of Delta State (2000) 7 SC (Part II) 1*

- *P.H.M.B v. Edosa (2001) 12 WRN 183 SC*

35. By virtue of section 109 of the Evidence Act, public documents are documents forming the acts or records of the acts of the sovereign authority, official bodies and tribunals; public officers, legislative, judicial and executive, whether of Nigeria or elsewhere; and public records kept in Nigeria of private documents.

- *Alataha v. Asin (1999) 5 NWLR (Pt. 601) 32 CA*

36. In the determination of responsibility or guilt, facts not otherwise relevant are by virtue of section 12(b) of the Evidence Act, relevant if, by themselves or in connection with other facts they make the existence or non-existence of any fact in issue or relevant fact probable or improbable. Thus, in the absence of direct evidence, the court can safely act upon circumstantial evidence in order to determine the responsibility or guilt of a party.

- *Akinmoju v. The State (2000) 4 SC (Part I) 64 at 78*

37. Circumstantial evidence can only ground a conviction if it irresistibly and unequivocally leads to the guilt of an accused person; there is no other reasonable inference that could be drawn from it; and there are no co-existing circumstances which could weaken the inference.

- *Okereke v. State (1998) 3 NWLR (Pt. 540) 75 CA*

- *Adepetu v. State (1998) 9 NWLR (Pt. 565) 185 SC*

- *Idowu v. State (1998) 11 NWLR (Pt. 574) 354 SC*

- *Akinmoju v. Atate (2000) 4 SC (Part I) 64*

- Durwode v. State (2000) 12 SC (Part I) 1

- The State v. Ogbubunjo (2001) 13 WRN 1 at 3 SC

38. Suspicion, no matter how grave it may be, cannot found a conviction.

- Idowu v. State (1998) 11 NWLR (Pt. 574) 354 SC

- Aigbadion v. The State (2000) 4 SC (Part I) 1

39. The question whether a person is an illiterate or not is an issue of fact and not law and has to be determined by hearing evidence on it to determine the preliminary issue.

- Girgiri v. Elf Marketing (Nig.) Ltd (1997) 2 NWLR (Pt. 487) 368 CA

40. The onus is on the party objecting to the admissibility of a document on the ground that the maker is an illiterate, to prove that the maker of such document is an illiterate and that there is no *jurat*.

- Mainagge v. Gwamna (1997) 11 NWLR (Pt. 528) 191 CA

41. Non-compliance with the requirement of the law that the writer of a document, signed or thumb-printed by an illiterate person, must write his name in the *jurat* does not render the document void but only voidable at the instance of the illiterate person. Section 3 of the Illiterates Protection Law, Cap. 47 Laws of Ogun State, 1978 considered.

- Olanloye v. Fatunbi (1999) 8 NWLR (Pt. 614) 203 CA

42. The Illiterates Protection Law does not render a document that fails to comply with the provisions of the law inadmissible or unenforceable. It is only the writer of such document that is prevented, at the instance of the illiterate, from taking a benefit under the document.

- Anaeze v. Anyaso (1993) 5 NWLR (Pt. 291) 1 SC

- Aighobahi v. Aifuwa (1999) 13 NWLR (Pt. 635) 412 CA

43. Where a letter or document is prepared by a legal practitioner at the request or on behalf of his client who is an illiterate, the legal practitioner need not interpret and explain the letter or document to the client prior to the client signing or making his mark on the letter or document. Section 5 of the Illiterates Protection Law Cap. 70, Laws of Bendel State, 1976 considered.

- *Edokpolo & Co. Ltd v. Ohenhen (1994) 7 NWLR (Pt. 358) 511 SC*
- *Aighobahi v. Aifuwa (1999) 13 NWLR (Pt. 635) 412 CA*

44. A jurat is for the protection of an illiterate and cannot be used against his interest. Absence of a jurat in a document signed by an illiterate does not render the document null and void.

- *Wilson v. Oshin (2000) 6 SC (Part III) 1*

45. "Judicial notice" refers to facts which a judge can be called upon to receive and to act upon either from his general knowledge of them or from inquiries to be made by him for his own information from sources to which it is proper for him to refer.

- *Gbadamosi v. Alete (1998) 12 NWLR (Pt. 578) 402 CA*
- *U.B.N. Plc. v. Scpok (Nig.) Ltd. (1998) 12 NWLR (Pt. 578) 439 CA*

10.3 Affidavit Evidence

1. Where there is a conflict in affidavit evidence before a court, the court should resolve such conflict by calling and hearing oral evidence from the deponents or such other witnesses as the parties may be advised to call.

- *Falobi v. Falobi (1976) NMLR 169 SC*
- *Gbadamosi v. Alete (1998) 12 NWLR (Pt. 578) 402 CA*
- *Habib (Nig.) Bank Ltd v. Oyebanji (1998) 13 NWLR (Pt. 580) 71 CA*
- *Akujobi v. Ekenan (1999) 1 NWLR (Pt. 585) 96 CA*
- *F.S.B. International Bank Ltd v. Imano Nigeria Ltd (2000) 7 SC (Part I) 1*

2. Where the opposing party does not challenge depositions in an affidavit, such evidence or depositions are deemed to stand and can be admitted as the true facts.

- *Long-John v. Blakk (1998) 6 NWLR (Pt. 555) 524 at 532 SC*
- *Umoh v. Tita (1999) 12 NWLR (Pt. 631) 427 CA*

3. **Documents attached to an affidavit constitute admissible evidence. They are entitled to be given weight where there is no conflict.**

> - *Shitta-Bey v. A-G., Federation (1998) 10 NWLR (Pt. 570) 392 SC*

4. **A court is expected to resolve conflicting affidavit evidence by calling oral evidence of the deponents to resolve the conflict and where the decision of the trial court is based on the conflicting affidavits in the absence of the oral evidence such decision will not be allowed to stand on appeal.**

> - *Gbadamosi v. Alete (1998) 12 NWLR (Pt. 578) 402 CA*
> - *Amiara v. Alo (1995) 7 NWLR (Pt. 409) 623 CA*

5. **Where the conflicts in affidavit evidence are not material to a case or where the facts therein are inadmissible in evidence, the court should not be saddled with the responsibility of calling oral evidence to resolve the conflict. The need to call oral evidence would also not arise if the areas of conflict are so narrow and are not significant.**

> - *Garba v. University of Maiduguri (1986) 1 NWLR (Pt. 18) 550 SC*
> - *L.S.D.P.C. v. Adold/Stamm Int. Ltd (1994) 7 NWLR (Pt. 358) 545 SC*
> - *Hyppolite v. Egharevba (1998) 11 NWLR (Pt. 575) 598 CA*

6. **Where a party files an affidavit deposing to certain vital facts which are material to the case in dispute, the opposing party has the duty to counter those facts by way of a counter affidavit and failure to do so, those facts must be deemed unchallenged.**

> - *Malgit v. Dachen (1998) 5 NWLR (Pt. 550) 384 CA*

10.4 Witness

1. **The word "witness" means any person who is legally competent to testify in a case. By virtue of section 159 of the Evidence Act, the definition includes an accused person.**

> - *Egboghonome v. State (1993) 7 NWLR (Pt. 306) 383 SC*

2. Anybody who is connected with a land in dispute whether due to family link with the land or as a witness to what happened to the land or as a party to a transaction on the land is definitely a competent witness.

- *Umeojiako v. Ezenamuo (1990) 1 NWLR (Pt. 126) 253 SC*

3. Under Islamic law, unlike the English law, parties are not competent witnesses in court in their respective claims. Hence, their statements in court are not regarded as evidence, but something akin to statements of claim or defence in court.

- *Hada v. Malumfashi (1993) 7 NWLR (Pt. 303) 1 SC*
- *Jatau v. Mailafiya (1998) 1 NWLR (Pt. 535) 682 SC*

4. A vital witness is a witness whose evidence may determine a case one way or another. Thus, failure to call a vital witness by a party, such as the prosecution, is fatal to the case of such party.

- *Framo (Nig.) Ltd v. Daodu (1993) 3 NWLR (Pt. 281) 372 CA*
- *State v. Nnolim (1994) 5 NWLR (Pt. 345) 394 SC*

5. It is trite law that a witness can be treated as unreliable when his evidence is materially contradictory with his former statements.

- *Ukut v. The State (1996) 1 NILR 1 SC*

6. An expert witness is a witness who is specially skilled in the field in which he is giving evidence. The question of whether or not a witness can be regarded as an expert is a question for the court to decide but the decision must be based on legal evidence before the court. Section 57(1) and (2) of the Evidence Act Cap. 112 Laws of the Federation of Nigeria, 1990 considered.

- *Azu v. State (1993) 6 NWLR (Pt. 299) 303 SC*
- *Ogiale v. Shell Pet. Dev. Co. (Nig.) Ltd (1997) 1 NWLR (Pt. 480) 148 CA*
- *Aigbadion v. State (1999) 1 NWLR (Pt. 586) 284 CA*

7. In law, a formal witness, such as a policeman giving evidence *qua* policeman, is under no compulsion to give evidence in court. He cannot also be compelled to give a particular kind or type of evidence. However, while the law gives him freedom to give only the kind or type of evidence he wants to, the same law

vests in the court the power to accept or refuse such evidence.

- *Na-Bature v. Mahuta (1992) 9 NWLR (Pt. 263) 85 CA*

8. A tainted witness is a witness who is either an accomplice or, by the evidence he gives, whether as a witness for the prosecution or defence, may and could be regarded as having some purpose of his own to serve.

- *Oguonzee v. State (1998) 5 NWLR (Pt. 551) 521 SC*
- *F.B.N. Plc v. Nwankwocha (1998) 5 NWLR (Pt. 551) 610 CA*
- *Effiong v. State (1998) 8 NWLR (Pt. 562) 362 SC*
- *Okoro v. State (1998) 14 NWLR (Pt. 584) 181 SC*
- *Ifejirika v. State (1999) 3 NWLR (Pt. 593) 59 CA*

9. The law allows a party to discredit his own witness if he applies to the court to treat him as a hostile witness. Once his application is successful, he now declares the witness as a hostile one, and the rest of the procedure is consistent with a declaration of overt enmity. The witness will be cross-examined with a view to discrediting him.

- *"K" Line Inc. v. K.R. Int. (Nig.) Ltd (1993) 5 NWLR (Pt. 292) 159 CA*

10. If a witness is treated as hostile by the party calling the witness, then the sworn evidence of that witness as well as the witness' previous unsworn statement becomes unreliable and both must be rejected.

- *Okonkwo v. State (1998) 8 NWLR (Pt. 561) 210 CA*

11. A court of law needs not take into account the number of witnesses for each side to a dispute as a relevant factor in deciding which side is to succeed. What is primarily relevant is the quality of the evidence adduced before the court.

- *Oguonzee v. State (1998) 5 NWLR (Pt. 551) 521 SC*

12. There is no rule which imposes an obligation on the prosecution to call a host of witnesses. All the prosecution need do is to call enough material witnesses to prove its case and in so doing it has a discretion in the matter.

- *Babuga v. State (1996) 7 NWLR (Pt. 460) 279 SC*
- *Oguonzee v. State (1998) 5 NWLR (Pt. 551) 521 SC*

- Jammal v. State (1999) 12 NWLR (Pt. 632) 582 CA

- Oduneye v. The State (2001) 13 WRN 88 SC

13. Where there are contradictions in the evidence of prosecution witnesses on a material fact, such contradictions ought to be explained by the prosecution, through evidence.

- Ahmed v. State (1999) 7 NWLR (Pt. 612) 641 SC

- Aigbadion v. State (2000) 4 SC (Part I) 1

14. Where a witness' real testimony in court contradicts or is inconsistent with his previous extra-judicial statement, the court should not only regard the sworn oral testimony as being unreliable but also the previous statement whether sworn or unsworn as not constituting evidence upon which it can act.

- Obri v. State (1997) 7 NWLR (Pt. 513) 352 SC

- Onuoha v. State (1998) 5 NWLR (Pt. 548) 118 CA

15. A trial judge cannot *suo motu* call a witness in a civil matter unless on application or consent of the parties.

- Udo v. Eshiet (1994) 8 NWLR (Pt. 363) 483 CA

16. A party may examine and re-examine his witness after the witness has been cross-examined by the opposing party in accordance with section 189(3) of the Evidence Act. However, a party cannot cross-examine his witness unless he is first declared a hostile witness.

- Amobi v. Amobi (1996) 8 NWLR (Pt. 469) 638 SC

17. A trial court has the discretion whether to accede to the request to recall a witness or not. However, the discretion is to be judicially exercised.

- Emodi v. Kwentoh (1996) 2 NWLR (Pt. 433) 656 SC

- Okoronkwo v. Chukweke (1992) 1 NWLR (Pt. 216) 175 CA

18. A witness who is served with a *subpoena duces tecum* is not under a duty to support the case of the party at whose instance he is summoned. It is however, not proper for such a witness to refuse to accept a witness summon served on him.

- Ojokolobo v. Alamu (1991) 1 NWLR (Pt. 165) 1 CA

19. The evidence of a single witness, if believed by the court, can establish a criminal case even if it is a murder charge.

> *- Effiong v. State (1998) 8 NWLR (Pt. 562) 362 SC*

10.5 Confessional Statement

1. The law is that a free and voluntary confession of guilt made by an accused person, if it is direct and positive is sufficient to warrant his conviction without any corroborative evidence as long as the court is satisfied of the truth of the confession.

> *- Effiong v. State (1998) 8 NWLR (Pt. 562) 362 SC*
> *- Ihuebeka v. State (2000) 4 SC (Part I) 203*
> *- Idowu v. State (2000) 7 SC (Pt. II) 50*
> *- Alarape v. The State (2001) 14 WRN 1 SC*

2. A true and voluntary confessional statement that was not read over or confirmed before a superior police officer does not *ipso facto* ceases to be a true or voluntary confessional statement or that it is thereby rendered weightless or inadmissible.

> *- Akpan v. State (1992) 6 NWLR (Pt. 248) 439 SC*
> *- Silas Ikpo v. The State (1996) 1 NILR 59 SC*
> *- Alarape v. The State (2001) 14 WRN 1 SC*

3. It is trite law that mere retraction of a voluntary confessional statement by an accused person does not render such statement inadmissible or worthless and untrue in considering his guilt.

> *- Silas Ikpo v. The State (1996) 1 NILR 59 SC*
> *- Ihuebeka v. State (2000) 4 SC (Pt. I) 203*
> *- Idowu v. State (2000) 7 SC (Pt. II) 50*

10.6 Corroboration

1. Corroborative evidence is defined as evidence given by an independent witness which confirmed in some material particular not only that a crime has been committed but also

that it was committed by the accused person.

- *Amadi v. State (1993) 8 NWLR (Pt. 314) 644 SC*
- *Siwobi v. C.O.P. (1997) 1 NWLR (Pt. 482) 411 CA*

2. Corroboration is not required by law in civil cases except in actions such as for breach of promise of marriage.

- *Onowhosa v. Odiuzou (1999) 1 NWLR (Pt. 586) 173 SC*

3. There is no rule of court or practice that a dying declaration must be corroborated.

- *Akinfe v. State (1988) 3 NWLR (Pt. 85) 729 SC*
- *Effia v. State (1998) 2 NWLR (Pt. 537) 275 CA*

4. It is the duty of a trial judge to warn himself of the danger of acting on the evidence of a co-accused without corroboration.

- *Ohuka v. State (No. 2) (1988) 4 NWLR (Pt. 86) 36 SC*

5. Since an accomplice is a suspect witness, it is not safe for a judge to convict an accused person based upon the evidence of such an accomplice without corroboration, except where the court is satisfied that the evidence is reliable. Section 178(1) of the Evidence Act considered.

- *Ozaki v. State (1990) 1 NWLR (Pt. 124) 92 SC*
- *Amadi v. State (1993) 8 NWLR (Pt. 314) 644 SC*

6. A trial judge can neither substitute the result of his personal observations at the *locus in quo* for evidence given on oath nor can he reach conclusions upon things he observed on the inspection in the absence of testimony on oath to the existence of those facts which he had observed.

- *Osolu v. Osolu (1998) 1 NWLR (Pt. 535) 532 CA*
- *Ogundele v. Fasu (1999) 12 NWLR (Pt. 632) 662 SC*

10.7 Res Judicata and Estoppel

1. Estoppel is a rule of evidence that prevents the party estopped from denying the existence of a fact. In other words, estoppel is part of the law of evidence and it is no other than a bar to

testimony.

   - *Ezewani v. Onwordi (1986) 4 NWLR (Pt. 33) 27 SC*

2. Estoppel may be classified into four main categories, namely: *estoppel per rem judicatam* or estoppel by matter of record; estoppel by deed; estoppel by representation or estoppel *in pais;* and promissory estoppel.

   - *Ukaegbu v. Ugoji (1991) 6 NWLR (Pt. 196) 127 SC*
   - *Oyerogba v. Olaopa (1998) 13 NWLR (Pt. 583) 509 SC*

3. "Estoppel by deed" occurs where a statement of facts is in a solemn deed made by parties and authenticated by their seals, whereby they cannot be heard to resile from the facts clearly set out therein. Those facts are binding on the parties thereto.

   - *Oyerogba v. Olaopa (1998) 13 NWLR (Pt. 583) 509 SC*

4. Where a person by words or deeds or by conduct made to another a clear and unequivocal representation of a fact either with knowledge of its falsehood or with the intention that it should be acted upon, or has so conducted himself that another would, as a reasonable man in his full faculties, understand that a certain representation of fact was intended to be acted upon, and that other person in fact acted upon that representation whereby his position was thereby altered to his detriment, an estoppel arises against that person who made the representation and he will not be allowed to aver that the representation is not what he presented it to be.

   - *Ude v. Osuji (1998) 13 NWLR (Pt. 580) 1 SC*
   - *Oyerogba v. Olaopa (1998) 13 NWLR (Pt. 583) 509 SC*

5. The principle of "estoppel by standing by" is that if a person is content to stand by and see his battle fought by somebody else in the same interest, he is bound by the result and should not be allowed to re-open the case.

   - *Bello v. Fayose (1999) 11 NWLR (Pt. 627) 510 SC*
   - *Wilson v. Oshin (2000) 6 SC (Pt. III) 1*

6. The principle of "promissory estoppel" is to the effect that where a party (a promissor) makes a promise to another party, which he knows the other party (the promisee) will act on, and the other party indeed alter his position by acting on the

promise, the promissor will be debarred from resiling from the promise. However, the principle can only be used as a defence and not as the basis of a cause of action.

- *Tika Tore Press v. Abina (1973) 12 SC 79*

- *M.I.A. & Sons Ltd v. F.H.A. (1991) 8 NWLR (Pt. 209) 295 CA*

- *Guinness (Nig.) Ltd v. Agoma (1992) 7 NWLR (Pt. 256) 728 CA*

7. It is not necessary to plead estoppel in any particular form so long as the matters constituting estoppel are stated in such a manner as to show that the party pleading relies upon it as a defence or answer.

- *Alakija v. Abdulai (1998) 6 NWLR (Pt. 552) 1 SC*

- *Ebba v. Ogodo (2000) 6 SC (Pt. I) 133*

8. There is a difference between *estoppel simpliciter* and *res judicata*. Estoppel is an admission of facts. By its very nature, it is so important, so conclusive that the party whom it affects is not allowed to plead against it, or adduce evidence to contradict it. *Res judicata*, on the other hand, operates not only against the party whom it affects but also against the jurisdiction of the court itself. The party affected is *estopped per rem judicatam* from bringing a fresh claim before the court and at the same time the jurisdiction of the court to hear such claim is ousted.

- *Ladimeji v. Salami (1998) 5 NWLR (Pt. 548) 1 SC*

9. "Issue estoppel" arises where an issue had earlier on been adjudicated upon by a court of competent jurisdiction and the same issue comes incidentally in question in a subsequent proceedings between the same parties or their privies.

- *Oyerogba v. Olaopa (1998) 13 NWLR (Pt. 583) 509 SC*

- *Akujobi v. Ekenan (1999) 1 NWLR (Pt. 585) 96 CA*

- *Ito v. Ekpe (2000) 2 SC 98*

- *Ebba v. Ogodo (2000) 6 SC (Pt. I) 133*

10. In relying on issue estoppel, a party is not required to prove, unlike an estoppel *per rem judicatam*, that the subject matter and the claims were identical in addition to the identity of the parties being the same.

- *Ezewani v. Onwordi (1986) 4 NWLR (Pt. 33) 27 SC*

11. Estoppel *per rem judicatam* or estoppel of record arises where an issue of fact has been judicially determined in a final manner between parties by a court or tribunal having jurisdiction, concurrent or exclusive in the matter and the same issue comes directly in question in subsequent proceedings between the parties or their privies. Thus, the parties affected are estopped from bringing a fresh action before any court on the same case and on the same issue already pronounced upon by the court in a previous action.

- *Osunrinde v. Ajamogun (1992) 6 NWLR (Pt. 246) 156 SC*
- *Igwego v. Ezeugo (1992) 6 NWLR (Pt. 249) 561 SC*
- *Dokubo v. Omoni (1999) 8 NWLR (Pt. 616) 647 SC*
- *Oshodi v. Eyifunmi (2000) 7 SC (Part II) 145*

12. For the plea of estoppel *per rem judicatam* to succeed, the party relying on it must establish that the parties or their privies, the claim or the issue in dispute, the subject matter of the litigation in the previous action were the same as those in the action in which the plea is raised. The party, in addition, must establish that the decision relied upon to support the plea is valid, subsisting and final, and that the court that gave the previous decision sought to be relied upon is a court of competent jurisdiction.

- *Igwego v. Ezeugo (1992) 6 NWLR (Pt. 249) 561 SC*
- *Dokubo v. Omoni (1999) 8 NWLR (Pt. 616) 647 SC*
- *Oshodi v. Eyifunmi (2000) 7 SC (Part II) 145*

13. The plea of *res judicata* is used as a shield and not as a sword. Thus, the plea is not open to a plaintiff in his statement of claim as he would thereby be impugning the jurisdiction of the court to which he has brought his action and since a successful plea of estoppel *per rem judicatam* ousts the jurisdiction of the court before which it is raised.

- *Igwego v. Ezeugo (1992) 6 NWLR (Pt. 249) 561 SC*
- *Ladimeji v. Salami (1998) 5 NWLR (Pt. 548) 1 SC*

14. The judgment of Native or Customary Courts can create estoppel *per rem judicatam*, since Native or Customary Courts are courts of competent jurisdiction.

- *Agbasi v. Obi (1998) 2 NWLR (Pt. 536) 1 at 5 SC*

- Agumuo v. Azubuike (1999) 5 NWLR (Pt. 604) 649 CA

15. It is trite law that a judgment obtained against a party in his personal capacity cannot constitute *res judicata* in a judgment action against the party in a representative capacity.

- Okukuje v. Akwido (2001) 10 WRN 1 SC

16. An order of dismissal or striking out for want of diligent prosecution of a case cannot operate as *res judicata* in a subsequent case.

- Obasi v. M.B.A.S. Ltd (2001) 8 WRN 52 CA

XI
Family Law & Matrimonial Causes

11.1 Family Law

1. In establishing whether or not two families are one and the same, one of the most important things to establish is whether they are blood relations.

   - *Kwan v. Sha (1994) 4 NWLR (Pt. 338) 365 CA*

2. In an action for declaration as to family status, the court should reject a line of succession which is not satisfactorily traced because it has gaps or mysterious linkages or no nexus.

   - *Balogun v. Oligbede (1991) 8 NWLR (Pt. 208) 223 CA*

3. A native law and custom which is to the effect that the eldest son succeeds to and inherits all the property of his deceased father to the exclusion of other children is not repugnant to natural justice, equity and good conscience.

   - *Lawal-Osula v. Lawal-Osula (1993) 2 NWLR (Pt. 274) 158 CA*

4. A person's birthplace does not necessarily make him an indigene of that place nor operate to disentitle him from a position in his ancestral home. The fact that a person resides outside his ancestral place does not render him ineligible to contest the headship of his town so far as he is shown to belong to the ruling family.

   - *Yongbish v. Bulus (1997) 2 NWLR (Pt. 489) 621 at 623 CA*

5. The head of a family can institute actions for and on behalf of the family. Contracts made by the head of the family for and on behalf of the family are valid. However, no individual member or collection of members of the family has a legal capacity to enter into contracts for and on behalf of the family, and unless the head of the family is a party to the contract, the contract is void. Consequently, no member without express mandate from

the family can institute action in court for and on behalf of the family.

- *Akapo v. Hakeem-Habeeb (1992) 6 NWLR (Pt. 247) 266 SC*

6. Where the issue of paternity of a child under the Yoruba customary law is in dispute, the evidence of acceptance of the pregnancy and the naming of the child by the father are sufficient and recognised acts of acknowledgment of the paternity of the child by the father.

- *Olanrewaju v Gov. of Oyo State (1992) 9 NWLR (Pt 265) 335 SC*

7. Little weight is attached to the evidence of a party as to circumstances of his birth and his mother's marriage because he can at best give evidence in accordance with what his mother and others told him.

- *Maduagwu v Maduagwu (1991) 8 NWLR (Pt. 212) 684 CA*

8. The dissolution of a customary marriage is not as stringent as that under the Marriage Act. A customary marriage can be dissolved without judicial pronouncement. However, there must be a formal act on the part of the party who is tired and not willing to continue with the union or association.

- *Nwangwa v Ubani (1997) 10 NWLR (Pt. 526) 559 CA*

9. A customary marriage is terminated in one of two ways, either by divorce which consists in the wife leaving the husband or being driven away by him and bride price being refunded, or the bride-price being paid into court, or by the death of the wife.

- *Nwangwa v. Ubani (1997) 10 NWLR (Pt. 526) 559 CA*

10. Customary marriage may be dissolved by mutual agreement between the husband (or his parents where he is young) and the parents of the wife in the presence of the marriage middlemen and one or more elders from each of the two families. Spouses who want divorce in this situation do not have to go to court to obtain it.

- *Nwangwa v. Ubani (1997) 10 NWLR (Pt. 526) 559 CA*

11. The fact that a woman lives with a man and has children for

him does not necessarily make the woman the wife of the man under native law and custom. Similarly, the mere fact that a wife, married under the native law and custom, leaves her husband and stays with another man and have children for him, will not amount to divorce.

> *- Lawal-Osula v. Lawal-Osula (1993) 2 NWLR (Pt. 274) 158 CA*

11.2 Matrimonial Causes

1. The principle of law that once there is a marriage, the husband and wife are one person in law, is limited only to a monogamous marriage and no other type of association. Nevertheless, the burden of proving a particular type of marriage is on a party alleging same.

> *- Owners M/V Baco Liner 3 v. Adeniji (1993) 2 NWLR (Pt. 274) 195 CA*

2. In law, where a man and a woman are proved to have lived together as man and wife, the law will presume, unless the contrary is proved, that they were living together in consequence of a valid marriage and not in a state of concubinage.

> *- Ogbole v. Onah (1990) 1 NWLR (Pt. 126) 357 CA*

3. Bigamy is committed when any person who, having a husband or wife living, marries another person during the life of such husband or wife. Bigamy can occur in various ways, namely: where both marriages are contracted under the Marriage Act and where there is a marriage under the Marriage Act and another under native law and custom. Section 370 of the Criminal Code considered.

> *- Lawal-Osula v. Lawal-Osula (1993) 2 NWLR (Pt. 274) 158 CA*

4. A person married under the Marriage Act commits bigamy where subsequently he marries a different person under a polygamous form of marriage.

> *- R v. Princewell (1963) N.R.N.L.R. 54*

5. Similarly, where a person marries another under the Marriage Act when his or her marriage to another person under the native law and custom is still subsisting, he or she is guilty of bigamy. Bigamy is a criminal offence and must therefore be proved beyond reasonable doubts.

   - *Lawal-Osula v. Lawal-Osula (1993) 2 NWLR (Pt. 274) 158 CA*

6. Where a husband and wife are first married under native law and custom but proceed subsequently to contract a marriage under Marriage Act, the latter takes precedence over the former and guides their rights and obligations.

   - *Okon v. Administrator-General, Cross-River (1992) 6 NWLR (Pt. 248) 473 CA*
   - *Jadesimi v. Okotie-Eboh (1996) 2 NWLR (Pt. 429) 128 SC*

7. Under Nigerian law, a man cannot be guilty of raping his wife. Sexual intercourse between a husband and wife cannot amount to rape until a *decree absolute* or possibly a *decree nisi* of divorce has been made. Under common law, the position is now different as a man has been found guilty of rape on his wife.

   - *Section 6 of the Criminal Code Act Cap 77, Laws of the Federation of Nigeria, 1990*

8. Where an injunction is granted against a husband, any sexual intercourse thereafter will be unlawful and will amount to rape unless the wife consented. Also, a separation order with a provision that the wife will no longer be obliged to co-habit with the husband has the effect of rendering sexual intercourse between spouses unlawful unless the wife consented.

   - *R v. Clarke (1949) 2 All E.R. 448*

9. A husband is not entitled to use force or violence in exercising his right to intercourse. Where he does, he may be guilty of wounding, doing grievous harm or assault according to the circumstances.

   - *R v. Miller (1954) 2 All E.R. 529*

10. The obligation of husband and wife to live together is mutual and negotiable. If they agree to live apart, neither party can be guilty of desertion in consequence of separation arising from

the agreement. If they cannot agree on account of unreasonableness of one or the other and this leads to separation then the party who caused the separation by reason of his or her unreasonable behaviour may be guilty of desertion.

> - *Theresa Ekanem v. Stanley Ekanem (1975) N.N.L.R. 158, High Court of North-Central State. Suit No. NCH/120/74*

11. The mere compliance with an order of transfer by a worker from his place of matrimonial home to another place, and his wife for one reason or another refuses to join him at the new place, does not render the worker guilty of desertion, for compliance with the order of transfer cannot be said to be unreasonable.

> - *Theresa Ekanem v. Stanley Ekanem (1975) N.N.L.R. 158, High Court of North-Central State. Suit No. NCH/120/74*

12. A man has a common law duty to maintain his wife and such a wife then has a right to be so maintained. This right is not contractual in nature. The husband is under an obligation to maintain his wife, and may by law be compelled to find her necessaries suitable to the husband's degree, estate or circumstance.

> - *Erhahon v. Erhahon (1997) 6 NWLR (pt. 510) 667 at 672-673 CA*

13. The general principle of law is that if a wife is deserted by her husband, or if he treats her with such cruelty that she is forced to leave him, she is entitled at common law to pledge his credit for necessaries, subject, however, to this qualification, that if she has earning power of her own, or money of her own which she could reasonably be expected to use to pay for the necessaries, she has no authority to pledge his credit for them.

> - *Biberfeld v. Berens (1952) 2 Q.B. 770 at 783*
> - *Albert Hutchinson v. Madam Omowumi Olajide (1970) N.N.L.R. 31 CA*

14. There is a distinction between necessaries and money. At common law, a wife only has authority to pledge her husband's credit for actual necessaries such as food, clothing and lodging, she has no authority to borrow money on his credit.

> - *Deare v. Soutten L.R. 9 Eq. 151*

- Albert Hutchinson v. Madam Omowumi Olajide (1970) N.N.L.R. 31 CA

15. There is a difference between the celebration of a statutory marriage and church marriage. Celebration of a church marriage is not one in accordance with the Marriage Act, and therefore has no statutory flavour. Church marriage merely gives divine blessing to the customary marriage, which for all intent and purpose remains a marriage under customary law. In order to convert a customary marriage into a statutory marriage, the parties must consciously take the steps to adopt the procedure contained in the Marriage Act.

- Nwangwa v. Ubani (1997) 10 NWLR (Pt. 526) 559 CA

16. Under Nigerian law, a monogamous marriage supported by a Registrar's certificate as well as a marriage certificate can only be characterised as a marriage under the Marriage Act. Excluding marriage under Muslim rites, there is no third type of marriage besides customary marriage and marriage under the Marriage Act.

- Chukwuma v. Chukwuma (1996) 1 NWLR (Pt. 426) 543 CA

17. A wilful celebration of a purported marriage under the Marriage Act without the parties first being armed with the Registrar's certificate is null and void. The only exception is where one of the spouses went through the purported statutory form of marriage but did not acquiesce to the irregularity of celebrating the marriage without first obtaining the Registrar's certificate because that spouse did not know of the mandatory requirement for that document and had at all material time intended to undergo a monogamous marriage.

- Chukwuma v. Chukwuma (1996) 1 NWLR (Pt. 426) 543 CA

18. By virtue of section 2 (1)(a) of the Matrimonial Causes Act, 1990 the High Court of any State in Nigeria has jurisdiction to hear and determine matrimonial causes instituted under the Act. It follows therefore that although there is no specific provisions in the Matrimonial Causes Rules for the transfer of a petition for dissolution of a marriage from one High Court of a State to another, such power can be inferred since the entire country constitutes one jurisdiction under the Act.

> - *Adegoroye v Adegoroye (1996) 2 NWLR (Pt. 433) 712 CA*

19. Under the Matrimonial Causes Act, 1970, (as amended) there is only one ground for the dissolution of marriage, and that is that the marriage has broken down irretrievably as provided under section 15(1) of the Act. See however, Section 15 (1) (2) (a-h) of the Matrimonial Causes Act, Cap. 220, LFN, 1990.

> - *Anagbado v Anagbado (1992) 1 NWLR (Pt. 216) 207 CA*

20. It is not unconstitutional to hear matrimonial proceedings in chambers. A court may exclude the public from matrimonial proceedings before it if satisfied that the circumstances of the case so warrant.

> - *Ononuju v Ononuju (1991) 5 NWLR (Pt. 192) 479 CA*

21. Adultery is consensual sexual intercourse between a married person and a person of the opposite sex other than the spouse. There must be some penetration of the woman by the man, although the act of sexual intercourse need not have been completed.

> - *Erhahon v. Erhahon (1997) 6 NWLR (Pt. 510) 667 at 670-671 CA*

22. Adultery per se is not a crime and proceedings with regard to adultery are civil not criminal. However, under the Penal Code applicable to Northern States of Nigeria, it is regarded as a criminal offence.

> - *Erhahon v. Erhahon (1997) 6 NWLR (Pt. 510) 667 CA*

23. While it is true that the standard of proof of adultery in a divorce case is not as high as that of rape or defilement in a criminal case which is beyond reasonable doubt, the Matrimonial Causes Act nevertheless puts proof of adultery in divorce cases in a class of its own as lying within the reasonable satisfaction of the trial court.

> - *Erhahon v. Erhahon (1997) 6 NWLR (Pt. 510) 667 at 670 CA*

24. A decree of divorce or of nullity of marriage must not be made absolute and a decree of judicial separation must not be granted unless the court is satisfied that arrangements have been made for the welfare of every child of the marriage. If possible before doing so, the court should consult the child's wishes in considering what order to make.

- *Odogwu v Odogwu (1992) 2 NWLR (Pt. 225) 539 SC*

25. "Custody" means the control, and the preservation and care of the child's person, physically, mentally and morally. It also concerns responsibility for a child as regards to his needs, food, clothing, instruction, etc.

- *Otti v. Otti (1992) 7 NWLR (Pt. 252) 187 CA*

26. In custody cases, where the parents are separated and the child of the union is of tender age, it is presumed that the child will be happier with the mother. The court will not make an order contrary to the above presumption unless it is abundantly clear that there is for instance, evidence of immorality or insanity against the mother, or infectious diseases, or of her cruelty to the child.

- *Odogwu v. Odogwu (1992) 2 NWLR (Pt. 225) 539 SC*

27. Where at the time of granting the decree of dissolution of marriage, the children of the marriage are already adults, such children as adults are no longer liable to be in the custody of either of the parties and the trial court ought not to make any order for custody.

- *Ononuju v. Ononuju (1991) 5 NWLR (Pt. 192) 479 CA*

28. There are strictly two types of domicile, namely, domicile of origin and domicile of choice. Domicile of origin depends on circumstances of birth or adoption. The law is that a domicile of origin is not lost until a domicile of choice is acquired. Indeed, a domicile of origin is never destroyed, but remains in abeyance when a new domicile is chosen, and revives and comes again into operation when the new domicile is abandoned.

- *Osibamowo v. Osibamowo (1991) 3 NWLR (Pt. 177) 85 CA*
- *Bhojwani v. Bhojwani (1995) 7 NWLR (Pt. 407) 349 CA*

29. It is the domicile of a person that confers jurisdiction on the court to entertain his or her petition for dissolution of marriage.

Where therefore the domicile of a petitioner is not established, the court will lack jurisdiction to decree dissolution of marriage.

- *Osibamowo v. Osibamowo (1991) 3 NWLR (Pt. 177) 85 CA*

- *Bhojwani v. Bhowani (1995) 7 NWLR (pt. 407) 349 CA*

30. The Married Women's Property Act, 1881 is inapplicable to marriages contracted under and governed by customary law.

- *Amadi v. Nwosu (1992) 5 NWLR (Pt. 241) 273 SC*

31. Where a decree *nisi* is made in compliance with the provisions of section 57 of the Matrimonial Causes Act, the decree *nisi* could, pursuant to the Act be made absolute by operation of law within a period of three months of the *decree nisi* or 28 days from the date of making that order unless special circumstances or reasons are shown why it should not be made absolute. Such special circumstances and reasons may include where one of the parties died before the decree is declared absolute; where the parties to the decree *nisi* have reconciled before the decree becomes absolute, and where the decree is rescinded on the grounds of miscarriage of justice.

- *Dejonwo v. Dejonwo (1993) 7 NWLR (Pt. 306) 483 CA*

32. Where similar or parallel divorce proceedings are maintained by two spouses in two sovereign and independent countries, neither of which in law is subordinated to the other; the very fact that one of the spouses succeeds in first obtaining a *decree nisi* in one country while the other spouse is still engaged in the preliminary 'skirmishes' of founding jurisdiction to pursue divorce proceedings in the other country; the best option of such spouse against whom the *decree nisi* is made, in order to prevent it being made absolute, is to appeal against the *decree nisi* in the country where such divorce proceedings have been pursued to near finality.

- *Bhojwani v. Bhojwani (1996) 6 NWLR (Pt. 457) 661 SC*

33. Under section 39(2) of the 1979 Constitution, no citizen of Nigeria shall be subjected to any disability or deprivation merely by reason of the circumstances of his birth. Since the coming into force of the 1979 Constitution therefore, the term 'Illegitimate children', used to describe children born out of

wedlock has been rendered illegal and unconstitutional.

- *Olympio v. Oluwole & Anor (1968) NNLR p.469*
- *Salubi v. Nwariaku (1997) 5 NWLR (Pt. 505) 442 at 454 CA*

34. It is trite law that in disputes about the paternity of a child born during the subsistence of a marriage, the court would presume paternity in favour of the husband. The onus of rebutting this presumption rests on the man who is claiming the child but is not married to the child's mother.

- *Megwalu v. Megwalu (1994) 7 NWLR (Pt. 359) 718 CA*

 # XII
Human Rights

12.1 *Nature of Rights*

1. The right to life under the Nigerian Law is not absolute but qualified. Thus, the law recognizes the death penalty as a form of punishment but only on the condition that it is in execution of the sentence of a court of law in a criminal offence of which an accused person has been found guilty in Nigeria. Section 30(1) of the Constitution of the Federal Republic of Nigeria, 1979 considered.

> - *Kalu v. State (1998) 13 NWLR (Pt. 583) 531 SC*

2. The right to life goes beyond the fundamental right to life. Thus, it was held that the right to life includes the right to live with human dignity and all that goes along with it, namely the bare necessity of life, such as adequate food, nutrition, clothing and shelter over the head.

> - *Maneka Ghandi v. Union of India (1978) 1 SCC 248 (Indian Supreme Court Judgment)*
> - *Franus v. Union Territory of Delhi, AIR 1981 SCC 7 (Indian Supreme Court Judgment)*

3. There is a close nexus between life and means of livelihood. Thus, what makes life liveable must be deemed to be an integral component of the right to life.

> - *Olga Tellis v. Bombay Municipal Corporation (1985) SCC 545 (Indian Supreme Court Judgment)*

4. By virtue of section 9 of the South African Constitution, the right to life is absolute and unqualified. Thus, death penalty violates the constitutional protection of freedom from cruel, inhuman and degrading treatment under section 11(2) of the Constitution and is, in consequence, invalid and unconstitutional.

> - *The State v. Makwanyane and Another (1995) (6) BCLR 665 (CC); (1995) SACLR LEXIS 218 (South African Supreme Court Judgment)*

5. The court has no power to abolish death penalty. The power to abolish or retain death penalty is within the exclusive jurisdiction of the legislature.

   - *Kalu v. State (1998) 13 NWLR (Pt. 583) 531 SC*

6. The rights to freedom of movement and residence guarantee unhindered residence and movement to all citizens all over Nigeria except on suspicion of commission of a criminal offence. The rights protect also against expulsion of citizens except in pursuance of valid extradition proceedings.

   - *Williams v. Majekodunmi (1962) 1 All NLR 413 SC*
   - *Federal Minister of Internal Affairs v. Shugaba Darman (1982) 3 NCLR 915*

7. The fundamental objectives of Government to provide equal and adequate educational opportunities at all levels enunciated under the Fundamental Objectives and Directive Principles of State Policy in section 18 of the 1979 Constitution, cannot be interpreted to mean that only schools established and operated by the government or its agencies could exist in the State. The objectives can be carried out by any government in the Federation without necessarily restricting the right of other persons or organisations to provide similar or different educational facilities at their own expenses.

   - *Archbishop Okogie v. A-G, Lagos State (1981) 2 NCLR 337*

8. The constitutional right to counsel of one's choice is not absolute. The counsel must have a right of audience in Nigerian courts and must not be under a disability of any kind.

   - *Awolowo and Ors. v. Minister of Internal Affairs and Anor. (1962) L.L.R. 177*

9. No person shall be required to perform forced or compulsory labour. It is a labour, which the person must perform whether he likes it or not.

   - *Uzoukwu v. Ezeonu II (1991) 6 NWLR (Pt. 200) 708 CA*

10. The concepts of 'fair trial' and 'fair hearing' are interchangeable. The true test of fair hearing is the impression of a reasonable person who was present at the trial whether from his observation, justice has been done in the case. Such a

bystander would be guided by two universally recognized principles. First, were the two sides to the case heard so as to fulfil the principle of *audi alteram partem*? Secondly, was the judge personally interested in the issue before him, thus violating the principle of *nemo judex in causa sua*?

> *- Isiyaku Muhammed v. Kano Native Authority SC 417/1967*
> *(Unreported) decided on 31 December, 1968*

11. While the 1979 Constitution guarantees every citizen the right to private and family life and to freedom of thought, conscience and religion, the law recognizes that a man does not normally live in isolation. Therefore, his family life or freedom of thought and religion may be interfered with by statute if such interference is dictated by reasons of defence, public health or where the need to promote the economic well being of the community so requires. Thus, it was held that the Northern Nigerian Children and Young Person Act, 1958, which prohibits juvenile, that is, a person under the age of sixteen, from engaging in political activities did not encroach upon the right of a father to educate his children politically.

> *- Olawoyin v. A.-G., Northern Region (1961) 1 All N.L.R.*
> *209*

12. It is legitimate and constitutional to discuss any grievance or to criticise the government and its policies by means of fair argument. What are not permitted are malignant criticisms, which could affect the public peace and order.

> *- D.P.P. v. Chike Obi (1961) 1 All N.L.R. 186*
> *- R. v. Amalgamated Press Limited (1961) 1 All N.L.R. 199*

13. Pursuant to the constitutional guarantee of freedom of speech, a journalist has a right not to disclose his sources of information.

> *- Tony Momoh v. Senate (1981) 1 NCLR 459*
> *- Innocent Adikwu v. The State (1982) 3 NCLR 394*

14. Every Nigerian citizen has a fundamental right to peaceful assembly and association. Section 37 of the 1979 Constitution considered.

> *- Akaniwon v. Nsirim (1997) 9 NWLR (Pt. 520) 255 CA*
> *- Okafor v. Asoh (1999) 3 NWLR (Pt. 593) 35 CA*

15. By virtue of section 37 of the Constitution of the Federal Republic of Nigeria, 1979 every person shall be entitled to assemble freely and associate with other persons, and in particular, he may form or belong to any political party, trade union or any other association for protection of his interest. However, this freedom is not absolute, but rather, it is restrictive. Thus, a person proposing to join an association must show how that association would protect his interest.

- *Sea Trucks (Nig.) Ltd v. Pyne (1999) 6 NWLR (Pt. 607) 514 CA*

16. A citizen's right to free movement and ownership of property be it movable or immovable is not absolute. Sections 38(1), (2)(a) and 40(1), (2)(c) & (k) of the 1979 Constitution considered.

- *Director, SSS v. Agbakoba (1999) 3 NWLR (Pt. 595) 314 SC*
- *Ikem v. Nwogwugwu (1999) 13 NWLR (Pt. 633) 140 at 142 CA*

17. By virtue of section 6 of the Passport (Miscellaneous Provisions) Act Cap. 343, Laws of the Federation of Nigeria, 1990, passport means a document of protection and authority to travel issued by the competent Nigerian officials to Nigerians wishing to travel outside Nigeria. The right of a person to leave any country, including his own and to return to his country, is therefore, subject to possession of a valid national passport. Thus, an unjustified denial of possession of a valid passport may amount to a denial of the right to travel outside one's country.

- *Director, SSS v. Agbakoba (1999) 3 NWLR (Pt. 595) 314 SC*

18. It is only the Minister of Internal Affairs who has the power to issue a passport and withdraw or cancel a passport already issued. This power must be exercised formally by notice in a Gazette or by some other form whereby the holder of such passport will know that his passport is being withdrawn, cancelled, etc. The officials of the State Security Service by virtue of the National Security Agencies Act, Cap. 278, Laws of the Federation of Nigeria, 1990, and being no servants or agents of the Minister vide section 6 of the Passport (Miscellaneous

Provisions) Act, have no power to seize, impound or withdraw a Nigerian citizen's passport.

> - *Director, SSS v. Agbakoba (1999) 3 NWLR (Pt. 595) 314 SC*

19. The Minister of Internal Affairs has power to cancel or withdraw a citizen's passport in any of four circumstances, namely: where a passport was obtained by fraud, or has expired, or the citizen holds more than one passport at the same time, or it is in the public interest to cancel or withdraw the same. Section 5(1)(a), (b), (c) or (d) of the Passport (Miscellaneous Provisions) Act Cap. 343 Laws of the Federation of Nigeria, 1990 considered.

> - *Director, SSS v. Agbakoba (1999) 3 NWLR (Pt. 595) 314 SC*

20. By virtue of Article 6 of the African Charter on Human and Peoples' Rights, every individual shall have the right to liberty and the security of his person. No one may be deprived of his freedom except for reasons and conditions previously laid down by law. In particular, no one may be arbitrarily arrested or detained.

> - *Ubani v. Director, SSS (1999) 11 NWLR (Pt. 625) 129 CA*

21. Once a citizen has shown that any of his fundamental rights has been infringed, the burden is on the infringing body or authority or person to establish that the denial of the right was justified by law.

> - *A.C.B. v. Okonkwo (1997) 1 NWLR (Pt. 480) 194 CA*
> - *Director, SSS v. Agbakoba (1999) 3 NWLR (Pt. 595) 314 SC*
> - *Nig. Soc. Ins. T.F.M.B v. Adebiyi (1999) 13 NWLR (Pt. 633) 16 CA*
> - *Abacha v. Fawehinmi (2000) 4 SC (Part II) 1*

12.2 Enforcement of Human Rights

1. The African Charter on Human and Peoples' Rights is part of Nigeria's domestic law by the enactment of the African Charter

on Human and Peoples' Rights (Ratification and Enforcement) Act, Cap 10, Laws of the Federation of Nigeria, 1990. As a result, the rights and obligations therein covered under the Charter are fully and legally enforceable by the Nigerian High Courts depending on the circumstances of each case and in accordance with the rules, practice and procedure of each court.

- Abacha v. Fawehinmi (2000) 4 SC (Part II) 1 at P. 34 & 63

2. Actions for wrongful dismissal from employment cannot be brought under Fundamental Rights (Enforcement Procedure) Rules 1979. A claim, which is based on wrongful dismissal from employment, is founded on contract.

- Egbuonu v. B.R.T.C. (1997) 12 NWLR (Pt. 531) 29 at 31 SC

3. The jurisdiction to entertain any suit which seeks to enforce the observance of a fundamental right under Chapter 4 of the 1979 Constitution, including the right of any person not to be subjected to torture, inhuman or degrading treatment, lies only with the High Court of a State or the Federal High Court in the exercise of its original jurisdiction. Thus, the jurisdiction of the Supreme Court on the matter is appellate and not original.

- Kalu v. State (1998) 13 NWLR (Pt. 583) 531 SC

12.3 Distinction between Human Rights and Fundamental Rights

1. There is a clear distinction between "'Fundamental Rights" and "Human Rights". Human rights are rights, which were derived from the wider concept of natural rights. They are rights which every civilised society must accept as belonging to each person as a human being irrespective of citizenship, race, religion and so on. Thus, Human rights have now formed part of International Law. Fundamental rights on the other hand, remain in the realm of domestic law. They are fundamental because they have been guaranteed by the fundamental law of the country, that is, the Constitution.

- Uzoukwu v. Ezeonu II (1991) 6 NWLR (Pt. 200) 708 CA

2. There are certain rights pertaining to a person, which are neither fundamental nor justiceable in the courts. These may include, for instance, rights given by the Constitution under the Fundamental Objectives and Directive Principles of State Policy contained in Chapter III of the Constitution of the Federal Republic of Nigeria, 1979.

- *Uzoukwu v. Ezeonu II (1991) 6 NWLR (Pt. 200) 708 CA*

XIII
Injunction

13.1 Nature of Injunction

1. An injunction is an equitable order restraining the party to whom it is directed from doing the things specified in the order or requiring in exceptional situations the performance of a specified act. In other words, the order of injunction is available to restrain a party from the repetition or continuation of the particular wrongful act complained of, with the aim of preserving the *res* or subject matter of the litigation.

> - *Adenuga v. Odumeru (2001) 10 WRN 104 SC*
> - *Odutola v. Lawal (2001) 11 WRN 34 CA*

2. It is a fundamental rule that the courts will only grant an injunction to support a legal right. Where a plaintiff has no legal right recognised by the courts, there will be no power to grant an injunction. Thus, a plaintiff seeking an injunction must prove that he has a legal right which is being threatened.

> - *Obeya Memorial Specialist Hospital & Anor. v. A. - G., Fed. & Anor. (1987) 2 NSCC 961*
> - *Morohunfola v. Kwara Tech. (1990) 4 NWLR (Pt. 145) 506 SC*
> - *Kele v. Nwerebere (1998) 3 NWLR (Pt. 543) 515 SC*
> - *DykTrade Limited v. Omnia Nigeria Limited (2000) 7 SC (Pt. 1) 56*

3. A court will not grant an injunction to restrain an act already executed. This is because an injunction is not a remedy for an act, which has already been carried out.

> - *Ajewole v. Adetimo (1996) 2 NWLR (Pt. 431) 391 SC*

4. For the purpose of granting an order of injunction where a continuing wrong is established, the *status quo* means the position prevailing when the defendant embarked upon the activities sought to be restrained.

> - *Ayorinde v. A-G., Oyo State (1996) 3 NWLR (Pt. 434) 20 SC*

5. Before a court can grant an injunction, an applicant needs to show that he has a right which ought to be protected pending the determination of the substantive suit, and that there is a serious issue to be determined on the evidence before the court, and that the balance of convenience is on his side.

- *Akapo v. Hakeem-Habeeb (1992) 6 NWLR (Pt. 247) 266 SC*

6. It is trite that leave of court is not required to appeal against the grant or refusal of an injunction. This is because an appeal against injunction lies as of right from the High Court to the Court of Appeal.

- *Ilechukwu v. Iwugo (1989) 2 NWLR (Pt. 101) 99 CA*
- *Shell Pet. Dev. Co. (Nig.) Ltd v. Lawson-Jack (1998) 4 NWLR (Pt. 545) 249 CA*

7. In an application for injunction, the power of the court hearing it is discretionary, and the law enjoins the court to exercise the discretion judicially and judiciously, and where it is not so exercised, the appellate court will interfere.

- *Ayoola v. Baruwa (1999) 11 NWLR (Pt. 628) 595 CA*

8. By virtue of sections 6(6)(b) and 236(1) of the Constitution of the Federal Republic of Nigeria, 1979, an injunction can be made against the State.

- *Commissioner for Works, Benue v. Devcon Ltd (1988) 3 NWLR (Pt. 83) 407 SC*

9. Where an order of injunction was issued as an ancillary relief to a declaratory/substantive relief, which has been set aside, the order of injunction must fail, being ancillary to the declaration which has been set-aside by the court's judgment.

- *Akuneziri v. Okenwa (2001) 8 WRN 114 SC*

10. A plaintiff, in a claim for injunction, has the burden to prove that the balance of convenience is in his favour, and that the inconvenience he will suffer by the refusal of the injunction is greater than that which the defendant will suffer, if it is granted.

- *Ilechukwu v. Iwugo (1989) 2 NWLR (Pt. 101) 99 CA*
- *Total (Nig.) Plc. v. Efakpokire (1998) 5 NWLR (Pt. 549) 307 CA*

11. On a clear proof that a tort is committed against the plaintiff and the defendant intends to repeat such tortious act, the plaintiff will generally be entitled both to recover damages for injury sustained and to obtain an injunction to restrain the continuance or repetition of the injury in the future.

> - *Busari v. Edo State Civil Service Commission (1999) 4 NWLR (Pt. 599) 365 CA*

12. A court will not grant an injunction to restrain a publisher from publishing an article that has not yet been pronounced to be defamatory of a person. After publication, where the book is libelous, the applicant then has a cause of action.

> - *Reg. Trustees of AMORC v. Awoniyi (1991) 3 NWLR (Pt. 178) 245 CA*

13. Notwithstanding the provisions of section 30(1)(a) of the Companies and Allied Matters Act, 1990, in order to restrain the registration of a new company with a name alleged to be similar to that of an existing company as to be calculated to deceive, it is imperative for the court to consider the business carried on by the existing company, and what is intended to be carried on by the new company. Therefore, before an injunction could be granted to restrain a company from using a trade name, the new company must carry on the same business as the old company.

> - *Motor Manufacturers and Traders Society Ltd v. Motor Manufacturers and Traders Mutual Insurance Co. Ltd (1925) All E.R. 616*
>
> - *Daily-Need Pharm. Ind. v. Daily-Needs Ind. Ltd. (1997) 3 NWLR (Pt. 491) 99 CA*

14. An injunction will not be granted where the words complained of in the name of a company are universally used to describe an organisation or words which are descriptive of the plaintiff rather than his goods or trade.

> - *Niger Chemists Ltd v. Nigeria Chemists Ltd (1961) 1 All NLR 171*
>
> - *Daily-Need Pharm. Ind. v. Daily-Needs Ind. Ltd. (1997) 3 NWLR (Pt. 491) 99 CA*

15. Where a petition for winding up is commenced against a company and the company seeks to obtain an order of

interlocutory injunction to restrain the petitioner from commencing its winding up, the court in the determination of whether to restrain the petitioner or not has to consider whether the petition was brought in good faith and/or whether the petition proceeded upon doubtful rights, such as where the debt outstanding still remains unresolved, and also whether the ensuing publication of the winding up proceedings would be productive or cause irreparable damage to the other party.

  - *U.B.N. Ltd v. Tropic Foods Ltd (1992) 3 NWLR (Pt. 228) 231 CA*

16. Where a plaintiff has established that he is in possession, it is necessary for an order of injunction to be obtained to protect the possession in him.

  - *Ajero v. Ugorji (1999) 10 NWLR (Pt. 621) 1 SC*

17. Trespass being an action against possession, postulates that the plaintiff who claims damages and injunction for trespass must, inter alia, aver and prove that he is in physical and constructive possession and that the defendant infringed that possessory right.

  - *Lawson v. Ajibulu (1997) 6 NWLR (Pt. 507) 14 SC*

18. In a claim for declaration of title to land, damages for trespass and injunction, once the claims for title and damages for trespass fail, the claim for injunction must also fail for an injunction is not granted in vain.

  - *Lawson v. Ajibulu (1997) 6 NWLR (Pt. 507) 14 SC*

19. In a claim for damages for trespass and an injunction to restrain further trespass, once there is a finding of trespass, the claims for damages and injunction must be awarded.

  - *Olorunfemi v. Asho (1999) 1 NWLR (Pt. 585) 1 SC*

20. Whenever an injunction is granted and it appears that considerable damage would be done to the defendant pending appeal by the stoppage of his business, which could not be compensated in cost, the injunction is stayed on terms. An appellate court can and must intervene by granting a stay of execution of the injunctive order pending appeal.

  - *Josien Holdings Ltd. v. Lornamead Ltd (1995) 1 NWLR (Pt. 371) 254 SC*

- *G.M.C. (UK) Ltd. v. Medicair W/A Ltd. (1998) 2 NWLR (Pt. 536) 86 CA*

21. Just as in a stay of execution, a plaintiff who was unsuccessful in a lower court can apply for an injunction to protect his right arising from reliefs sought by him in the lower court pending the determination of an appeal he has lodged.

- *Onuzulike v. Commissioner for Special Duties, Anambra State (1990) 7 NWLR (Pt. 161) 252 CA*

- *Oyelami v. Mil. Adm., Osun State (1999) 8 NWLR (Pt. 613) 45 CA*

22. A court has the power, on the application of a respondent, to discharge an injunction where it becomes subsequently apparent that the injunction was founded on a decision, which was wrong in law. Also, an injunction may, by application to do so, be suspended.

- *Shell Pet. Dev. Co. (Nig.) Ltd v. Omu (1998) 9 NWLR (Pt. 567) 672 CA*

23. There are many grounds for the discharge of an injunction. These include, where the plaintiffs have not used their administrative powers that might have resolved the difficulty; where default has been made in giving security for costs; if the affidavit had not been filed when the injunction was moved; where an order for injunction was granted on a suppression or misrepresentation of material facts; where it was irregularly granted; if the plaintiff failed to attend to be cross-examined; and if there had been delay in complying with an undertaking to amend the writ by adding a party as plaintiff.

- *Nwakonobi v. Udeorah (1991) 9 NWLR (Pt. 213) 85 CA*

24. There are different kinds of injunction. These are namely: *ex-parte / interim* injunction, interlocutory injunction, perpetual injunction, mareva injunction, and Anton Piller injunction. Apart from interlocutory and perpetual injunctions, the rest have limited application and are conceived of being of extremely short duration.

- *G.M.C. (UK) Ltd v. Medicair W/A Ltd (1998) 2 NWLR (Pt. 536) 86 CA*

13.2 Ex-Parte Injunction

1. *Ex-parte* injunctions are for cases of real emergency or urgency where it is not possible to give notice of motion.

> - *Attamah v. Anglican Bishop of the Niger (1999) 13 NWLR (Pt. 633) 6 at 9 SC*

2. The courts in order to prevent abuse of the use of *ex-parte* order of injunction do not grant it unless in very urgent circumstances.

> - *Badejo v. Fed. Min of Education (1996) 8 NWLR (Pt. 464) 15 SC*

3. Where a party to be affected is present in court at the hearing of a motion for *ex-parte* injunction, the court has a duty to hear him before making its ruling on the motion.

> - *Adebisi v. Odukoya (1997) 11 NWLR (Pt. 527) 83 CA*

4. An *ex-parte* injunction does not usually subsist for a long time before the merit of the injunction is determined in an interlocutory proceeding upon a motion on notice. However, the party against whom such an order subsists reserves the right to move the court to discharge such *ex-parte* order of injunction even before the date named for the expiration of the order, or before the motion on notice comes up for hearing.

> - *Urhobo v. Oteri (1999) 2 NWLR (Pt. 589) 147 CA*

5. Where there is a delay in bringing an application for *ex-parte* injunction, and there has been insufficient explanation for such delay, the application will be refused, unless the applicant has an overwhelming case on the merits.

> - *Okechukwu v. Okechukwu (1989) 3 NWLR (Pt. 108) 234 CA*

6. The suppression and misrepresentation of material facts in an application for an *ex-parte* injunction is sufficient reason to have the *ex-parte* injunction discharged *ex debito justitiae* by the court.

> - *Okechukwu v. Okechukwu (1989) 3 NWLR (Pt. 108) 234 CA*

13.3 Interim Injunction

1. The object of an interim injunction is to maintain the *status quo* pending the motion on notice. Where the *status quo* ceases, the court is obliged to discharge the interim injunction notwithstanding that the substantive suit had not been withdrawn.

- *Orji v. Zaria Ind. Ltd (1992) 1 NWLR (Pt. 216) 124 SC*
- *Awofeso v. Oyenuga (1996) 7 NWLR (Pt. 460) 360 CA*

2. Ordinarily, where an interim injunction is considered desirable, the court does not grant it without an undertaking as to damages.

- *Anike v. Emehelu (1990) 1 NWLR (Pt. 128) 603 CA*
- *Wema Bank v. Adebowale (2001) 4 WRN 1 CA*

3. A court, without hearing the parties to a case, cannot make an order of interim injunction *suo motu*. The court, upon application properly filed before it by a party to the case can only make such order.

- *Ude v. Bassey (1991) 7 NWLR (Pt. 206) 771 CA*

4. It is an improper exercise of jurisdiction to make an interim order of injunction on an *ex-parte* application to last until the final determination of the substantive action.

- *Chief Land Officer v. Alor (1991) 4 NWLR (Pt. 187) 617 CA*

5. The effect of failure on the applicant's part to establish urgency in an application for interim/interlocutory injunction is that such an application would be refused by the court.

- *Ajewole v. Adetimo (1996) 2 NWLR (Pt. 431) 391 SC*

6. Where an application for interim injunction is filed in the court to restrain a party from doing an act or from continuing the act which the party has commenced before the application is filed in court, it behoves the party against whom the order of injunction is sought to accord respect to that court before which the application is pending so as not to foist upon the court a position of helplessness or paralysis.

- *Opara v. Ihejirika (1990) 6 NWLR (Pt. 156) 291 CA*

7. Pleadings are not necessary before an application for interim or interlocutory injunction can be brought or granted.

- *Opara v. Ihejirika (1990) 6 NWLR (Pt. 156) 291 CA*
- *A.C.B. Ltd v. Awogboro (1996) 3 NWLR (Pt. 437) 383 SC*

8. An injunction sought, pending the determination of the substantive suit can only be interlocutory and not interim, as an interim injunction is one that can be discharged during the pendency of the substantive action.

- *Globe Fishing Ind. Ltd v. Coker (1990) 7 NWLR (Pt. 162) 265 SC*

13.4 Interlocutory Injunction

1. An order of interlocutory injunction is one which a court of law grants on notice in a course or during the pendency of a matter, and which lasts until the final determination of the matter.

- *Ezebilo v. Chinwuba (1997) 7 NWLR (Pt. 511) 108 CA*

2. The purpose of an application for interlocutory injunction pending the determination of the substantive suit is to keep the parties in *status quo* in which they were before the judgment or act complained of.

- *Saraki v. Kotoye (1990) 4 NWLR (Pt. 143) 144 SC*
- *Globe Fishing Ind. Ltd. v. Coker (1990) 7 NWLR (Pt. 162) 265 SC*

3. In an application for interlocutory injunction, the first issue to be determined is whether there is a question of law or legal right or serious issue to be determined in the substantive action. There is no rule requiring an applicant to establish a *prima facie* case before he can get an interlocutory injunction, so long as the court is satisfied that his case is not frivolous or vexatious and that there is a serious question to be tried.

- *Ayorinde v. A-G, Oyo State (1996) 3 NWLR (Pt. 434) 20 SC*
- *A.C.B. Ltd. v. Awogboro (1996) 3 NWLR (Pt. 437) 383 SC*
- *Falomo v. Banigbe (1998) 7 NWLR (Pt. 559) 679 SC*

4. Before an applicant for interlocutory injunction can succeed, he must establish the following, namely: that there is a serious question to be tried in the substantive action; that the balance of convenience is on his side; that damages cannot be adequate compensation for his damage or injury if he succeeds at the end of the day; that his conduct is not reprehensible, for instance, that he is not liable for any delay; and that the injunction is necessary to preserve the *res*, which is in imminent danger of being destroyed.

> - *Commissioner for Works, Benue v. Devcon Ltd (1988) 3 NWLR (Pt. 83) 407 SC*
>
> - *Kotoye v. C.B.N. (1989) 1 NWLR (Pt. 98) 419 SC*
>
> - *Queen v. Adaroh (1999) 1 NWLR (Pt. 586) 330 CA*

5. The governing principle in considering the question of balance of convenience in an application for interlocutory injunction is whether, in case the applicant succeeds in his claim, he would not be adequately compensated by an award of damages against the respondent, and that the respondent is financially in a position to pay the damages awarded.

> - *Orji v. Zaria Ind. Ltd (1992) 1 NWLR (Pt. 216) 124 SC*
>
> - *Union Beverages Ltd. v. Pepsicola Int. Ltd. (1994) 3 NWLR (Pt. 330) 1 SC*

6. An interlocutory injunction may be granted in all cases in which it appears to the court to be just and convenient to do so. It is not granted as a matter of course. The remedy is entirely discretionary and the governing principles, depending on the facts and the issue in a given case, admit some element of flexibility. The discretion is however one that must be exercised judicially and judiciously.

> - *Ayorinde v. A-G, Oyo State (1996) 3 NWLR (Pt. 434) 20 SC*

7. The failure of an applicant for interlocutory injunction to give an undertaking as to damages does not render the order made, in the absence of such undertaking, incompetent. It only renders the order liable to be set aside and whether it will be set aside in any case will depend upon the facts of the particular case.

> - *Onyesoh v. Nnebedun (1992) 3 NWLR (Pt. 229) 315 at 323 SC*

8. An application for interlocutory injunction can be determined in the absence of pleading and oral evidence.

- *Mobil Oil (Nig.) Ltd. v. Agadaigho (1988) 2 NWLR (Pt. 77) 383 SC*

- *A.C.B. Ltd. v. Awogboro (1996) 3 NWLR (Pt. 437) 383 SC*

9. Where in an application for interlocutory injunction to restrain one party from doing an act, and the parties agree that the injunction may issue against all parties concerned or a definite case is made out that it is in the overall interest of justice that both parties should be restrained, the court would be entitled to issue such order. The court must however, clearly state the facts and circumstances which make it compelling and imperative to extend the order of injunction to both parties.

- *Falomo v. Banigbe (1998) 7 NWLR (Pt. 559) 679 SC*

10. Whenever it is possible to accelerate the hearing of a case, instead of wading through massive affidavits and hearing lengthy arguments on interlocutory injunction, the court should accelerate the hearing and decide finally on the rights of the parties.

- *Onyesoh v. Nnebedun (1992) 3 NWLR (Pt. 229) 315 SC*
- *Ezebilo v. Chinwuba (1997) 7 NWLR (Pt. 511) 108 CA*

11. An applicant for an interlocutory injunction must satisfy the court, if he is to succeed that there is a serious question to be tried, in addition to his satisfying the court that he has a right, which ought to be protected.

- *Union Beverages Ltd. v. Pepsicola Int. Ltd (1994) 3 NWLR (Pt. 330) 1 SC*

12. A plaintiff who claims only pecuniary damages ought not to be granted an interlocutory injunction.

- *Queen v. Adaroh (1999) 1 NWLR (Pt. 586) 330 CA*

13. A person applying for an interlocutory injunction must show the court clearly that he has an interest to be protected in the case. It follows, therefore, that a defendant who has not filed a

counter-claim will per se be deemed as having no interest to be protected if he applies to the court for an interlocutory injunction.

- *Ubani v. Ogolo (1998) 3 NWLR (Pt. 540) 120 CA*
- *Oyubu v. Akpobarojero (1998) 4 NWLR (Pt. 546) 422 CA*

14. Where a Judge dismisses an interlocutory motion for an injunction, he still has jurisdiction to grant the unsuccessful applicant an injunction pending an appeal against the dismissal. The fact that the interlocutory application for injunction was dismissed does not deprive him of the jurisdiction to grant the injunction pending appeal against his decision.

- *Okoya v. Santilli (1990) 2 NWLR (Pt. 131) 172 SC*

15. An application for an interlocutory injunction is not the same as that for a perpetual injunction. Whereas a perpetual injunction can only be granted after a trial, and the applicant has established his right and an actual or threatened infringement of it, an interlocutory injunction is granted pending the trial of the action in order to keep matters in *status quo* until the issues in controversy between the parties can be tried and determined. An applicant can therefore properly obtain an order of interlocutory injunction even though he has not made out a case that will necessarily entitle him to one of perpetual injunction.

- *Globe Fishing Ind. Ltd. v. Coker (1990) 7 NWLR (Pt. 162) 265 SC*

16. An order of interlocutory injunction cannot be made in respect of an area of land whose boundaries are not properly identified. Such an order may only be made and tied to a plan or to a clearly defined area but must be refused if the area of land to which it relates is uncertain. The onus is on the plaintiff who seeks a declaration of title to land and/or injunction to show clearly the area of land to which he claims. He may discharge this onus by oral description of the land in dispute, that any surveyor, acting on such description, can produce a plan of the land in issue. He may also file and tender before the trial court, an accurate survey plan of the land in dispute drawn to scale by a licensed surveyor reflecting all the features on the land and

showing clearly the boundaries, especially on the side in dispute.

- *Dabup v. Kolo (1993) 9 NWLR (Pt. 317) 254 SC*
- *Agba v. B.H. I. Holdings Ltd (1998) 1 NWLR (Pt. 535) 696 CA*
- *Adesanya v. Aderonmu (2000) 6 SC (Pt. II) 18 at 30-31*

17. It is a general principle of law that an interlocutory injunction or any other types of injunction should not be granted against a person who is not a party to litigation in court.

- *Fawehinmi v. N.B.A. (No. 1) (1989) 2 NWLR (Pt. 105) 494 SC*
- *Union Beverages Ltd v. Pepsicola Int. Ltd (1994) 3 NWLR (Pt. 330) 1 SC*
- *Onyekwulunne v. Ndulue (1997) 7 NWLR (Pt. 512) 250 CA*
- *Uzondu v. Uzondu (1997) 9 NWLR (Pt. 521) 466 CA*

18. In an application for the grant of interlocutory injunction pending the determination of the substantive claim, the judge has a duty to ensure that he does not in the determination of the application determine the same issues or rights that would arise for determination in the substantive suit. It is not proper for the court at that stage to express any opinion as to such rights, as such an opinion might give the impression that the court has made up its mind on the substantive issues on trial before it.

- *Akapo v. Hakeem-Habeeb (1992) 6 NWLR (Pt. 247) 266 SC*
- *A.C.B. Ltd. v. Awogboro (1996) 3 NWLR (Pt. 437) 383 SC*

19. It is trite that if a court lacks jurisdiction to hear a substantive suit, it would also lack jurisdiction to make an order of interlocutory injunction.

- *Uzondu v. Uzondu (1997) 9 NWLR (Pt. 521) 466 CA*

20. In an application for interlocutory injunction pending the determination of the substantive suit, the pertinent considerations are whether the claims are frivolous and whether a case is made out which requires to be tried. Where it seems to the court that a triable issue is made out, it has the discretion to

grant an injunction pending the determination of the substantive suit.

- *Globe Fishing Ind. Ltd. v. Coker (1990) 7 NWLR (Pt. 162) 265 SC*

13.5 Perpetual Injunction

1. A court will only grant a perpetual injunction at the suit of a plaintiff in support of a right known to law or equity. The plaintiff's conduct must also be taken into consideration in determining whether or not to grant the injunction.

- *Biyo v. Aku (1996) 1 NWLR (Pt. 422) 1 CA*
- *Afrotec v. MIA (2001) 6 WRN 65 SC*

2. A perpetual injunction can only be granted after a trial, when the applicant has established both his right and the actual or threatened infringement thereof.

- *Globe Fishing Ind. Ltd. v. Coker (1990) 7 NWLR (Pt. 162) 265 SC*

3. Perpetual injunction will be ordered, whenever the tort of trespass to property is committed, under two main circumstances, namely: where there would be an irreparable damage or if the act complained of would be destructive where an injunction to restrain it is not ordered; and where a failure to exercise the jurisdiction would lead to multiplicity of suits.

- *Onabanjo v. Efunpitan (1996) 7 NWLR (Pt. 463) 756 CA*

13.6 Mandatory Injunction

1. A mandatory injunction is a different type of injunction. It is positive in nature and is usually targeted upon a completed act unlike an order of interlocutory injunction, which is negative and restrictive in nature and is made to preserve the *res* pending litigation or to prevent breach.

- *C.B.N. v. U.T.B. (Nig.) Ltd (1996) 4 NWLR (Pt. 445) 694 CA*

- *Abubakar v. J.M.D.B. (1997) 10 NWLR (Pt. 524) 242 CA*

2. **Mandatory injunction may be granted in some of the following circumstances, namely: where the injury done to the plaintiff cannot be estimated and sufficiently compensated for by damages; where the injury to the plaintiff is so serious and material that the restoration of things to their former condition is the only way justice can be adequately done; where the injury complained of is in breach of an express agreement; where the act done is simple and can be easily remedied; and where the defendant attempts to foist upon the plaintiff a *fait accompli*.**

- *C.B.N. v. U.T.B. (Nig.) Ltd (1996) 4 NWLR (Pt. 445) 694 CA*
- *Abubakar v. J.M.D.B. (1997) 10 NWLR (Pt. 524) 242 CA*

3. **Mandatory injunction is usually targeted upon a completed act. It will lie to reverse a step already taken by a party to litigation. It may be made, for instance, to order a building which had been erected to be pulled down if it is established that the defendant erected it in order to foist upon the plaintiff a *fait accompli*, on having notice that an injunction was to be taken out against him.**

- *A.G., Anambra State v. Okafor (1992) 2 NWLR (Pt. 224) 396 SC*
- *Unipetrol (Nig.) Plc. v. Abubakar (1997) 6 NWLR (Pt. 509) 470 CA*

4. **Courts are slow to make an order of mandatory injunction in view of its irreversible nature. As such, the order should be made only in very special cases.**

- *Okefi v. Ogu (1996) 2 NWLR (Pt. 432) 603 CA*
- *A.- G., Anambra State v. Okafor (1992) 2 NWLR (Pt. 224) 396 SC*

5. **A mandatory injunction can be granted on an interlocutory application as well as at the hearing. However, in the absence of special circumstances, it will not normally be granted.**

- *C.B.N. v. U.T.B. (Nig.) Ltd (1996) 4 NWLR (Pt. 445) 694 CA*

13.7 Mareva Injunction

1. A mareva injunction is an anticipatory injunction which should be granted where it appears likely that the plaintiff would obtain judgment against the defendant for a certain or approximate sum; and there are reasons to believe that the defendant has assets within the jurisdiction of the court to meet the judgment, wholly or in part, but might deal with them so that they will not be available or traceable when judgment is given against him.

> - *Sotuminu v. Ocean Steamship (Nig.) Ltd (1992) 5 NWLR (Pt. 239) 1 SC*

2. By its very nature, a mareva injunction could be open to abuses. Before it could be granted, the applicant must show that he has a cause of action against the defendant which is justiciable; that there is a real and imminent risk of the defendant removing his assets from jurisdiction and thereby rendering nugatory any judgment which the plaintiff may obtain; that the applicant has made a full disclosure of all material facts relevant to the application; that he has given full particulars of the assets within the jurisdiction; that the balance of convenience is on the side of the applicant; and that he is prepared to give an undertaking as to damages. The mareva injunction would not be granted where the applicant fails to satisfy the court in any of the above pre-conditions.

> - *Sotuminu v. Ocean Steamship (Nig.) Ltd (1992) 5 NWLR (Pt. 239) 1 SC*
>
> - *Durojaiye v. Continental Feeders Nig. Ltd (2001) 14 WRN 141 CA*

3. A court of law is entitled to invoke its mareva jurisdiction by granting a mareva injunction where there is a danger or likelihood that the *res* will be destroyed, or damaged by the adverse party before the issues joined by the parties are heard on their merits.

> - *A.C.B. Ltd v. Awogboro (1991) 2 NWLR (Pt. 176) 711 CA*

XIV
Insurance Law

14.1 Meaning and Nature of Insurance Contract

1. A contract of insurance is a contract whereby one person called the "insurer" undertakes in return for agreed consideration called "premium" to pay another person called the "insured" a sum of money or its equivalent on the happening of a specific event. Most contracts of insurance are contracts of indemnity whereby the insurer agrees to compensate the insured for the loss that the latter may sustain through the happening of the event upon which the insurer's liability may arise.

   - *Liberty Ins. Co. Ltd v. John (1996) 1 NWLR (Pt. 423) 192 CA*

2. Any person who is capable of contracting may be the assured under a contract of insurance. Consequently, a minor may enter into a contract of insurance as the assured, if it is for his benefit, otherwise, the contract will not be binding upon him.

   - *Clements v. London and North Western RLY Co. (1894) 2 QB 482 CA*
   - *Imperial Life Insurance Co. v. Charlebois (1902) 2Z CLT 417*

3. A contract of insurance made by a person of unsound mind or drunken person is, in certain circumstances, voidable.

   - *Imperial Life Assurance of Canada v. Audeft (1912) 20 WLR 372*

4. Insurance contracts may be made without following a particular form. For instance, non-marine insurance contract can be made orally or by telephone or inferred from common course of business. Such oral or informal contracts are deemed to be subject to the usual terms of a standard cover.

   - *Esewe v. Asiomo & Anor (1974) 4 UILR 335*
   - *Murfitt v. Royal Insurance Co. (1922) 38 TLR 344*

- *Stockton v. Mason (1978) 1 WLR 1*
- *Salako v. Lombard Insurance Co. Ltd (1976) 10-12 CCHCJ 215*

5. Generally, the agent of an insurance company, in completing a proposal form for a proposer is acting on behalf of the proposer and not on behalf of the insurance company.

- *Newsholme Bros v. Road Transport and General Insurance Co. Ltd (1929) All ER Rep 442*
- *Northern Assurance Co. Ltd v. Idugboe (1966) 2 All N.L.R. 88 SC*

6. There is no insurance contract if premium is not paid. Thus, the receipt of an insurance premium is a condition precedent to a valid contract in respect of an insurance risk, unless the premium is paid in advance. Section 50(1) of the Insurance Decree No. 2 of 1997 considered.

- *Charles Chime v. United Nigeria Co. Ltd (1972) 2 ECSLR 808*
- *Irukwu v. T.M.I.B. (1997) 12 NWLR (Pt. 531) 113 CA*

7. The purpose of a cover note is to give insurance cover whilst the proposal is being considered until a policy is granted or refused.

- *Julien Praet et Cie SA v. HG Poland Ltd (1960) 1 Lloyd's Report 420*

8. Where the policy is illegal, the premium cannot be recovered if the insured is in *pari delicto*, that is, in equal fault with the insurers.

- *Harse v. Pearl Life Assurance Co. (1904) 90 LT 245*

9. Under a contract of insurance, where an offer is made and accepted on the condition that the insurer will not be indemnifying the assured until the premium is paid within a specified time, a contract of some sort may have been entered but the insurer will escape liability if the premium is not paid.

- *Liberty Ins. Co. Ltd v. John (1996) 1 NWLR (Pt. 423) 192 CA*

10. The rule is that, before a person can institute an action in court against an insurance company, such person must serve a

notice of his intention to sue on the company and, one clear month, at least from the date of the service of the said notice, must elapse before necessary court processes can be filed in court. This is *sine qua non* to taking out a writ of summons against an insurance company. Where he fails to comply with this provision, the suit shall be incompetent, and a court of law, for that reason, lacks jurisdictional power to entertain it. Section 58(1) and (2) of the Insurance Decree No. 58 of 1991 considered.

- *Liberty Ins. Co. Ltd v. John (1996) 1 NWLR (Pt. 423) 192 CA*

- *Irukwu v. T.M.I.B (1997) 12 NWLR (Pt. 531) 113 CA*

- *IAL 361 Inc. v. Mobil Oil (Nig.) Plc (1999) 5 NWLR (Pt. 601) 9 CA*

- *Aliyu v. Aturu (1999) 7 NWLR (Pt. 612) 536 CA*

14.2 Insurable Interest

1. Every contract of insurance requires an insurable interest to support it; otherwise it will be invalid.

- *Prudential Insurance Co. v. IRC (1904) 2 KB 658*

2. A person can sue on a policy of insurance, if only he has an insurable interest except, where, by special provisions, the law allows it, or where the policy is made for the sake of another person(s), or where a statute provides that the policy shall ensure for the benefit of somebody else.

- *Anctil v. Manufacturers Life Insurance Co. (1899) AC 604 PC*

3. A person has an insurable interest in a thing if he will be prejudiced by its loss. Thus, a person who would foreseeably suffer financial loss from the occurrence of an event has an insurable interest in the subject matter which it is sought to insure against the event. The event must either cast upon the assured a legally binding liability or it must affect a right of the assured, which is recognised and protected by the courts.

- *Lucena v. Craufurd (1806) 2 BOS & PNR 269*
- *Law Union and Rock Ins. v. Onuoha (1998) 6 NWLR (Pt.*

555) 576 CA

- *C.C.B. Ltd v. Nwokocha (1998) 9 NWLR (Pt. 564) 98 CA*

4. As a legal owner of a trust property, a trustee has an insurable interest in the trust property. Where the property in question is a house or similar structure, a policy covering the risk of fire, storm, or flood may be obtained.

- *Waters and Another v. Monarch Fire & Life Assurance Co. (1856) 25 LJ QB 102*

5. A registered company is a corporate entity and a juristic person with perpetual succession. Its personality is distinct from those of the shareholders. Consequently, the company's assets cannot be described as the assets of the shareholders. A shareholder has, therefore, no insurable interest in the assets of a company.

- *Macaura v. Northern Assurance Co. Ltd (1925) All ER Rep 51*

14.3 Disclosure of Material Facts

1. A contract of insurance is a contract of the utmost good faith (*uberrima fides*). It is the duty of the parties to help each other to come to a right conclusion. It is the duty of the assured not only to be honest and straightforward but also at all times to make a full disclosure of all material facts within his actual knowledge. In the same vein, it is the duty of the insurers and their agents to disclose all material facts within their knowledge.

- *London General Omnibus Co. Ltd v. Holloway (1911-13) All ER Rep 518*
- *Tabs Ass. Ltd v. Akwuzie Ind. (Nig.) Ltd (1995) 4 NWLR (Pt. 388) 223 CA*
- *U.N.I.C. v. U.C.I. C Ltd (1999) 3 NWLR (Pt. 593) 17 CA*

2. There is no duty on the insured to disclose facts which he could not reasonably be expected to know.

- *Joel v. Law Union and Crown Insurance Co. (1908) 99 LT 712 at 718 CA*

3. Although the insured is under a duty to disclose material facts to the insurer, he needs not disclose facts, which the insurer

knows or is deemed to know.

> - *Carter v. Boehm (1766) 3 Burr 1905*

4. There is sometimes no need to call evidence to prove the materiality of a fact, if the fact is so obvious in the eyes of the court. Thus, where an insured failed to disclose that he had been refused burglary insurance by another insurance company, the court held that in a case of burglary insurance, the fact was material.

> - *Glicksman v. Lancashire and General Assurance Co. Ltd (1925) 133 LT 688 CA*

5. The duty to disclose material facts is to last till the first premium is paid.

> - *Looker v. Law Union and Rock Insurance Co. Ltd (1927) 137 LT 648*

6. When the answers, which the proposer gives are inconsistent or unsatisfactory, and no further inquiries are made by the insurers, and a policy is issued, the insurers cannot repudiate liability on the ground that there has not been a full disclosure, for it will be held that they have waived their right to do so.

> - *Keeling v. Pearl Assurance Co. Ltd (1923) 129 LT 573*

7. Every material representation made by the assured or his agent during the negotiations and before the contract of insurance is concluded, must be true. If it is untrue, the insurer may avoid the contract.

> - *Demetriades and Company v. Northern Assurance Company (1925) 21 Ll L Rep. 265*
> - *Bamidele & Another v. Nigerian General Insurance Co. Ltd (1973) 3 UILR Part IV P. 418*

8. Where a space for an answer in a proposal form is left blank, the court may infer that the answer is a negative one.

> - *Roberts v. Avon Insurance Co. Ltd (1956) 2 Lloyd's Rep 240*

14.4 The Conduct of the Insured

1. Unless there is a provision in the policy to the contrary, for instance exception clause, an insurance company must indemnify an insured who is insured against third party risks, even when the third party's death has been caused by the drunkenness of the insured.

> - *James v. British General Insurance Co. Ltd (1927) All ER Rep 442*

2. The court will not enforce a contract of insurance in respect of goods, which are knowingly imported by the insured in breach of the customs regulations, because to enforce the contract would be contrary to public policy.

> - *Geismar v. Sun Alliance and London Insurance Ltd (1977) 3 All ER 570*

14.5 Claims

1. An insurer is liable for a loss proximately caused by a peril insured against. The cause, which is truly proximate, is that which is proximate in efficiency.

> *Leyland Shipping Co. Ltd v. Norwich Union Fire Insurance Society Ltd (1918-19) All ER Rep 443*

2. The "proximate cause" rule may be excluded by the use of the words 'directly or indirectly caused by'.

> - *Coxe v. Employers' Liability Assurance Corporation Ltd (1916) 114 LT 1180*

3. In all cases of claims, the burden of proving a loss is on the insured.

> - *Regina Fur Co. Ltd v. Bossom (1958) 2 Lloyd's Rep 425*

4. A victim of accident or tortious act, in addition to obtaining compensation for bodily injuries, may also claim compensation for his financial loss. The principle applicable here is that of restitution (*restitutio in integrum*).

> - *Livingstone v. Rawyards Coal Co. (1880) AC 25*

5. Under the tort law, "working life" is the basic criterion used in determining the assessment of damages in personal injury claims.

- *Ekrebe v. Efeizomor II (1993) 7 NWLR (Pt. 307) 588 CA*

6. Compensation for loss of earnings suffered by a victim of an accident is recoverable from the tortfeasor. The amount payable covers the actual loss of earnings already suffered and which is capable of being assessed as well as an estimated loss of future earnings.

- *Road v. Fates (1937) 3 All ER 442*

7. A plaintiff who brings an action under the Fatal Accident Law must give full particulars not only of the nature of the claim, but also of the person or persons for whom or on whose behalf he brings the action.

- *Okafor v. Nnodi (1963) 1 All NLR 373*

8. Where property is lost or destroyed by the wrongful act of another person other than the owner, the measure of damages payable to the owner is the value of the goods at the time and place of its destruction or loss.

- *Liesbosch Dredger v. SS Edision (1933) AC 448*

9. Where a claimant has been awarded reasonable and adequate compensation under specific heads, he is not entitled to compensation for "general damages" as such an award will lead to double compensation.

- *Soetan & Anor v. Ogunwo (1975) 6 SC 67*

10. An arbitration clause does not in any way oust the jurisdiction of the courts, nor does it prevent parties from putting in a claim in spite of its existence; it merely enables the other party to apply for a stay of legal proceedings pending such arbitration. Such application is made by way of motion on notice and even then the grant or refusal of a stay is within the court's discretion.

- *Alhaji Garba Oshifisan v. Leadway Assurance Co. Ltd (1977) N.N.L.R. 92, High Court of Borno State*

14.6 Life Assurance

1. A wife has insurable interest in the life of her husband and vice versa. It is not necessary for the wife to prove that she has any pecuniary interest in the life of her husband. The interest is presumed by law.

   - Griffths v. Fleming (1909) 1 KB 805

2. An employee, who is under contract to serve his employer for a fixed period, has an insurable interest in his employer's life up to the amount of his salary to be paid during the period.

   - Hebdon v. West (1863) 3 B & S 579

3. A creditor has an insurable interest in the life of his debtor to the extent of his debt.

   - Godsall v. Boldero (1807) 9 East 72

4. Suicide is a criminal offence. It is, therefore, an implied term of life assurance contract that the assured will not commit suicide.

   - Beresford v. Royal Insurance Co. Ltd (1938) AC 595

14.7 Fire and Property Insurance

1. To constitute a loss by "fire", actual ignition of the insured property is necessary. Destruction by heat is not enough.

   - Austin v. Drew (1815) 4 Camp 360

2. The fact that the proposer has suffered a loss by fire on a previous occasion is usually a material one, which he should disclose.

   - Condogians v. Guardian Assurance Co. Ltd (1921) 125 LT 610

3. Where a fire causes an explosion, which in its turn causes a second fire, the insured is entitled to recover for the loss caused by the first fire. An exception clause may preclude him from recovering for the loss caused by the second fire.

   - Stanley v. Western Insurance Co. (1868) 17 LT 513

14.8 Motor Insurance

1. Drivers of motor vehicles owe a duty of care to other users of the road and are, therefore liable for any injury or damage which they may cause to other road users as a result of their negligence or recklessness.

> *- Nance v. British Columbia Railway Co. Ltd (1915) A.C. 601 at 611*

2. A person who leaves an unlighted obstruction on a road at night may be liable for negligence. It may not avail the defaulting party to argue that a careful driver ought to see the obstruction and must therefore be liable for contributory negligence.

> *- Adams v. Ibadan District Council (1961) WRNLR 67*

3. If the condition on a road is adverse, for example, as a result of down pour, a motorist ought to adjust his driving and exercise greater caution. Indeed, if necessary, he must stop altogether if it is too dangerous to proceed.

> *- Thompson & Another v. Adefope (1969) 1 All NLR 322*

4. In considering the tortious liability of a motorist, evidence of conviction for motoring offence arising out of an accident which later becomes the subject of civil litigation to which that person is a party is inadmissible in a civil trial. The civil court must base its findings on the facts placed before it without any regard to the proceedings before another court or tribunal.

> *- Oyewole v. Kelani (1948) 12 WACA 327*

5. The measure of damages where there is a total loss of vehicle belonging to a third party is the value of the vehicle at the time of the accident, in addition to a further sum as would compensate the owner for loss of earning and the inconvenience experienced by him for being without a vehicle during the period reasonably required for procuring another vehicle.

> *- Okosun v. Katsina and Another (1976) 8 CCHCJ 2225*

6. Where a claim is based on cost of repairs of a vehicle, a plaintiff would be entitled to not only cost of repairs but also the amount of income lost to the plaintiff, if the vehicle was a commercial vehicle for the period when the vehicle was under repairs. If

the period of repairs claimed was unreasonably long the court will not award for the whole period, but for only a reasonable period that would mitigate the plaintiff's losses.

> - *Palm Beach Insurance Co. Ltd v. Bruhns (1997) 9 NWLR (Pt. 519) 80 CA*

7. Normally, contracts of insurance which provide cover for loss or damage are construed so as to cover only the loss of or damage to the subject matter of the insurance itself. Thus, loss of profit and other consequential losses such as loss of rents where a house is burnt down or loss of salary after an accident are not covered unless expressly stipulated.

> - *F.B.N. Plc v. Abba (1998) 10 NWLR (Pt. 569) 227 CA*

8. A tripartite agreement is one to which there are three parties, namely the owner of the car, the repairer and the insurer. Thus, in a situation where the owner of a vehicle takes it to a repairer for repairs and indicates that the cost of repairs would be settled by the insurer and introduces his said insurer to the repairer, there exists a tripartite contract involving the owner of the vehicle, the repairer and the insurer and each can acquire rights and come under obligations thereunder.

> - *J.E. Oshevire Ltd v. Tripoli Motors (1997) 5 NWLR (Pt. 503) 1 SC*

14.9 Marine Insurance

1. As a general rule, a contract of marine insurance is not admissible in evidence unless it is embodied in a marine policy in accordance with the form in the schedule to the Marine Insurance Act. This general rule is, however, subject to the provisions of any statute in force. Section 24(1) of the Marine Insurance Act, 1961 considered.

> - *Jessica Trading Co. Ltd v. Bendel Ins. Co. Ltd (1996) 10 NWLR (Pt. 476) 1 SC*

2. There is a distinction between a "'voyage policy" and a "time policy" of Marine Insurance. Where the contract is to insure the subject matters "at and from" or from one place to another or

others, the policy is called a voyage policy; where the contract is to insure the subject matter for a definite period of time the policy is called time policy. It should be noted, however, that a contract for a voyage policy and contract for time policy are not mutually exclusive. Thus, a contract for both voyage and time may be included in the same policy.

> *- Jessica Trading Co. Ltd v. Bendel Ins. Co. Ltd (1996) 10 NWLR (Pt. 476) 1 SC*

3. The general rule is that where the place of departure is specified in an insurance policy, and the ship instead of sailing from that place, sails from any other place, the risk does not attach, nor does it usually attach when the destination is specified in the policy, and the ship, instead of sailing for that destination, sails for another.

> *- Edokpolor & Co. Ltd v. Bendel Insurance Co. Ltd. (1997) 2 NWLR (Pt. 486) 131 SC*

4. To succeed in an action under a voyage policy, the insured has a duty to establish that the vessel sailed from the port of loading or departure as stipulated in the policy of insurance. The burden of proving, therefore, that there was alteration of port of departure or loading under section 44 of the Marine Insurance Act, 1961 would fall on the insurer.

> *- Edokpolor & Co. Ltd v. Bendel Insurance Co. Ltd. (1997) 2 NWLR (Pt. 486) 131 SC*

XV
International Law

15.1 Sources of International Law

1. The sources of international law are namely: international conventions, whether general or particular, establishing rules expressly recognised by the contesting States; international custom, as evidence of a general practice accepted as law; the general principles of law recognised by civilised nations; judicial decisions; and the teaching of qualified publicists.

> - *Article 38(1) of the I.C.J. Charter*
> - *Asylum Case: Columbia v. Peru (1950) I.C.J. Rep. p. 266*
> - *Anglo-Norwegian Fisheries Case (UK v. Norway) (1951)*
>   *I.C.J. Rep. p. 116*

2. Custom has been described as a constant and uniform usage, accepted as law.

> - *Asylum Case: Columbia v. Peru (1950) I.C.J. Rep. p. 266*

3. The recognition of a particular rule of international law by a large number of States raises the presumption that the rule is generally recognised. Such a rule will be binding on States generally and an individual State may only oppose its application by showing that it has persistently objected to the rule from the date of its first formulation.

> - *Anglo-Norwegian Fisheries Case (UK v. Norway) (1951)*
>   *I.C.J. Rep. p. 116*

4. The rule is that a State cannot rely upon the provisions or deficiencies of its municipal law to avoid its obligations under international law.

> - *Alabama Claims Arbitration (1872) Moore, I Int. Arb. 495*

5. The principle of primacy of international law over municipal law before international tribunals applies to all aspects of a State municipal law, its constitutional provisions, its ordinary legislation and to the decisions of its courts.

> - *UN Headquarters Agreement Case (1988) I.C.J. Rep.*

6. The fact that an international treaty, like the African Charter on Human and Peoples' Rights is superior to municipal laws on questions of human rights does not derogate from the sovereignty of a State as a sovereign entity.

> - *Comptroller of Nigerian Prisons v. Adekanye (1999) 10 NWLR (Pt. 623) 400 at 407 CA*

7. One of the attributes of a nation State under international law is the competence to make laws within its defined borders. However, the State may sometimes voluntarily surrender aspects of its sovereignty for the collective good of a larger community of States. The true import of this voluntary act of surrender is the assertion of the sovereignty of the nation State concerned. It is only a truly sovereign nation State that can limit its sovereignty.

> - *Comptroller of Nigerian Prisons v. Adekanye (1999) 10 NWLR (Pt. 623) 400 at 407 CA*

15.2 *International Personality*

1. The traditional view is that only States are subjects of international law. They alone are capable of possessing international rights and duties and they alone have the capacity to maintain those rights by bringing international claims.

> - *The Nuremberg Trial, Comd. 6964 (1946) p. 13*

2. The State as a person of international law should possess the following qualifications, namely: a permanent population; a defined territory; government; and capacity to enter into relations with other States.

> - *Article 1 of the Montevideo Convention on Rights and Duties of States 1933*

3. International organisations, such as the United Nations are subjects of international law and capable of possessing international rights and duties and they have capacity to maintain their rights by bringing international claims.

> - *Reparation for Injuries Suffered in the Service of the United Nations Case (1949) I.C.J. Rep. 174*

4. Individuals who commit crimes against humanity or war crimes and are brought before an international tribunal for trial may have some degree of international personality.

  - *The Nuremberg Trial, Comd. 6964 (1946) p. 13*

15.3 Sovereignty and Equality of States

1. All States are equal in law, despite their obvious inequalities in other respects, such as inequality of size, wealth, population, strength or degree of civilisation.

  - *Article 2(1) of the Charter of the United Nations*

2. It is well established in international law that no State can, without its consent be compelled to submit its dispute, with other States either to mediation or to arbitration, or to any other kind of pacific settlement.

  - *Eastern Carelia Case (1923) P.C.I.J. Rep. Series B No. 5*

3. Territorial sovereignty is the right to exercise therein, to the exclusion of any other State, the functions of a sovereign.

  - *Island of Palms Case: The Netherlands v. US (1928) 2 RIAA 829*

4. A State has the exclusive right of sovereignty over any additions made to its territory as a result of silting or other deposits or resulting from the formation of island within its territorial waters.

  - *Louisiana v. Mississipi (1931) United States Supreme Court Judgment*

5. Cession is the transfer of territory, usually by treaty, from one State to another. In order to effect a valid cession there should normally be both a treaty and actual transfer of possession.

  - *Iloilo Case (1925) cited in Public Int. Law Textbook 15Ed. 1993 p.85 (MacLean)*

6. The territory of a State shall not be the object of military occupation resulting from the use of force in contravention of the provisions of the United Nations Charter. Similarly, the territory of a State shall not be the object of acquisition by

another State resulting from the threat or use of force.

> - UN Security Council Resolution 662 (1990) of 9 August, 1990

15.4 State Jurisdiction

1. In international law the presumption is that a statute is presumed to apply only within the territorial jurisdiction of the promulgating State unless the contrary intent is stated.

> - AM-Banana Co. v. United Fruit Co., U.S. Supreme Court 1909

2. A State cannot take measures on the territory of another State by way of enforcement of its national laws without that other State's consent. Consequently, neither can a person be arrested nor police investigations be mounted, nor summonses be served on the territory of another State except under the terms of a treaty or with the other State's consent.

> - A.G., of Israel v. Eichmann (1962) 36 I.L.R 5

3. Every State has jurisdiction over crimes committed in its own territory.

> - Lotus Case: France v. Turkey (1927) P.C.I.J. Rep. Series A No. 10

4. A State may prosecute its nationals in its territory for crimes committed anywhere in the world. Similarly, a State may assume jurisdiction to punish within its territory acts prejudicial to its security even where they are committed by aliens abroad. Such acts, include spying, plots to overthrow the government, forging currency, immigration and economic offences.

> - Article 7 of the French Criminal Code
> - Joyce v. D.P.P. (1946) A.C. 347

5. Every person who voluntarily brings himself within the jurisdiction of a State, whether permanently or temporarily, is subject to the operation of the laws of that State whether he is a citizen or a mere resident, so long as, in the case of an alien resident, no principle of customary or treaty law is contravened.

- *U.S. (Gelbrunk Claim) v. Salvador (1902) U.S. Foreign Relation p. 877*

15.5 Nationality

1. Nationality is defined as a legal bond between a State and its subject having as its basis a social fact of attachment, a genuine connection of existence and sentiments, together with the existence of reciprocal rights and duties.

   - *Nottebohm Case: Liechtenstein v. Guatemala (1955) I.C.J. Rep. p. 4*

2. The laws of every State provide for the acquisition of its nationality. Generally, two principles are applied. These are *jus sanguinis* (acquisition of nationality by descent or by being born of parents who are nationals) and *jus soli* (acquisition of nationality by being born in the territory of the State itself).

   - *Section 25 of the 1999 Constitution of the Federal Republic of Nigeria*
   - *British Nationality Act 1981*

3. Ships have the nationality of the State whose flag they fly. There must exist a genuine link between the State and the ship.

   - *Article 91 of the 1982 Law of the Sea Convention*

4. A ship which sails under the flags of two or more States, using them according to convenience, may not be able to claim any of the nationalities of the States in question, and may be assimilated to a ship without nationality.

   - *Article 91 of the 1982 Law of the Sea Convention*

5. Aircraft have the nationality of the State in which they are registered.

   - *Article 17 of the Chicago Convention of International Civil Aviation, 1944*

6. A contracting State which is not the State of registration may not interfere with an aircraft in flight in order to exercise its criminal jurisdiction over an offence committed on board the

aircraft except in the following cases, namely: where the offence has effect on the territory of such State; where the offence has been committed by or against a national or permanent resident of such State; where the offence consists of a breach of any rules or regulations relating to the flight or manoeuvre of aircraft in force in such State; and where the exercise of jurisdiction is necessary to ensure the observance of any obligation of such State under multilateral international agreement.

> - *Article 4 of the Chicago Convention of International Civil Aviation 1944*

7. The general rule is that a corporation has the nationality of the State under the laws of which it has its virgin incorporation and in whose territory it has its registered office.

> - *Barcelona Traction, Light and Power Co Case: Belgium v. Spain (1970) I.C.J. Rep. p. 3*

8. A State does not commit an international delinquency in inflicting an injury upon an individual lacking nationality and consequently, no State is empowered to intervene or complain on his behalf either before or after the injury.

> - *Dickson Car Wheel Company Case: United States v. Mexico (1931) 4 R.I.A.A. 669*

15.6 Immunity from Jurisdiction

1. There are certain categories of persons and bodies to whom international law accords immunity from jurisdiction of municipal courts. The two principal categories are: foreign States (State immunity) and diplomatic agents (diplomatic immunity)

> - *The Schooner Exchange v. McFadden (1812) 7 Cranch 116*

2. The basic principle behind the doctrine of State immunity is that since States are independent and equal they should not be subjected to the jurisdiction of other States without their consent.

> - *De Haber v. Queen of Portugal (1851) 17 Q.B. 196*

3. State immunity ensures that a State cannot be impleaded before the courts of another State without its consent.

> - *Mighell v. Sultan of Johore L.R. (1984) 1 Q.B.D. 149*
> - *Kramer Italo Ltd v. The Government of the Kingdom of Belgium (1987), Suit No. LD/1689/86, High Court of Lagos State Judgment*

4. State immunity is rooted upon two principles of international law namely: the principle of *par in parem non-habet jurisdictionem*, that is, legal persons of equal standing cannot have their disputes settled in the courts of one of them, and the principle of non-intervention in the internal affairs of other States.

> - *Buck v. A.-G., (1965) Ch. 745*

5. The law is that a Head of State loses his State immunity when he ceased to be Head of State. However, he cannot be held liable in respect of acts performed as part of his official duties when he was in office as Head of State.

> - *R v. Bow Street Metropolitan Stipendiary Magistrate & Ors, Ex-parte Pinochet Ugarte (No. 3) (1999) 2 WLR 827*

6. The new rule of international law is to the effect that a claim to State immunity is not absolute. Therefore, a former Head of State who committed crimes against humanity such as torture, war crimes or any other international crimes whether those crimes were acts done in the cause of his official duties or not, shall be liable for prosecution before any court of competent jurisdiction.

> - *R v. Bow Street Metropolitan Stipendiary Magistrate & Ors, Ex-parte Pinochet Ugarte (No. 3) (1999) 2 WLR 827*

7. There is a distinction between acts *jure imperii* (acts of a sovereign nature) and acts *jure gestionis* (acts of a commercial nature). While absolute immunity would be granted in respect of act jure *imperii*, an act of a commercial nature would not attract immunity. This approach is known as the doctrine of restrictive immunity.

> - *Trendtex Trading Corp. v. Central Bank of Nigeria (1977) Q.B. 527*

8. The person of a diplomatic agent shall be inviolable. He shall

not be liable to any form of arrest or detention. The receiving State shall treat him with due respect and shall take all appropriate steps to prevent any attack on his person, freedom or dignity.

> - Article 29 of the Vienna Convention on Diplomatic Relations 1961

9. The premises of a sovereign mission shall be inviolable. The agents of the receiving State may not enter them, except with the consent of the Head of the mission. Similarly, the premises of the mission, their furnishings and other property thereon and the means of transport of the mission shall be immuned from search, requisition, attachment or execution.

> - Article 22 of the Vienna Convention on Diplomatic Relations 1961
> - Hostage Case: US v. Iran (1980) I.C.J. Rep. p. 3

10. Foreign diplomats and their families are not entitled to diplomatic immunity, or the right to residence or to expedited immigration procedure, after the expiry of their secondment to their mission.

> - R v. Secretary of State for the Home Department, Ex-parte Bagga (1990) 3 W.L.R. 1013

11. A diplomatic agent has diplomatic immunity only from the time the receiving State accepts him as *persona grata*, and not from the time he is appointed.

> - R v. Lambeth JJ, Ex-parte Yusufu (1985) Crim. L. R. 510 Q.B.D.

15.7 Extradition and Asylum

1. A person who is suspected to have committed a crime may seek refuge in a State which has no jurisdictional competence to try him, or is unwilling to try him in respect of the crimes committed by him within the territory of another State. International law allows the State in which a suspected or convicted criminal has sought refuge to extradite him by surrendering him to the State which has jurisdiction to try him.

However, in the absence of a treaty of extradition between the States concerned, there is no duty under customary international law to extradite.

- *The United Kingdom Extradition Act 1989*

- *M v. Secretary of State for the Home Department (1995) Times 7 November (Court of Appeal: Millett and Ward LJJ)*

- *R v. Governor of Brixton Prison, Ex-parte Levin (1996) Times 11 March (Queen's Bench Division: Beldam LJ and Morison J)*

- *In the Matter of Chetta (1996) Times 11 July (Queen's Bench Division: Henry LJ and Ebsworth J)*

- *R v. Bow Street Metropolitan Stipendiary Magistrate & Ors, Ex-parte Pinochet Ugarte (No. 3) (1999) 2 WLR 837*

2. Everyone has the right to seek asylum in other countries from persecution. This right may not be invoked in the case of prosecutions genuinely arising from non-political crimes or from acts contrary to the purposes and principles of the United Nations.

- *Article 14 of the Universal Declaration of Human Rights 1948*

- *R v. Special Adjudicator Ex-parte Babatinca (1995) Imm AR 484 (Queen's Bench Division: Turner J)*

- *R v. Secretary of State for Home Department, Ex-parte Mehari (1944) Imm AR 151*

- *Sekhon v. Secretary of State for the Home Department (1955) Imm AR 507 (Court of Appeal: Stuart-Smith, Hobhouse and Phill LJJ)*

3. There is no rule of international customary law that recognises the right of a person to seek asylum on diplomatic premises, on board foreign warships or other public vessels merely for reasons of political expediency.

- *Montevideo Conventions on Political Asylum, 1933 and 1939*

- *Asylum Case: Columbia v. Peru (1950) ICJ Reports p. 266*

15.8 State Responsibility

1. All States are responsible in law for their illegal acts.

> - *Spanish Zones of Morocco Claims: Great Britain v. Spain (1925) 2 R.I.A.A. 615*

2. The conduct of an organ of an insurrectional movement, which is established in the territory of a State or in any other territory under its administration shall not be considered as an act of that State under international law.

> - *Article 14 of the International Law Commission Draft Articles on State Responsibility*
> - *Samaggio Case: Italy v. Venezuela (1903) 10 R.I.A.A. 499*
> - *Short v. Iran (U.S. v. Iran) (1987) 16 Iran-U.S.C.T.R. 76*

3. The conduct of an organ of a State empowered to exercise elements of the governmental authority, and such organ having acted in that capacity, shall be considered as an act of the State under international law even if, in the particular case, the organ exceeded its competence according to international law or contravened instructions concerning its activity.

> - *Article 10 of the International Law Commission Draft Articles on State Responsibility*
> - *Youmans Claim: United States v. Mexico (1926) 4 R.I.A.A. 110*

4. A State is responsible for the acts of its security services.

> - *Rainbow Warrior Case (1987) 26 I.L.M. 1346*
> - *Yeager v. Iran (U.S. v. Iran) (1987) 17 Iran-U.S.C.T.R. 92*

5. As a general rule, if a State, through the activities of its organs or representative commits a wrongful act against the person or property of a foreign national within its territory, then that act will *prima facie* constitute a breach of international law.

> - *Massey Case: US v. Mexico (1927) 4 R.I.A.A. 155*
> - *Fisheries Jurisdiction Case: UK v. Iceland (Jurisdiction) (1973) I.C.J. Rep. p. 3*

6. States may be held responsible for *ultra vires* acts of their officials if committed within the scope of their apparent authority.

> - *Union Bridge Company Claim: United States v. Great Britain (1924) 6 R.I.A.A. 138*

7. Where persons employed by government abused the governmental powers entrusted to them, their State may be liable.

> - *Caire Claim: France v. Mexico (1929) 5 R.I.A.A. 516*

8. The conduct of a person or a group of persons not acting on behalf of the State shall not be considered as an act of the State under international law. However, if it is subsequently established that the person(s) were in fact acting on behalf of the State, where for instance, the State adopts the acts in question, then responsibility will arise.

> - *Article 11 of the International Law Commission Draft Articles on State Responsibility*
> - *Hostage Case: US v. Iran (1980) I.C.J. Rep. p. 3*

9. If a State, through its acts or omissions, is the direct cause of damage to the property of a foreign State, then the State is liable to pay reparation for the damage so caused.

> - *Corfu Channel Case: United Kingdom v. Albania (1949) I.C.J. Rep. p. 15*

10. Failure to respect the territorial rights of another State may occur in a number of ways namely: invasion or other use of force against a State; the unlawful arrest of a wanted criminal on the territory of another State; illegal flights in the airspace of another State; the carrying out of activities in the territorial waters of a State; and by allowing toxic fumes to escape into the territory of another State.

> - *Article 2(4) of the Charter of the United Nations*
> - *Eichmann Case (1962) 36 I.L.R. 5*
> - *U-2 Incident of May 1960*
> - *Corfu Channel Case (Merits): United Kingdom v. Albania (1949) I.C.J. Rep. p. 15*
> - *Trial Smelter Arbitration: United States v. Canada (1938 and 1941) 3 R.I.A.A. 1905*

11. It is an elementary principle of international law that a State

is entitled to protect its subjects, when injured by acts contrary to international law committed by another State, from whom they have been unable to obtain satisfaction through the ordinary channels. By taking up the case of one of its subjects and by resorting to diplomatic action or international judicial proceedings on his behalf, a State is in reality asserting its own right, that is, its right to ensure, in the person of its subjects, respect for the rules of international law.

> - *Mavronmmatis Palestine Concessions Case (Jurisdiction): Greece v. United Kingdom (1924) P.C.I.J. Rep. Series A No. 2 p. 12*

12. One of the rights possessed by the supreme power in every State is the right to refuse to permit an alien to enter that State, to formulate the conditions for entry, and to expel or deport from the State, at pleasure, even a friendly alien, especially if it considers his presence in the State is detrimental to its peace, order and good government, or to its social or internal interests.

> - *A.-G., of Canada v. Cain (1906) A.C. 542*

13. Although it is generally agreed that expropriation of foreign property by a State is lawful, the wide divergence of political and economic beliefs among States has resulted in little agreement as to the rules to be applied in cases of expropriation. The developing States believe the matter should be left to the expropriating State to decide in accordance with its national law. Western capital exporting States have, however, advocated an international minimum standard based on three principles of non-discrimination, the principle that the expropriation must be for a public purpose; and the principle that expropriation must be followed by adequate compensation.

> - *Certain German Interests in Polish Upper Silesia Case (1926) P.C.I.J. Rep. Series A No. 7 p. 22*
> - *BP v. Libya (1974) 53 I.L.R. 297*
> - *LIAMCO v. Libya Case (1981) 20 I.L.M. 1*
> - *Aminoil v. Kuwait (1982) 21 I.L.M. 976*

14. If a host State expropriates foreign owned property contrary to international law, it will be liable in international law to the State of nationality of the injured party. However, international law does not prohibit expropriation of foreign property.

- O'keefe (1976) 25 I.C.L.Q. 329

15. Nationalisation, expropriation or requisitioning shall be based on grounds or reasons of public utility, security or the national interests which are recognised as overriding purely individual or private interests, both domestic and foreign. In such cases, the owner shall be paid appriopriate compensation in accordance with the rules in force in the State taking such measures in the exercise of its sovereignty and in accordance with international law. In any case, where the question of compensation gives rise to a controversy, the national jurisdiction of the State taking such measures shall be exhausted. However, upon agreement by sovereign States and other parties concerned, settlement of the dispute should be made through arbitration or international adjudication.

- The General Assembly Resolution on Permanent Sovereignty over Natural Resources (1962) (GAR 1803)

16. In order to nationalise, expropriate or transfer ownership of foreign property adequate compensation should be paid by the State adopting such measures, taking into account its relevant laws and regulations and all circumstances that the State considers pertinent. In any case, where the question of compensation gives rise to a controversy, it shall be settled under the domestic laws of the nationalising State and by its tribunals, unless it is freely and mutually agreed by all States concerned that peaceful means be sought on the basis of the sovereign equality of States and in accordance with the principle of free choice of means.

- Article 2(c) of the Charter of Economic Rights and Duties of States (1974) (GAR 3281)

17. Generally, a State cannot intervene on behalf of a foreign corporation solely on the basis that some of its nationals are shareholders in the company. The shareholders must rely upon the diplomatic protection available to the corporation itself.

- Barcelona Traction, Light and Power Co. Case: Belgium v. Spain (1970) I.C.J. Rep. p. 3

18. It is a general rule of international law that it is the national State of a company concerned which is entitled to exercise diplomatic protection and seek redress for an international wrong done to the company.

> - *Barcelona Traction, Light and Power Co. Case: Belgium v. Spain (1970) I.C.J. Rep. p. 3*

19. It is an established principle of international law that a claim brought by a State on behalf of its national will not be admissible before an international tribunal unless the foreign national has exhausted all legal remedies available to him under the local courts of the defendant State.

> - *Aerial Incident of 27th July, 1955 Case (1960) I.C.J. Rep. p. 146*

20. Where a foreign national fails to present his claim effectively or pursue it fully there will be no exhaustion of local remedies.

> - *Ambatielos Arbitration: Greece v. United Kingdom (1956) 12 R.I.A.A. 83*

21. Generally, local remedies will not be exhausted until the injured party has pursued his claim through the various channels of appeal available to him under the municipal law. Until the highest appellate tribunal determines the issue, the local remedies are not exhausted. However, there is no need to resort to the municipal courts if the result would be a repetition of a decision already given.

> - *Panevezys Saldutiskis Railway Case: Estonia v. Lithuania (1939) PCIJ Rep Series A/B ND 76*

22. If the conditions within the State are such that the processes available for pursuing local remedies are corrupt or insufficient and unreliable, a foreign national may be excused of recourse to such processes. In other words, a claimant in a foreign State is not required to exhaust justice in such State when there is no justice to exhaust.

> - *Robert E. Brown Case: United States v. Great Britain (1923) 6 R.I.A.A. 120*

23. Where a claim arises out of interference with property, the amount of the award depends not only upon the value of the property but also upon the degree of interference.

> - *Union Bridge Company Claim: United State v. Great Britain (1924) 6 R.I.A.A. 138*

24. Where there has been a denial of justice, the value of the award may depend upon the degree of misconduct by the respondent State, that is, the degree of shock, outrage, and suffering inflicted upon the claimants by the wrongful acts.

- *Maal Case: Netherlands v. Venezuela (1903), RIAA, 10 p.730*

15.9 Treatment of Aliens

1. States have adopted two approaches in the treatment of nationals of other States. The first approach which developed States of Western Europe and North America have generally supported is to the effect that there is an international minimum standard of treatment which must be accorded aliens by all States irrespective of how they treat their own nationals. The second approach, the standard of national treatment which is supported by the developing countries is to the effect that aliens are not entitled to more favourable treatment than that enjoyed by the nationals of the State concerned.

- *Neer Claim: United States v. Mexico (1926) 4 R.I.A.A. 60*
- *Roberts Claim: United States v. Mexico (1926) 4 R.I.A.A. 77*

2. An alien who finds himself in a country other than his own, is considered to have cast in his lot with the citizens of that State, subject always that no principle of international law protecting the alien is contravened.

- *U.S. (Gelbrunk Claim) v. Salvador (1902) U.S. Foreign Relations p. 877*

15.10 Remedies under International Law

1. Potential remedies available under international law include satisfaction, declaration, injunction, restitution and damages.

- *Chorzow Factory Case (Indemnity) (Merits): Germany v. Poland (1927) PCIJ Rep Series A No. 17*

- *I'M Alone Case: Canada v. U.S. (1935) 3 R.I.A.A. 1609*
- *Borchgrave Case: Belgium v. Spain (1937) PCIJ Rep. Series A/B No. 71*
- *Corfu Channel Case (Merits): U.K. v. Albania (1949) ICJ Report p. 4*
- *Nuclear Test Case: Australia v. France; New Zealand v. France (1974) ICJ Report pp. 253, 457*

2. Satisfaction has been defined as any measure which the author of a breach of duty is bound to take under an agreement by the parties to a dispute, apart from restitution or compensation. Satisfaction may take the form of apology, payment of an indemnity, the punishment of the individuals concerned, or the taking of measures to prevent a recurrence of the harm.

- *Borchgrave Case: Belgium v. Spain (1937) PCIJ Rep Series A/B No. 71*

3. A declaration by a court or tribunal that a State has acted illegally may in itself be a sufficient satisfaction.

- *Corfu Channel Case (Merits): U.K. v. Albania (1949) ICJ Rep. p. 4*

4. The International Court of Justice has power under its statute to grant interim measure of protection. It may, for instance, enjoin a party from taking any steps, which may prejudice the position of the other party to the dispute before the case can be heard on its merits.

- *Nuclear Test Cases: Australia v. France; New Zealand v. France (1974) ICJ Rep. pp.253, 457*

5. Reparation must, as far as possible, wipe out all the consequences of the illegal act and re-establish the situation which would, in all probability, have existed if that act had not been committed.

- *Chorzow Factory Case (Indemnity) (Merits): Germany v. Poland (1928) PCIJ Rep. Series A No. 17 p.29*

6. Damages may be awarded to compensate for the actual loss resulting from the damage or injury suffered.

- *Corfu Channel Case (Merits): U.K. v. Albania (1949) ICJ Rep. p. 4*

7. Damages may be awarded in respect of the insult to the national honour of the claimant State.

> - *I'M Alone Case: Canada v. U.S. (1935) 3 R.I.A.A. 1609*

15.11 Treaties

1. A treaty is an international agreement concluded between States in written form and governed by international law, whether embodied in a single instrument or in two or more related instruments, and whatever its particular designation. To qualify as a "treaty" therefore, the agreement must satisfy the following criteria: it should be a written instrument or instruments between two or more parties; the parties must be endowed with international personality; it must be governed by international law; and it should be intended to create legal obligations.

> - *Article 2(1)(a) of the Vienna Convention on the Law of Treaties 1969*

2. Individuals or corporations have no capacity to make treaties, whether with States, other individuals or with other international persons, with treaty-making capacity. It is possible for a State to enter into a contract with an individual or a corporation, but such an agreement will not have the status of a treaty under international law.

> - *Anglo-Iranian Oil Company Case (Pleadings) 1952 I.C.J. Pleadings p. 81*

3. Where a treaty is subject to ratification, acceptance or approval, it will not be enforceable against a party until it is formally ratified.

> - *North Sea Continental Shelf Cases (1969) I.C.J. Rep. p. 3*

4. Where a treaty is not subject to ratification, mere signature will signify consent of the parties to be bound.

> - *Article 12(1) of the Vienna Convention on the Law of Treaties 1969*

5. It is an established rule of law that the plea of error cannot be allowed as an element vitiating consent if the party advancing

it contributed by its own conduct to the error, or could have avoided it, or if the circumstances were such as to put that party on notice of a possible error.

- *Temple of Preah Vihear Case: Cambodia v. Thailand (1962) I.C.J. Rep. p. 6*

6. If a State has been induced to conclude a treaty by the fraudulent conduct of another negotiating State, the injured State may invoke the fraud as invalidating its consent to be bound by the treaty.

- *Article 49 of the Vienna Convention on the Law of Treaties 1969*

7. The first duty of a tribunal which is called upon to interpret and apply the provisions of a treaty, is to endeavour to give effect to them in their natural and ordinary meaning in the context in which they occur. In addition, attention should be given to the objects and purposes of the treaty.

- *Competence of the General Assembly Case (1950) I.C.J. Rep. p. 4*
- *Peace Treaties Case (I.C.J. AO 1949)*

8. The duty of the court is to interpret treaties, not to revise them.

- *Peace Treaties Case (I.C.J. AO 1949)*

9. Every treaty in force is binding upon the parties to it and must be performed by them in good faith. Consequently, a State cannot release itself from its obligations whenever it feels like.

- *Article 26 of the Vienna Convention on the Law of Treaties 1969*

10. The termination of a treaty or the withdrawal of a party from a treaty may take place in conformity with the provisions of the treaty, by agreement, by denunciation/withdrawal, or by implied termination where the parties enter into a similar treaty on the same subject matter.

- *Articles 54(a)(b), 56 and 59 of the Vienna Convention on the Law of Treaties 1969*

15.12 Peaceful Settlement of Disputes

1. The rule is that parties to a dispute shall seek a solution by negotiation, mediation, inquiry, conciliation, arbitration, judicial settlement, and the resort to regional agencies or by other peaceful means.

- *Article 33 of the Charter of the United Nations*

2. The International Court of Justice shall be open to a State which is not a party to the statute of the International Court of Justice upon the following conditions, namely: that such State shall previously have deposited with the Registrar of the court a declaration by which it accepts the jurisdiction of the court, in accordance with the Charter of the United Nations and with the terms and subject to the conditions of the Statute and Rules of the Court, and undertakes to comply in good faith with the decision or decisions of the court and to accept all the obligations of a member of the United Nations under Article 94 of the Charter.

- *Article 35(2) of the Statute of I.C.J.*
- *Corfu Channel Case (Merits): UK v. Albania (1949) I.C.J. Rep. p. 4*
- *Monetary Gold Case (1954) I.C.J. Rep p. 19*
- *North Sea Continental Shelf Cases: (1969) I.C.J. Rep. p. 3*

3. The jurisdiction of the International Court of Justice covers all cases, which the parties refer to it and all matters specially provided for in the Charter of the United Nations or in treaties and conventions in force.

- *Article 36(1) of the Statute of I.C.J.*

4. The Statute of the International Court of Justice contains no express provisions relating to a period within which a case must be brought to its attention. However, this is not to say that such a period of limitation does not exist, for clearly the Court would be reluctant to adjudicate disputes that have their origins other than in the recent past.

- *Certain Phosphate Lands in Nauru Case (Preliminary Objections) (1992) I.C.J. Rep. p. 240*

5. The judgment of the International Court of Justice is final

and without appeal. In the event of a dispute as to the meaning or scope of its judgment, the Court shall construe it upon the request of any party.

- Article 60 of the Statute of the I.C.J.

6. In addition to its jurisdiction to decide cases brought by States under Article 36 of its statute, the International Court of Justice may give advisory opinion on any legal question.

- Article 65(1) of the Statute of the I.C.J.

7. The International Court of Justice may in the exercise of its advisory jurisdiction, determine questions of fact.

- Namibia Case ICJ AO (1971)

8. The International Court of Justice may in the exercise of its advisory jurisdiction, deal with questions involving a political element.

- Conditions of Admission of a State to Membership in the United Nations Case (1948) I.C.J. Rep. p. 57

- Certain Expenses of the United Nations Case (1962) I.C.J. Rep. p. 151

XVI

Islamic Law & Procedure

16.1 Sources and Application of the Principles of Islamic Law

1. The primary source of Islamic law is the Holy Quran.

- *Wali v. Ibrahim (1997) 9 NWLR (Pt. 519) 160 CA*

2. Principles of Islamic law are not applicable to parties who are not Moslems and are not applicable in the Customary Court of Appeal.

- *Ango v. Awawa (1998) 1 NWLR (Pt. 532) 146 CA*
- *Korau v. Korau (1998) 4 NWLR (Pt. 545) 212 CA*

16.2 Court System, Jurisdiction and Appeal under Islamic Law

1. Under Islamic law, appellate courts are not restricted to issues raised by the parties. They can rehear or retry a case in whole or in part.

- *Aski v. Alu (1999) 2 NWLR (Pt. 589) 53 CA*

2. Upper Area Courts in Nigeria have dual powers both as appellate and first instance courts.

- *Ige v. Dobi (1999) 3 NWLR (Pt. 596) 550 CA*

3. The jurisdiction of the Sharia Court of Appeal is provided for under Section 242 of the 1979 Constitution in addition to or subject to the jurisdiction conferred on it by the law of a State.

- *Abdulkadir v. Musa (1999) 1 NWLR (Pt. 587) 348 CA*

4. Land dispute or action for recovery of premises can only be heard by Sharia Court of Appeal if it involves issues of Islamic Personal Law such as wakf, gift, will or succession.

- *Magaji v. Matari (2000) 5 SC 46*
- *Korau v. Korau (1998) 4 NWLR (Pt. 545) 212 at 214 CA*

5. The inspector of an Area Court has the power to initiate an appeal at the Sharia Court of Appeal on his own motion or upon the application of any person concerned where in his opinion there has been a miscarriage of justice in a case before an Area Court to which he has access.

- *Adamu v. Bashiru (1997) 10 NWLR (Pt. 523) 81 CA*

6. An appeal lies from decisions of the Sharia Court of Appeal to the Court of Appeal as of right in accordance with Acts of the National Assembly and Rules of Court in any civil proceedings with respect to question of Islamic Personal Law.

- *Adamu v. Bashiru (1997) 10 NWLR (Pt. 523) 81 CA*

7. Granting leave to appeal out of time after inordinate delay, without any convincing reason will amount to misuse of judicial powers.

- *Akanke v. Atanda (1990) 1 I.L.R. 94 CA*

8. Court has the duty to conduct proper investigation or receive evidence before giving judgment in accordance with chapter 49 verse 6 of the Holy Quran.

- *Fakka v. Mamman (1997) 4 NWLR (Pt. 499) 335 CA*
- *Wali v. Ibrahim (1997) 9 NWLR (Pt. 519) 160 CA*

16.3 Burden of Proof under Islamic Law

1. Under Islamic law, adducing evidence of two male credible witnesses discharges the burden of proof.

- *Umaru v. Abdul-Mutallabi (1998) 11 NWLR (Pt. 573) 247 SC*

2. The burden of proof is on a plaintiff who claims ownership

of a property in possession of another person under Islamic law.

- *Garba v. Dogon Yaro (1991) 1 NWLR (Pt. 165) 102 at 104 CA*

- *Balarabe v. Abdu (1997) 10 NWLR (Pt. 524) 299 at 301 CA*

3. In civil cases under Islamic law, where each party is a plaintiff in his own case, each will be entitled to call witnesses to prove his case. The Court shall now decide whose witnesses are more pious and trustworthy. This is what is called "Tarjih" in the Islamic Law of Procedure.

- *Usman v. Kusfa (1997) 1 NWLR (Pt. 483) 525 SC*

4. The burden of proof under Islamic law is on the plaintiff and failure to discharge, the defendant is called upon to take an oath of rebuttal.

- *Abdullahi v. Bataganawa (1997) 5 NWLR (Pt. 506) 650 CA*

5. Where a plaintiff fails to prove his case and the property subject matter of dispute is in possession of the defendant such that the doctrine of Hauzi is applicable, it shall not be necessary for the defendant to subscribe to the rebuttal oath except where the property was loaned to him.

- *Sule v. Kera (1998) 13 NWLR (Pt. 581) 300 CA*

6. Burden of proof in civil cases, under Islamic law, is on the plaintiff to adduce evidence to establish his claim and he cannot do so by testifying in his own case.

- *Dandume v. Adamu (1997) 10 NWLR (Pt. 525) 452 CA*

7. The substantial procedural difference between English law and Islamic law is that in the former, the judge exercises a judicial discretion in deciding the credibility of witnesses; while in the latter he does not. In English law, the discretion cannot be exercised judicially unless the judge has heard all the witnesses of both the parties. In Islamic law, once the party asserting has perfected the proof of his case, there is no further discretion left to the judge.

- *S.A. Shittu v. M. Ibrahim Biu (1973) N.N.L.R. 195 CA*

8. A confession or admission by a sane Moslem adult is binding on him and there may be no need to call any witness.

- Issa v. Alabi (1961-1989) 1 SLRN, 177

- Wali v. Ibrahim (1997) 9 NWLR (Pt. 519) 160 CA

9. An oath of judgment is administered to a person who makes a claim over a deceased person's property. It is also proffered where the claim involves the property of a person who has been absent and his whereabouts are unknown or a claim, which involves a minor.

- Kada v. Yawa (1998) 10 NWLR (Pt. 569) 196 SC

10. In Islamic law, where both parties to a suit decline to take an oath to establish their claims in respect of a property then the person in possession of the property shall hold on to it.

- Gaya v. Ali (1990) 1 I.L.R. 76 CA

11. The law is that where evidence presented in court is unchallenged by the parties to the dispute, the court would be right to rely on it.

- Waziri v. Waziri (1998) 1 NWLR (Pt. 533) 322 CA

12. Oath taking becomes necessary under Islamic law where there is evidence in favour of a party, which undermines the evidence of the other party. In such a situation, it becomes necessary for the other party to take oath to rebut the evidence against him. Failure to take the oath will be detrimental to his case.

- Umma v. Bafullace (1997) 11 NWLR (Pt. 529) 363 CA

13. In Islamic law, he who asserts must prove and failure to so do, the defendant takes oath of denial of such assertion. Judicial proof is effected by the evidence of either two male unimpeachable witnesses; or one male witness and an oath; or one male witness and at least two female witnesses; or at least two female witnesses and an oath; or admission by the defendant.

- Issa v. Alabi (1990) 1 I.L.R. 84 CA

14. The Islamic civil procedure is based on the maxim "he who avers must prove by witnesses; he who denies may take

an oath".

> *- Uwar Zoramawa v. Daje Alkanci (1972) N.N.L.R. 15 CA*

16.4 Witness under Islamic Law

1. A plaintiff can only prove his case, under Islamic law, by evidence of two unimpeachable male witnesses; or an unimpeachable male or two or more unimpeachable female witnesses; or a male witness or two or more female witnesses plus the plaintiff's complimentary oath.

> *- Manu v. Muhammad (1997) 11 NWLR (Pt. 528) 323 CA*

2. Under Islamic law, the evidence of a blood relation, such as grandmother, sister, uncle, in-laws of a party to a suit is not acceptable in favour of the party.

> *- Kwaire v. Kola (1990) 1 I.L.R. 55 CA*
> *- Manu v. Muhammad (1997) 11 NWLR (Pt. 528) 323 CA*

3. It is permissible under Islamic law for a witness to give evidence for both parties in a case.

> *- Umma v. Bafullace (1997) 11 NWLR (Pt. 529) 363 CA*

4. Under Islamic law, parties to a dispute are not competent witnesses in their respective claims. Their statements in court would not be regarded as evidence, but something akin to statement of claim or defence. Their statement must be supported by the testimony of two male unimpeachable witnesses or one male and an oath, or one male and two female witnesses or two female witnesses and an oath.

> *- Jatau v. Mailafiya (1998) 1 NWLR (Pt. 535) 682 SC*

5. In case of impeachment of a witness, two male witnesses are required to confirm the impeachment before the court can approve it.

> *- Ahmad v. Umaru (1997) 5 NWLR (Pt. 503) 103 CA*

16.5 Title to Land under Islamic Law

1. A forest in Islamic law belongs to no one and whoever

cultivates it acquires exclusive ownership over it against the whole world.

- *Balarabe v. Abdu (1997) 10 NWLR (Pt. 524) 299 CA*

2. Under Islamic law, the claimant has the burden of proof in respect of title to land.

- *Ige v. Dobi (1999) 3 NWLR (Pt. 596) 550 CA*

3. The onus of proof of purchase of immovable property is on the defendant who is in possession and ascertaining valid purchase thereof.

- *Abubakar v. Gama (1999) 1 NWLR (Pt. 588) 547 CA*

4. The Islamic principle of "*Hauzi*" or prescription as stated in Hadith is to the effect that whoever is in peaceful possession of a thing (real property) for 10 years becomes its owner except where there is a cogent reason for not complaining in time, or in the case of a minor, or a free or paying tenant, or a trustee, or where the claimant is a partner or co-proprietor to the person in possession.

- *Gwabro v. Gwabro (1998) 4 NWLR (Pt. 544) 60 CA*

5. The Islamic doctrine of "*Hauzi*" (prescription) does not apply to undistributed property.

- *Gewayau v. Dushi (1997) 8 NWLR (Pt. 517) 522 CA*

6. The limitation period under Islamic law for challenging a sale of property in the presence and to the knowledge of the owner without any objection from him is one year.

- *Umma v. Bafullace (1997) 11 NWLR (Pt. 529) 363 CA*

7. A valid sale of land under Islamic law must establish the price, identity and features of the landed property.

- *Abdullahi v. Bataganawa (1997) 5 NWLR (Pt. 506) 650 CA*

8. Under Islamic law, where a vendor agrees to sell a property to another but then in breach of his agreement, sells the property to a third party, the sale or purported sale to the third party may be set aside and the vendor may be ordered to carry out his

agreement to sell to the purchaser at the agreed price and, when payment has been made, to give the purchaser and not the third party possession of the property.

- *Samu'ila Dan Tanko v. Danlami Maidaka (1971) N.N.L.R. 116 CA*

16.6 Matrimonial Causes under Islamic Law

1. The "*Idda*" period under Islamic law is a period of probation before a divorced woman or widow can remarry and any marriage contracted during such period is void.

- *Akanke v. Atanda (1990) 1 I.L.R. 94 CA*

2. The paternity of a child born by a divorced woman or widow during the "idda" period belongs to the husband for whom she kept the "*Idda*".

- *Atanke v. Atanda (1990) 1 I.L.R. 94 CA*

3. Under Islamic law, the evidence of two male unimpeachable witnesses is sufficient to grant a divorce on ground of defamation.

- *Kwaire v. Kola (1990) I.L.R. 55 CA*

4. The onus is on a wife or her representatives claiming that her husband has divorced her to adduce evidence of one male unimpeachable witness or two female unimpeachable witnesses.

- *Ngbdobe v. Dubrare (1997) 11 NWLR (Pt. 529) 382 CA*

5. Gifts, dresses or ornaments given to a wife by her husband during the subsistence of their marriage are not refundable.

- *Issa v. Alabi (1990) 1 I.L.R. 84 CA*

16.7 Succession and Inheritance

1. For a gift to be valid under Islamic law, there must be a

declaration of the gift by the donor, acceptance by the donee or by his agent and the donee must be put in possession by the donor.

- *Aiyo v. Da'ado (1990) I.L.R. 60 CA*

2. For succession to be valid under Islamic law there must be preliminary payments of funeral expenses, debts and other outgoing made from the estate of the deceased.

- *Baka v. Dandare (1997) 4 NWLR (Pt. 498) 244 CA*

3. Succession under Islamic law confers an inalienable right on its claimant and once the right is proved, "*Hauzi*" (prescription), sale (bay), loan (*ariya*) or even usurpation (*ghasb*), etcetera, cannot defeat the claimant's right to succeed a deceased.

- *Dantani v. Daji (1998) 3 NWLR (Pt. 543) 649 CA*

4. Under Islamic law, a deceased's heirs are permitted to appoint a person learned in Islamic law to share his estate among them according to law and the court has power to enforce the sharing.

- *Jiddun v. Abuna (2000) 10-11 SC 19*

5. The claim as to who pre-deceased the other for purposes of inheritance where two spouses died almost at the same time is to be established by the evidence of one male unimpeachable witness plus that of two female unimpeachable witnesses or by evidence of one of the two with the claimant's complimentary oath.

- *Jiddun v. Abuna (2000) 10-11 SC 19*

6. Only male children of an emancipated slave can inherit his estate.

- *Baraya v. Belel (1999) 1 NWLR (Pt. 585) 105 CA*

7. Entitlement to inherit the estate of a deceased under Islamic law can only be proved by the establishment of three fundamental conditions namely: the death of the deceased; the survival of a heir to the deceased and the establishment of inheritable estate.

- *Jatau v. Mailafiya (1998) 1 NWLR (Pt. 535) 682 SC*

8. An orphaned grandchild can inherit, by way of bequest or *wakf* or gift, his grandfather's property in place of his late father.

- Ahmad v. Umaru (1997) 5 NWLR (Pt. 503) 103 CA

9. A father can inherit the property of his deceased son in accordance with Chapter 4 verses 8-12 of the Holy Quran.

- Ahmad v. Umaru (1997) 5 NWLR (Pt. 503) 103 CA

10. Death of a "*mafqud*" (missing person) can be established by the production of a decree of death issued by a court and by giving evidence which will eventually lead to the issuance of the said decree of death.

- Jatau v. Mailafiya (1998) 1 NWLR (Pt. 535) 682 SC

XVII
Judgment and Orders

17.1 Nature of Court Judgment

1. A judgment is what may be described as the *ratio decidendi* of a case in contrast to the passing remarks otherwise made by the court in the course of preparing the judgment. *Ratio decidendi* contained in the lead judgment or in a judgment of the trial court constitutes the authority for which the case stands while the *obiter dicta* are other expressions contained in the judgment and they only have a persuasive effect in other occasions.

- *Abacha v. Fawehinmi (2000) 4 SC (Part II) 1*
- *Awoniyi v. Registered Trustees of the Rosicrucian Order, AMORC (Nigeria) (2000) 6 SC (Part I) 103*

2. A good judgment should set out the nature of the action before the court and the issue in controversy; review the cases for parties; consider the relevant laws raised and applicable to the case; make specific findings of fact and conclusion; and give reasons for arriving at those decisions.

- *Ciroma v. Ali (1999) 2 NWLR (Pt. 590) 317 CA*

3. The judgment of a trial court or any court of law must contain all the elements of fairness and a dispassionate consideration of issues in controversy between the parties. Where a finding of fact by a trial court does not correctly reflect the claims of the parties before it, it results in a miscarriage of justice and constitutes sufficient reason to allow an appeal against such a decision.

- *Oyewale v. Oyesoro (1998) 2 NWLR (Pt. 539) 663 CA*

4. A court which has delivered its judgment becomes *functus officio* and ceases to have powers to tamper with the judgment in any way except in a situation like correction of clerical mistakes and arithmetical errors.

- *Bako v. Mai-Adashi (1997) 4 NWLR (Pt. 497) 116 CA*

5. Although a court must deliver its judgment within three months after the conclusion of evidence and final addresses in accordance with the provisions of section 258(1) of the 1979 Constitution, it is permissible to deliver judgment outside this period for certain reasons. For instance, the illness of a judge is a pardonable exception to the mandatory provision.

   - Korobotei v. Obubo (1999) 9 NWLR (Pt. 620) 655 CA

6. The combined reading of section 258(1) and (4) of the 1979 Constitution is to the effect that delivery of judgment outside the prescribed period of three months would not ordinarily render the judgment a nullity unless the appellant could show that the delay had occasioned a miscarriage of justice.

   - Mika'ilu v. State (2001) 5 WRN 74 CA

7. Once a trial court delivers its judgment in a suit, it becomes *functus officio* with respect to the suit. Thereafter, the court can only make ancilliary orders such as an order for stay of execution of the judgment or payment of the judgment debt by instalment by virtue of the relevant provisions.

   - Kaduna Textiles Ltd v. Obi (1999) 10 NWLR (Pt. 621) 138 CA

8. An unsigned and undated judgment is null and void and of no effect whatsoever.

   - Awoniyi v. Aleshinloye (1998) 9 NWLR (Pt. 564) 71 CA

9. Any judgment, however well written, if given without jurisdiction is no judgment at all.

   - Ajayi v. Mil. Adm., Ondo State (1997) 5 NWLR (Pt. 504) 237 CA

10. A judgment of a court is said to be perverse when it runs counter to the evidence, or where it has been shown that the trial court took into account matters which it ought not to have taken into account or shuts its eyes to the obvious; or when it has occasioned a miscarriage of justice.

   - Agbomeji v. Bakare (1998) 9 NWLR (Pt. 564) 1 SC
   - Ige v. Adegbola (1998) 10 NWLR (Pt. 571) 662 CA
   - State v. Ajie (2000) 7 SC (Pt. 1) 24

11. A miscarriage of justice occurs where there are substantial errors in adjudication, with the resultant effect that the party relying on such errors may likely have a judgment in his favour.

- Amadi v. N.N.P.C. (2000) 6 SC (Pt. 1) 66

12. A person whose property was wrongfully sold in execution of a judgment debt has the following remedies namely: an action for the recovery of the property; an action for declaration of his title to the property; and an action for declaration that the sale is void and be set aside.

- Hakuri Sarkin Tsha v. Alhaji Awwa Ali (1975) N.N.L.R. 149, High Court of North-Central State. Suit No. NCH/26/ 75

17.2 Types of Court Judgments

1.Executory judgment declares the respective rights of the parties and then proceeds to order the defendant to act in a particular way, for example, to pay damages or refrain from interfering with the plaintiff's rights; such order being enforceable by execution if disobeyed.

- Adedoyin v. Sonuga (1999) 13 NWLR (Pt. 635) 355 CA

2. Declaratory judgments on the other hand, merely proclaim the existence of a legal relationship and do not contain any order, which may be enforced against the defendant. It may be the ground of subsequent proceedings in which the right, having been violated receives enforcement but in the meantime, there is neither enforcement nor any claim to it.

- Adedoyin v. Sonuga (1999) 13 NWLR (Pt. 635) 355 CA

3. When a judgment is executory in nature, it becomes enforceable by writs of attachment and committal if disobeyed. On the other hand, a declaratory judgment may be ground of subsequent proceedings in which any alleged right, having been violated receives enforcement, but till such violation, there is no enforcement or any claim on such judgment.

- Awoniyi v. Registered Trustees of the Rosicrucian Order, AMORC (Nigeria) (2000) 6 SC (Pt. 1) 103

4. Generally, a court of coordinate jurisdiction does not have the jurisdiction to set aside the judgment of another court of similar jurisdiction but it can do so where the said judgment is *ab initio* void; when the order is a nullity it can be set aside *ex debito justitiae*; and when it is a default judgment.

- *Koden v. Shidon (1998) 10 NWLR (Pt. 571) 662 CA*

5. A court has the power to set aside a default judgment given in the absence of a party, and any judge of the High Court can exercise this power and not necessarily by the judge who gave the judgment.

- *Emodi v. Kwentoh (1996) 2 NWLR (Pt. 433) 656 SC*

6. A consent judgment is a judgment, the provisions and terms of which are settled and agreed to by the parties to the action and due effect may be given to it by the court. It is a final judgment and being final, it cannot be set aside by the court, which gave the judgment.

- *Spectra Ltd. v. Stablini Visioni Ltd (1999) 6 NWLR (Pt. 608) 631 CA*
- *Lamurde v. Adamawa State J.S.C (1999) 12 NWLR (Pt. 629) 86 CA*

7. There are exceptional cases where a consent judgment will be set aside by the court that gave it. These are where it was obtained by fraud; where it was obtained by misrepresentation or nondisclosure of a material fact which there was an obligation to disclose; where it was obtained by duress or concluded under a mutual mistake of fact; and where it was obtained without proper authority.

- *Spectra Ltd. v. Stablini Visioni Ltd (1999) 6 NWLR (Pt. 608) 631 CA*
- *Lamurde v. Adamawa State J.S.C (1999) 12 NWLR (Pt. 629) 86 CA*

8. By section 220(1) of the 1979 Constitution, appeal against consent judgment shall lie to the Court of Appeal only by leave of a High Court or Court of Appeal.

- *Enigbokan v. Baruwa (1998) 8 NWLR (Pt. 560) 96 CA*

17.3 Review of Judgment

1. A review of judgment is a re-examination or reconsideration for purposes of correction of an issue decided. It is done by an appeal court with a view to correcting where the trial court went wrong. Such a review, which is an appeal, must be initiated through the due process of law for the appeal court to act judicially.

> - N.I.D.B. v. Limani (Nig.) Enterp. Ltd (1998) 10 NWLR (Pt. 568) 97 CA

2. An action for review of judgment in an action already concluded is maintainable where fresh evidence is discovered. However, it must be shown that the evidence could not have been obtained with reasonable diligence for use at the trial; the evidence must be such that, if given, it would probably have an important influence on the result of the case, although it need not be decisive; and the evidence must be such as is presumably to be believed, or it must be apparently credible, although it need not be incontrovertible.

> - Anatogu v. Iweka II (1995) 8 NWLR (Pt. 415) 547 SC

3. A court shall not review any judgment once given and delivered by it save to correct any clerical mistake or some error arising from any accidental slip or omission or to vary the judgment or order so as to give effect to its meaning or intention. Also, where an appropriate Law or Decree provides for finality of such decision, it cannot be interfered with either by way of appeal or by the employment of a prerogative writ or proceedings.

> - Okpala v. Ezeani (1999) 4 NWLR (Pt. 598) 250 CA
> - Onwuchekwa v. C.C.B. (Nig.) Ltd. (1999) 5 NWLR (Pt. 603) 409 CA

4. The exercise of the power of court to amend or vary its judgment or order is not open only to the very judge who delivered the judgment or who made the order. Any other judge in the same jurisdiction can exercise that power.

> - Bola v. St. Latunde (1993) 1 SCNLR 288
> - Ogwuegbu v. Agomuo (1999) 7 NWLR (Pt. 609) 144 CA

5. A State High Court, like any other superior court of record,

has an inherent jurisdiction to amend or vary its own judgment or order in order to bring out its own meaning and to give effect to its plain intention. This inherent power is limited only to situations where, there is a clerical mistake in the judgment or order; where there is an error arising from an accidental slip or omission; or where it is necessary to do so to bring out its meaning and to make its intention plain.

- *F.B.N. Plc. v. Obande & Sons Ent. Ltd. (1998) 2 NWLR (Pt. 538) 410 CA*
- *Ovenseri v. Osagiede (1998) 11 NWLR (Pt. 572) 1 SC*
- *Pavex International Co. (Nig.) Ltd v. I.B.W.A. (2000) 4 SC (Pt. II) 196*

6. The Supreme Court is always reluctant to overturn the concurrent judgment of the High Court and Court of Appeal. Where, however, a concurrent judgment of the two lower courts appears unreasonable and against the evidence adduced at the trial, the Supreme Court cannot allow it to stand.

- *Bayol v. Ahemba (2001) 2 WRN 109 SC*
- *Dogo v. The State (2001) 9 WRN 70 SC*

7. By virtue of section 251(1) of the 1979 Constitution, decisions of the Supreme Court must be enforced in any part of the Federation by all authorities and persons and by courts with subordinate jurisdiction to that of the Supreme Court. The Judgment (Enforcement) Rules made under the Sheriffs and Civil Process Act and the provisions of Order 8 Rule 15 of the Supreme Court Rules 1985 govern the enforcement of the judgment of the Supreme Court.

- *Ajiboye v. Olabanji (1998) 7 NWLR (Pt. 558) 464 CA*
- *Alesinloye v. Oyediran (1999) 12 NWLR (Pt. 631) 481 CA*

8. The procedure for enforcement under the Judgment (Enforcement) Rules and the Supreme Court Rules 1985 is that a certified copy of the judgment shall be sent by the Registrar of the Supreme Court to the court below; a sealed or certified copy of the order shall be sent by the Registrar to the court below. The judgment may be enforced by the Supreme Court or by the court below or any other court which has been seized of the matter as the Supreme Court may direct and where the Supreme

Court directs its judgment to be enforced by another court, then a certificate under the seal of the court and the hand of the presiding justice shall be transmitted by the Registrar which shall enforce such judgment in terms of the certificate.

- *Ajiboye v. Olabanji (1998) 7 NWLR (Pt. 558) 464 CA*

- *Alesinloye v. Oyediran (1999) 12 NWLR (Pt. 631) 481 CA*

9. A judgment delivered by a trial court before the expiration of the time allowed on the writ of summons for a defendant to enter appearance is invalid and ought to be set aside.

- *Aderonke Bakery Ltd v. M/S .D. Onyejekwe Ltd (1999) 2 NWLR (Pt. 590) 228 CA*

10. There is a presumption of the validity and bindingness of a previous judgment until it is upturned on appeal.

- *Kamalu v. Umunna (1997) 5 NWLR (Pt. 505) 321 SC*

- *Nwanwata v. Esumei (1998) 8 NWLR (Pt. 563) 650 CA*

- *Babatunde v. Olatunji (2000) 2 SC 9*

- *Ogiugo v. Ogiugo (2001) 1 WRN 131 SC*

11. By virtue of section 6 of the Foreign Judgment (Reciprocal Enforcement) Act, 1961, where a party against whom a registered judgment is made duly applies to have it set aside, the registration of the judgment shall be set aside if the registering court is satisfied that the court of the country of original court has no jurisdiction in the circumstances of the case. The judgment debtor who intends to set aside a registration of a foreign judgment is entitled to examine the materials on which the registration was based to see if all the antecedent legal requirements were satisfied.

- *Hyppolite v. Egharevba (1998) 11 NWLR (Pt. 575) 598 CA*

12. An allegation of fraud must be proved with particularity and established before a court will allow a judgment to be set aside on the ground of fraud. A judgment obtained by fraud can be set aside on an action brought afterwards.

- *A.-G., Federation v. Ijewere (1995) 8 NWLR (Pt. 415) 618 CA*

- *Ikyaawan v. Ajivah (1997) 4 NWLR (Pt. 499) 365 CA*

13. It is not every error or mistake on the part of a lower court that will vitiate a judgment but only where such error or mistake is so fundamental as to occasion a miscarriage of justice.

- *State v. Ogbubunjo (2001) 13 WRN 1 SC*

14. Once the Supreme Court in its decision has effectively decided on a matter before it and there is no ambiguity or slip to be corrected, it becomes *functus officio* of the powers of the court to reopen it. The inherent powers of the court can only be invoked if there is a missing link in the main body of the judgment and some steps must be taken to fill the gaps or ambiguity so that the justice of the issues will be clear.

- *Adigun v. The Secretary, Iwo Local Govt. (1999) 8 NWLR (Pt. 613) 30 SC*
- *Alao v. African Continental Bank Ltd (2000) 6 SC (Part I) 27*
- *Okegbe v. Chikere (2000) 7 SC (Part 1) 106*

15. A conclusive native court judgment may operate as *estoppel per rem judicatam* or issue estoppel.

- *Kamalu v. Umunna (1997) 5 NWLR (Pt. 505) 321 SC*

16. Where an appeal is withdrawn, the resultant position is as if there was never an appeal filed. Under the Supreme Court Rules, 1985, as amended, an appeal, which has been withdrawn shall be deemed to have been dismissed. However, the judgment dismissing the appeal is not a judgment on the merits. A judgment on the merits is a decision that was rendered on the basis of the evidence and facts introduced.

- *Akuneziri v. Okenwa (2000) 12 SC (Part II) 75*

17. Wrongful exclusion of evidence is not of itself a ground for the reversal of any decision if it appears to the Court of Appeal that, had the evidence excluded been admitted, the decision would reasonably nevertheless have been the same.

- *Waziri v. State (1997) 3 NWLR (Pt. 496) 689 CA*

17.4 Orders

1. An order of court is one which directs a party to a case to do something in relation to the case.

- *Chia v. Uma (1998) 7 NWLR (Pt. 556) 95 CA*
- *Bello v. Fayose (1999) 11 NWLR (Pt. 627) 510 SC*

2. A consequential order is an order necessarily flowing directly and naturally from, and inevitably consequent upon, the judgment already given.

- *Liman v. Mohammed (1999) 9 NWLR (Pt. 617) 116 SC*
- *Momah v. Vab Petroleum Inc. (2000) 2 SC 142*
- *A-G., Federation v. A.I.C. Ltd. (2000) 6 SC (Pt. 1) 175*
- *Broad Bank of Nigeria Ltd v. Odjemu (2001) 12 WRN 40 CA*

3. An order of a court of competent jurisdiction subsists until it is set aside.

- *Gomwalk v. Mil. Adm. Plateau State (1998) 7 NWLR (Pt. 558) 413 CA*
- *Ezeokafor v. Ezeilo (1999) 9 NWLR (Pt. 619) 513 SC*

4. Once the principal order sought in an action is refused, no order incidental to the principal order can be granted.

- *Awoniyi v. Registered Trustees of the Rosicrucian Order, AMORC (2000) 6 SC (Pt. 1) 103*

5. Where an order has been made against a person in his absence without notifying him of such proceedings, he has the right to have the order set aside on the ground that a condition precedent to the order taking effect has not been fulfilled.

- *Atser v. Gachi (1997) 6 NWLR (Pt. 510) 609 CA*

6. Judicial orders when used inappropriately lose their potency as deterrence.

- *Sandra v. Adeniran (1998) 8 NWLR (Pt. 560) 167 CA*
- *Wema Bank Plc v. Balogun (1999) 7 NWLR (Pt. 610) 242 CA*

7. An order for non-suit is a final order. Although it disposes of

the rights of parties temporarily, the parties are at liberty to commence proceedings afresh in respect of the same subject matter.

- *Trans Nab Ltd v. Joseph (1997) 5 NWLR (Pt. 504) 176 CA*

8. A final order is one which puts an end to the action by declaring that the plaintiff has or has not entitled himself to the remedy he sued for, so that, nothing remains to be done to execute the judgment. The court becomes *functus officio* after a final order has been made. In determining whether an order is final or interlocutory, what should be considered is what effect the order appealed against has on the right of the parties. If the order determines finally the rights of the parties, then it is a final order. If not, it is an interlocutory order.

- *Ndigwe v. Ibekendu (1998) 7 NWLR (Pt. 558) 486 CA*
- *Gomwalk v. Okwosa (1999) 1 NWLR (Pt. 586) 225 CA*
- *Nwoke v. Ebeogu (1999) 6 NWLR (Pt. 606) 228 CA*

9. *Ex-parte* orders should be cautiously and sparingly made, and when made in the compelling interest of justice, should not be kept in existence for longer than necessary.

- *Bettinni Homes Ltd v. Internorth Nigeria Ltd (1999) 13 NWLR (Pt. 634) 333 CA*

10. Dismissal of an action is one of the gravest sanctions a plaintiff can face. A court of law should be most reluctant in invoking its power of dismissal. A court should embark on this remedy as a last resort and should do so when there are no other avenues to remedy that situation by way of judicial sanction.

- *Emesim v. Nwachukwu (1999) 6 NWLR (Pt. 605) 154 CA*

11. Whether a court will adjourn a matter for a considered ruling in an application depends on the nature of the application and the facts and law relevant to a particular application. If the answer in an application is so obvious that the court considers it a waste of its time to adjourn, it is entitled to give its ruling instantly. The important thing is ensuring that justice is done. A complaint based on the fact that an adjournment is not given to consider the ruling *simpliciter* is not well founded.

- *Mba v. Mba (1999) 10 NWLR (Pt. 623) 503 CA*

12. Interest on a judgment of the court can arise where the interest claimed is contemplated in the agreement between the parties and where it arises in equity. The tenets of equity modify the severity of the common law and presumes that an interest should be accruable having regard to the mercantile nature of the transaction. A court may grant an order for installmental payment of a judgment debt. It may also order that interest be paid on the debt from the date afterwards.

- *Kano Textiles Printers Plc v. Tukur (1999) 2 NWLR (Pt. 589) 78 CA*

- *N.I.D.B. v. De Easy Life Electronics (1999) 4 NWLR (Pt. 597) 8 CA*

13. The court cannot make an order for interest to be paid unless there is an application for installmental payment of the judgment debt concerned and the application is being granted.

- *K.S.T.A v. Ofodile (1999) 10 NWLR (Pt. 622) 259 CA*
- *Jeric Nigeria Limited v. Union Bank of Nigeria Plc (2000) 12 SC (Part II) 133*

14. A party is entitled to make a claim in court in either the local currency or in foreign currency if the basis of the contract between the parties sought to be enforced by order of specific performance is in foreign currency, and the court can make award in foreign currency.

- *Pan African Bank Ltd v. Ede (1998) 7 NWLR (Pt. 558) 422 CA*
- *Saegby v. Olaogun (2001) 11 WRN 179 SC*

15. A court has power to set aside a default judgment. In doing this, the court takes certain factors into consideration. These include whether an applicant has shown good reasons for being absent at the hearing; whether the application was brought within the prescribed period of six days; whether in an application for extension of time to bring the application, the applicant gave good reason for his inability to bring the application to set aside the judgment within six days prescribed under the rule; whether he has shown there is an arguable defence to the action which is not manifestly unsupportable; whether his conduct at trial is deserving of sympathy; whether

judgment was given for an amount in excess of what was due and claimed; whether the respondent will not suffer any prejudice if the judgment is set aside; and whether the judgment is tainted with fraud or is irregularly obtained.

- *Odunsi v. U.N.M.I.C. (1998) 2 NWLR (Pt. 536) 95 CA*
- *Akinriboya v. Akinsole (1998) 3 NWLR (Pt. 540) 101 CA*

16. The service of notice of attachment of immovable property of a judgment debtor is so fundamental that any irregularity in respect of such service would vitiate the sale of the attached property; where an application for leave to attach immovable property of judgment debtor is granted *ex-parte*, the *ex-parte* order is a nullity.

- *Bayero v. Crusader Ins. Co. Ltd (1998) 6 NWLR (Pt. 553) 214 CA*
- *Ndigwe v. Ibekendu (1998) 7 NWLR (Pt. 558) 486 CA*
- *Akpunonu v. Beakart Overseas (2000) 7 SC (Part I) 49*

17. A decree of specific performance is a form of relief that is purely equitable in origin and the fundamental rule is that specific performance will not be decreed if there is an absolute remedy at law in answer to the plaintiff's claim. The jurisdiction in specific performance is based on the inadequacy of the remedy at law.

- *Afrotec v. MIA & Ors (2001) 6 WRN 65 SC*

18. Where there is no appeal against a foreign judgment a party cannot competently seek a stay of execution of the said judgment. What a party may do is to resist the grant of an order of registration or obtain an order to stay the order of registration.

- *Momah v. Vab. Petroleum Inc. (2000) 2 SC 142*

19. The grant of a declaration of right is at the discretion of the court but it is a discretion that must be exercised judicially. Ordinarily, the Appellate Court would not question the exercise of discretion of the trial judge merely because it would have exercised the discretion in a different way if it had been in the position of the trial court. It would however, do so if as a result of such exercise injustice is meted out to either of the parties or

that the trial judge gave no weight or gave insufficient weight to important considerations.

- *Dantata v. Mohammed (2000) 5 SC 1*
- *Owodunni v Registered Trustees of C.C.C (2000) 6 SC (Part III) 60*

20. **Where special or peculiar facts are taken into account in determining an issue and there is departure from the general rule, there is a duty in the interest of clarity to state the reasons why there is such a departure.**

- *NV Scheep v. MV "S. Araz" (2001) 4 WRN 105 SC*

21. **A party, who knows of an order, whether null or valid, regular or irregular, cannot be permitted to disobey it. He should apply to the court to have it discharged and as long as it exists, it must not be disobeyed.**

- *Babatunde v. Olatunji (2000) 2 SC 9*

22. **The principle of slip rule, which permits a court to correct clerical errors in its judgment, does not extend to clerical errors made by counsel in his submission.**

- *Alao v. A.C.B. Ltd (2000) 6 SC (Pt. 1) 27*
- *Okegbe v. Chikere (2000) 7 SC (Pt. 1) 106*

23. **A court has no power to make an order which has not been asked for and which the person against whom it is made had no opportunity for resisting.**

- *Oladunjoye v. Akinterinwa (2000) 4 SC (Pt. 1) 19*
- *A-G Federation v. A.I.C. Ltd (2000) 6 SC (Pt. 1) 175*
- *Dyktrade Limited v. Omnia Nigeria Limited (2000) 7 SC (Pt. 1) 56*
- *Afrotec. Technical Services (Nig.) Ltd v. MIA & Sons Ltd (2000) 12 SC (Part II) 1*
- *Badmus v. Abegunde (2001) 3 WRN 40 SC*

24. **A case is decided *per incuriam* where a statute or rule having statutory effect or other binding authority, which would have affected the decision, had not been brought to the attention of the court.**

- *Adisa v. Oyinwola (2000) 6 SC (Part II) 47*

25. It is the duty of parties to a case, once they are put on notice of the judgment date, to be in court to receive copies of the judgment of the court and it is not the function of the court to search for the litigants in order to hand over its judgment.

- *Oruche v. C.O.P. (1997) 4 NWLR (Pt. 497) 1 SC*

26. The applicable law on public holidays is the Public Holidays Act, 1990 and, under the schedule to this Act, Saturday is not considered a public holiday.

- *Shugaba v. U.B.N. Plc (1997) 4 NWLR (Pt. 500) 481 CA*

27. An order, striking out a suit under Order 29 Rule 3(1) of the High Court (Civil Procedure) Rules of Niger State, 1987 with a condition that the plaintiff should not file another action against the defendant based on the same cause of action, finally disposes of the right of the parties. It is therefore appellable as of right under section 220(1)(a) of the 1979 Constitution and not under section 221(1) of the Constitution which would necessitate a party to seek and obtain leave before filing a competent appeal.

- *Trans Nab Ltd v. Joseph (1997) 5 NWLR (Pt. 504) 176 CA*

28. When an action is struck out, it is still alive and could be resuscitated by the plaintiff. A dismissal brings the matters to an end and the particular claim or relief dies. Generally, a case would be struck out in the following circumstances, namely: when the court lacks jurisdiction or competence to hear it; when there is inexplicable absence of the plaintiff in court on the date the case is fixed for hearing; and when it is in the interest of justice to do so.

- *Oko v. Igweshi (1997) 4 NWLR (Pt. 497) 48 CA*

29. A retrial order should not be made where an Appellate Court, on proper consideration of the case before it comes to the conclusion that it can do complete justice between the parties.

- *Salami v. Gbodoolu (1997) 4 NWLR (Pt. 499) 277 SC*

17.5 Discretion

1. Judicial discretion is a term applied to the discretionary action

of a judge or court and means discretion bounded by the rules and principles of law and not arbitrary, capricious or unrestrained. It is a legal discretion to be exercised in discerning the course prescribed by law and is not to give effect to the will of the judge, but to that of the law

> - *Mohammed v. C.O.P. (1999) 12 NWLR (Pt. 630) 331 CA*

2. A proper exercise of discretion should be according to law and not humour. It is not to be arbitrary, vague and fanciful but legal and regular. It must be upon facts and circumstances presented to the court, from which it must draw a conclusion governed by law.

> - *U.B.N. Plc v. Adjarho (1997) 6 NWLR (Pt. 507) 112 CA*

3. A court's exercise of its discretion without averting to all the peculiar facts and circumstance of the particular case before it, is as bad as its exercise upon a wrong principle. Also, if there is any miscarriage of justice in the exercise of a judicial discretion, it is within the competence of an appellate court to have it reviewed.

> - *Oduba v. Houtmangracht (1997) 6 NWLR (Pt. 508) 185 SC*

4. It is within the discretion of a court hearing a case to award cost.

> - *Afribank (Nig.) Plc v. Geneva (1999) 12 NWLR (Pt. 632) 567 CA*

5. The Court of Appeal will not interfere with a proper exercise of discretion of a lower court. However, where the exercise of discretion tends to do injustice to one of the parties, the appeal court must employ its judicial sledge hammer to salvage the situation.

> - *Guda v. Kitta (1999) 12 NWLR (Pt. 629) 21 CA*
> - *Imani & Sons Ltd v. Bil Const. Co. Ltd (1999) 12 NWLR (Pt. 630) 254 CA*
> - *Mohammed v. C.O.P. (1999) 12 NWLR (Pt. 630) 331 CA*
> - *Ehidimhen v. Musa (2000) 4 SC (Pt II) 166*
> - *Oyekanmi v. NEPA (2000) 12 SC (Pt. 1) 70*
> - *Biocon Agro Chemicals v. Kudu Holding (2000) 12 SC (Pt. 1) 139*

6. Where the judgment of the Supreme Court has charted a path on the general principles to be followed in the exercise of a judicial discretion, the lower Court in the hierarchy cannot depart from such principles by viewing the judgment of the Supreme Court as a fetter in the exercise of discretion.

- *Afribank (Nig.) Plc v. Geneva (1999) 12 NWLR (Pt. 632) 567 CA*

XVIII
Jurisdiction

1. Jurisdiction is defined as the limits imposed on the power of a validly constituted court to hear and determine issues between persons seeking to avail themselves of its process by reference to the subject matter of the issues, or to the persons between whom the issues are joined, or to the kind of relief sought.

> - *A-G., Lagos State v. Dosunmu (1989) 3 NWLR (Pt. 111) 552 SC*

2. The question of jurisdiction is very fundamental that it should be determined first by the courts before starting any proceedings. If the court proceeds without jurisdiction, all proceedings however well conducted amount to a nullity. It is trite law that the issue of jurisdiction can be raised at any time by a party even on appeal in the Supreme Court.

> - *Ukwu v. Bunge (1997) 8 NWLR (Pt. 518) 527 SC*
> - *Ezechigbo v. Gov. Anambra State (1999) 9 NWLR (Pt. 619) 386 CA*
> - *Messrs N.V Scheep v. The M.V. "S. Araz" 2000) 12 SC (Part I) 164*
> - *Jeric Nig. Ltd. v. U.B.N. Plc. (2000) 12 SC (Part II) 133*

3. When a court's jurisdiction is challenged, it is neater and better for the court to settle that issue one way or the other before proceeding to the hearing of the case on the merits.

> - *A-G., Lagos State v. Dosunmu (1989) 3 NWLR (Pt. 111) 552 SC*
> - *Nokoprise Int. Co. Ltd v. Dobest Trading Corporation (1997) 9 NWLR (Pt. 520) 334 CA*

4. When a court's jurisdiction is challenged, the court must first of all assume jurisdiction to decide whether in clear and

unequivocal terms, it has or lacks jurisdiction.

- *A-G., Lagos State v. Dosunmu (1989) 3 NWLR (Pt. 111) 552 SC*

- *Nokoprise Int. Co. Ltd v. Dobest Trading Corporation (1997) 9 NWLR (Pt. 520) 334 CA*

5. Where the jurisdiction of a court is challenged, the court should expeditiously attend to it particularly at the trial stage and even on appeal. The court can also raise the issue of jurisdiction *suo motu* so long as the parties are accorded the opportunity to react to the issue. Where the court's jurisdiction is challenged irregularly by a preliminary objection, the irregularity does not affect the fundamental nature of jurisdiction and a court has a duty to consider the issue. Jurisdiction cannot be assumed in the interest of justice. A court either has or does not have jurisdiction.

- *Ajayi v. Mil. Adm., Ondo State (1997) 5 NWLR (Pt. 504) 237 CA*

- *Amadi v. NNPC (2000) 6 SC (Part I) 66*

- *Galadima v.Tambai (2000) 6 SC (Part I) 196 at 207*

6. The courts guard their jurisdiction jealously. Where a statute ousts the jurisdiction of the court, the language of such statute must be construed rather strictly but once it is crystal clear that an ouster or restriction is intended or imposed and that the facts of a particular case comes squarely within the four corners of the cold embrace of the ouster statute, the hands of the court are tied and has no alternative except to hold that it lacks jurisdiction.

- *Ajayi v. Mil. Adm., Ondo State (1997) 5 NWLR (Pt. 504) 237 CA*

- *Amadi v. N.N.P.C (2000) 6 SC (Part I) 66 at 95*

7. In considering whether a court has jurisdiction to entertain a matter, the court is guided by the claim before it by critically looking at the writ of summons and the statement of claim.

- *Tukur v. Govt. of Gongola State (1989) 4 NWLR (Pt. 117) 517 SC*

- *Onyenucheya v. Mil. Adm., Imo State (1997) 1 NWLR (Pt. 482) 429 CA*

- *Multi-Purpose Ventures Ltd v. A.-G., Rivers State (1997) 9 NWLR (Pt. 522) 642 CA*

8. Where a court declines jurisdiction in the absence of a plaintiff's statement of claim, it amounts to a denial of the fundamental right of fair hearing of the plaintiff as enshrined in section 33(1) of the 1979 Constitution of the Federal Republic of Nigeria.

- *Republic Bank Ltd v. C.B.N. (1998) 13 NWLR (Pt. 581) 306 CA*

9. Where a court decides that it lacks the jurisdiction to entertain a suit, the proper order it should make is one of striking out the matter and not of dismissal.

- *Republic Bank Ltd v. C.B.N. (1998) 13 NWLR (Pt. 581) 306 CA*

10. Any order made without jurisdiction is a nullity and a court has inherent powers to set aside any order made by it, which amounts to a nullity.

- *Uwamu v. Uwamu (1998) 10 NWLR (Pt. 569) 240 CA*
- *Galadima v. Tambai (2000) 6 SC (Part I) 196*

11. Every court of record has an inherent power to set aside its judgment or order, which is a nullity.

- *Alao v. African Continental Bank Ltd (2000) 6 SC (Part I) 27*

12. Any party to a suit can raise the issue of jurisdiction and a court *suo motu* can raise same issue provided the parties are given the opportunity to react to the issue.

- *Waniko v. Ade-John (1999) 9 NWLR (Pt. 619) 401 CA*
- *Galadima v. Tambai (2000) 6 SC (Part I) 196 at 207*

13. A court lacks jurisdiction to give judgment for reliefs not sought without hearing parties to the case. Where such judgment is given, it should be set aside.

- *S.G.B. (Nig.) Ltd v. Western Electrodes Co. Ltd (1998) 5 NWLR (Pt. 550) 512 CA*

14. It is proper for a party on appeal to raise the issue of jurisdiction without obtaining the leave of the appellate court.

The issue of jurisdiction being fundamental can be raised at any stage of the proceedings without leave of court.

- *Makinde v. Ojeyinka (1997) 4 NWLR (Pt. 497) 80 CA*

15. Failure of a plaintiff to obtain the leave of court to issue and serve a writ of summons on a defendant outside the jurisdiction of the court renders the issuance and service of such writ void notwithstanding the appearance and participation of the defendant in the proceedings. This is because, a writ unlike other processes is an originating court process and it requires the Registrar's endorsement.

- *N.N.P.C. v. Elumah (1997) 3 NWLR (Pt. 492) 195 CA*
- *B.B.N v. Olayiwola (2001) 6 WRN 141 CA*

16. Territorial jurisdiction of a trial court and the composition of the court are both aspects of jurisdiction, both of which are relevant for the validity of any proceedings before a court.

- *Wuyep v. Wuyep (1997) 10 NWLR (Pt. 523) 154 CA*

17. It is settled that a court is competent when the court is properly constituted as regards numbers and qualifications of the members of the bench and no member is disqualified for one reason or the other; the subject matter of the case is within its jurisdiction, and there is no feature in the case which prevents the court from exercising its jurisdiction; and the case comes before the court initiated by due process of law and upon fulfillment of any condition precedent to the exercise of jurisdiction.

- *Madukolu v. Nkemdilim (1962) 1 All NLR 587 SC*
- *Skenconsult v. Ukey (1981) 1 SC 6*
- *Benin Rubber Producers Ltd v. Ojo (1997) 9 NWLR (Pt. 521) 388 SC*
- *Magaji v. Matari (2000) 5 SC 46*
- *Alao v. African Continental Bank Ltd (2000) 6 SC (Pt. 1) 27*
- *Galadima v. Tambai (2000) 6 SC (Part I) 196*
- *Araka v. Ejeagwu (2000) 12 SC (Pt. I) 99*

18. Failure to serve process where service is required is a failure, which goes to the root of jurisdiction of the court. Any

proceeding in such a case is a nullity.

- *Atser v. Gachi (1997) 6 NWLR (Pt. 510) 609 CA*

19. In an action for the enforcement of fundamental rights, where the main or principal claim is not the enforcement or securing the enforcement of a fundamental right, the jurisdiction of the court cannot be properly exercised, as it will be incompetent. Also, where a court lacks jurisdiction to entertain principal or main claims in an action, that court cannot adjudicate over the incidental or ancillary claims where a determination of such incidental claims must involve a consideration of the main claim.

- *Tukur v. Govt. of Taraba State (1997) 6 NWLR (Pt. 510) 549 SC*

20. Courts are creatures of statute and it is the statute that created a particular court that will also confer on it, its jurisdiction. Jurisdiction may be extended, not by the courts, but by the legislature, for it is part of interpretation functions of the courts to expound the jurisdiction of the court but not to expand it.

- *Gov. of Kwara State v. Gafar (1997) 7 NWLR (Pt. 511) 51 CA*
- *Okulate v. Awosanya (2000) 1 SC 107*
- *Messrs NV Scheep v. The MV 'S. Araz' (2000) 12 SC (Part I) 164*

21. By virtue of section 6 of Decree No. 41 of 1991, the continued exercise of jurisdiction by a court to hear a matter when the subject of a case is in another state due to the creation of new states is valid.

- *Chime v. Chime (2001) 9 WRN 113 SC*

22. The High Court of a state does not have criminal jurisdiction in respect of an offence wholly committed outside the state except where any of the elements of the offence occurs in the state.

- *Waziri v. State (1997) 3 NWLR (Pt. 496) 689 CA*

23. The High Court of a State is by virtue of section 236(1) of the 1979 Constitution conferred with unlimited jurisdiction to hear and determine civil and criminal matters unless such matters are specifically precluded by the Constitution. A state law cannot therefore derogate from the jurisdiction conferred on the High Court.

> - *Salami v. Chairman, L.E.D.B. (1989) 5 NWLR (Pt. 123) 539 SC*
> - *Okulate v. Awosanya (2000) 1 SC 107*

24. By virtue of section 41 of the Land Use Act, 1978, the State High Courts, alongside the Area Courts and Customary Courts, have unfettered concurrent original jurisdiction in respect of claims pertaining to land in non-urban areas, which is subject to customary right of occupancy granted by a Local Government under the Act.

> - *Adisa v. Oyinwola (2000) 6 SC (Part II) 47 at 110*

25. The Sharia Court of Appeal has no jurisdiction to determine any matter which is not an issue of Islamic personal law.

> - *Abuja v. Bizi (1989) 5 NWLR (Pt. 119) 120 CA*
> - *Magaji v. Matari (2000) 5 SC 46*

26. By virtue of section 230(1)(r) and (s) of the 1979 Constitution as amended by Decree 107 of 1993, the Federal High Court has exclusive jurisdiction in civil causes and matters arising from the operation and interpretation of the Constitution in so far as it affects the Federal Government or any of its agencies.

> - *University of Ilorin v. Olutola (1998) 12 NWLR (Pt. 576) 72 CA*

27. Section 230 (1)(a)-(s) of the 1979 Constitution as amended by Decree No. 107 of 1993 confers on the Federal High Court exclusive jurisdiction to entertain matters which in one form or the other affects or reflects the vital interests of the Federal Government as regards revenue and other fiscal measures, financial institutions such as banks. However, this exclusivity is relaxed by section 230(1)(d) of the Constitution as regards matters between an individual customer and his bank or between two banks, taking into account the nature of the transaction and the capacity in which one of the banks dealt with the other.

> - *N.D.I.C. v. F.M.B (1997) 2 NWLR (Pt. 490) 735 CA*

28. By virtue of the combined provisions of section 230(1)(e) of the 1979 Constitution, as amended by Decree No. 107 of 1993 and section 7(1)(b) of the Federal High Court Act, 1973 as amended, the Federal High Court has exclusive jurisdiction in any civil matter arising from the operation of any Act or Decree relating to company and allied matters.

> - *Daily Times (Nig.) Plc v. Akindiji (1998) 13 NWLR (Pt. 580) 22 CA*

29. The admiralty jurisdiction of the Federal High Court cannot be invoked for the sole purpose of obtaining security for the satisfaction of an award that might be made in foreign arbitration proceedings. Section 7(1)(a) of the Federal High Court Act, Cap 134 Laws of the Federation 1990 and section 1(1) of the Admiralty Jurisdiction Act, 1991 considered.

> - *Messrs. NV Scheep v. The MV "S. Araz" 2000) 12 SC (Part I) 164*

30. By virtue of section 7(1)(l) of Decree No. 60 of 1991 and section 230(1)(k) of the 1979 Constitution as amended by Decree No. 107 of 1993, the Federal High Court is the only court vested with original exclusive jurisdiction on aviation matters, including carriage of goods and passengers by air.

> - *Sudan Airways Co. Ltd v. Abdullahi (1998) 1 NWLR (Pt. 532) 156 CA*
>
> - *Kabo Air Ltd v. Oladipo (1999) 10 NWLR (Pt. 623) 517 CA*

31. Although the Supreme Court is the Court of last resort, it is nevertheless a court of appellate jurisdiction. Its jurisdiction is clearly laid down in the Constitution and except for the original jurisdiction conferred on it in section 232 of the 1999 Constitution, its jurisdiction is appellate only, with incidental original jurisdiction conferred on it by subsection (6)(a) of section 6 of the Constitution for the purpose of exercising that appellate jurisdiction.

> - *Alao v. A.C.B. Ltd (2000) 6 SC (Pt. 1) 27*

XIX
Labour Law

19.1 Nature of Contract of Employment

1. A 'worker' is defined generically as any person not being a minor but employed under certain terms of a contract of employment. Consequently, a worker includes a casual worker.

- *Phoenix Motors Ltd v. National Provident Fund Management Board (1993) 1 NWLR (Pt. 272) 718 CA*

2. A contract of employment is usually governed by service agreement or the conditions of service. It is this agreement or conditions of service that regulate the relationship between an employer and his employee.

- *Union Bank of Nigeria Ltd v. Edet (1993) 4 NWLR (Pt. 287) 288 CA*

3. A contract of employment can be divided into two broad categories. The first is the common law ordinary relationship of master and servant with all its normal incidents. The second, is a contract in which the tenure of the employee is protected in one form or the other by a statute. This type of contract of employment enjoys what is called statutory flavour.

- *Central Bank of Nigeria (CBN) v. Jidda (2001) 7 WRN 24 at 27 CA*
- *Shell Pet. Dev. Co. (Nig.) Ltd v. Lawson-Jack (1998) 4 NWLR (Pt. 545) 249 CA*

4. A contract of employment with statutory flavour is one where the conditions for appointment or the determination of such employment are governed by a prescribed conditions in the enabling statute, so that a valid determination of appointment is predicated upon the satisfaction of the statutory provisions.

- *Fakuade v. O.A.U.T.H. (1993) 5 NWLR (Pt. 291) 47 SC*

5. As a general rule, specific performance or reinstatement is not the remedy for breach of contract of service. However, in "special circumstances", specific performance may be granted in contract of service. The special circumstances depend upon the particular facts of each case and on the discretion of the court. Such special circumstances will arise where the contract of employment has a legal or statutory flavour.

- *Chukwumah v. Shell Petroleum (1993) 4 NWLR (Pt. 289) 512 SC*
- *U.B.N. Ltd v. Ogboh (1995) 2 NWLR (Pt. 380) 647 SC*
- *Afribank (Nig.) Plc v. Nwanze (1998) 6 NWLR (Pt. 553) 283 CA*

6. The law is that where an office or employment enjoys a statutory flavour in the sense that its conditions of service are provided for and protected by statute or regulations made thereunder, any person in that office or employment enjoys a special status over and above the ordinary master and servant relationship. In matters of discipline, tenure of office or termination of appointment of such an employee, the procedure laid down by the applicable statute or regulations must be fully complied with. Failure to do so will render null and void any decision that affects the right, reputation or tenure of office of that employee.

- *U.N.T.H.M.B v. Nnoli (1994) 8 NWLR (Pt. 363) 376 SC*
- *Tionsha v. Judicial Service Committee, Benue State (1997) 6 NWLR (Pt. 508) 307 at 313 CA*
- *Bamgboye v. University of Ilorin (1999) 10 NWLR (Pt. 622) 290 at 298 & 299 SC*
- *Psychiatric Hospital Management Board (PHMB) v. Edosa (2001) 12 WRN 183 SC*

7. The law is that where an employee is alleged to have committed a crime by his employer, the employee must be given adequate opportunity to explain himself before a tribunal vested with criminal jurisdiction before any disciplinary action is taken against him by his employer.

- *Denloye v. Medical and Dental Practitioners Disciplinary Committee (1968) All NLR 306*
- *Okpeke v. N.S.P. & M.C. Ltd (1999) 12 NWLR (Pt. 629) 160 CA*

19.2 Vicarious Liability

1. The doctrine of vicarious liability is to the effect that where the relationship of master and servant exists, the master is liable for the wrongful or tortious acts of the servant so long as they are committed in the course of the servant's employment.

- *James v. Mid-West Motors Nigeria Ltd (1978) 11-12 SC 31 at 51*
- *Odebunmi v. Abdullahi (1997) 2 NWLR (Pt. 489) 526 at 529 SC*
- *Osondu v. Boneh (2000) 3 SC 42 at 48 & 49*

2. The "course of the servant's employment" can be extended to acts, which are outside the employee's working hours and outside the employer's premises, provided the acts are done for the purpose of the employer's business.

- *Ruddiman & Co. v. Smith (1889) 60 LT 708*

3. A servant's wrongful act is deemed to be in the course of his employment if it is either a wrongful act authorized by the master, or a wrongful and unauthorized mode of doing some act authorised by the master.

- *N.B.N. v. T.A.S.A. Ltd (1996) 8 NWLR (Pt. 468) 511 at 513 CA*

4. In an action for vicarious liability, the plaintiff must establish that the relationship of master and servant exists and that the servant is liable for the wrongful act. Similarly, the servant has to be joined as a party to a suit against his master. If the servant is not joined in the action, the action is incompetent *ab initio*.

- *Chukwu v. Solel Boneh (Nig.) Ltd (1993) 3 NWLR (Pt. 280) 246 CA*
- *Obi v. Biwater Shellabear (Nig.) Ltd (1997) 1 NWLR (Pt. 484) 722 CA*

19.3 Redundancy

1. Redundancy in service is a mode of removing an employee from service when his post is declared redundant by his employer. It is not a voluntary or forced retirement, nor is it a dismissal from service. It is not a voluntary or forced resignation, nor is it a termination of appointment. It is rather, a unique procedure whereby an employee is quietly and lawfully relieved of his post. Consequently, the conditions applicable to redundancy are quite distinct from those applicable to retirement or other conventional modes of relieving an employee from active service, such as termination, resignation or dismissal.

P.A.N. Ltd v. Oje (1997) 11 NWLR (Pt. 530) 625 at 627 CA

2. The principle of "last in, first out" (LIFO) is applicable in the discharge of a particular category of workers, subject to such factors of relative merit, such as skill, ability and reliability. The principle relates to re-engagement of workers. It does not apply to redundancy of workers. Section 20(1)(b) of the Labour Act, Cap. 198 Laws of the Federation of Nigeria, 1990 considered

- Agoma v. Guinness (Nig.) Ltd (1995) 2 NWLR (Pt. 380) 672 SC

19.4 Retirement

1. It is a well known practice, that only an employee in public office that can elect to retire voluntarily at the age of 45 or compulsorily at the age of 60.

- Ejitagha v. Psychiatric Hospital Management Board (1995) 2 NWLR (Pt. 376) 189 CA

2. A public officer, who wishes to retire from the public service is under a mandatory duty to either give three-month notice of his intention to retire or pay three-month salary in lieu of the notice. It is either one or the other. Where he elects to give three month notice, he shall remain in the service until the expiration of the three-month notice. Within that period, he is entitled to

all the benefits and advantages of a serving officer. Similarly, he is subject to any disciplinary measures that his employer may wish to take against any serving officer, including himself.

> - *Amokeodo v. I.G.P. (1999) 6 NWLR (Pt. 607) 467 at 471 SC*

3. A public servant who has been in service for 15 years and aged 45 years at the time of his retirement is qualified for pension. Sections 3(2)(a) & (b) and 4(2) of the Pensions Act, Cap 346, Laws of the Federation of Nigeria, 1990 considered.

> - *Achimugu v. Minister, F.C.T. (1998) 11 NWLR (Pt. 574) 467 CA*

4. A public servant is not qualified for pension merely because a court had awarded damages for a period covering the time he would have remained in service had his services not been terminated.

> - *Achimugu v. Minister, F.C.T. (1998) 11 NWLR (Pt. 574) 467 CA*

5. The fact that a person is employed in public office does not *ipso facto* entitle him to pension or bring his service under the Pensions Act, Cap. 346, Laws of the Federation of Nigeria, 1990, so as to subject his appointment to the provisions of the Act.

> - *Ejitagha v. Psychiatric Hospital Management Board (1995) 2 NWLR (Pt. 376) 189 CA*

19.5 Termination/Dismissal at Common Law

1. The rule is that before an employer can terminate the appointment of his employee, such an employee must be given the opportunity of being heard, even where the allegation for which the employee sought to be removed, involves accusation of crime.

> - *Afribank (Nig.) Plc v. Nwanze (1998) 6 NWLR (Pt. 553) 283 CA*

2. A master can terminate the employment of his servant at any

time and for any reason or for no reason at all, provided the termination is in accordance with the terms of their contract. The motive, which impels the master to terminate a contract of employment with his servant, is irrelevant. Consequently, the exercise of a right to terminate a contract of employment by a master cannot be vitiated by proof of malice or improper motive.

- *Fakuade v. O.A.U.T.H. (1993) 5 NWLR (Pt. 291) 47 SC*
- *Ekpeogu v. Ashaka Cement Co. Plc (1997) 6 NWLR (Pt. 508) 280 CA*
- *WR & PC Ltd v. Onwo (1999) 12 NWLR (Pt. 630) 312 CA*

3. Where the termination of a contract of employment is unlawful or wrongful, it only entitles the employee to damages. It would be wrong for a court to declare such a wrongful termination of contract of employment null and void, and to hold that the contract is still subsisting on the ground that the termination was done in breach of the terms of the contract between the employer and the employee. This is because, a court of law has no power to impose an employee on an unwilling employer.

- *Ekpeogu v. Ashaka Cement Co. Plc (1997) 6 NWLR (Pt. 508) 280 CA*
- *WR & PC Ltd v. Onwo (1999) 12 NWLR (Pt. 630) 312 CA*

4. The law is that where an employee accepts or collects his entitlements, which includes salary in lieu of notice of termination of his appointment, he cannot be heard to complain later that his contract of employment was not validly and properly determined. The employee can no longer maintain an action after collecting his benefits.

- *Agoma v. Guinness (Nig.) Ltd (1995) 2 NWLR (Pt. 380) 672 SC*

5. Where a contract of employment is silent as to the required notice for termination, the court will imply that a reasonable notice is necessary. It is within the powers of the judge to decide what a reasonable notice is, having regard to certain factors, such as, the nature of the employment, the length of service, and other circumstances of the case.

- Akumechiel v. B.C.C. Ltd (1997) 1 NWLR (Pt. 484) 695 CA

6. There is a difference between wrongful dismissal and unlawful dismissal. Wrongful dismissal applies only to a master and servant relationship, which merely entitles an employee to the usual damages in terms of what he would have earned for the period of notice he is entitled to, for the termination of his employment. Unlawful dismissal, on the other hand, applies to employment governed and protected by statute.

- Shell Pet. Dev. Co. (Nig.) Ltd. v. Lawson-Jack (1998) 4 NWLR (Pt. 545) 249 CA

7. It is a well established principle of law, that ordinarily, a master is entitled to dismiss his servant from his employment for any reason or for no reason at all. Likewise, the court will not impose an employee on an employer.

- Chukwumah v. Shell Petroleum (1993) 4 NWLR (Pt. 289) 512 SC

8. Except in employment governed by statute, wherein the procedure for employment and discipline including dismissal of an employee are clearly spelt out, any other employment outside the statute is governed by the terms under which the parties agreed to be master and servant.

- U.B.N. Ltd v. Ogboh (1995) 2 NWLR (Pt. 380) 647 SC

9. Disobedience of an employer's lawful order and, or insubordination by an employee is an act of misconduct which may justifiably attract the penalty of summary dismissal, termination or compulsory retirement of the said employee.

- University of Calabar v. Essien (1996) 10 NWLR (Pt. 477) 225 SC

10. Where an employee is guilty of gross misconduct, he could be lawfully dismissed summarily without notice and without wages.

- U.B.N. Ltd v. Ogboh (1995) 2 NWLR (Pt. 380) 647 SC

11. "Gross misconduct" is defined as conduct of a grave and weighty character as to undermine the confidence, which exists between the employee and his employer, or which work against

the deep interest of the employer.

- *U.B.N. Ltd v. Ogboh (1995) 2 NWLR (Pt. 380) 647 SC*

12. Conviction for criminal offence, corruption, conduct likely to endanger the lives and safety of other people or the property of the employer, appropriation of the employer's property to personal use without his consent, stealing of employer's money, drunkenness, indulgence in violence, etc., are examples of acts which the law considers as gross misconduct and can lead to summary dismissal of a servant.

- *Osakwe v. Nigerian Paper Mill Ltd (1998) 10 NWLR (Pt. 568) 1 at 5 SC*

13. A servant who is purportedly dismissed summarily by his master where a notice of not less than three months is required, can recover as damages for breach of contract three months remuneration and no more. Once the agreed or specified period of notice or payment of salary in lieu of notice has been given, it prevents the termination of the contract of employment from being wrongful or actionable.

- *Odiase v. Auchi Polytechnic (1998) 4 NWLR (Pt. 546) 477 CA*

14. An employee is not entitled to obtain an injunction or a court order with the aim of restraining his master from dismissing him. He can only claim damages for wrongful dismissal.

- *Shell Pet. Dev. Co. (Nig.) Ltd v. Lawson-Jack (1998) 4 NWLR (Pt. 545) 249 CA*

15. A wrongful dismissal of an employee in complete disregard of the terms of his contract of employment is a repudiation of the contract by the employer. Therefore, the only remedy available to the employee is a claim for damages for the wrongful dismissal.

- *Francis v. Municipal Councillors of Kuala Lumpur (1962) 2 All ER 633*

- *Ilodibia v. Nigerian Cement Company Ltd (1997) 7 NWLR (Pt. 512) 174 at Pages 176 & 177 SC*

- *Olafimihan v. Nova Lay-Tech Ltd (1998) 4 NWLR (Pt. 547) 608 CA*

16. A claim for wrongful dismissal from employment is founded on the basis of contract of employment. It is, therefore, improper to bring an action for wrongful dismissal from employment under the Fundamental Rights (Enforcement Procedure) Rules 1979.

> - *Egbuonu v. Borno Radio Television Corporation (1997) 12 NWLR (Pt. 531) 29 at 42 SC*
>
> - *Sea Trucks v. Anigboro (2001) 10 WRN 78 at 81 SC*

19.6 Termination/Dismissal under Statutes

1. For an employer to successfully justify the termination of the employment of his employee which is with statutory flavour, such employer must prove to the satisfaction of the trial court that the allegation made against the employee was disclosed to him, whereby he was given a fair hearing, and that the disciplinary panel believed that the employee committed the offence after hearing him.

> - *Bamgboye v. University of Ilorin (1999) 10 NWLR (Pt. 622) 290 SC*

2. Specific performance of the contract of employment or reinstatement of the servant to his position in the master's employ may be ordered where such employment enjoys statutory flavour.

> - *U.N.T.H.M.B. v. Nnoli (1994) 8 NWLR (Pt. 363) 376 SC*

3. An appointment is said to be with statutory flavour if a servant's conditions of service are governed by a statute, regulations and rules made under it.

> - *Odiase v, Auchi Polytechnic (1998) 4 NWLR (Pt. 546) 477 CA*

4. Where a contract of employment makes explicit provision for termination of appointment, the termination of the appointment of a servant must be done in accordance with the prescribed procedure. The motive or reason for the termination may not be quite relevant.

> - *Odiase v. Auchi Polytechnic (1998) 4 NWLR (Pt. 546) 477 CA*

5. A plaintiff who seeks a declaration that the termination of his contract of employment is a nullity must plead and prove the following material facts. First, that he is an employee of the defendant. Secondly, he must show how he was appointed and the terms and conditions of his appointment. Thirdly, he must prove the person or authority who can appoint and remove him from his employment. Fourthly, he must plead and prove the circumstances under which his employment can be terminated and; Finally, he must prove that his appointment can only be terminated by a person or authority other than the defendant.

> - *Morohunfola v. Kwara Tech. (1990) 4 NWLR (Pt. 145) 506 SC*

> - *Okoebor v. Police Council (1998) 9 NWLR (Pt. 566) 534 CA*

6. Before a civil servant can be dismissed from service, certain steps must be taken, in accordance with the Civil Service Commission Regulations. For instance, the civil servant concerned must have been either convicted of a criminal offence based on fraud or dishonesty, or have been found guilty, after a thorough hearing according to the civil service rules, of some offences bordering on dereliction of duty, incompetence, or deliberate act or omission that caused loss to government, etc.

> - *Ebohon v. A-G, Edo State (1997) 5 NWLR (Pt. 505) 298 SC*

19.7 Trade Union Matters

1. "Trade dispute" means any dispute between employers and workers or between workers and workers, which is connected with the employment or non-employment, or the terms of employment or conditions of work of any person. Section 25 of the Trade Union Act, Cap 437, Laws of the Federation of Nigeria, 1990 considered.

> - *Anigboro v. Sea Trucks (Nig.) Ltd (1995) 6 NWLR (Pt. 399) 35 CA*

2. A case of wrongful dismissal between a master and a servant,

based on the terms of their contract of employment cannot be treated as a trade dispute.

> - *Sea Trucks (Nig.) Ltd v. Pyne (1995) 6 NWLR (Pt. 400) 166 CA*

3. The law is that no action relating to trade disputes whether intra or inter-union dispute can be commenced in a court of law. The jurisdiction of courts to entertain such action was ousted with effect from 1st January 1992. Section 1A of the Trade Disputes (Amendment) Decree No. 47 of 1992 considered.

> - *Udoh v. Orthopaedic Hospital Management Board (1993) 7 NWLR (Pt. 304) 139 SC*

4. The relationship between a member of a trade union and the union itself is contractual, and the terms of the contract are to be found in the rules of the union. A member of a trade union has, in general the right to take proceedings to enforce compliance with the union's own rules in relation to matters, such as election of officers and other internal regulations.

> - *Elufioye v. Halilu (1993) 6 NWLR (Pt. 301) 570 SC*

5. It is trite law that collective labour agreements, except where they have been adopted as forming part of the terms of employment, are not intended to give, or capable of giving individual employees a right of action over an alleged breach of their terms of employment as may be conceived by them to have affected their interest. Similarly, the collective agreements are not meant to supplant or even supplement their contract of service.

> - *Union Bank of Nigeria Ltd v. Edet (1993) 4 NWLR (Pt. 287) 288 CA*

6. The failure to act in strict compliance with a collective labour agreement is not justiciable. The enforcement of such agreement lies in negotiation between the union and the employer. Consequently, if an employer ignores or breaches a term of collective labour agreement, resort could be had, if at all, to negotiation between the union and the employer, and ultimately, to a strike action, should the need arise and if it is appropriate to do so.

> - *Union Bank of Nigeria Ltd v. Edet (1993) 4 NWLR (Pt. 287) 288 CA*

7. The right to freedom of association is well protected by section 37 of the Constitution of the Federal Republic of Nigeria, 1979. Consequently, the right to form or join any political party or trade union is exclusively that of the individual citizen and not that of his employer. Indeed, an employer has no business forming a trade union, let alone compelling his workers to join it.

   - *Anigboro v. Sea Trucks (Nig.) Ltd (1995) 6 NWLR (Pt. 399) 35 CA*

XX
Land Law

20.1 Proof of Title to Land

1. There are five ways of proving or establishing title to or ownership of land. These are by traditional evidence; production of documents of title duly authenticated in the sense that their due execution must be proved; by positive acts of ownership extending over a sufficient length of time; by acts of long possession and enjoyment of the land; by proof of possession of connected or adjacent land in circumstances rendering it probable that the owner of such connected or adjacent land, would in addition, be the owner of the land in dispute.

> - *Nkado v. Obiano (1997) 5 NWLR (Pt. 503) 31 at 34 SC*
> - *Nkwo v. Iboe (1998) 7 NWLR (Pt. 558) 354 SC*
> - *Chukwu v. Diala (1999) 6 NWLR (Pt. 608) 674 CA*
> - *Inwelegbu v. Ezeani (1999) 12 NWLR (Pt. 630) 266 CA*
> - *Adesanya v. Aderounmu (2000) 6 SC (Part II) 18*
> - *Adeosun v. Jibesin (2001) 14 WRN 106 at 108 CA*

2. There is a difference between a grant of land and a settlement on land. A grant comes from a previous titleholder to a subsequent person called the grantee but a settlement does not recognise any previous titleholder. Where a plaintiff establishes a grant of land in evidence, he cannot be said to have proved his title. Also, the party who led evidence as to a grant cannot seek to plead settlement in place of a grant.

> - *Kode v. Yussuf (2001) 14 WRN 153 CA*

3. Section 46 of the Evidence Act raises a presumption in favour of a person who exercises acts of possession and enjoyment over a piece of land to be the owner of the said land. However, for this presumption to apply, the party relying on it must adduce evidence in proof of positive and numerous acts to warrant the inference that he is the exclusive owner of the land.

> - *Okwaranonobi v. Mbadugha (1998) 7 NWLR (Pt. 558) 471 CA*

- Nwosu v. Okoli (1999) 2 NWLR (Pt. 592) 598 CA

- Ikwuje v. Elenu (2001) 13 WRN 43 CA

4. Where a party's claim for title to land is founded upon a grant by a particular person, family or community, under native law and custom, that party must plead and prove the origin of the title of such person, family or community unless that title has been admitted.

- Inko-Tariah v. Goodhead (1997) 4 NWLR (Pt. 500) 453 CA

- Ekpechi v. Owhonda (1998) 3 NWLR (Pt. 543) 618 CA

5. In an action for declaration of title to land based on communal ownership, there is need for the plaintiff to plead facts showing how the land in question became communal property and also the identity of the communal ancestor ought to be established.

- Echi v. Nnamani (2000) 5 SC 62 at 78

6. Where both parties agree that the title to a land in dispute belongs to a common vendor, for either side to succeed, he must be able to trace his root of title to the common vendor.

- Adebo v. Saki Estates Ltd. (1999) 7 NWLR (Pt. 612) 525 SC

7. Where a party to a land in dispute has directly traced his title to a person whose title to ownership had been established, it would not be necessary for him to prove his ownership of the said land.

- Bunyan v. Akingboye (1999) 7 NWLR (Pt. 609) 31 SC

8. In an action for a declaration of statutory right of occupancy to land, the dismissal of the plaintiff's claim does not automatically confer the statutory right of occupancy on the defendant. This is because the grant of a statutory right of occupancy to the defendant is not directly in issue.

- Yusuf v. Matthew (1999) 13 NWLR (Pt. 633) 30 at 32 CA

9. A plaintiff who seeks declaration of title to land must prove his root of title to the land. Where he traces his title to a particular person, he must further prove how that person got his own title or came to have the title vested in him, including, where necessary, the family that originally owned the land. The burden

of proof on the plaintiff is not discharged even where the scales are evenly weighted between the parties.

    - Dike v. Okoloedo (1999) 10 NWLR (Pt. 623) 359 SC

10. In a claim for declaration of title to land, a plaintiff has the burden of proving his case upon his own evidence and cannot rely on the weakness of the defendant's case. However, a plaintiff can take advantage of evidence by the defence, which supports his case.

    - Nze v. Unakalamba (1998) 2 NWLR (Pt. 537) 308 CA

    - Ibe v. Auta (1998) 2 NWLR (Pt. 538) 497 CA

    - Nwosu v. Okoli (1999) 2 NWLR (Pt. 592) 598 CA

    - Dike v. Okoloedo (1999) 10 NWLR (Pt. 623) 359 SC

    - Ojo v. Anibire (1999) 11 NWLR (Pt. 628) 630 CA

    - Orubon v. Gbondu (1999) 11 NWLR (Pt. 628) 661 CA

    - Madubuonwu v. Nnalue (1999) 11 NWLR (Pt. 628) 673 SC

    - Eze v. Atasie (2000) 6 SC (Part I) 214

    - Elema v. Akenzua (2000) 6 SC (Part III) 26 at 29-30

    - Itauma v. Akpe-Ime (2000) 7 SC (Part II) 24 at 30-31

    - Gbadamosi v. Dairo (2001) 11 WRN 129 CA

11. A party who relies on a document in proof of his title to land must tender the document in evidence, as extrinsic evidence of its contents is not admissible in evidence.

    - Adelaja v. Alade (1999) 6 NWLR (Pt. 608) 544 SC

    - Jiaza v. Bamgbose (1999) 7 NWLR (Pt. 610) 182 SC

12. The fact that a person has acquired rights of possession over parts of a piece of land in dispute will not affect the right of any other person to seek a declaration of title to the whole piece of land.

    - Uzochukwu v. Eri (1997) 7 NWLR (Pt. 514) 535 SC

    - Dokubo v. Omoni (1999) 8 NWLR (Pt. 616) 647 SC

13. Under Bini native law and custom, all Bini lands are communal property of the entire Bini people and the legal estate in such lands is vested and resides in the Oba of Benin as trustee for Bini people. In order to succeed in proving acquisition of title under Bini law, the plaintiff must prove that he got the

allocation or grant of the land through the Oba of Benin who is the only authority competent to allocate land.

- *Enabulele v. Agbonlahor (1999) 4 NWLR (Pt. 598) 166 SC*
- *Ojo v. Azama (2001) 12 WRN 1 SC*

14. A court of law will not reject a traditional history tainted with sentiment and emphasis as long as such sentiment and emphasis do not disturb the natural flow of the evidence in terms of accuracy in details.

- *Odunukwe v. Ofomata (1999) 6 NWLR (Pt. 607) 416 CA*

15. Where there is a conflict in the evidence led by parties based on traditional history, the court is to test the traditional history by reference to the facts in recent years as established by evidence and, ascertain which of the two is the more probable. The court may visit the *locus in quo* to remove any doubt in its mind as to the ownership of the land.

- *Adeyeri v. Okobi (1997) 6 NWLR (Pt. 510) 534 SC*

16. A plaintiff relying on evidence of traditional history to prove ownership of land needs to give a credible evidence which is consistent and leaves no gap as to the chain of succession. The traditional evidence tendered must in addition to making consistent sense be linked with the plaintiff.

- *Idesoh v. Ordia (1997) 3 NWLR (Pt. 491) 17 CA*
- *Salami v. Gbodoolu (1997) 4 NWLR (Pt. 499) 277 SC*
- *Ojokolobo v. Alamu (1998) 9 NWLR (Pt. 565) 226 SC*
- *Sanni v. Hughes (1999) 7 NWLR (Pt. 611) 474 CA*
- *Olohunde v. Adeyoju (2000) 6 SC (Pt. III) 118*

17. To plead traditional history as root of title in a claim for declaration of title, there must be averments as to the devolution of the land right from the original founder to the present party without leaving any unexplained or unexplainable gaps in the line of successors. An insufficient averment as to the founding of the land in dispute will not found such a claim on traditional history.

- *Uchendu v. Ogboni (1999) 5 NWLR (Pt. 603) 337 SC*
- *Eze v. Atasie (2000) 6 SC (Pt. 1) 214*

18. A survey plan is not a *sine qua non* in a claim for declaration

of title to land. All that is required is a clear description to make a disputed land ascertainable. However, by way of common practice, parties in land dispute file a detailed and accurate survey plan of the land showing the various features on such land sufficient to point to the clear boundaries thereof.

- *Oyefeso v. Coker (1999) 1 NWLR (Pt. 588) 654 CA*
- *Emiri v. Imieyeh (1999) 4 NWLR (Pt. 599) 442 SC*
- *Gbadamosi v. Dairo (2001) 11 WRN 129 CA*

19. Where a plaintiff tenders a survey plan of disputed land in evidence without an objection and the defendant fails to file a counter-plan, the defendant cannot be heard to contend that the plaintiff did not prove with certainty the boundaries of the land in dispute.

- *Adepoju v. Oke (1999) 3 NWLR (Pt. 594) 154 SC*

20. The act of vesting legal title in respect of a piece of land in a person is a matter of law to be deduced from the facts and evidence admitted.

- *Nasiru v. Abubakar (1997) 4 NWLR (Pt. 497) 32 CA*

21. A plaintiff who pleads a particular root of title and fails to prove that particular root of title cannot rely on another mode of acquisition of land not pleaded by him as his root of title to support his claim.

- *Ude v. Chimbo (1998) 12 NWLR (Pt. 577) 169 at 172-173 SC*

22. Possession in law means exclusive possession. The law does not protect possession, which is not exclusive. What constitutes acts of possession depends on the merits of each case.

- *Igwegbe v. Ezuma (1999) 6 NWLR (Pt. 606) 228 at 230 CA*
- *Ajero v. Ugorji (1999) 10 NWLR (Pt. 621) 1 at 4 SC*

23. A plaintiff in exclusive though adverse possession of land may institute an action in trespass to protect his right to retain and to undisturbed enjoyment of the land against all wrongdoers except a person who can establish a better title thereto.

- *Odekilekun v. Hassan (1997) 12 NWLR (Pt. 531) 56 SC*
- *Akanbi v. Raji (1998) 12 NWLR (Pt. 578) 360 CA*

- Shomefun v. Shade (1999) 12 NWLR (Pt. 632) 531 CA

24. A party claiming reversionary interest on land has a duty to first identify and establish his title to the land in dispute before the question of reversion arises.

- Dikko v. Ibadan South West L.G. (1997) 2 NWLR (Pt. 486) 235 CA

25. The grant of a statutory right of occupancy over land extinguishes any previous licence granted in respect of the same piece of land by virtue of section 5(2) of the Land Use Act, 1978.

- Kari v. Ganaram (1997) 2 NWLR (Pt. 488) 380 SC

26. Under the Yoruba customary law, *Ishakole* is a tribute paid to an overlord by tenants put on a land. *Ishakole* could be in kind or in cash. Payment of *Ishakole* may be dispensed with in so far as the tenants are loyal and admit their overlordship.

- Adesanoye v. Akinwale (1997) 3 NWLR (Pt. 496) 664 CA

- Makinde v. Akinwale (2000) 1 SC 89

27. In a claim for easement, a plaintiff must establish that the access road is one for which a public right of way has been created; and show actual interference by the defendant with the plaintiff's right of use of the said access road by way of obstruction.

- Amachree v. Isokariari (1998) 11 NWLR (Pt. 572) 52 at 53-54 CA

28. A person in lawful possession ought to be served with a notice for recovery of possession. It is mandatory to serve all those in actual possession of land, in an action for recovery of possession. This is to avoid a situation where parties may collude to dispossess someone in lawful possession by not serving him thereby making him unaware of the action taken to dispossess him.

- Oduola v. Nabham (1981) N.S.C.C. Vol. 12 P.180 at 194

- In Re: Arowolo (1993) 2 NWLR (Pt. 275) 317 CA

20.2 Trespass to Land

1. Trespass to land constitutes the slightest disturbance to the possession of land by a person who cannot show a better right to possession.

> - *Imona-Russel v. Niger Construction Ltd (1987) 3 NWLR (Pt. 60) 298 SC*
> - *Ojomo v. Ibrahim (1999) 12 NWLR (Pt. 631) 415 at 417 CA*

2. Trespass to land is actionable at the instance of the person in possession. Exclusive possession gives the person in possession the right to retain the land and to undisturbed enjoyment of it against all wrong doers except a person who can establish a better title. Nevertheless, if a land is in possession of a tenant, it is the tenant and not the landlord who can sue for trespass because in almost all cases, it is the person in possession of the property who can sue for trespass.

> - *Agu v. Nnadi (1999) 2 NWLR (Pt. 589) 131 CA*
> - *Adepoju v. Oke (1999) 3 NWLR (Pt. 594) 154 SC*

3. Although a claim for trespass is rooted in exclusive possession, once the defendant asserts ownership of the land in dispute, title thereto is automatically put in issue and for the plaintiff to succeed, he must establish a better title than that of the defendant.

> - *Fasikun II v. Oluronke II (1999) 2 NWLR (Pt. 589) 1 at 4 SC*
> - *Ichu v. Ibezue (1999) 2 NWLR (Pt. 591) 437 CA*

4. In an action for trespass, to defeat the plaintiff's claim, a defendant must show either that he is the one in actual possession or that he has a right to such possession.

> - *Ojomo v. Ibrahim (1999) 12 NWLR (Pt. 631) 415 CA*

5. A person other than the true owner of a piece of land can bring an action for trespass if he has exclusive possession of the said land.

> - *Ekennia v. Nkpakara (1997) 5 NWLR (Pt. 504) 152 SC*
> - *Nkume v. The Regt. Trustees of the Diocese of Aba (1998) 10 NWLR (Pt. 570) 514 CA*

6. There are different ingredients for establishing trespass to land and title to land. For trespass, once the plaintiff establishes exclusive possession, he can sustain an action for trespass but for a declaration of title to land, the plaintiff must prove his case based on satisfactory and emphatic evidence.

- *Abasi v. Onido (1998) 5 NWLR (Pt. 548) 89 CA*

7. A court can only grant a party specific reliefs claimed. A court cannot grant to a party a relief more than he claimed. Therefore, although an action for trespass to land coupled with a claim for injunction automatically puts in issue the title of the parties, this does not mean the plaintiff in such an action is entitled to an award of title to the land in dispute without a specific relief for title before the court.

- *Agbaisi v. Ebikorefe (1997) 4 NWLR (Pt. 502) 630 SC*
- *Udih v. Idemudia (1998) 4 NWLR (Pt. 545) 231 SC*

8. By virtue of section 4(1) of the Limitation Law of Bendel State, Cap. 89 of 1976 actions founded on simple contract or on tort shall not be brought after the expiration of six years from the date, which the cause of action accrued. Therefore, trespass being a tortious act is statute barred after 6 years.

- *Amata v. Omofuma (1997) 2 NWLR (Pt. 485) 93 CA*

9. An act of trespass can never become an act of possession and the rightful owner of the land is entitled to complain once he becomes aware of the trespass.

- *Chukwueke v. Okoronkwo (1999) 1 NWLR (Pt. 587) 410 at 412 SC*

10. There is nothing like "partial or continuing trespass". One is either a trespasser or not a trespasser. Even though one might have entered premises lawfully and with full consent of the owner, he becomes a trespasser *ab initio* from the moment he begins to dispute the title of the true owner or commits other acts of trespass.

- *Grains Prod. Agency v. Ezegbulem (1999) 1 NWLR (Pt. 587) 399 CA*

20.3 Proof of Identity of Land

1. Before a claim for declaration of title to land is granted, the land being claimed must be ascertained with certainty, the test being whether a surveyor can, from the record, produce an accurate plan of such land.

- *Igyuse v. Ocholi (1997) 2 NWLR (Pt. 487) 352 CA*
- *Anakaa v. Chako (1997) 2 NWLR (Pt. 488) 488 CA*
- *Idehen v. Osemwenkhae (1997) 10 NWLR (Pt. 525) 358 SC*
- *Pever v. Adaa (1998) 3 NWLR (Pt. 540) 129 CA*
- *Iordye v. Ihyambe (2000) 12 SC Part II) 126*

2. Where in a land case, the area of land in dispute is well known to both sides, the issue of proof of it does not arise, as the court cannot possibly reach a conclusion that the area claimed is not certain.

- *Osho v. Ape (1998) 8 NWLR (Pt. 562) 492 at 495 SC*

20.4 Sale of Land

1. Under native law and custom, the requirements for a valid sale of land are the payment of the agreed purchase money by the purchaser and delivery of possession of the land by the vendor to him. It is not necessary to have a written contract or conveyance as under English law.

- *Yusuf v. Matthew (1999) 13 NWLR (Pt. 633) 30 CA*
- *Adesanya v. Aderounmu (2000) 6 SC (Part II) 18*
- *Elema v. Akenzua (2000) 6 SC (Part III) 26 at 37*

2. Refusal by the vendor to execute a power of attorney or deed of assignment in favour of the purchaser pursuant to a contract of sale is an unequivocal breach of his undertaking to the purchaser.

- *Lawal v. Ejidike (1997) 2 NWLR (Pt. 487) 319 CA*

3. Under customary law, if the purchase price of land is not fully paid, there can be no valid sale notwithstanding that the purchaser is in possession. The possession cannot defeat the

title of the vendor.

- *Odusoga v. Ricketts (1997) 7 NWLR (Pt. 511) 1 SC*

4. Where there is no evidence of distribution of a jointly owned land, one of the joint owners cannot validly dispose of such land by way of sale. Where one of the joint owners of undistributed land, which is jointly owned, sells, the sale is not valid in law.

- *Ige v. Dobi (1999) 3 NWLR (Pt. 596) 550 CA*

5. The principles governing ownership and use of lake are that a family owning land which abuts on a lake automatically has a fishing right in that lake; no part of the lake is exclusively owned by anybody or family and; the lake cannot become the private property of any particular family, so as to ensure that the right of any other family is not denied and, in the cause of rotation, to ensure the order of rotation is maintained.

- *Ebimotureh v. Inekembagha (1998) 3 NWLR (Pt. 543) 548 CA*

6. The purport of the doctrine of *lis pendens* is to prevent a party to litigation in respect of real property from transferring the property, the subject matter of the litigation to a third party during the pendency of the case. This doctrine aims at avoiding pre-emption of the result of the action to the prejudice of the opposing party. A sale under such circumstance will be set aside.

- *Alakija v. Abdulai (1998) 6 NWLR (Pt. 552) 1 at 4 SC*
- *Bua v. Dauda (1999) 12 NWLR (Pt. 629) 59 CA*
- *Umoh v. Tita (1999) 12 NWLR (Pt. 631) 427 CA*

7. The doctrine of *quic quid plantatur solo solo cedit* is to the effect that whoever owns land also owns what is on the land, attached to the land, fixed to the land or found on the land.

- *Ikyaawan v. Ajivah (1997) 4 NWLR (Pt. 499) 365 CA*

8. An instrument means a document affecting land whereby one party confers, transfers, limits, charges or extinguishes in favour of another party any right or title to or interest in the land. For an instrument to be pleaded or given in evidence in any court as affecting land, such instrument must be registered. However, an unregistered registrable instrument, though not admissible to prove title, is admissible to prove payment of money and

coupled with possession of land by the purchaser, it may give rise to an equitable interest.

- *Olanrewaju v. Ogunleye (1997) 2 NWLR (Pt. 485) 12 SC*
- *Lawal v. Ejidike (1997) 2 NWLR (Pt. 487) 319 CA*
- *Alaya v. Akinduro (1998) 4 NWLR (Pt. 545) 311 CA*
- *Adeyemo v. Ida (1998) 4 NWLR (Pt. 546) 504 CA*
- *Nnubia v. A-G, Rivers State (1999) 3 NWLR (Pt. 593) 82 CA*

9. The doctrine *nemo dat quod non habet* is to the effect that a person cannot give what he does not have. Therefore, a vendor cannot subsequently sell land, which he already sold to another person.

- *Adeagbo v. Williams (1998) 2 NWLR (Pt. 536) 120 CA*

10. *Jus tertii* means the right of a third party. A tenant or bailee who pleads that the title to a disputed land is in some other person other than his landlord or bailor is said to set up a *jus tertii*. A party cannot rely on the title of a third person unless he is claiming by or on the strength of such title.

- *Audu v. Ndubuisi (1997) 3 NWLR (Pt. 493) 306 CA*

11. A body corporate in law is a juristic person having legal personality and it can be an occupier of premises.

- *Laban-kowa v. Alkali (1999) 9 NWLR (Pt. 620) 601 CA*

20.5 Family Property

1. A family member and, *a fortiori*, a family head, who becomes aware of a threat to family land from external sources can take necessary action to protect and preserve the family property.

- *Afoezioha v. Nwokoro (1999) 8 NWLR (Pt. 615) 393 at 395 CA*

2. A partition of family land, which is made without the consent of the head and principal members of the family, is clearly defective.

- *Odekilekun v. Hassan (1997) 12 NWLR (Pt. 531) 56 at 63 SC*

3. A sale of unpartitioned family land is valid only when the principal members of the family consent to it. This is because family land ceases to be family land only after partition. Mere allotment does not give the allotee right to sell family land. Therefore, where there is no consent of majority of family members, any purported sale is invalid.

   - *Agboke v. Igbira (1997) 9 NWLR (Pt. 519) 40 CA*

4. A grantee of a partitioned portion of family property becomes the owner of the specific portion of land granted. He can therefore exercise exclusive right of ownership over such land including right to alienate.

   - *Etim v. Butt (1997) 11 NWLR (Pt. 527) 69 CA*
   - *Akinsanya v. Soyemi (1998) 8 NWLR (Pt. 560) 49 CA*

5. The legal term 'partition' is applied to the division of land, tenements and hereditaments belonging to co-owners, and the allotment among them of parts. Partition brings to an end the community of ownership between some or all of the joint owners of land. It may be made by agreement where all parties are either *sui juris* or have power conferred on them either by statute or by an instrument. The effect of partition is to make each former tenant a separate owner of a specific portion of land. It completely terminates the co-ownership.

   - *Akinsanya v. Soyemi (1998) 8 NWLR (Pt. 560) 49 at 51 CA*

6. There is a distinction between partition and allotment of land. Partition results in the determination of co-ownership of family land and is based on equality of quantum of shares. There is an agreement to divide. However, allotment involves a cession of part of family land to a branch of the family while the remaining part continues to be held as such in co-ownership.

   - *Baruwa v. Osoba (1997) 3 NWLR (Pt. 492) 164 CA*
   - *Akinsanya v. Soyemi (1998) 8 NWLR (Pt. 560) 49 CA*

7. Under the law, unanimity of concurrence of the members of a family is not required for a valid sale of family land. Where the head of the family secures the concurrence of the principal members of the family, he can validly alienate the family property.

   - *Odekilekun v. Hassan (1997) 12 NWLR (Pt. 531) 56 SC*

- *Okonkwo v. Okonkwo (1998) 10 NWLR (Pt. 571) 554 at 557 SC*

- *Oladunjoye v. Akinterinwa (2000) 4 SC (Pat I) 19*

8. Where the head of a family alone sells family land without the consent of the principal members of the family, the sale is not void but *prima facie* voidable. However such sale can only be set aside at the instance of the family provided the non-consenting members act timeously and are not caught by laches.

- *Salako v. Dosunmu (1997) 8 NWLR (Pt. 517) 371 at 374 SC*

- *Odekilekun v. Hassan (1997) 12 NWLR (Pt. 531) 56 SC*

- *Odukwe v. Ogunbiyi (1998) 8 NWLR (Pt. 561) 339 at 342 SC*

- *Babayeju v. Ashamu (1998) 9 NWLR (Pt. 567) 546 SC*

- *Kobuwa v. Lamudu (1998) 9 NWLR (Pt. 567) 709 CA*

- *Teniola v. Olohunkun (1999) 5 NWLR (Pt. 602) 280 SC*

- *Fayehun v. Fadoju (2000) 4 SC (Part I) 48 at 62*

9. A sale of family land by a member of the family without the consent of the head and the principal members of the family is void *ab initio*.

- *Odukwe v. Ogunbiyi (1998) 8 NWLR (Pt. 561) 339 SC*

10. A gift *inter-vivos* is an act whereby something is voluntarily transferred from the true possessor to another person, with full intention that the thing shall not return to the donor, and with the full intention on the part of the receiver to retain the thing entirely as his own without restoring it to the giver. Where a gift of land is made *inter-vivos*, even after the death of the donor, the land remains the exclusive property of the donee.

- *Oguejiofor v. Osaka (2000) 3 SC 1 at 14*

20.6 Mortgage

1. A mortgage is a legal or equitable conveyance of title as a security for the payment of debt or the discharge of some other obligations for which it is given, subject to a condition that the

title shall be reconveyed if the mortgage debt is liquidated.

- Nigerian Law of Secured Credit by I.O. Smith, 2001 p. 35

2. There is a distinction between a legal mortgage and an equitable mortgage. A legal mortgage transfers title in the property to the mortgagee and the term of the mortgage may give a right of sale to the mortgagee without court order. However, an equitable mortgage by way of deposit of title deed does not transfer title in the property to the mortgagee and the equitable mortgagee can only enforce his right of sale upon an order of court.

- Okuneye v. F.B.N. Plc (1996) 6 NWLR (Pt. 457) 749 CA

3. Where consent is required to a deed of legal mortgage and such consent was obtained at the creation of the mortgage, no further consent would be required for the upstamping of the mortgage if further facility is granted on it.

- Moses Ola & Sons Ltd v. Bank of the North Ltd (1992) 3 NWLR (Pt. 229) 377 CA

4. Where a mortgage which should have been registered, is not registered within the statutory period of six months, the mortgage becomes void and any purported sale is of no effect and will not convey a legal estate to any purchaser.

- Onashile v. Idowu & Ors (1969) All NLR (Pt. 2) 313

5. An equitable mortgage may be created in any of the following ways: by mere deposit of title deeds with a clear intention that the deeds should be taken or retained as security for a loan; or by any agreement to create a legal mortgage; or by mere equitable charge on the mortgagor's property.

- Okuneye v. F.B.N. Plc (1996) 6 NWLR (Pt. 457) 749 CA

6. Mere deposit of title deed with a bank will not create an equitable mortgage unless and until the borrower signs a memorandum under seal contemporaneously with the delivery of the deed.

- African Continental Bank Ltd v. Yesufu (1977) NCLR 212

- Section 5(1)(c) of the Law Reform (Contracts) Law Cap. 114 Laws of Lagos State, 1994

- Section 78(1)(c) Property and Conveyancing Law of Western Nigeria, 1959

7. While land may be pledged at customary law, a deposit of title deeds creates an equitable mortgage over the land in favour of the creditor.

- *Ogundana v. Araba & Anor (1978) 11 NSCC 334*

8. It is trite law that the right of a mortgagor to redeem his mortgaged property cannot be taken away even by an express agreement of the parties. The right continues unless and until the mortgagor's title is extinguished or his interest is destroyed by sale either under the process of the court or of a power in the mortgage deed.

- *Ejikeme v. Okonkwo (1994) 8 NWLR (Pt. 362) 266 SC*
- *Rafukka v. Kurfi (1996) 6 NWLR (Pt. 453) 235 CA*

9. It is a settled rule of equity that any agreement which, directly bars the mortgagor's right to redemption, is ineffectual. Similarly, stipulations which, even indirectly tend to have the effect of making a mortgage irredeemable, are equally void and unenforceable as clogging the equity of redemption.

- *Ejikeme v. Okonkwo (1994) 8 NWLR (Pt. 362) 266 SC*

10. Where a mortgagee, in the exercise of his powers under a legal mortgage, sells the mortgaged property, the mortgagor's equity of redemption is extinguished and the mortgagor from then on is only entitled to surplus proceeds of sale.

- *Ikeanyi v. A.C.B. Ltd (1991) 7 NWLR (Pt. 205) 626 CA*

11. It is trite that the right to exercise the power of sale under a mortgage must have arisen, that is, the mortgage debt must have fallen due, before the mortgagee can pass a good title to a purchaser free from the equity of redemption.

- *Oguchi v. F.M.B. (Nig.) Ltd (1990) 6 NWLR (Pt. 156) 330 CA*

12. It is well settled that where a mortgagee exercise his power of sale *bona fide* for the purpose of realising his debt and without collusion with the purchaser, the court will not interfere even though the sale is disadvantageous, unless the price is so low as to constitute in itself evidence of fraud.

- *Rafukka v. Kurfi (1996) NWLR (Pt. 453) 235 SC*

13. The law is that a mortgagee exercising his power of sale under

a mortgage has a duty to take reasonable care to obtain the true market value of the property in order to realise his security. The mortgagee has no obligation to wait for a favourable moment in the property market before exercising his right of sale.

- *Temco Eng. & Co. Ltd v. S.B.N. Ltd (1995) 5 NWLR (Pt. 397) 607 CA*

14. There is a duty on a prospective purchaser to make inquiries as to any prior interest before purchase and failure to so do often attracts a fatal consequence where there is an existing interest prior to his own and which would have been discovered if diligence was applied.

- *Okoye v. Dumez (Nig.) Ltd (1983) 1 NWLR 783*

15. Foreclosure is a remedy available only to an equitable mortgagee; whereas a legal mortgagee who has a power of sale does not need to foreclose.

- *Ikeanyi v. A.C.B. Ltd (1991) 7 NWLR (Pt. 205) 626 CA*

16. A statutory corporation, which has authority to build houses and sell on terms to people, is in some way a mortgagee to the buyer. As such, the corporation cannot just revoke an allotment when the allottee fails to keep up his installmental payment for some weeks as the mortgagor (allottee) is entitled to retain his equity of redemption even after the contractual date for payment of an instalment had passed.

- *Anambra State Housing Development Corporation v. Emekwue (1996) 1 NWLR (Pt. 426) 505*

XXI
Landlord and Tenant Relations

21.1 Meaning of Landlord, Tenant and Squatter

1. A landlord, in relation to premises, is the person entitled to the immediate reversion of the premises, or if the property is held in joint tenancy or tenancy in common, any of the persons entitled to the immediate reversion and this includes the attorney or agent of any such landlord. Section 40 of the Rent Control and Recovery of Residential Premises Edict No. 9 of Lagos State 1976 considered.

> - *Coker v. Adetayo (1996) 6 NWLR (Pt. 454) 258 SC*
> - *Erhunmunse v. Ehanire (1998) 10 NWLR (Pt. 568) 53 at 55 CA*

2. A tenant is any person who occupies premises lawfully. It includes a sub-tenant or any person occupying any premises whether on payment of rent or otherwise but does not include a person occupying premises under a *bona fide* claim to be the owner of the premises. The most important ingredient of tenancy is lawful occupation. It is immaterial whether the tenant pays regular rent, subsidised rent or indeed no rent so long as the initial occupation is lawful.

> - *African Petroleum Ltd v. Owodunni (1991) 8 NWLR (Pt. 210) 391 SC*
> - *Ejiwunmi v. Costain (W.A) Plc (1998) 12 NWLR (Pt. 576) 149 at 154 CA*

3. There is a distinction between a tenant and a squatter. A squatter is one who without any colour of right, enters on an unoccupied premises or land intending to stay there as long as he can. A landlord or an owner of the premises or land occupied by a squatter is entitled, if he so desires, to forcibly evict the squatter without recourse to the courts. However, such a step is not always recommended.

> - *Elakhame v. Osemobor (1991) 6 NWLR (Pt. 196) 170 CA*

21.2 Nature of Landlord and Tenant Relationship

1. The relationship between a landlord and a tenant is a contractual one and being a matter of contract, its terms cannot be altered by either party without the agreement of the other. This is, however, subject to the provisions of any statute governing the type of tenancy.

- *Udih v. Izedonmwen (1990) 2 NWLR (Pt. 132) 357 CA*

2. A relationship of landlord and tenant is brought into being by an agreement between the parties. The agreement may be express or implied. Similarly, there is nothing wrong in relying on an oral tenancy agreement where the parties are in consensus.

- *Conac Optical (Nig.) Ltd v. Akinyede (1995) 6 NWLR (Pt. 400) 212 CA*
- *Erhunmunse v. Ehanire (1998) 10 NWLR (Pt. 568) 53 CA*

21.3 Types of Tenancy

1. The law recognises two classes of tenants for the purpose of the Rent Control and Recovery of Premises. These are namely, contractual tenants and statutory tenants.

- *Pan Asian African Co. Ltd v. N.I.C.O.N. (1982) 9 SC 1*
- *African Petroleum Ltd v. Owodunni (1991) 8 NWLR (Pt. 210) 391 SC*

2. A contractual tenant is a tenant who enters upon premises by reason of a contract between him and the landlord. On the other hand, a statutory tenant is one whose contractual tenancy with the landlord has expired but holds on to the premises by virtue of the provisions of statute such as the Rent Control and Recovery of Residential Premises Law, No. 9 of 1976, Lagos State.

- *African Petroleum Ltd v. Owodunni (1991) 8 NWLR (Pt. 210) 391 SC*

3. A statutory tenant is entitled to all the benefits and is subject to all the terms and conditions of the original tenancy. Although

he no longer has an estate in the property, his tenure is protected by law.

> - *African Petroleum Ltd v. Owodunni (1991) 8 NWLR (Pt. 210) 391 SC*

4. The rule is that an agent or servant who occupies premises belonging to his principal or employer in order to be able to perform his duties acquires no estate in the property whatsoever apart from physical possession. At common law, he is regarded as a licensee because the owner that is, the employer has not given up possession for term certain.

> - *F.C.D.A. v. Nwanna (1998) 4 NWLR (Pt. 544) 73 CA*

5. A tenancy at sufferance is one in which the original grant by the landlord to the tenant has expired, usually by effluxion of time, but the tenant holds over the premises. Thus, where the original grant by the landlord to the tenant has expired, but the tenant holds over and remains in possession of the premises without the landlord assenting or dissenting, and pays no rents, he becomes a tenant at sufferance, having come upon the land lawfully in the first place. He is liable for use and occupation of the land but could rely upon his possession of the land against, the whole world until the lessor recovers possession from him in the manner authorized by law.

> - *African Petroleum Ltd v. Owodunni (1991) 8 NWLR (Pt. 210) 391 SC*
> - *Ude v. Nwara (1993) 2 NWLR (Pt. 278) 638 SC*
> - *Obioha v. Date (1994) 2 NWLR (Pt. 325) 157 CA*

6. A tenancy at will arises when a person with the consent of the owner occupies land or premises as tenant on terms that either party may determine the tenancy at any time. A tenancy at will may be created in any of the following ways namely; by express agreement of the parties; where a tenant holds over with the landlord's permit without paying rent on a periodic basis; where a tenant takes possession under a void lease or under a mere agreement for a lease and has not yet paid rent; where a person is allowed to occupy a house, rent free and for an indefinite period and finally, where a purchaser has been let into possession pending completion of sale. However, a tenant at will becomes a trespasser when he commits voluntary waste

or takes it upon himself to do those things which only the owner of the land or premises can do.

- *Elakhame v. Osemobor (1991) 6 NWLR (Pt. 196) 170 CA*
- *African Petroleum Ltd v. Owodunni (1991) 8 NWLR (Pt. 210) 391 SC*

7. A customary tenant is entitled to possession and occupation of the land, which is the subject matter of the tenancy. The tenant's right is, however, subject to the overlord's right of reversion which is exercisable if and when the tenant denied the title of the overlord or he misbehaves by failing to comply with the terms of the grant or if he abandons the land.

- *Akintola v. Oyelade (1993) 3 NWLR (Pt. 282) 379 SC*

8. The law is that once land is granted to a tenant in accordance with native law and custom, whatever may be the consideration, full rights of possession are conveyed to the grantee. The only right remaining in the grantor is that of reversion, should the grantee deny title or abandon or attempt to alienate.

- *Okegbe v. Chikere (2000) 7 SC (Part I) 106 at 113-114*

9. The law is that possession of land, no matter how long, cannot convert a customary tenant into an owner. In other words, it was not the intention of the Land Use Act to convert a tenant into an owner merely because such tenant was in occupation of his landlord's land before the inception of the Act or when it came into force.

- *Nyagba v. Mbahan (1996) 9 NWLR (Pt. 471) 207 CA*

10. A customary tenant who turns round to challenge the title of his landlord has committed a gross misconduct. The misconduct is aggravated where there is a subsisting decision of the court that he is nothing but a tenant. In such a case, he automatically forfeits his right to possession, should the landlord claim it.

- *Olugbode v. Sangodeyi (1996) 4 NWLR (Pt. 444) 500 SC*
- *Nyagba v. Mbahan (1996) 9 NWLR (Pt. 471) 207 CA*
- *Fasonu v. Fawehinmi (1997) 3 NWLR (Pt. 492) 182 CA*
- *Esiaba v. Ojiegbe (1999) 10 NWLR (Pt. 623) 463 CA*
- *Makinde v. Akinwale (2000) 1 SC 89 at 95*

11. The relief of forfeiture of customary tenancy is not automatic. Therefore, when there is an action, which warrants forfeiture, the proper remedy for the overlord is to ask the court to forfeit the interest of the tenant and to make an order for possession.

- *Akintola v. Oyelade (1993) 3 NWLR (Pt. 282) 379 SC*
- *Ogun v. Akinyelu (1999) 10 NWLR (Pt. 624) 671 CA*

12. It is trite law that failure by a customary tenant to pay tribute to his landlord, as and when due, is a recognized ground for forfeiting the customary tenancy.

- *Okpala v. Okpu (1996) 8 NWLR (Pt. 468) 589 CA*

13. A customary tenant against whom a claim for forfeiture of tenancy is brought and who wishes to seek a relief from forfeiture in the action has to explain the circumstances that led to his misbehaviour. The countenance of the tenant and language of his counsel must all reflect penitence or remorse. The tenant must specifically ask for the relief. He must adopt a procedure, which ensures that both sides to the dispute are heard. He must show the nature of the hardship that will result to him from the order of forfeiture and such hardship must be such that cannot be mitigated or removed by leaving the tenant to find an alternative land and this evidence must be strong, verifiable and cogent.

- *Nwaokoro v. Egbenoma (1997) 11 NWLR (Pt. 528) 238 CA*
- *Oshoboja v. Dada (1999) 12 NWLR (Pt. 629) 102 CA*
- *Dehinsilu v. Olowu (1999) 12 NWLR (Pt. 632) 641 CA*

14. The doctrine of laches, acquiescence and standing by are very alien to Yoruba Native Law and Custom because possession, however long, cannot be converted to title.

- *Olugbode v. Sangodeyi (1996) 4 NWLR (Pt. 444) 500 SC*

21.4 Lease

1. A lease is the demise by the landlord of a less estate than that which he himself possesses on the land. The estate created in a lease is designated *terminus* owing to its duration or continuance

as being defined and limited.

  - *Opara v. D.S. (Nig.) Ltd (1995) 4 NWLR (Pt. 390) 440 CA*
  - *Iragunima v. Uchendu (1996) 2 NWLR (Pt. 428) 30 CA*

2. A valid lease must embody the following essential elements namely: the words of demise; it must be a complete agreement; there must be an identification of lessor and lessee; the premises and dimensions of the property to be leased; and, finally, commencement and duration of the term. All the essential elements stipulated above must co-exist and any break in the chain will render the lease invalid.

  - *Osho v. Foreign Finance Corporation (1991) 4 NWLR (Pt. 184) 157 SC*
  - *Opara v. D.S. (Nig.) Ltd (1995) 4 NWLR (Pt. 390) 440 CA*
  - *Okechukwu v. Onuorah (2000) 12 SC (Pt. II) 104*

3. An agreement for a lease is defined as an instrument, which binds the parties wherein one party creates and the other accepts.

  - *Opara v. D.S. (Nig.) Ltd (1995) 4 NWLR (Pt. 390) 440 CA*

4. In order to establish the existence of a valid agreement for a lease, there must be definite understanding in respect of the parties to the lease, the property involved, the rent payable, the length of the term and the commencement date.

  - *Int. Textile Ind. (Nig.) Ltd. v. Aderemi (1999) 8 NWLR (Pt. 614) 268 at 282 SC*

5. A term of years in a lease agreement must be certain or ascertainable. When a term is made to commence upon the occurrence of a future contingent event, the test as to the certainty of the commencement of the term, is based on whether the happening of the contingent event itself is certain.

  - *Okechukwu v. Onuorah (2000) 12 SC (Part II) 104 at 123-124*

6. A sublease is valid if the term granted is sufficiently defined to be certain or ascertainable as regards its commencement and duration. More so, a thing shall not be regarded as omitted or uncertain in a sublease if the sublease contains sufficient facts or materials from which it can reasonably be supplied or

ascertained.

- *Okechukwu v. Onuorah (2000) 12 SC (Part II) 104 at 114*

7. An agreement for a lease is as good as a lease and is a registrable instrument under the Nigerian laws.

- *Osho v. Foreign Finance Corporation (1991) 4 NWLR (Pt. 184) 157 SC*

8. A lease may take effect without actual occupation. However, to be effectual an agreed rent must be reached between the parties.

- *Opara v. D.S. (Nig.) Ltd (1995) 4 NWLR (Pt. 390) 440 CA*

9. Leasehold title to land entitles the lessee to exclusive possession of the land for the period of the life of the instrument.

- *Kukoyi v. Aina (1999) 10 NWLR (Pt. 624) 633 at 636 CA*

10. There are instances where the law recognizes that leasehold may terminate before the expiration of its term. One of such instances is where the tenant breaches the covenant to pay rent. In such a case, a landlord can take action for re-entry, if such a right is expressly reserved in the lease. Another instance is where a tenant breaches an undertaking, which is a condition.

- *A.-G., Lagos State v. Sowande (1992) 8 NWLR (Pt. 261) 589 CA*

11. The remedy available to a landlord or a lessor where a tenant holds over after the term of a lease has expired, without paying rent, is to file an action in the High Court to recover possession as provided by the law. When the court finds that the lessee does not establish any right or title to the possession of the land, the court has the discretion to either order him to surrender possession forthwith or to surrender possession on or before a named date.

- *Obioha v. Dafe (1994) 2 NWLR (Pt. 325) 157 CA*

12. In Lagos State, relief against forfeiture of a lease can only be granted when there has been a breach for non-payment of rent. However, there is no relief against forfeiture in respect of other breaches of covenant in a lease. Conveyancing and Law of Property Act 1881-1892 considered.

- *Chigbu v. Tonimas (Nig.) Ltd. (1999) 3 NWLR (Pt. 593) 115 at 120 CA*

13. The law is that where a grant of lease had expired and the tenant holds over, pays rent and the landlord accepts the rent, the law will recognise such instance as a renewal of the lease on the same terms and conditions as the original lease.

- *Ude v. Nwara (1993) 2 NWLR (Pt. 278) 638 SC*

21.5 Rent

1. The law is that where parties to a tenancy agreement fail to agree on specific amount of rent to be paid, the court has the power to order that the rent payable is the fair market rent. To determine what is a fair market or reasonable rent, there must be evidence adduced before the court.

- *Awaye Motors Co. Ltd v. Adewunmi (1993) 5 NWLR (Pt. 292) 236 CA*

2. A unilateral decision by a landlord to increase the amount of rent payable under a tenancy agreement is invalid unless there is an agreement to that effect between the landlord and the tenant. A unilateral increase of rent is, at best, an offer or proposal and where the tenant refuses to pay the increased rent, the landlord is required to take necessary steps as required by law to terminate the tenancy.

- *Udi v. Izedonmwen (1990) 2 NWLR (Pt. 132) 357 CA*

3. The court has the power to *suo motu* order the payment of rents in respect of a disputed property into court pending the final determination of the dispute.

- *Ahmadu v. Attorney-General, Rivers State (1996) 7 NWLR (Pt. 459) 236 CA*

4. 'Mesne profits' are the rents and profits which a trespasser has, or might have received or made during his occupation of the premises, and which he must, therefore, pay over to the true owner as compensation for the tort which he has committed. A claim for 'mesne profits' can only be made when the tenancy of

the tenant has been duly determined and he becomes a trespasser.

- *African Petroleum Ltd v. Owodunni (1991) 8 NWLR (Pt. 210) 391 SC*

- *Metal Construction (W.A.) v. Aboderin (1998) 8 NWLR (Pt. 563) 568 SC*

21.6 Recovery of Premises

1. It is settled law that before a tenant is ejected from the premises he lawfully occupies, he must first be served with the prescribed statutory notice to determine the tenancy. This is known as the "Notice to quit". The duration of the notice will depend on the nature of the tenancy or such period otherwise agreed by the parties. On the expiration of a notice to quit, if the tenant remains adamant and fails to deliver up possession of the premises, a further notice titled "Notice to Tenant of Owner's intention to apply to recover possession", will be issued. It is only after the expiration of the second notice, that is the seven (7) days notice that the landlord can take out a writ of summons or plaint against the tenant or person refusing to deliver up possession.

- *Gambari v. Gambari (1990) 5 NWLR (Pt. 152) 572 CA*
- *Ihenacho v. Uzochukwu (1997) 2 NWLR (Pt. 487) 257 at 259-260 SC*

2. In order to be effective, a notice to quit should determine a tenancy at the end of the current term of the tenancy. For instance, a notice of six months is necessary to determine a yearly tenancy and such notice must terminate the tenancy at the end of the current term of the tenancy. Thus, any notice given and due to end at the middle of the term of the tenancy will be invalid.

- *Omotesho v. Oloriegbe (1988) 4 NWLR (Pt. 87) 225 CA*
- *African Petroleum Ltd. v. Owodunni (1991) 8 NWLR (Pt. 210) 391 SC*

3. The law is that a letter of instruction by a landlord instructing

a solicitor to recover possession of premises on the landlord's behalf must be issued before the notice to quit is issued by the solicitor otherwise, the solicitor has no authority to act. Consequently, any notice to quit or notice of intention to apply to recover possession issued by any such solicitor before the letter of instruction is null and void and of no effect.

- *Coker v. Adetayo (1992) 6 NWLR (Pt. 249) 612 CA*

4. The law does not protect a landlord who resorts to self-help in ejecting a tenant. Thus, where a landlord unilaterally enters into the premises of his tenant and takes possession of the property or goods of the tenant, he has committed an act of trespass.

- *National Salt Company of Nigeria Ltd v. Innis-Palmer (1992) 1 NWLR (Pt. 218) 422 CA*

5. A court may award damages for unlawful ejectment of a tenant by his landlord where the ejectment was not in accordance with the tenancy agreement or where the landlord employs self-help in the ejection or eviction of the tenant.

- *National Salt Company of Nigeria Ltd v. Innis-Palmer (1992) 1 NWLR (Pt. 218) 422 CA*

6. The law in Nigeria protects a person who is in physical and peaceful possession with a claim of right. This means that resort to self help by a landlord to eject a tenant in lawful occupation does not come within the purview and provision of our law. This rule also operates to protect a sub-tenant, so that whether there is privity of contract or not, attornment of tenancy or not, a sub-tenant is for the purposes of ejectment, a tenant and the provisions of the law must be followed before ejecting him. In other words, only the courts can order ejectment. The recovery of possession from a tenant in lawful occupation must, therefore, be obtained by the help of an order of court made after hearing the parties.

- *Calabar East Co-op v. Ikot (1993) 8 NWLR (Pt. 311) 324 CA*

7. In an action for recovery of possession of premises, the service of notice of intention to recover premises on the tenant is a condition precedent to the exercise of court's jurisdiction. In other words, in the absence of service of valid quit notices under

the law, the claim of a plaintiff landlord is not properly constituted and such claim should be struck out so as to afford him the opportunity of bringing a new action after complying with the requirement of serving valid quit notice.

- *Eleja v. Bangudu (1994) 3 NWLR (Pt. 334) 534 CA*

8. The law is that a State Government must institute proceedings in the State High Court in order to recover possession of state land from a lessee of such land. If the State Government finds a compelling need to determine a lease, it must follow the due process of law.

- *Obioha v. Dafe (1994) 2 NWLR (Pt. 325) 157 CA*

9. The proof of service of statutory notices is the determining factor as to whether or not a writ of recovery of possession is valid. Such a proof is essentially based on a preponderance of evidence.

- *Sovcchi M. & F. Co. Ltd v. Alabi (1996) 7 NWLR (Pt. 462) 627 CA*

10. Customary courts are specifically excluded from exercising jurisdiction over matters relating to recovery of premises. It is only the High Courts and Magistrate Courts that can exercise jurisdiction over such matters. Section 142(1) of the Landlord and Tenant Law of Anambra State, 1986 considered.

- *Nzegwu v. Omata (1999) 2 NWLR (Pt. 592) 537 CA*

XXII
Land Use Act

22.1 Rights of Occupancy

1. The State High Court has original jurisdiction in respect of lands subject to customary right of occupancy. This is because by virtue of section 41 of the Land Use Act, 1978 customary or area courts have no exclusive jurisdiction over land in non-urban areas.

   - *Oyeniran v. Egbetola (1997) 5 NWLR (Pt. 504) 122 at 124-125 SC*

   - *Ogigie v. Obiyan (1997) 10 NWLR (Pt. 524) 179 SC*

   - *Adisa v. Oyinwola (2000) 6 SC (Pt. 2) 47*

2. The Governor, by virtue of section 5(1) of the Land Use Act, 1978 has the overall powers to grant statutory rights of occupancy over any land whether or not in an urban area of a state.

   - *Iywev v. Uli (1999) 13 NWLR (Pt. 634) 189 CA*

3. The Governor's power to grant a statutory right of occupancy shall not be exercised to deny a prior holder of his title before the coming into force of the Land Use Act. Such a prior holder is a deemed holder of a statutory or customary right of occupancy if the land is situate in urban or non-urban areas respectively. This is pursuant to sections 34 and 36 of the Land Use Act, 1978.

   - *Agundo v. Gberbo (1999) 9 NWLR (Pt. 617) 71 at 78-79 CA*

4. A major reason for setting aside a grant of statutory right of occupancy is where there had been a prior holder whose interest in the land was subsisting at the time the certificate of occupancy was given to a different person.

   - *Teniola v. Olohunkun (1999) 5 NWLR (Pt. 602) 280 at 290 SC*

5. The Governor may delegate all or any of his powers to the

State Commissioner subject to such restrictions, conditions and qualifications as may be specified by him, which are consistent with the provisions of the Land Use Act, 1978.

- *F.M.B.N. v. Babatunde (1999) 12 NWLR (Pt. 632) 683 CA*

6. A certificate of occupancy must contain an accurate description of the land to which it relates or even better, should have attached to it a survey plan of the said land.

- *Usman v. Garke (1999) 1 NWLR (Pt. 587) 466 at 473 CA*

7. The grant of a certificate of occupancy to a person does not extinguish the right of an existing customary owner. This is because the prior holder is deemed to be the holder of a customary right of occupancy over such land. Unless and until such a prior holder's interest is revoked, a subsequent grant is not valid.

- *Macaulay v. Omiyale (1997) 4 NWLR (Pt. 497) 94 CA*

8. The grant of a statutory right of occupancy over land extinguishes any previous licence granted in respect of the same land by virtue of section 5(2) of the Land Use Act, 1978.

- *Kari v. Ganaram (1997) 2 NWLR (Pt. 488) 380 SC*

9. Where a competent authority properly issues a certificate of occupancy, it raises the presumption that the holder is the owner in exclusive possession of the land to which the certificate relates. It also raises the presumption that at the time it was issued, there was not in existence a customary owner whose title has not been revoked. However, these presumptions are rebuttable. Where it is proved by evidence that another person had a better title to the land before the issuance of the certificate of occupancy, the court can revoke it.

- *Osazuwa v. Ojo (1999) 13 NWLR (Pt. 634) 286 at 287 CA*

10. Unlike section 39 of the Land Use Act, 1978 which gives the State High Court exclusive jurisdiction over land in urban areas, section 41 of the same law does not give exclusive jurisdiction to Area or Customary court over land in non-urban areas.

- *Nelson v. Ebanga (1998) 8 NWLR (Pt. 563) 701 at 704 CA*

11. The State High Court by virtue of section 39(1) of the Land Use Act, 1978 has exclusive jurisdiction over land subject of

statutory right of occupancy.

> *- Nzegwu v. Omata (1999) 2 NWLR (Pt. 592) 537 at 539 CA*

12. The law recognizes two distinct stages in transactions involving the transfer or sale of an estate in land. First, is the contract stage, which must end with the formation of a binding contract for sale. Second, is the conveyance stage, which should confer title in the purchaser by means of appropriate instrument. It follows, therefore, that it is only after a binding contract for sale is concluded that the need to pursue the procedure for acquiring title will arise. The contract stage does not require the Governor's consent.

> *- F.M.B. v. Akinola (1998) 4 NWLR (Pt. 545) 325 at 327 CA*
> *- Int. Textile Ind. (Nig.) Ltd. v. Aderemi (1999) 8 NWLR (Pt. 614) 268 at 277 SC*

13. Pursuant to section 22(1) of the Land Use Act, 1978 a holder of a statutory right of occupancy is prohibited from alienating his right or any part of it by assignment, mortgage, transfer of possession, sublease or otherwise without first seeking and obtaining the Governor's consent. Where such alienation is done without the Governor's consent first had and obtained, section 26 of the same law makes the purported transfer void.

> *- F.M.B. v. Akinola (1998) 4 NWLR (Pt. 545) 325 at 327 CA*
> *- Int. Textile Ind. (Nig.) Ltd. v. Aderemi (1999) 8 NWLR (Pt. 614) 268 at 277 SC*

14. By virtue of sections 22 and 26 of the Land Use Act, 1978 any transaction regarding subleasing of land or mortgage requires the consent of the State Governor. Such consent must be obtained before alienation of interest in the said land.

> *- Okusanya v. Ogunfowora (1997) 9 NWLR (Pt. 520) 347 at 348 CA*
> *- Isichei v. Allagoa (1998) 12 NWLR (Pt. 577) 196 at 200 CA*

15. By virtue of section 28(5)(a) and (b) of the Land Use Act, 1978, the Governor has power to revoke a certificate of occupancy for a breach of the terms, which is deemed to be contained in a certificate of occupancy and, a breach of any term contained in the certificate or any special contract made under section 8 of

the Act. The reason for revoking a person's right of occupancy must be stated in the notice of revocation notwithstanding that the Act does not expressly state that the specific ground of the revocation must be stated in the notice. Also, where there is a failure to serve the notice of intention to revoke a right of occupancy personally on the holder before such notice is published in the gazette, it amounts to a substantial non-compliance with the law, which renders any acquisition pursuant to such revocation a nullity.

> - N.E.W. Ltd v. Denap Ltd (1997) 10 NWLR (Pt.525) 481 at 487-488 CA

16. Notwithstanding the Land Use Act, 1978, the doctrine of *quic quid plantatur solo solo cedit*, which is to the effect that whoever owns land also owns what is on the land, attached to the land, fixed to the land or found on the land, is still part of Nigerian Law.

> - Ikyaawan v. Ajivah (1997) 4 NWLR (Pt. 499) 365 at 369 CA

17. At the coming into force of the Land Use Act, title in all lands in each state in Nigeria became vested in the Governor. The nature of entitlement a court can award to a party in a land dispute is a right of occupation, and no more. A right of occupancy is either statutory or customary. The Governor is the only person empowered to grant a statutory right of occupancy in any part of the state, whether in the urban or non-urban area. On the other hand, a customary right of occupancy is grantable by a Local Government and this must only be in respect of land in a non-urban area.

> - Arhurhu v. Delta Steel Co. Ltd. (1997) 3 NWLR (Pt. 491) 82 at 84-85 CA

18. In the Federal Capital Territory, customary right of occupancy has been abolished.

> - Ona v. Atenda (2000) 5 NWLR (Pt. 656) 244 CA

22.2 Acquisition of Land

1. The government cannot acquire land from an individual without adequate compensation. However, section 109 of the Public Lands Acquisition Law of Western Nigeria, 1959 provides for a limitation period of six weeks within which to lodge with the Governor, a claim for compensation, failure of which the claim shall be settled by the High Court. The six weeks start running after the service and publication of the notice of acquisition in the gazette.

> - *N.H.R.I v. Ayoade (1997) 11 NWLR (Pt. 530) 541 SC*
> - *Kukoyi v. Aina (1999) 10 NWLR (Pt. 624) 633 at 637 CA*

2. In the absence of any statutory provision to the contrary, the issuance of a public notice of acquisition does not immediately vest title to the land in government. The government acquires title after satisfying the provisions of the Public Land Acquisition Act, which requires that a land certificate should be obtained as proof of title.

> - *Edun v. Provost, Lagos State College of Education (LACOED) (1998) 13 NWLR (Pt. 580) 52 at 55 CA*

3. Under the Public Lands Acquisition Law Cap. 105 Laws of Bendel State, 1976, land may be acquired for public purpose. By section 2(h) of the Law, the establishment of an industrial/residential layout is a public purpose for which land may be acquired.

> - *Integrated Rubber Products Ltd v. Oviawe (1992) 5 NWLR (Pt. 243) 572 CA*
> - *Ononuju v. A.-G., Anambra State (1998) 11 NWLR (Pt. 573) 304 at 309 CA*

XXIII

Law of Armed Conflict

23.1 Non-Intervention

1. The principle of non-intervention forbids all States or group of States to intervene directly or indirectly in the internal or external affairs of other States. Non-intervention includes the use of force either in the direct form of military action or in the indirect form of support for subversive or terrorist armed activities within another State, choice of political, economic, social and cultural system, and the formulation of foreign policy.

> - Nicaragua Case (Merits) (Nicaragua v. United States) I.C.J. Reports 1986, p. 14

2. The laying of mines by another State in the internal or territorial waters of a sovereign State is a breach of international customary law that prohibits a State from intervening in the internal affairs of another State.

> - Nicaragua Case (Merits) (Nicaragua v. United States) I.C.J. Reports 1986, p. 14

23.2 Meaning of War/Armed Attack/Armed Conflict

1. The word "war" refers not only to declared war but also to other cases of armed conflict and to the occupation of another State's territory even if the occupation meets with no armed resistance.

> - Judgment of the International Military Tribunal for the Trial of German Major War Criminals (Cmd. 6964 H.M.S.O. 1946) 125

2. "Attack" means act of violence against the enemy or adversary, whether in offence or in defence.

> - Article 49(1) Protocol I of the Protocols Additional to the Geneva Conventions of 12 August 1949

3. War is essentially an evil thing. Its consequences are not confined to the belligerent States alone, but affect the whole world. To initiate a war of aggression, therefore, is not only an international crime, but a supreme international crime differing only from other war crimes, in that it contains within itself the accumulated evil of the whole.

 - *The Nuremberg Trial, Comd. 6964 (1946) p. 13*

4. An armed attack means military action by regular forces across an international border. It includes also the sending by or on behalf of a State of armed bands, groups, irregulars or mercenaries, which carry out acts of armed force against another State of such gravity as to amount to actual armed attack conducted by regular forces.

 - *Nicaragua Case (Merits) (Nicaragua v. United States) I.C.J. Reports 1986, p. 14*

5. While the concept of an armed attack includes the despatch by one State of an armed bands into the territory of another State, the supply of arms and other support to such bands cannot be equated with armed attack.

 - *Nicaragua Case (Merits) (Nicaragua v. United States) I.C.J. Reports 1986, p. 14*

6. An armed conflict arises whenever there is a resort to armed force between States or protracted armed violence between government authorities and organized armed groups or between such groups within a State.

 - *Prosecutor v. Tadic (Jurisdiction) I.L.R. 105 (1997) 419*

7. There are two major kinds of armed conflict namely: an armed conflict of international character, and an armed conflict of non-international character.

 - *Case Concerning Military and Para-Military Activity, Nicaragua I.C.J Reports 1986, 14; I.L.R 76 (1988)*

8. International humanitarian law applies from the initiation of armed conflicts and extends beyond the ceasation of hostilities until a general conclusion of peace is reached, or, in the case of internal conflicts, a peaceful settlement is achieved. Until that moment, international humanitarian law continues to apply in the whole territory of the warring States or, in the

case of internal conflicts, the whole territory under the control of a party, whether or not actual combat takes place.

> - *Prosecutor v. Tadic (Jurisdiction) I.L.R. 105 (1997) 419*

23.3 Self-Defence

1. Every sovereign State has the inherent right of self-defence in the event of an armed attack. This right covers both collective and individual self-defence.

> - *Nicaragua Case (Merits) (Nicaragua v. United States) I.C.J. Reports 1986, p. 14*

2. Self-defence is justified only in the case of an instant and overwhelming necessity for self-defence, leaving no choice of means and no moment of deliberation.

> - *The Caroline Case, Moore's Digest of International, II 412*

3. A State which is actively engaged in an armed conflict is entitled to exercise inherent right of self-defence to stop and search a foreign merchant ship on the high seas if there are reasonable grounds for suspecting that the ship is taking arms to the other side for use in the conflict. If the suspicion proves to be unfounded and if the ship has not committed acts calculated to give rise to suspicion, then the ship owners have a good claim to compensation for loss caused by the delay.

> - *The Caroline Case (1938) 3 A.J.I.L. 82*

4. The exercise of the right of collective self-defence pre-supposes that an armed attack has occurred. It is the duty of the victim State to draw attention to its plight. If the victim State wishes another State to come to its help in the exercise of the right of collective self-defence it has to make an express request to that effect.

> - *Nicaragua Case (Merits) (Nicaragua v. United States) I.C.J. Reports 1986, p. 14*

5. Generally, the threat or use of nuclear weapons is contrary to the rules of international law applicable in armed conflict, and in particular the principles and rules of humanitarian law.

However, what is much less certain is whether the threat or use of nuclear weapons would be lawful or unlawful in an extreme circumstance of self-defence.

> - *Legality of the Threat or Use of Nuclear Weapons Case. ICJ Advisory Opinion (1997) 35 I.L.M. 809 & 1343*

23.4 Combatants/Prisoners of War

1. Combatants are members of the armed forces of a Party to a conflict (other than medical personnel and chaplains). Combatants shall be commanded by a person responsible for his subordinates, wear a fixed distinctive emblem recognisable at distance, carry arms openly and conduct their operations in accordance with the laws and customs of war.

> - *Ex-parte Quirin et Al. (1942) 317 U.S 1 at 31*
> - *Article 43 of Protocol I, Protocols Additional to the Geneva Conventions of 12 August 1949*

2. Any combatant who falls into the power of an enemy or the opposing military forces shall be a prisoner of war.

> - *Article 44 of Protocol I, Protocols Additional to the Geneva Conventions of 12 August 1949*
> - *Article 4 of the Third Geneva Convention Relative to the Treatment of Prisoners of War, 12 August 1949*

3. Prisoners of war shall at all times be humanely treated. In particular, no prisoner of war may be subject to physical mutilation or to medical or scientific experiments of any kind. Likewise, prisoners of war must at all times be protected particularly against acts of violence or intimidation, insults and public curiosity.

> - *Article 13 of the Third Geneva Convention Relative to the Treatment of Prisoners of War, 12 August 1949*
> - *Ex-parte Quirin et Al. (1942) 317 U.S 1 at 31*

4. Every prisoner of war, when questioned upon being captured is bound to give only his surname, first name and rank, date of birth, and army, regimental, personal and serial number. No physical or mental torture, or any other form of coercion shall

be inflicted on a prisoner of war to secure from him information of any kind whatsoever. Similarly, a prisoner of war who refuses to answer questions may not be threatened, insulted, or exposed to unpleasant or disadvantageous treatment of any kind.

> - *Article 17 of the Third Geneva Convention Relative to the Treatment of Prisoners of War, 12 August 1949*

5. The law does not strictly prohibit the use of the enemy uniform and equipment in order to deceive the enemy in battle. However, the individual soldiers so disguising their true character are not entitled to be treated as prisoners of war, if captured.

> - *United States v. Skorzeny et Al. (1947), War Crimes Reports, ix (1949) 90*

23.5 Spy/Mercenary/Guerrilla

1. Spies are persons acting under false pretences or in a deliberate clandestine manner so as to acquire information about the enemy. Spies are not entitled to the status of prisoner of war. Consequently, they may be subject to trial and punishment by military tribunals.

> - *Ex-parte Quirin et Al., (1942) 317 U.S 1 at 31*
> - *Article 46 of Protocol I, Third Geneva Convention Relative to the Treatment of Prisoners of War, 1949*

2. Persons who carry on secret warfare, sabotage and who do not conduct their military operations in accordance with the laws and customs of war are not combatants. If captured, they may be subject to trial and punishment by military tribunals for acts, which render their belligerency unlawful.

> - *Ex-parte Quirin et Al., (1942) 317 U.S 1 at 31*

3. A member of the armed forces of a Party to the conflict who, on behalf of his unit and in territory controlled by an enemy gathers or attempts to gather information shall not be considered as engaging in espionage if, while so acting, he is in uniform of his armed forces.

> - *Article 46 of Protocol I, Third Geneva Convention Relative*

to the Treatment of Prisoners of War, 1949

4. A mercenary is any person who is specially recruited locally or abroad to fight in an armed conflict. He is neither a national of a Party to the conflict nor a resident of the territory controlled by a Party to the conflict. Similarly, he is not a member of the armed forces of a Party to the conflict. He is solely motivated to take part in the conflict by his desire for private gains.

> *- Article 47(2) of Protocol I, Protocols Additional to the Geneva Convention of 12 August 1949*

5. A mercenary shall not have the right to be treated as a combatant or a prisoner of war upon capture.

> *- Article 47(1) of Protocol I, Protocols Additional to the Geneva Convention of 12 August 1949*

6. The word "guerrilla" is not intended to signify a category of conflict, but a particular method of waging war.

> *- International Committee of the Red Cross (ICRC) (Document D 1153 of August 1970, p. 4*

7. The basic rule, as affirmed by Article 4 of the Third Geneva Convention Relative to the Treatment of Prisoners of War, 1949 is that guerrilla forces enjoy the status of prisoners of war only if they conduct their military operations in accordance with the laws and customs of war.

> *- Article 43 of Protocol I, Third Geneva Convention Relative to the Treatment of Prisoners of War, 1949*

8. The rule is that members of resistance movement who comply with the rules of conduct of war, namely: that they be commanded by a person responsible for his subordinates, wear a fixed distinctive sign recognisable at a distance, carry arms openly, and conduct their operations in accordance with the laws and customs of war, even in occupied areas, are entitled to be treated as prisoners of war upon capture.

> *- Article 4 of Third Geneva Convention Relative to the Treatment of Prisoners of War, 1949*

23.6 War Crimes

1. War crimes are defined as violations of the laws and customs of war. Such violations shall include, but not limited to: employment of poisonous weapons or other weapons calculated to cause unnecessary suffering; wanton destruction of cities, towns or villages, or devastation not justified by military necessity; attack, or bombardment, by whatever means, of undefended towns, villages, dwellings or buildings; seizure of, destruction or wilful damage done to institutions, dedicated to religion, charity and education, the arts and sciences, historic monuments and works of art and science; plunder of public or private propety.

> - *Article 6(6) of the International Military Tribunal for the Trial of German Major War Criminals (Nuremberg Charter) Cmd. 6903 (1946) p. 5*
>
> - *Article 5(6) of the International Military Tribunal for the Far East (Tokyo Charter) (The Occupation of Japan)1948, p.149*
>
> - *Article 3 of the Statute of the International Criminal Tribunal for the former Yugoslavia, 1993*

2. Crime against peace consists of any of the following acts namely: planning a war of aggression, or a war in breach of international treaties agreements or assurances; preparation of such a war; initiation of such a war; waging such a war; participation in a common plan or conspiracy for the accomplishment of any of the aforesaid.

> - *Article 6(6) of the International Military Tribunal for the Trial of German Major War Criminals (Nuremberg Charter) Cmd. 6903 (1946), p. 5*
>
> - *Article 5(6) of the International Military Tribunal for the Far East (Tokyo Charter) (The Occupation of Japan), 1948 p. 149*
>
> - *The Eichman Case (1961) International Law Reports, Vol. 36, p. 5*

3. Crimes against humanity include murder, extermination, enslavement, deportation and other inhumane acts committed against any civilian population before or during war, or persecutions on political, racial or religious grounds.

> - *The Eichman Case (1961) International Law Reports Vol. 36, p. 5*

23.7 Defences to War Crimes

1. Where grievous and extensive crimes have been committed consciously, ruthelessly and without military excuse or justification, the defence of superior orders cannot be considered in mitigation of guilt.

> - *Article 8 of the International Military Tribunal for the Trial of German Major War Criminals (Nuremberg Charter) Cmd. 6964 (1946) p. 92*

2. An order of a superior officer does not provide absolute immunity. However, where the interest of justice demands, superior orders may be admitted as defence in mitigation of guilt.

> - *Article 8 of the International Military Tribunal for the Trial of German Major War Criminals (Nuremberg Charter) Cmd. 6668 (1946), p. 51)*
> - *Article 6 of the International Military Tribunal for the Far East (Tokyo Charter) (The Occupation of Japan), 1948 p.149*

3. The personal immunity of Heads of State from the civil and criminal law of other States is a rule of the law of peace. It does not apply to a state of war.

> - *The International Military Tribunal for the Trial of German Major War Criminals (Nuremberg Charter, 1946)*
> - *The International Military Tribunal for the Far East (Tokyo Charter, 1948)*

4. A Head of State, who has a military rank and is captured by the enemy, becomes a prisoner of war. If he lacks military status, he is liable to be treated as an enemy civilian. Any additional consideration the captor State may show him, rests on international custom or courtesy.

> - *The International Military Tribunal for the Trial of German Major War Criminals (Nuremberg Charter, 1946)*
> - *The International Military Tribunal for the Far East (Tokyo Charter, 1948)*

5. In times of war, diplomatic privilege does not import immunity from legal liability but only exemption from trial by the court of the State to which an ambassador or a diplomatic

staff is accredited.

- *The International Military Tribunal for the Trial of German Major War Criminals (Nuremberg Charter, 1946)*
- *The International Military Tribunal for the Far East (Tokyo Charter, 1948)*

23.8 Sea Warfare

1. A war-time blockade need not be restricted to any particular port or roadstead, but may extend to the whole of the enemy coast.

- *Orinoco Steamship Company (1903) 1 R.T.A.A. p. 102-103*

2. The term "warship" includes any vessel which is commissioned as part of the naval forces of a recognized State; bears the external marks distinguishing warships of her nationality; commanded by a member of the armed services of the belligerent concerned and manned by a crew subject to naval discipline.

- *Article 8(2) of the Convention on the High Seas, April 27, 1958*
- *Article 29 of the Convention on the Law of the Sea, 1982*

3. The term 'materials' from the military point of view, includes any objects pertaining to either the naval or land forces and impressed with a military character. Such materials range from hand grenades to a completed and fully equipped warship.

- *Galland Steamship Corporation Claim (1924) 7 R.I.A.A. p. 73 at 77*

4. Postal correspondence of neutrals or belligerents, whatever its official or private character may be, is inviolable if found on the high seas on board a neutral or enemy ship. If the ship is detained, the correspondence is to be forwarded by the captor with the least delay.

- *Article 1 of Hague Convention XI of 1907*
- *The Case of Carthage (1913) Hague Court Reports, Vol. 1 p. 329*

5. While a merchant ship may not use armaments for offensive purposes, she is entitled to carry and employ armaments for purposes of self-defence.

- *Garland Steamship Corporation Claim (1924) 7 R.I.A.A., p. 73 at 82*

6. If an armed merchant ship actually uses her armament for defensive purposes, she becomes assimilated to a warship. Her master and crew become legitimate combatants and, if captured, are entitled to all the privileges of combatants and prisoners of war.

- *Article 1 of Hague Convention XI of 1907*

- *Garland Steamship Corporation Claim (1924) 7 R.I.A.A., p. 73 at 82*

7. If a merchant ship takes offensive action against an enemy warship, her master and crew become illegitimate combatants and are, consequently, treated as unprivileged prisoners of war if captured. Although if they are shipwrecked the enemy must do his best to rescue them.

- *Garland Steamship Corporation Claim (1924) 7 R.I.A.A., p. 73*
- *Article 13 of the Geneva Convention II of 1949*
- *Article 4 of the Geneva Convention III of 1949*

8. A neutral merchant ship in convoy under the escort of one or several enemy warships may be treated as an enemy warship. Consequently, the destruction of such merchant ship in convoy is lawful.

- *Garland Steamship Corporation Claim (1924) 7 R.I.A.A., p. 73*
- *Kyriakides v. Germany (The Georgios -1928) 8 M.A.T., p. 349 at 350-351*

9. Neutral merchant ships and aircraft operating directly under enemy control, orders, charter employment or direction are liable to the same treatment as enemy merchant ships and aircraft. They may be destroyed without prior warning.

- *Costonmenis and Another v. Germany (The India, 1929) 8 M.A.T. p. 848*

- *Embiricos v. Germany (The Eirini, 1930) 8 M.A.T. p. 104*

10. Naval bombardment is lawful, to the extent that it is required to overcome enemy resistance.

- *American Electric and Manufacturing Company Claim (1903-United States, Venezuelan Commission) 9 R.I.A.A. p. 145 at 146*

11. An excessive or unnecessary bombardment is illegal.

- *De Lemos Claim (1903-United States, Venezuelan Commission) 9 R.I.A.A. p. 360 at 378-379*

12. A defended place may be bombarded to the extent that it is required to overcome armed resistance.

- *Bembelista Claim (1903-Netherlands, Venezuelan Commission) 10 R.I.A.A. p. 717*

23.9 Air Warfare

1. An attack or bombardment, "by whatever means" of towns, villages, dwellings or building, which are undefended, is prohibited. A place is defended if it is capable of opposing an enemy attack.

- *Article 25 of Hague Regulations of 1907 on Land Warfare*

2. One of the principles generally recognised by international law is that the belligerents must respect, as far as possible, the civilian population and their property.

- *Article 26 of Hague Regulations of 1907 on Land Warfare*
- *Article 6 of Hague Convention IX of 1907 on Bombardments by Naval Forces in Time of War*
- *Articles 50, 51 and 52 of Protocol I, Protocols Additional to the Geneva Convention of 12 August 1949*
- *Coenca Brothers v. Germany (1927) 7 M.A.T. 683*
- *Kiriadolou v. Germany (1903) 7 M.A.T. 687-688*

3. Aerial bombardment for the purpose of terrorising the civilian population, destroying or damaging private property not of military character, or of injuring non-combatants is prohibited.

- Article 22 of Hague Rules of Aerial Warfare, 1923
- Article 51 of Protocol I, Protocols Additional to the Geneva Convention of 12 August 1949

23.10 Armistice/Peace Treaty

1. Armistice is a mere cessation of hostilities and not peace.

- Artilio Regolo and Other Vessels (1945) 12 R.I.A.A. p. 7 at p. 8

2. In the absence of express provisions to the contrary, the primary intention of parties to armistice is to suspend military operations.

- Article 36 of the Hague Regulations of 1907
- The International Military Tribunal for the Far East (Tokyo Charter, 1948)

3. In the case of a serious breach of an armistice agreement by one of the parties, the other party may denounce it and may even recommence hostilities without warning.

- The International Military Tribunal for the Far East (Tokyo Charter, 1948)

4. The primary object of a peace treaty is the re-establishment of a state of peace between the belligerents

- The Wimbledon Case (1923) A1, p. 38 (Judgment of the Permanent Court of International Justice) 1923-1930

5. A "state of war", in the legal meaning of the term, continues, until the conclusion of peace treaty

- Ahmed Emir Bey (1927) 7 M.A.T. p. 920

XXIV
Law of Contract

24.1 Definition of Contract

1. A contract may be defined as a legally binding agreement between two or more persons by which rights are acquired by one party in return for acts or forbearances on the part of the other.

> - Orient Bank (Nig.) Plc. v. Bilante Int'l Ltd (1997) 8 NWLR (Pt. 515) 37 at 41 CA
>
> - Societe Generale Bank (Nig.) Ltd. v. Safa Steel and Chemical Manufacturing Ltd. (1998) 5 NWLR (Pt. 548) 168 CA

2. There are five important factors that must be present in a valid contract. These are offer, acceptance, consideration, intention to create legal relationship, and capacity to contract.

> - Okubule v. Oyagbola (1990) 4 NWLR (Pt. 147) 723 SC
>
> - Orient Bank (Nig.) Plc v. Bilante Int'l Ltd (1997) 8 NWLR (Pt. 515) 37 CA
>
> - Obaike v. B.C.C. Plc (1997) 10 NWLR (Pt. 525) 435 CA

3. In order to create a binding contract, the parties must express their agreement in a form, which is sufficiently certain for the courts to enforce.

> - Scammell and Nephwe Ltd v. Ouston (1914) AC 251
>
> - Orient Bank (Nig.) Plc v. Bilante International Ltd (1997) 8 NWLR (Pt. 515) 37 CA

4. The procedure of formal contract and the recourse to "subject to contract" do not at the moment fit into the Nigerian system of sale of land particularly as Nigeria does not have the equivalent of any special conditions. Therefore, the use of the phrase "subject to contract" appears to be irrelevant and perhaps meaningless in contract for sale of land.

> - Int. Textile Ind. (Nig.) Ltd v. Aderemi (1999) 8 NWLR (Pt. 614) 268 at 272-275 SC

24.2. Offer

1. An offer may be defined as a definite indication by one person to another that he is willing to conclude a contract on the terms proposed which, when accepted, will create a binding legal obligation. The offer may be verbal, written, or even implied from the conduct of the offeror.

- *Majekodunmi v. National Bank of Nigeria (1978) 3 SC 119 at 129*
- *Union Bank v. Ozigi (1991) 2 NWLR (Pt. 176) 677 at 679 CA*
- *Obaike v. B.C.C Plc (1997) 10 NWLR (Pt. 525) 435 at 437 CA*

2. An offer may be addressed to the general public. For example, where the owner of a lost dog offers a reward of N2,000 to anyone who finds and returns the animal to him, such an offer is capable of acceptance by anyone who fulfils the conditions set out in the advertisement.

- *Carlill v. Carbolic Smoke Ball Co. (1893) 1 QB 256*

3. The offeror must communicate his offer to the offeree so that he has an opportunity to accept or reject it. The offeree cannot be contractually bound to pay for services rendered to him without his consent or knowledge.

- *Taylor v. Laird (1856) 25 LJ Ex. 329*

24.3 Invitation to Treat

1. An offer must be distinguished from an invitation to treat. Invitation to treat is the first step in negotiations between the parties to a contract. It may or may not lead to a definite offer being made by one of the parties to the negotiations.

- *Fisher v. Bell (1960) 3 All ER 73*
- *Gibson v. Manchester City Council (1978) 1 WLR 520 CA*
- *Orient Bank (Nig.) Plc v. Bilante International Ltd (1997) 8 NWLR (Pt. 515) 37 CA*

2. A shopkeeper who displays goods in his shop with ticket

attached stating the price, is not offering them for sale, but merely inviting a member of the general public to make an offer to purchase by selecting an item and taking it to the cash desk. The shopkeeper may accept or reject the customer's offer.

- *Pharmaceutical Society of Great Britain v. Boots Cash Chemists (1953) 1 QB 401*
- *Partridge v. Crittenden (1968) All ER 421*

3. The rule is that an auctioneer's request for a bid is not an offer but an invitation to treat. The bid constitutes an offer, which the auctioneer may accept or reject. Acceptance is usually manifested by the fall of the hammer. Section 58(3) of Sales of Goods Act, 1893 considered.

- *Pane v. Cave (1789) 3 Term. Rep 148*

24.4 Termination of Offer

1. There are five principal methods by which an offer may be terminated before it can be accepted by the offeree, thereby preventing a contract from coming into existence. An offer may be revoked before acceptance; it may be terminated by a rejection by the offeree; it may be terminated by lapse of time; an offer which is stated to come to an end if certain event occurs cannot be accepted after that event has actually taken place; and finally, an offer may be terminated by the death of the offeror.

- *Hyde v. Wrench (1840) 3 Bear 334*
- *Dickinson v. Dodds (1876) 2 ChD 463*
- *Byrne v. Leon van Tienhoven (1880) 5 CPD 344*

2. An offer may be revoked at any time before notification of acceptance even if the stipulated period for acceptance has not ended. The offeror's decision to revoke is ineffective until it has been communicated to the offeree. It is however, not essential that the offeror himself should make the communication, provided the offeree is made aware of revocation from a reliable source. Consequently, once the person to whom the offer was made knows that the property has been sold to someone else it becomes late for him to accept the offer.

- *Dickinson v. Dodds (1876) 2 Ch. 463*

3. When an offeree expressly rejects an offer made to him it becomes effective when notice of rejection actually reaches the offeror. An offer is impliedly rejected if the offeree instead of accepting the original offer makes a counter offer which varies the terms proposed by the offeror.

- *Hyde v. Wrench (1840) 3 Beav. 334*
- *Major General George Innih (rtd) & Ors v. Ferado Agro and Consortium Ltd (1990) 5 NWLR (Pt. 152) 604 CA*

4. The legal effect of a counter-offer is to "kill off" the original offer so that it cannot subsequently be accepted by the offeree.

- *Hyde v. Wrench (1840) 3 Bear 334*
- *Okubule v. Oyagbola (1990) 4 NWLR (Pt. 147) 723 SC*
- *Gadzama v. Rims Merchant Bank Ltd (1997) 4 NWLR (Pt. 498) 234 at 237 CA*
- *Afrotec Technical Services (Nig.) Ltd v. MIA & Sons Ltd (2000) 12 SC (Pt. II) 1 at 24*

5. An offer lapses if it is not accepted within the period stated by the offeror. If a precise period of time is not stipulated then acceptance must be made within a reasonable time which depends upon the circumstances of the individual case under consideration. A relatively short period of time will be allowed in cases involving the sale of property, such as perishable goods, or the sale of security, like shares, where the market price may fluctuate considerably from day to day.

- *Ramsgate Victoria Hotel Co. v. Montefiore (1866) LR Exch. 109*

6. An offer addressed to a specified offeree who dies before accepting it, cannot be accepted by another person instead. Consequently, an acceptance of an offer to buy annuities by the solicitors of the annuitant in ignorance of the fact that the annuitant had died was invalid on the ground that the solicitors' authority was terminated by their client's death.

- *Reynolds v. Atherton (1921) 125 L.T. 690*

24.5 Acceptance

1. Acceptance may be defined as any act signifying the offeree's

consent to the terms proposed by the offeror. An enforceable contract will not come into existence unless an acceptance has been brought to the notice of the offeror, corresponding precisely with the terms proposed in the offer. Any form of acceptance is valid, whether it is verbal, written or merely inferred from the conduct of the parties.

> - *Carlill v. Cabolic Smoke Ball Co. (1893) 1 QB 256*
> - *Orient Bank (Nig.) Plc v. Bilante International Ltd (1997) 8 NWLR (Pt. 515) 37 CA*
> - *Obaike v. B.C.C Plc (1997) 10 NWLR (Pt. 525) 435 at 437 CA*

2. The general rule is that an acceptance must be communicated to the offeror. The acceptance is validly communicated when it is actually brought to the attention of the offeror.

> - *Entores v. Miles Far East Corporation (1955) 2 QB 327*
> - *Okubule v. Oyagbola (1990) 4 NWLR (Pt. 147) 723 SC*

3. The rule that acceptance must be communicated to the offeror is not an absolute one. For instance, the terms of the offer may demonstrate that the offeror does not insist that the acceptance be communicated to him.

> - *Carlill v. Carbolic Smoke Ball Co. (1893) 1 QB 256*

4. The general rule is that acceptance by post takes effect when the letter of acceptance, properly addressed and stamped, is posted. However, the court may not apply the postal rule where it would lead to manifest inconvenience and absurdity.

> - *Adams v. Lindsell (1818) 1 B & Ald 681*
> - *Holwell Securities Ltd v. Hughes (1974) 1 WLR 155*
> - *Orient Bank (Nig.) Plc v. Bilante International Ltd (1997) 8 NWLR (Pt. 515) 37 CA*

5. A conditional acceptance of an offer does not in law constitute an acceptance of the offer in question.

> - *Okubule v. Oyagbola (1990) 4 NWLR (Pt. 147) 723 SC*
> - *Orient Bank (Nig.) Plc v. Bilante International Ltd (1997) 8 NWLR (Pt. 515) 37 CA*

6. Acceptance is ineffective unless there is complete agreement on all material terms and it is not the function of the court to

make a contract for parties who are too lazy to negotiate their own agreement.

- *Scammell Ltd v. Ouston (1914) 1 All ER 14*

24.6 Consideration

1. Consideration is defined as some right, interest, profit or benefit accruing to one party, or some forbearance, detriment, loss or responsibility given, suffered or undertaken by the other. In essence, each party to the contract must suffer a loss or detriment in return for the advantage or benefit conferred as where goods are sold in return for cash. All simple contracts must be supported by consideration if they are to be valid and enforceable. However, contracts under seal are an exception to the general rule, being valid and enforceable though not supported by consideration.

- *Currie v. Misa (1875) LR 10 Ex 153*
- *B. Stabilini & Co. Ltd v. Obasi (1997) 9 NWLR (Pt. 520) 293 at 296 & 297 CA*

2. Past consideration will not support a contractual claim, where for instance, a contract is wholly executed and completed before a promise is made to do or give something in return.

- *Re McArdle (1951) Ch. 669*
- *Akenzua II, Oba of Benin v. Benin Divisional Council (1959) W.R.N.L.R. 1*
- *A.G., Bendel State v. Okwumabua (Unreported) Bendel State High Court, Benin, 1980*

3. A person wishing to enforce a contract must show that he personally provided consideration. If the consideration is provided by a third party, the promisee cannot enforce the promise.

- *Twaddle v. Atkinson (1861) 1 B & S 393*

4. In law the parties to a contract are free to conclude their bargain on whatever terms as are deemed to be appropriate. Once, the consideration is of some value in the eye of the law, the courts have no jurisdiction to determine whether it is

adequate or inadequate. In principle, therefore, no consideration is too small or too much or unfair, in the absence of fraud, duress or misrepresentation.

- *African Petroleum Ltd v. Owodunni (1991) 8 NWLR (Pt. 210) 391 SC*
- *Faloughi v. Faloughi (1995) 3 NWLR (Pt. 384) 434 at 451*

5. The law is settled that consideration must be real but need not be adequate. However, a patently or grossly inadequate consideration may in an appropriate case amounts to strong evidence of fraud.

- *Spasco Vehicle & Plant Hire Co. v. Alraine (Nig.) Ltd (1995) 8 NWLR (Pt. 416) p. 665 at 672 SC*

6. Whilst consideration need not be adequate, it must, however, have some value in the eyes of the law. In other words, it must contain some element, which can be regarded as the price of the defendant's promise.

- *Chappel & Co. Ltd v. Nestle (1960) AC 87*
- *Younis v. Chidiak (1970) All N.L.R. 188 SC*

7. A complaint about insufficiency of consideration where the contract is fully executed on both sides is bound to fail because the parties can no longer return to *status quo.*

- *Okafor v. Igwilo (1997) 11 NWLR (Pt. 527) 36 at 40 CA*

8. The general rule is that a party cannot enforce a promise made to him in return for his performance of, or promise to perform, a public duty or duty imposed by law.

- *Collins v. Godetroy (1831) 1 B. & Ad. 950*

9. The principle of promissory estoppel, is that, where one party has by his words or conduct made to the other, a promise or assurance which was intended to affect the legal relations between them and to be acted on accordingly, then, once the other party has taken him at his words and acted upon them, the one who gave the promise or assurance cannot afterwards be allowed to revert to the previous legal relations as if no such promise or assurance had been made by him. He must accept their legal relations subject to the qualifications which, he himself has introduced, even though it is not supported in point

of law by any consideration, but only by his words.

- *Central London Property Trust Ltd v. High Trees House Ltd (1947) K.B. 130*

- *Combe v. Combe (1951) 1 All ER 767*

- *Offiong v. African Development Corporation Ltd (1964) 2 All N.L.R. 75, High Court of Lagos*

- *Tika Tore Press v. Abina (1974) 4 U.I.L.R. 145 SC*

- *Prospect Textile Mills v. I.C.I. Plc England, (1996) 6 NWLR (Pt. 457) 668 CA*

- *Onamade v. African Continental Bank (1997) 1 NWLR (Pt. 480) 123 at 126-127 SC*

10. A complete failure of consideration in a contract occurs where one of the contracting parties fails to receive the benefits. Where there is a claim of total failure of consideration, the innocent party is entitled to restitution.

- *Dantata v. Mohammed (2000) 5 SC 1 at 11*

11. Valuable consideration must be distinguished from consideration in the moral sense. Where a father promises to buy a house for his daughter who is homeless after her husband's death, such a promise is not enforceable in law.

- *Eastwood v. Henyon (1840) 11 A & E 438*
- *Faloughi v. Faloughi (1995) 3 NWLR (Pt. 384) 434 CA*

12. A mere promise, which is not supported by consideration, is unenforceable.

- *Combe v. Combe (1951) 2 KB 215*
- *B. Stabilini & Co. Ltd v. Obasi (1977) 9 NWLR (Pt. 520) 193 CA*

24.7 Intention to Create Legal Relations

1. As a general principle of law, domestic and social arrangements are not intended to be legally binding unless the court reaches a contrary conclusion after examining words used and surrounding circumstances. A promise by a husband to buy his wife a car in order to improve their strained relations is, for

example, purely domestic arrangement not intended to create any legal relation.

- *Simpkins v. Pays (1955) 3 All ER 10*

2. When one spouse asserts that an enforceable contract exists with the other spouse, the intention to create a legally binding agreement must be proved. The presumption being that such an intention is absent.

- *Balfour v. Balfour (1919) 2 K.B. 571*
- *Spellman v. Spellman (1961) 1 WLR 921*

3. A domestic arrangement will often be legally binding when one of the parties had detrimentally altered his position by relying on a promise made by the other party.

- *Parker v. Clarke (1960) 1 All ER 93*

4. The usual presumption that agreements between spouses living together are not legally enforceable does not apply where they are unhappily married, or about to separate, or already separated. Consequently, any arrangements governing their mutual rights and obligations may be binding at law.

- *Merrit v. Merrit (1970) 1 WLR 1121*

5. If a husband and wife wish to enter into a contract, it is advisable to record the terms clearly and unequivocally in written form with the parties' signature attached. Where a husband, on leaving his wife, orally promised to pay her as long as he could manage it the sum of £15 a week as maintenance allowance for herself and their two children, the court held that a contract did not exist, since the husband's qualifying words "as long as I can manage it", made the whole agreement uncertain.

- *Gould v. Gould (1969) 3 All ER 728*

6. The presumption is that parties to commercial agreements do intend to create legal relations. The presumption may however, be rebutted by an express term in the contract, which states that the parties do not intend to create legal relations. This may be demonstrated by such express terms such as "subject to contract" or "honour clause".

- *Rose & Frand Co. v. JR Crompton and Bros Ltd (1925) AC 445*

- *Esso Petroleum Ltd v. Commissioners of Custom and Excise (1976) 1 WLR 1*

7. The honour clause contained in football pool agreements expressly excludes any intention to enter into legal relations between the stakers and the pool companies.

- *T.K. Amadi v. Pool House Group (Nig.) Ltd & Nigerian Pools Company Ltd (1966) 2 All N.L.R. 254*
- *S.A. Bako v. Nigerian Pools Company Ltd (1968) N.M.L.R. 196*

24.8 Capacity to Contract

1. A minor is a person under the age of 18. The general rule is that a minor is not bound by a contract, which he enters into during minority. But this general rule is subject to certain exceptions, such as, contracts for necessaries and education, and contracts for beneficial service.

- *Roberts v. Gray (1913) 1 KB 520*
- *Slade v. Metrodent Ltd (1953) 2 QB 112*

2. A contract of apprenticeship negotiated while under age is usually binding on the minor provided that as a whole the agreement can be regarded as beneficial to the minor.

- *Clements v. London and North Western Railway Co. (1894) 2 Q.B. 482*

3. Any trading contract to which a minor is a party is void even though its terms are beneficial to him on the ground that a minor who trades may lose the capital he has invested in the business enterprise.

- *Cowern v. Nield (1912) 2 K.B. 419*

4. If a party is suffering from such a degree of mental disorder that he is incapable of understanding the nature of the contract then it is voidable at his instance, provided his disability was known or ought to have been known to the other party. However, a mentally disordered person must always pay a reasonable price for necessaries supplied to him and he is always bound by contracts made during a lucid interval. Also, if one party is so

drunk that he does not know what he is doing, the contract is voidable at his instance, provided the other party knew of his condition. A similar duty to pay a reasonable price for necessaries is imposed on him as on the mentally disordered person by virtue of section 2 of the Sale of Goods Act 1893.

- *Gore v. Gibson (1843) 13 M & W 623*
- *Imperial Loan Co. v. Stone (1892) 1 QB 599*
- *Chaplin v. Leslie Frewin (1966) Ch. 71*

24.9 Privity of Contract

1. One basic rule of law of contract is that a person who is not originally a party to a contract, cannot be bound by its terms, nor can he receive any benefit from it. This is known as the doctrine of privity of contract. There are exceptions to this rule, the main one being agency where, if A makes a contract with B, C can intervene provided he can establish that one of the original parties was acting on his behalf, and that he is in fact the principal.

- *Twaddle v. Atkinson (1861) 1 B & S 393*
- *Dunlop Pnuematic Tyre Company Ltd v. Selfridge (1915) AC 847*
- *A-G, Federation v. A.I.C. Ltd (2000) 6 SC (Pt. I) 175 at 183*

2. It is a general principle of law that a master is liable for a contract entered into on his behalf by his servant if the servant has express, apparent or implied authority of the master to enter into such contract.

- *B.Visinoni Ltd v. National Bank of Nigeria Ltd (1975) N.N.L.R. 15, High Court of North-Central State. Suit No. NCH/103/74*

3. A master is not liable for a contract entered into on his behalf by his servant if the servant has no authority to enter into such contract and the other contracting party is aware of the absence of authority.

- *B.Visinoni Ltd v. National Bank of Nigeria Ltd (1975) N.N.L.R. 15, High Court of North-Central State. Suit No.*

NCH/103/74

4. A third party who was not privy to a contract cannot ordinarily be held responsible for the damages incurred by default of one of the parties.

- *African Insurance Development Corporation v Nigeria LGN Ltd (2000) 2 SC 57 at 66*

5. A contract, which is concluded under a tripartite agreement, is one, which involves three parties, and each party can acquire rights and each can come under obligations. For instance, where an owner of a car, the repairer and the insurers enter into an agreement, each can acquire rights and come under obligations thereunder.

- *Abed Bros. Ltd. v. Niger Insurance Co. Ltd (1976) NNLR 1 SC*
- *J.E. Oshevire Ltd v. Tripoli Motors (1997) 5 NWLR (Pt. 503) 1 SC*

6. In giving effect to the agreement of contracting parties, the court has a duty not only to look at what the parties wrote or said but also at what they did, their conduct or "modus operandi".

- *Nwobi v. Anukam (2001) 14 WRN 38 at 39 CA*

7. The law is that an agreement between a contractor and his employer prohibiting subcontracting does not bind a subsequent subcontractor, who is not a party to the agreement.

- *Kyaure Const. Ltd v. Agbana (1998) 2 NWLR (Pt. 539) 581 CA*

24.10 Terms of Contract

1. It is an established rule of law that contracts may be in writing, oral or implied. Consequently, a contract between parties may be expressed by words or by an agreement in writing signed by the parties. Also, a contract could be implied by the conduct of the parties themselves.

- *Majekodunmi v. National Bank of Nigeria Ltd (1978) 3 SC 119 at 127*

- *B. Stabilini & Co. Ltd v. Obasi (1997) 9 NWLR (Pt. 520) 293 at 297 CA*

2. Parties are bound by the terms of contract contained in an agreement without any subtraction or addition. The court has no power to rewrite the contract.

- *Afrotech v. MIA & Sons Ltd (2000) 12 SC (Part II) 1 at 15*

3. A party who induced another party to enter into a contract and has indeed benefited from the contract cannot subsequently deny the validity of that contract.

- *Okechukwu v. Onuorah (2000) 12 SC (Part II) 104 at 109*

4. It is a general rule that where parties enter into a contract, they are bound by the terms thereof and the court will not allow to be read into such a contract, terms on which there is no agreement.

- *Baba v. Nigerian Civil Aviation Training Centre (1991) 5 NWLR (Pt. 192) 388 SC*
- *Koiki v. Magnusson (1999) 8 NWLR (Pt. 615) 492 at 494 SC*

5. Where the term of a contract is silent as to the time for the performance or satisfaction of a condition, the law shall imply that the obligation is performed within a reasonable time. However, where the parties have, by their mutual agreement, provided for the time for the satisfaction of a condition, time becomes of the essence of the agreement and thus, any breach of that condition has the effect of putting an end to the contract.

- *Niger Insurance v. Abed Brothers (1976) 7 SC 35*
- *Leyland (Nig.) Ltd v. Dizengoff (1990) 2 NWLR (Pt. 134) 610 CA*
- *Gamla (Nig.) Ltd v. New (Nig.) Bank Plc (1999) 12 NWLR (Pt. 631) 408 at 409 CA*

6. The general law and the rules of court have provided principles for the purposes of determining the right venue or forum in which actions with respect to contract may be heard and determined. The principles consist of the following, namely: where the contract was made or entered into - *lex loci contractus*; where the contract ought to have been performed - *lex loci*; where the defendant resides - *lex loci domicili*; where payment ought

to be made - *lex loci solutionis;* and where, in land matters, the land is situate - *lex loci rei sitae/lex situs.*

- *I.K. Martins (Nig.) Ltd v. U.P.L. (1992) 1 NWLR (Pt. 217) 322 CA*
- *Ndaeye v. Ogunnaya (1997) 1 SC 11 at 25*
- *Societe Generale Bank (Nig.) Ltd v. Safa Steel and Chemical Manufacturing Ltd (1998) 5 NWLR (Pt. 548) 168 at 170 CA*

7. A contract may be subject to terms that are implied by custom or trade usage.

- *British Crane Hire Corporation v. Ipswich Plant Hire Ltd (1975) Q.B. 303; (1974) All ER 1059 CA*

8. The rule is that no evidence of custom can override the terms of written contract.

- *Leyland (Nig.) Ltd v. Dizengoff (1990) 2 NWLR (Pt. 134) 610 CA*

9. In a contract for sale of goods by description there is implied condition that the goods shall correspond with that description. This usually covers cases where the buyer has not seen the goods and relies on the seller's description. Section 13(1) of the Sale of Goods Act, 1893 considered.

- *Varley v. Whipp (1900) 1 Q.B. 513*
- *Boshalli v. Allied Commercial Exporters LA (1961) 1 All N.L.R. 917 P.C.*

10. Where goods are sold in the course of business, there is an implied condition that they are of merchantable quality, except where the defect is specifically drawn to the buyer's attention before the contract is made, or, the buyer examined the goods before contracting and the defect ought to have been revealed upon examination.

- *Godley v. Perry (1960) 1 All ER 36*
- *Khalil and Dibbo v. Mastronikolis (1949) 12 W.A.C.A. 462*

11. The courts do not have powers to intervene in contracts and impose terms arbitrarily. However, courts may imply a term in order to fill a gap left by the parties in the terms expressly agreed upon which fail to regulate their respective rights and liabilities

in the situation that had arisen. Where, for instance, the plaintiff claimed that "bush clearing" did not cover the felling of trees, the court held that although the contract did not expressly stipulate that the plaintiff were to cut down the trees on the route, there was an implied terms to that effect.

- *Okotete v. Electricity Corporation of Nigeria (Unreported) High Court of Midwest, Warri, May 29, 1970*

- *Mazin Eng. Ltd v. Tower Aluminium (1993) 5 NWLR (Pt. 295) 526 at 567 SC*

12. Where goods are required for various purposes, the buyer is obliged to indicate the particular purpose for which he needs the goods.

- *D.I.C. Industries v. Jimfat (Nig.) Ltd (1975) 2 C.C.H.C.J. 175, High Court of Lagos, Casebook, p. 152*

13. Where however, there is only one particular purpose, for which goods can be used, there will be no need to specify the purpose for which a buyer needed the goods. For instance, where a plaintiff was afflicted by dermatitis (a skin disease) after wearing underpants manufactured by the defendants, the court held that there was no need to specify the particular purpose for which the plaintiff needed the goods.

- *Preist v. Last (1903) 2 K.B. 148*

- *Grant v. Australian Knitting Mills Ltd (1936) A.C. 85*

24.11 Forms of Contract

1. In a contract of sale of land, the agreement to sell is concluded when both parties agree on the subject matter, the nature of the transaction and the consideration.

- *Doherty v. Ighodaro (1997) 11 NWLR (Pt. 530) 694 at 696 CA*

2. In a contract of guarantee, the surety receives no benefit and no consideration. He is bound, therefore, strictly to the proper meaning and effect of the written engagement. If there is any alteration afterwards, notwithstanding the fact that it was altered for his benefit, or innocently altered, the surety is at liberty to

protest that the contract is no longer that which he was engaged to be a surety and that his obligation be put to an end.

> - *Gurara Securities and Finance Ltd v. T.I.C. Ltd (1999) 2 NWLR (Pt. 589) 29 at 31 CA*

3. As a general rule, a contract of service cannot be presumed. There must be express evidence that there was a contract of employment between the parties. It cannot be presumed from the circumstances of the case nor can it be inferred from the evidence that a person's salaries are being paid by another. Thus, a plaintiff seeking a declaration that the termination of his appointment is a nullity must plead and prove that he is an employee of the defendant, by producing relevant letter of appointment, if the contract is written; the terms and conditions of his appointment; and the circumstances under which his appointment can be terminated.

> - *NITEL v. Oshodin (1999) 8 NWLR (Pt. 616) 528 at 531 & 532 CA*

4. There is a difference between a contract of sale and an agreement to sell. Where the property in the goods is transferred from the seller to the buyer, it is called a contract of sale. However, where the transfer of the property in the goods is to take place at a future time or subject to some conditions thereafter to be fulfilled, it is called an agreement to sell. An agreement to sell becomes a sale when the conditions are fulfilled subject to which the property in the goods is to be transferred. Section 1(2), (3) and (4) Sale of Goods Act, 1893 considered.

> - *Afrotec Technical Services (Nig.) Ltd v. MIA & Sons Ltd (2000) 12 SC (Pt. II) 1 at 34 & 35*

5. The law is that no sale by auction shall take place until after at least seven days public notice has been given in the city and at the place of intended sale. Also, before beginning any auction, the auctioneer shall affix or suspend and during the auction keep affixed or suspended in some conspicuous part of the place, a ticket or board containing his true and full names and residence printed or written in large letters. Furthermore, within sixty hours after the sale, the auctioneer shall deliver to the state commissioner, a complete account of the sale verified by oath or affirmation of the auction. Sections 19, 20 and 21 of Sales by

Auction Law, Cap. 126, Laws of Lagos State, 1973 (as amended) considered.

> - *Leventis Motors Ltd v. Nunieh (1999) 13 NWLR (Pt. 634) 235 at 239 CA*

6. A hire purchase agreement must satisfy two major conditions for it to be valid in the eyes of the law. The person giving out the goods must be the owner, and the transaction must be reduced into writing in the form of a note or memorandum of agreement. Section 2(1) and (2) of the Hire Purchase Act, Cap 169, Laws of the Federation of Nigeria, 1990 construed.

> - *Yusuf v. Mobolaji (1999) 12 NWLR (Pt. 631) 374 at 377 CA*

7. Under a hire purchase agreement, the hirer can only become the owner of the property if, after all the installments and other moneys payable under the hire purchase agreement have been paid and provided there was no breach of the provisions of the agreement. A hirer is not entitled to ownership of the hired goods if he fails to pay all installments and is in breach of the provisions of the agreement.

> - *Incar (Nig.) Plc v. Uralo General Enterprises Ltd (1998) 13 NWLR (Pt. 582) 346 at 349 CA*

8. Under the law of agency, an estate agent is an independent person engaged by the vendor on a commission basis to find and introduce a willing purchaser. He is not an agent of the vendor to contract on his behalf. His actions are attributable to the vendor only in a limited case, for example, the making of representations as to the condition of the property. Therefore, an estate agent has neither actual nor implied authority to ask for or receive a pre-contract deposit, as agent for the vendor.

> - *Ezenwa v. Ekong (1999) 11 NWLR (Pt. 625) 55 at 60 CA*

9. An estate agent is not entitled to retain a commission on a sale which a court of law has set aside.

> - *Taiwo v. Danbare Agency Ltd. (2001) 14 WRN 52 at 55 CA*

24.12 Exemption Clause

1. The simplest means of ensuring that a particular clause is included in an agreement is to write down the terms of the contract and have the other party sign the document. The clause is then binding on the signatory even if he fails to read it or fails to appreciate its significance.

- *L'Estrange v. Graucob (1934) 2 K.B. 394*

2. A person is, as a general rule, bound by the contents of a document signed by him, whether he read it or not, except it is procured by fraud or misrepresentation.

- *L'Estrange v. Graucob (1934) 2 K.B. 394*
- *George Chagoury v. Adebayo, 3 U.I.L.R. 532*

3. Where a person is induced by fraud to sign a document, he may deny the validity of the contract by pleading "non est factum" in any action brought against him to enforce the contract.

- *Foster v. Makinnon (1869) L.R. 4*

4. A person making a plea of *non est factum* must prove and satisfy two important conditions namely: that there is a radical or fundamental difference between what he signed and what he had intended to sign, and that he was not negligent in signing the document.

- *Foster v. Makinnon (1869) L.R. 4*
- *Gallie v. Lee (1969) 2 Ch. 31*
- *Barclays Bank of Nigeria Ltd v. Okotie-Eboh (Unreported) High Court of Lagos, Taylor, C.J. Suit No. LD/1233/71*

5. It is trite law that if an exclusion clause is to be effective, notice of it must be given to the other party before the contract is concluded.

- *Imo Concorde Hotel Ltd v. Anya (1992) 4 NWLR (Pt. 234) 210 CA*

6. The law is that the degree of notice required to make an exemption clause applicable to an illiterate person is higher than normal.

- *Richardson Spence & Co. v. Rowntree (1894) A.C. 217*
- *Otegbeye v. Little (1900) 1 N.L.R. 70*

7. Where statutory provisions are expressly incorporated into a contract by parties under the doctrine of incorporation by reference, the parties would be deemed to have had actual notice of the existence of the statutory provisions at the time the contract was entered into.

- *Iwuoha v. N.R.C (1997) 4 NWLR (Pt. 500) 419 at 422 SC*

8. General words in an exemption clause do not ordinarily absolve the party seeking to rely on the exemption from liability for his own negligence or that of his employees. Consequently, words such as "for loss of or damage to goods, which can be covered by insurance" do not cover loss or damage due to the party's negligence. Similarly, where garage owners stated that they are "not responsible for damage caused by fire to customers' cars on the premises", they are by the words, not protected against their negligence.

- *Price and Co. v. The Union Lighterance Co. (1904) I.B.B. 412*
- *Hollier v. Rambles Motors (A.M.C.) Ltd (1972) 2 QB 71*
- *F.B.N. Plc v. Associated Motors Co. Ltd (1998) 10 NWLR (Pt. 570) 441 CA*

9. In order to exclude liability for negligence effectively, appropriate and comprehensive words should be used. It was therefore held that words such as any loss "however arising" or from "any cause whatever", would cover losses by negligence.

- *Joseph Travers & Sons Ltd v. Cooper (1915) 1 KB 73*
- *Rutter v. Palmer (1922) 2 KB 87*

10. The law is that a party to a contract cannot rely on exemption clause if he fails to carry out the contract in its essential aspect. A breach, which goes to the root of a contract, disentitles a party from relying on the exemption clause.

- *Karsale (Harrow) Ltd v. Wallis (1956) 2 All E.R. 866*
- *Harbutt's Plasticine Ltd v. Wayne Tank Pump Co. Ltd (1970) 1 QB 477*
- *Photo Production Ltd v. Securicor Ltd.(1980) AC 827*

24.13 *Illegal Contract*

1. An illegal contract may be defined as a contract, which the law forbids, for example, a contract to commit murder, or to obstruct a highway.

- *Thirwell v. Oyewumi (1990) 4 NWLR (Pt. 144) 384 CA*

2. A contract is illegal at common law if it is harmful to the interest of the society and prejudicial to the social and economic interest of the community. The following contracts are generally regarded as illegal at common law, namely: a contract to commit a crime, tort or a fraud; a contract prejudicial to the status of marriage; a contract prejudicial to public safety; a contract prejudicial to the administration of justice; a contract that tends to promote corruption in public life; and a contract to defraud Inland Revenue or local authority of taxes or rates.

- *Alexander v. Rayson (1936) 1 K.B. 169*
- *Regazzoni v. K.C. Sethia Ltd (1958) A.C. 301*
- *Golden Okoronkwo v. P.O. Nwoga (1972) 2 E.C.S.L.R. 615*
- *R v. Andrew (1973) Q.B. 422*
- *Alake v. Chief Oderinlo (Unreported) High Court of Western State, Abeokuta Judicial Division, Suit No. 23A/74 delivered on January 24, 1975*
- *A.C.B. v. Alao (1994) 7 NWLR (Pt. 358) 614 CA*

3. The provision of a statute or a statutory instrument may expressly or impliedly declare certain contracts illegal with the result that they are void. The Exchange Control Act of 1962, for instance, expressly prohibits certain types of contracts or transactions involving foreign exchange.

- *Sodipo v. Lemminkainen (1986) 1 NWLR (Pt. 15) 220 SC*
- *Melwani v. Chanhira Corp. (1995) 6 NWLR (Pt. 402) 438 CA*

4. Where a contract is *ex facie* illegal, that is illegal as formed and, therefore completely prohibited either by statute or at common law, neither party can derive any right or interest from it. It is void *ab initio*.

- *Rivway Lines Ltd v. Rhein Mas Und See (1993) 7 NWLR (Pt. 308) 692 CA*

- *Melwani v. Chanhira Corp. (1995) 6 NWLR (Pt. 402) 438 CA*

5. As a general rule the courts will neither enforce a contract which is illegal or which is otherwise contrary to public policy, nor permit the recovery of benefits conferred under such a contract.

- *Pearce v. Brooks (1866) LR 1 Ex 213*

- *Alao v. A.C.B. Ltd (1998) 3 NWLR (Pt. 542) 339 SC*

6. Generally, the consequence of illegality is that the court will not come to the assistance of any party to an illegal contract who wishes to enforce it. This position of the law is founded on the principle of public policy and is expressed in the maxim *ex turpi causa non oritur actio*, meaning that an action does not arise from a bad cause.

- *Pan Bisbilder (Nig.) Ltd v. First Bank of Nigeria Ltd (2000) 1 SC 71 at 76, 79, 83*

7. A contract is illegal if the consideration involves doing something illegal or contrary to public policy or if the intention of the parties in making the contract is to promote or enhance something, which is illegal or contrary to public policy.

- *Sodipo v. Lemminkainen OY (No.1)(1985) 2 NWLR (Pt. 8) 547 SC*

- *Alao v. A.C.B Ltd (1998) 3 NWLR (Pt. 542) 339 at 346 SC*

24.14 *Void Contract*

1. Contracts that are sexually immoral are void contracts. A prostitute cannot, for instance, sue for her fees. Similarly, an action cannot be maintained to recover lodging knowingly let for prostitution.

- *Uptill v. Wright (1911) 1 K.B. 506*

2. A contract in restraint of trade is one in which a party covenants to restrict his future liberty to exercise his trade, business or profession in such a manner and with such person as he chooses. *Prima facie*, such contracts are void. However, a

contract in restraint of trade is valid and binding if, it is reasonably necessary to protect the interests of the person in whose favour it is imposed; it is not unreasonable as regards the person restrained; and it is not injurious to the public.

> - *Leontaritis v. Nigerian Textile Mills Ltd (1967) N.C.L.R. 114*

3. The rule is that where the whole of the agreement is void, the contract as a whole cannot be enforced. But, where a contract contains partly valid terms and partly void terms, the valid terms can be enforced by applying the doctrine of severance.

> - *Adesanya v. Otuewu (1993) 1 NWLR (Pt. 270) 414 SC*

24.15 Duress, Undue Influence and Mistake

1. At common law, duress means actual violence or threats of violence to the person, or to his personal freedom. That is, threats calculated to produce fear of loss of life or bodily harm, or fear of imprisonment. The subject of such threats must be the plaintiff himself, or his wife, parent, child or other near relative.

> - *Sear v. Cohen (1881) 45 L.T. 589*
> - *Williams v. Bayley (1886) L.R. 1 H.L. 200*
> - *Kaufman v. Gerson (1904) 1 K.B. 591*

2. The rule is that a contract concluded under duress is voidable at the option of the coerced person, since that person does not freely consent to the agreement made between him and the other party.

> - *Cumming v. Ince (1847) 11 Q.B.D. 112*

3. The courts have widened the scope of the common law doctrine of duress to include amongst others, economic duress. Where, for instance, the defendant ship builders forced the plaintiffs for whom they were building a ship to pay an extra 10 per cent over and above the agreed cost of the ship by threatening to abandon the construction of the ship midway, knowing that the plaintiffs had already concluded a lucrative contract to lease the ship to a third party on completion of the construction, the court held that the action of the defendants

constituted economic duress.

- *North Ocean Shipping Co. Ltd v. Hyundai Construction Co. Ltd (1979) Q.B. 705*

4. Undue influence simply means inequality of bargaining power.

- *Lloyd's Bank Ltd v. Bundy (1975) Q.B. 326*

5. The concept of undue influence may arise from two circumstances namely: where there is a special relationship between the parties, and where there is no special relationship between the parties. Where there is a special relationship between the parties, equity will presume the existence of undue influence, and will set aside any contract advantageous to the party in a superior position to the other. The onus is on that party to establish that the agreement was free from undue influence.

- *Tate v. Williamson (1886) L.R. 2 Ch. App. 55*

6. The rule is that where there is no special relationship between the parties, undue influence has to be proved by the person alleging that he entered into the bargain as a result of it. He has to prove, therefore, that there was actual coercion by the defendant or that the defendant exercised such a degree of domination and control over him that his independence of decision was substantially undermined.

- *Williams v. Bayley (1866) L.R. 1 H.L. 200*

7. Undue influence may be implied in the following relationships namely: parent and child; guardian and ward; doctor and patient; religious leader and disciple; solicitor and client; and teacher and student.

- *Itylton v. Itylton (1754) Ves. Sen. 547*
- *Allcard v. Skinner (1887) 36 Ch.D. 145*
- *Powell v. Powell (1900) 1 Ch. 243*
- *Wright v. Carter (1903) 1 Ch. 27*
- *Radelife v. Price (1908) 18 T.L.R. 466*

8. The presumption of undue influence may be rebutted if the defendant can prove that the plaintiff acted independently of his influence. This can be established by showing, for example,

that the plaintiff had competent and independent advice.

- *Lloyd's Bank v. Bundy (1975) Q.B. 326*

9. Where undue influence is alleged, the onus lies on the party seeking to set aside the contract to show that undue means had been used to obtain the contract.

- *Pan Bisbilder (Nig.) Ltd v. First Bank of Nigeria Ltd (2000) 1 SC 71 at 83*

10. Where parties have reached an agreement, but that agreement is based upon a fundamental mistaken assumption by both parties, the court may nullify the consent of the parties by holding their contract void. An agreement between parties, for instance, to purchase a specific article is void if in fact the article had perished before the date of the sale.

- *Bell v. Lever Brothers Ltd (1932) AC 161*

11. A mistake may be sufficiently fundamental to avoid a contract where both parties are mistaken as to the existence of the subject matter of the contract.

- *Galloway v. Galloway (1914) 30 TLR 531*

12. A mistake as to the identity of the subject matter of the contract may be sufficiently fundamental to avoid a contract if both parties thought that in fact they were dealing with another subject matter.

- *Diamond v. British Colombia Thoroughbred Breeders' Society (1966) 52 DLR (2d) 146 (Canadian Case)*

13. A mistake may be sufficiently fundamental to avoid a contract where both parties believe that the contract is capable of being performed when, in fact, it is not. Mistake as to the possibility of performing the contract may be due to physical impossibility, legal impossibility or commercial impossibility.

- *Cooper v. Phibbs (1867) LR 2HL 149*
- *Griffth v. Brymer (1903) 19 TLR 434*
- *Sherikh Brothers Ltd v. Ochsner (1957) AC 136*

14. A mistake as to the quality of the subject matter of the contract may be sufficiently fundamental to avoid a contract. But the courts are extremely reluctant to conclude that a mistake

as to quality renders a contract void.

> - *Bell v. Lever Brothers (1932) AC 161*
> - *Leaf v. International Galleries (1950) 2 KB 86*
> - *Harrison and Jones v. Burton and Lancaster (1953) 1 QB 646*

24.16 Misrepresentation

1. Misrepresentation may be defined as an unambiguous false statement of fact, which is addressed to the party misled and which materially induces the contract. Thus, misrepresentation under the law of contract, may be broken down into three distinct elements, viz: the representation must be an unambiguous false statement of fact, it must be addressed to the party misled and, it must be a material inducement to enter into the contract.

> - *Edgington v. Fitzmaurice (1885) 29 Ch D 459*
> - *Bisset v. Wilkinson (1927) AC 177*
> - *Commercial Banking Co of Sydney v. RH Brown and Co (1972) 2 Lloyds Rep 360*
> - *Esso Petroleum Ltd v. Mardon (1976) QB 801*

2. Fraudulent misrepresentation has been defined as a false statement made knowingly, or without belief in its truth, or recklessly, or carelessly whether it be true or false.

> - *Derry v. Peek (1889) 14 App. Cas. 337*

3. A representor is defined as the person who makes a statement of fact and a representee is a person to whom the statement is directed and the latter must have been induced to enter into the contract by the statement. There are three classes of representees namely: a person to whom the representation is made and his authorized agents; persons to whom the representor intended the representation to be passed on, and; members of a class at which the representation is directed, for example, the public at large or a particular class. The question whether the plaintiff comes within a particular category of representees, depends to a large extent on the purpose of the representation or the

intention of the representor.

- *Peek v. Gurney (1837) L.R. 6 H.L. 377*

4. The rule is that mere silence is not misrepresentation. However, if a person conducts himself in a manner which suggests that a particular state of affairs exists, that person would be guilty of misrepresentation if the conduct turns out to be misleading. It was thus, held that a person who sits in a restaurant and orders a meal impliedly represents that he has the means to pay.

- *D.P.P. v. Ray (Ray v. Sempres) (1974) A.C. 370*

5. The doctrine of misrepresentation by conduct has been extended by the courts to include the use of cheques and credit cards. It was, thus held that the use of a cheque will amount to a false representation if it is, in the circumstances, unauthorized by the bank. Similarly, it has been held that the use of credit card to purchase goods amounts to a representation that the user has the authority of the credit card company to use the card.

- *R v. Charles (1977) A.C. 177*
- *R v. Lambie (1981) 1 WLR 78*

6. A misrepresentation becomes a ground for rescission of contract if it is intended to cause and in fact causes the representee to enter into the contract. The burden of proving this lies on the representee who is alleging misrepresentation. Therefore, if a misrepresentation did not affect the mind of a representee, because he was unaware it had been made; or because even though he was aware, he had not been influenced by it; or because he knew that it was false, he would have no remedy.

- *Udogwu v. Oki (1990) 5 NWLR (Pt. 153) 721 CA*

7. At common law, misrepresentation may be fraudulent, negligent or innocent.

- *Hedley Byrne v. Heller (1964) AC 465*

8. The rule is that once it is established that the representor is guilty of a fraudulent misrepresentation, it is no defence that the representee could have discovered the fraud if he had been

more diligent.

> - *Redgrave v. Hurd (1881) 20 Ch.D. 1*
> - *Sule v. Aromire (1951) 20 N.L.R. 20*

9. A negligent misrepresentation is one made carelessly, or without reasonable grounds for believing it to be true. As a rule, negligent misrepresentation cannot give rise to liability on the part of the representor unless, he owes a duty of care to the representee or where there is a fiduciary relationship between the parties.

> - *Nocton v. Ashburton (1914) A.C. 932*
> - *Chandler v. Crane, Christmas & Co. (1951) 2 K.B. 164*
> - *Imarsel Chemical Co. Ltd v. National Bank of Nigeria (1974) 4 E.C.S.L.R. 355*
> - *Esso Petroleum Co. Ltd v. Mardon (1976) Q.B. 801; (1976) 2 All ER 5*

10. As a general rule, the effect of misrepresentation on a transaction is that it entitles the injured party to avoid the transaction induced by the misrepresentation. For instance, in the case of a contract, the injured party has the right to have it rescinded or to recover damages for injury. Similarly, it gives rise to a defence to any action brought by the fraudulent party to enforce the contract or other transaction. However, it does not make a contract or transaction void. It only makes it voidable.

> - *Udogwu v. Oki (1990) 5 NWLR (Pt. 153) 721 CA*

11. There are two principal remedies available once the existence of misrepresentation is established before a court of law or a tribunal. The first is the setting aside of the contract induced by the misrepresentation, that is rescission. The second is that the party who was induced to enter into the contract may claim damages in tort where the misrepresentation was made fraudulently or negligently.

> - *Redgrave v. Hurd (1881) 20 Ch D 1*
> - *Car and Universal Finance Co. v. Caldwell (1965) 1 QB 525*
> - *Doyle v. Olby (1969) 2 QB*
> - *Smith Kline & French Laboratories Ltd v. Long (1989) 1 WLR 1*

24.17 Discharge of Contract: Performance, Frustration and Breach

1. A contract may be discharged through the following, namely: by performance, if both parties have done all that is required of them; by agreement, if both parties have mutually agreed to put an end to their contractual relationship; by frustration, if some event outside the control of the parties takes place, making performance impossible; and, by breach, when the innocent party alone is relieved of liability, future or past, and the party in default may be liable for damages.

> - *Westac v. Sokoto State Government (S.S.G) (2001) 1 WRN 113 at 118 CA*

2. A contractual obligation can be effectively discharged by full and precise performance in accordance with the strict letter of the agreement. Partial performance does not result in a discharge.

> - *Re Moore & Co. and Lander & Co. (1921) 2 K.B. 519*

3. A party who partially performs his contractual obligations cannot recover anything for the benefit conferred on the other party as a result of the work carried out. However, there are exceptions to this general rule. For example, where one party is prevented from fully carrying out his contractual duties because of some act or omission by the other party which effectively prevents the contract from being duly performed as anticipated. In such a case, the party who partially implemented the agreed terms may sue on *quantum meruit*, or for damages for breach of contract in order to recover compensation for the amount of work actually completed.

> - *Planche v. Colburn (1831) 8 Bing. 14*

4. A party who has substantially performed his contractual duties in the manner stipulated, even though some small part of the work had been badly done, or not done at all, may recover the agreed price, less a deduction to remedy the minor defects or lapses. The injured party, may, also have an action for any damages he may have sustained.

> - *Hoening v. Isaacs (1952) 2 All ER 176*
> - *Ekwunife v. Wayne (W.A.) Ltd (1989) 5 NWLR (Pt. 122) 422 at 441-2 SC*

5. The common law view is that time is of the essence where the parties have expressly made it so, or where circumstances show that it is intended to be of the essence, or where a definite time is fixed for execution of a mercantile contract even though time is not expressly made of the essence. Thus, failure to perform the contract within the time limit will constitute a breach. Performance must be rendered within a reasonable time in the absence of any specification as to time in the contract itself.

- *Mazin Eng. Ltd v. Tower Aluminium (1993) 5 NWLR (Pt. 295) 526 SC*

6. Frustration occurs whenever the law recognises that, without default of either party, a contractual obligation has become incapable of being performed because the circumstances in which performance is called for would render it radically different from what was undertaken by the contract.

- *Davis Contractors Ltd v. Fareham D.C. (1956) A.C. 696*

- *Akanmu v. Olugbode (2001) 13 WRN 132 CA*

7. The underlisted situations or events have been held by the courts at one time or the other to constitute frustrating events namely: subsequent legal changes; outbreak of war; destruction of the subject matter of the contract; government requisition of the subject matter of the contract; and the cancellation of an expected event.

- *Krell v. Henry (1903) 2 K.B. 740*

- *Bentworth Finance Ltd v. Alhaji Sani Bakori (Unreported) High Court of North Central State, Kaduna Judicial Division. Suit No. NCH/46/71 delivered on 12 February, 1973*

- *Ajuna Uche Johnson v. U.A.C. Nigeria Ltd (Unreported) High Court of Lagos State Suit No. C0/1443/72 delivered on 23 May, 1975*

- *Obayuwana v. The Governor of Bendel State (1982) Selected Judgments of the Supreme Court, p. 167*

8. The rule is that it is not for the parties, but for the court to state whether and when frustration has occurred, and the court has the power to determine the existence of frustration even where the parties have showed otherwise.

- *Denny, Mott & Dickinson v. James B. Fraser & Co. Ltd (1944) A.C. 265; (1944) 1 All ER 678*

9. The doctrine of frustration is applicable to all categories of contracts; sales of land, leases, and tenancies inclusive.

- *Araka v. Monier Construction Company Ltd (1978) 2 L.N.R. 60*
- *National Carriers Ltd v. Pannalpina (Northern) Ltd (1981) A.C. 675; (1981) 1 All ER 161*

10. A contract of employment may be frustrated by the illness or innate inability of one party to perform the contract in the manner anticipated.

- *Condor v. The Barron Knights (1966)7 WLR 89*

11. The rule is that self-induced frustration is no frustration but a breach of contract.

- *Western Nigerian Finance Corporation v. West Coast Builders Ltd (1971) 1 U.I.L.R. 93*

12. A contract is not frustrated merely because its execution becomes more difficult or more expensive than either party originally anticipated and has to be carried out in a manner not envisaged at the time of its negotiation.

- *Davies Contractors Ltd v. Fareham UDC (1956) AC 696*
- *Tsakiroglou & Co. v. Noblee Thorh G.m.b.h. (1962) A.C. 93*

13. A contract is frustrated where after the contract was concluded, events occur which make performance of the contract impossible, illegal or something radically different from that which was in the contemplation of the parties at the time they entered into the contract. A contract, which is discharged on the ground of frustration, is brought to an end automatically by the operation of law, irrespective of the wishes of the parties.

- *Hirji Mulji v. Cheong Yue SS Co (1926) AC 497*

14. A contract can be discharged by breach. A breach of contract means that the party in breach has acted contrary to the terms of the contract either by non-performance or by performing the contract not in accordance with its terms or by a wrongful repudiation of the contract. Therefore, a party who has performed the contract in consonance with its terms cannot be said to have been in breach thereof.

- *Pan Bisbilder (Nigeria) Ltd v. First Bank of Nigeria Ltd (2000) 1 SC 71 at 86/87*

15. In an action for breach of contract, the cause of action accrues for the plaintiff's benefit from the time the breach is committed and not when the damage is suffered. Thus, the period of limitation begins to run from the date the cause of action accrues.

> - *Sanda v. Kukawa Local Government (1991) 2 NWLR (Pt. 174) 379 at 381 SC*
> - *Iweka v. S.C.O.A. (Nigeria) Ltd (2000) 3 SC 21 at 30*

16. Where one party has committed a serious breach of contract, the innocent party has a right to rescind the contract. One of the consequences is that the innocent party who has elected to rescind the contract is released from further obligation under the contract.

> - *Dantata v. Mohammed (2000) 5 SC 1 at 10, 11 & 28*

17. Where an innocent party treats the contract as still in force, the *status quo ante* is maintained. In such a case, each party is entitled to sue for both past and future breaches. Therefore a seller, who refuses to treat a breach by the buyer as terminating the contract, will remain liable for the delivery of the goods to the buyer and, where a buyer refuses to treat non-delivery by the seller as discharging the contract, he will remain liable to take delivery and pay for the goods.

> - *Udom v. Michelette & Sons Ltd (1997) 8 NWLR (Pt. 516) 187 SC*

24.18 Remedies for Breach of Contract: Damages, Specific Performance

1. If one party to a contract is in breach of its terms, the other party is entitled to bring an action for damages so as to be placed in the same financial position as if the contractual terms had been duly carried out. If the innocent party does not suffer any monetary loss at all, he may still successfully sue the defaulting party for breach of contract, although only nominal damages will be awarded to reflect infringement of his legal right.

> - *Hadley v. Baxendale (1854) 9 Exch. 341*

2. Under the first branch of the rule in *Hadley v. Baxendale*,

damages are recoverable by the injured party if the loss may be fairly and reasonably considered to arise naturally. The loss must be reasonably supposed, at the time of making the contract, to have been in the contemplation of both parties as the probable consequence of its breach. Under the second branch of the rule, exceptional and unusual losses are recoverable from the defaulting party, if, owing to special circumstances, actually or constructively known to him at the time of making the contract he contemplated that its breach would cause losses outside the usual course of things.

- *Victoria Landry v. Newman Industries (1949) 2 K.B. 528*
- *Cottrill v. Steyning & Littlehampton Building Society (1966) 1 WLR 753*
- *Ajufor v. Trans Arab Ltd (Unreported) Western State Court of Appeal, Ibadan, delivered on 8 December, 1972*
- *Olagunju v. Raji (1986) 5 NWLR (Pt. 42) 408 CA*

3. The rule governing the time of assessment of damages is that damages are to be assessed as at the time when the cause of action arose, that is, the date of the breach. However, this is not an absolute rule. The courts have power to fix any other appropriate day if the date of breach will work injustice.

- *Johnson v. Agnew (1980) A.C. 367*

4. In an action for breach of contract, damages may be awarded for physical inconvenience and mental distress suffered as a result of that breach.

- *Jarvis v. Swan Tours Ltd (1972) 1 All ER 71*
- *Eweka v. Midwest Newspapers Corporation (1976) E.C.S.L.R. 280*

5. A duty is imposed upon a plaintiff to take all reasonable steps to mitigate any loss caused to him by the defendant's breach of contract. Compensation will not be awarded for any damage incurred which the plaintiff had a reasonable opportunity to avoid.

- *British Westinghouse Electric and Manufacturing Co. v. Underground Electric Railways Co. of London (1912) A.C. 673*
- *Victor Oladapo Taiwo v. F.B.A. Princewell (1961) All N.L.R.*

(Pt. 406) 184 CA

- *Obasuyi v. Business Ventures Ltd (1995) 7 NWLR (Pt. 406) 184 CA*

6. Where contracts of international nature involve different currencies, damages should be awarded in the currency that most truly represents the loss sustained.

- *Services Europe Atlantique v. Stockholms R.S. (1978) 2 WLR 887*

7. The rule is that in an action for breach of contract, the terms "special" and "general" damages are not applicable. Consequently, there is no distinction between special and general damages in law of contract.

- *Chanrai v. Khawan (1965) 1 All N.L.R. 182 SC*
- *Shell B.P. v. Jammal Eng. Ltd (1974) 1 All N.L.R. (pt. 1) 542 SC*
- *Okeke v. Oche (1994) 2 NWLR (Pt. 329) 688 CA*
- *Steyer (Nig.) Ltd v. Gadzama (1995) 7 NWLR (Pt. 407) 305 at 339 CA*

8. The rule is that a plaintiff is entitled to nominal damages even though he has suffered no actual damage. The violation or infraction of his legal right *per se* will entitle him to nominal damages without proof of any loss incurred by him as a consequence of the breach.

- *Obere v. Board of Management, Eko Hospital (1978) 1 L.R.N. 246 at 250 SC*

9. A claim for damages and breach of contract must be filed in the same suit in order to avoid the effect of the rule of *res judicata*. Consequently, the claims for breach of contract and damages constitute one cause of action.

- *Alhaji Bature Gafai v. U.A.C. (1962) N.N.L.R. 78*

10. The burden of proof of damages for breach of contract is on the plaintiff. Where his evidence is unchallenged, the burden of proof is discharged upon a minimum of proof.

- *Steyer (Nig.) Ltd v. Gadzama (1995) 7 NWLR (Pt. 407) 305 at 311-312 CA*
- *Medical and Dental Council of Nigeria v. System Informatix*

Ltd (1998) 12 NWLR (Pt. 577) 258 at 260- 261 CA

11. There are two alternative remedies available to a victim of breach of a partly performed contract. These remedies are, namely: damages for breach of contract, or reasonable remuneration in *quantum meruit* for the work already done.

- *Olaopa v. Obafemi Awolowo University (O.A.U) Ile-Ife (1997) 7 NWLR (Pt. 512) 204 at 207-209 SC*

12. The general rule is that where a contract is wrongfully terminated by one party, the other party has a choice of either accepting the termination and suing for damages for wrongful termination of the contract or ignore the wrongful termination and perform his own part of the contract and claim thereafter against the other party.

- *Savoia v. Sonubi (2000) 7 (Pt. I) 36 at 46 SC*

13. In awarding damages in an action founded on breach of contract, the rule to be applied is *restitutio in integrum*, that is, in so far as the damages are not too remote, the plaintiff shall be restored, as far as money can do it, to the position in which he would have been if the breach had not occurred.

- *Okongwu v. N.N.P.C (1989) 4 NWLR (Pt. 115) 296 SC*
- *Oshin & Oshin Ltd v. Livestock Feed Ltd (1997) 2 NWLR (Pt. 486) 162 at 165 CA*

14. The principles guiding the award of damages in tort are different from those guiding the award of damages in contract. The object of tort damages is to put the plaintiff in that position he would have been in, if the tort has not been committed whereas, the object of contract damages is to put the plaintiff in the position he would have been in, if the contract had been satisfactorily performed.

- *Agbanelo v. Union Bank of Nigeria Ltd (2000) 4 SC (Pt. 1) 233 at 245*

15. Where a contract is wrongfully terminated, the rule is that an aggrieved contractor is entitled to any balance of payment for work done and also for loss of profit on the work he has been prevented from doing.

- *ACME Builders Ltd v. Kaduna State Water Board (1999) 2 NWLR (Pt. 590) 288 at 293 & 294 SC*

16. The basic rule is that the courts will not decree an order of specific performance if there is an absolute remedy at law in answer to the plaintiff's claim, that is to say, where the plaintiff could be adequately compensated by the common law remedy of damages. Similarly, the court may not order specific performance of a contract if the claimant thereof is guilty of delay in performing his own part of the contract where time is of the essence of the contract or the delay by the plaintiff was such as may be regarded as evidence of abandonment of the contract between the parties.

> - *Universal Insurance Company Ltd v. Hammond Nigeria Ltd (1998) 9 NWLR (Pt. 565) 340 at 344 & 345 CA*
> - *Afrotec Technical Services v. MIA & Sons Ltd (2000) 12 SC (Pt. II) 1 at 41/42*

17. The law is that a person who is seeking to enforce his right under a contractual agreement must show that he has fulfilled all the conditions precedent and that he has performed all those terms which ought to have been performed by him. Consequently, a plaintiff, in an action for specific performance of an agreement, must fail if there is default on his part to discharge his own obligations under that contract.

> - *Ezenwa v. Ekong (1999) 11 NWLR (Pt. 625) 55 at 62 CA*

18. The doctrine of part performance cannot transfer possession of land. However, it creates a cause for the specific performance of the contract.

> - *International Textile Industries (Nig.) Ltd v. Aderemi (1999) 8 NWLR (Pt. 614) 268 at 276 SC*

19. The order of specific performance is more frequently granted where the contract is for the sale of land than in any other case. This is not because of any distinction between the jural nature of a right to purchase land and other contractual rights but because damages are less often a complete remedy for the breach of the sale of land than for the breach of other contracts.

> - *Fakoya v. St. Paul's Church Shagamu (1966) 1 A.L.R. Comm. 459 SC*

- Paye v. Gaji (1996) 5 NWLR (Pt. 450) 589 at 605 CA

20. The court will not make an order of specific performance of a contract of personal service unless it is one with a statutory flavour.

- Ondo State University v. Folayan (1994) 7 NWLR (Pt. 334) 1 at 10 SC

- Chukwu v. NITEL (1996) 2 NWLR (Pt. 430) 290 CA

21. By virtue of the Limitation Law or Act, a right of action for breach of contract is extinguished six years after the date on which the cause of action accrued.

- Egbe v. Adefarasin (1987) 1 NWLR (Pt. 47) p. 20 SC

- British Airways v. Akinyosoye (1995) 1 NWLR (Pt. 374) 722 CA

22. As a general rule, the limitation period shall not begin to run where there is a case of fraud. In other words, the period of limitation will not begin to run until the plaintiff has discovered the fraud, or could with reasonable diligence have discovered it.

- Arowolo v. Fabiyi (1995) 8 NWLR (Pt. 414) 496 CA

23. Under the law of contract, a compromise means arrangement or agreement made by the parties as a way of settling a dispute, whether the dispute is already in court or out of court. Usually, a compromise does not involve an admission of liability. Its real essence is concession on both sides to avoid the necessity of determining liability.

- Central Bank of Nigeria v. Beckiti Construction Ltd (1998) 6 NWLR (Pt. 553) 238 at 240-241 CA

XXV
Law of Information Technology

25.1. Information Law

1. The unjustified interception of communications infringes a right to privacy guaranteed by the Irish Constitution.

> - *Kennedy v. Reland (1987) 1 R. 587*

2. Tapping a suspect's telephone in the course of criminal investigation does not amount to violation of his right to privacy.

> - *Nalon v. Metropolitan Police Commissioner (No. 2) (1979) 2 AER 620*
> - *Kaye v. Roberts (1991) FSR 62 at 70*

3. Article 8 of the European Convention on Human Rights, which provides that everyone has the right to respect for his private and family life, his home and correspondence has been held to include right of access to personal data.

> - *Gaskin v. U.K. (1990) 12 EHRR 36*

4. Under the American law, information may add value to physical objects when determining the value of stolen item in a theft case.

> - *Hancock v. Texas 402 SW 2d 906 (1966) Tex. Crim. App*
> - *U.S v. Girard and Lambest 601 F. 2d*

5. Under the English law, confidential information is not regarded as property as defined in Theft Act of 1968.

> - *R v. Asolon (1979) 68 Cr. App. R 183*

6. The Theft Act of 1968 applies to theft of "property" as defined in the 1968 Act. Copyright is not contemplated by the definition of property under the Act.

> - *Rank Film Distributors Ltd. v. Video Information Centre (1982) AC 380 at 387*

7. Under the Canadian law, information, even confidential

information is not regarded as property.

- *R v. Stawart 138 DLR (3d) 73; 149 DLR (3d) 583; 50 DLR (4th) 1*

25.2 *Computer Law*

1. A computer consists of two major parts namely, hardware and software. Hardware has been defined as the physical part of the computer and the ancillary equipment.

- *DPCE v. ICL Ltd. Lexis Report 31 July 1985 CDB*

2. Software denotes the information loaded into the machine and the directions given to the machine (usually by card or teleprompter) as to what it is to do and upon what material. Software is also frequently used to include "support", that is, advice, assistance, counselling and sometimes engineering help furnished by the vendor in loading the machine for a certain programme such as inventory control or preparation of payroll.

- *Honeywell Inc. v. Lithonia Lighting Inc. 317 F.Supp. 406 (N.D 1970) 408*

3. Software is not a commodity, which is delivered once, but one, which will necessarily be accompanied by a degree of testing and modification.

- *Saphena Computing v Allied Collection Agencies Ltd. (1995) FSR 616*

4. Although the customer should not expect software to work perfectly from the moment it was supplied, this cannot provide a defence in a situation where software proves incapable of meeting its basic purposes.

- *St. Albans DC. v. ICL (1996) 4 AER 481 or (1995) FSR 686*

5. It is not an unusual business practice to supply computer programme including system software containing errors and bugs. However, the vendor has a duty to correct errors and bugs that may prevent the product from being properly used. Therefore, it is not every bug or error in a computer programme

that can be categorised as a breach of contract.

> - *Eurodynamic Systems v. General Automation Ltd. (Unreported) 6th September 1988, QBD*

6. The rule is that a person is not allowed to exceed the level of his authorised access to information stored in a computer. Thus, a person who knowingly and intentionally exceeds the level of his authorised access commits an offence under the Computer Misuse Act of the United States of America.

> - *Lovable Corp v. Honeywell Inc. 431 F. 2d 668 (5thCir, 1970) 677*

7. It is a serious misconduct for an employee to seek to obtain unauthorised access to information held on the employer's computer. Such misconduct can ground his summary dismissal from his master's employment.

> - *Denco v. Johnson (1992) 1AER 463*

8. It is the law that computer generated evidence will be admissible where the court is satisfied that there has been no improper use of the computer and that at all material times, the computer was operating properly.

> - *R v. Ewing (1983) 2 AER 645*
> - *R v. Wood (1983) 76 Cr. App. R. 23 at 29*
> - *R v. Shepherd (1993) 1 AER 225 at 231*

9. A statement in a document produced by a computer is not admissible of any fact stated therein unless it is shown that there are no reasonable grounds for believing that the statement is inaccurate because of improper use of the computer.

> - *Section 69(1)(a) of the British Police and Criminal Evidence Act 1984*

XXVI
Law of the Sea

26.1 Delimitation

1. Every State has the right to establish the breadth of its territorial sea up to a limit not exceeding 12 nautical miles. Article 3 of the Convention on the Law of the Sea 1982 considered.

- *Anglo-Norwegian Fisheries Case (U.K. v. Norway) I.C.J. Reports 1951, p. 24-26*

2. Delimitation of continental shelf is to be effected by agreement in accordance with equitable principles, taking into account all the relevant circumstances in such a way as to leave as much as possible to each party all those parts of the continental shelf that constitute a natural prolongation of its land territory into and under the sea, without encroachment on the natural prolongation of the land territory of the other.

- *The North Sea Continental Shelf Cases (1969) I.C.J. Rep. p. 53*
- *Anglo-French Continental Shelf Case (1979) I.L.M. 397, p. 8*
- *The Continental Shelf (Tunisia v. Libya) Case (1982) I.C.J. Rep. p. 18 at 59*
- *Libya v. Malta (1985) I.C.J. Rep. p. 35*

26.2 Jurisdiction

1. The Exclusive Economic Zone is a zone of the sea adjacent to a coastal State's territorial sea within which the coastal State has exclusive jurisdiction over fishing.

- *Fisheries Jurisdiction (Merits) Cases: (United Kingdom v. Iceland); (Federal Republic of Germany v. Iceland) (1974) I.C.J. Rep. pp. 3,175*

2. The rule is that when a merchant vessel of one country enters

the ports of another for the purpose of trade, it subjects itself to the law of the place to which it goes, unless by treaty or otherwise the two countries have come to some different understanding or agreement.

- *R v. Anderson (1868) 11 Cox's Criminal Cases, 198, Court of Criminal Appeal*
- *Wildenhus's Case 120 U.S. 1 (1887) US Supreme Court*

3. The rule of international law requires every ship sailing the high seas to fly the flag of the State whose nationality it possesses.

- *Article 91 of the 1982 United Nations Convention on the Law of the Sea*

4. The rule of international law is that the law of the flag State ordinarily governs the internal affairs of a ship. Consequently, all matters of discipline and all things done on board which do not involve the peace or dignity of the port State or the tranquility of the port should be left by the port State to be dealt with by the authorities of the flag State.

- *Cunnard SS Co. v. Mellon (1923) 262 U.S. 100, 124*
- *McCulloch v. Sociedad Nacional (1963) 372 U.S. 10, I.L.R. 34, p. 5*
- *State v. Jannopoulous (1974) I.L.R. 77, p. 559*

5. Coastal States are empowered to exercise sovereignty over the territorial sea up to a distance of 12 nautical miles, its seabed, subsoil and superjacent airspace. This sovereignty is, however, subject to the right of innocent passage of foreign ships through the territorial sea. Articles 2 and 17 of the Convention on the Law of the Sea, 1982 considered.

- *Corfu Channel Case (Merits): U.K. v. Albania (1949) I.C.J. Rep. p. 4*

26.3 The Regime of the High Seas

1. The basic rule of customary international law is that vessels on the high seas are subject to no authority except that of the State whose flag they fly.

- *The Lotus Case (France v. Turkey) (1927) P.C.I.J. Reports, Series A, No. 10*

2. A ship may however, be subject to the authority or jurisdiction of a State other than its State of nationality in the following situations, namely: where the ship is engaged in piracy, slave trade or engaged in unauthorised broadcasting, or subject to the general right conferred on warships to stop and verify the nationality of any merchant ship (right of approach). Article 110 of the Convention on the Law of the Sea, 1982 considered.

- *The Lotus Case (France v. Turkey) (1927) P.C.I.J. Reports, Series A, No. 10*

3. It is well settled that there would be no breach of international law if a ship sails on the high seas without a flag. However, such a ship shall be treated as a stateless vessel and shall not be entitled to the protection of any State.

- *Naim Molvan v. Att.-Gen. for Palestine [The Asya] (1948) A.C. 351*

4. Stateless or flagless vessels are international pariahs. They have no internationally recognised right to navigate freely on the high seas. They are, indeed subject to the jurisdiction of every State.

- *United States v. Cortes, 588 F. 2d, 106 (1979)*
- *United States v. Marino-Garcia 679, F. 2d, 1373 (1982)*

5. The high seas shall be reserved for peaceful purposes. Testing of nuclear weapons on the high seas is, therefore, a violation of Article 88 of the Convention on the Law of the Sea, 1982 and the provisions of the Nuclear Test Ban Treaty 1963. What is less certain is whether the right of testing nuclear weapons is prohibited by customary international law.

- *Australia v. France, I.C.J. Report, 1974 p. 253*
- *New Zealand v. France, I.C.J Report, 1974, p. 457*

6. The right of hot pursuit implies that, subject to certain conditions, a government enforcement vessel (not necessarily a warship) of a coastal State may pursue unto the high seas a foreign merchant ship, where the competent authorities of the coastal State have good reason to believe that the ship has violated that State's laws and regulations, whilst in waters

within the State's jurisdiction, and has escaped from those waters. Article 111 of the Convention on the Law of the Sea, 1982 considered.

- *I'm Alone Case (Canada v. United States) (1935) 29 A.J. I.L. 326*
- *The Red Crusade Case (1962) 35 I.L.R. 485*
- *U.S. v. Fishing Vessel Taiyo (1976) 70 A.J.I.L. 95*
- *R v. Mills (1995) 44 I.C.L.Q. 949*

7. For the right of hot pursuit to be lawful, it must be continuous. The continuous quality is not broken simply because one vessel takes over the pursuit from another. Once the pursuit has been broken off it may not be resumed. Also, the right of pursuit ceases as soon as the ship being pursued enters the territorial sea of its own country or of a third State.

- *I'm Alone Case (Canada v. United States) (1935) 29 A.J. I.L. 326*

8. Where there is good reason to believe a foreign ship has violated the law of a coastal State in its internal waters or territorial seas, the competent authorities of that State are entitled to engage in hot pursuit and to arrest the ship on the high seas. The pursuing vessel might use necessary and reasonable force for the purpose of effecting the objects of boarding, searching, seizing and bringing into port the suspected vessel; and if sinking should occur incidentally, as a result of the exercise of necessary and reasonable force, the pursuing vessel might be entirely blameless.

- *I'm Alone Case (Canada v. United States) (1935) 29 A.J. I.L. 326*

9. "Piracy" has been defined as every unauthorized act of violence committed by a private vessel on the high seas against another vessel with the intent to plunder (*animo furandi*). Piracy *jure gentium* must be distinguished from some acts which particular municipal laws may denominate as piracy and which, therefore, are not of universal cognizance, so as to be punishable by all nations. Article 101 of the Convention on Law of the Sea, 1982 considered.

- *In Re Piracy Jure Gentium (1934) A.C. 586*

10. Piracy is a universal crime. Therefore, every State has, by international law, the right, on the high seas or in any other place outside the jurisdiction of any State to seize a pirate ship or aircraft or a ship taken by piracy and under the control of pirates, arrest the persons and property on board. Each State may also prescribe its own penalties for acts of piracy.

- *In Re Piracy Jure Gentium (1934) A.C. 586*
- *Santa Maria Incident (1961) 4 Whiteman 665*
- *Achille Lauro Incident (1988) 82 A.J.I.L. 269*

26.4 Salvage

1. "Salvage" is defined as a compensation allowed to persons by whose assistance a ship or its cargo has been saved in whole or in part from impending danger, or recovered from actual loss in cases of shipwreck, derelict or recapture.

- *The Oceanic Grandeur (1872) 2 Lloyd's Report 496 (High Court of Australia)*

2. At common law, to claim salvage, the services rendered to the property in peril have to be voluntary, that is, without any pre-existing contractual or other legal duty. Consequently, voluntariness of the services rendered is a pre-requisite to a salvage award.

- *The Oceanic Grandeur (1872) 2 Lloyd's Report 496 (High Court of Australia)*
- *The National Defender (1970) 1 Lloyd's Report 40 (U.S. District Court)*

3. "Success" is an essential ingredient in a claim for salvage. Consequently, a person rendering salvage services voluntarily, is not entitled to any remuneration unless he saves the property in whole or in part. In other words, no remuneration is due if the services rendered have no beneficial effect. Article 2 of the Brussels Convention on Salvage, 1910 considered.

- *The Tojo Maru (1972) A.C. 242, 293*

4. There is an exception to the general rule that for the right to salvage to accrue, the salvor must have saved the property in

whole or in part. This exception is called "engaged services" or "services at request".

- The Undaunted (1860) Lush. 90, 92

5. There is a distinction between salvors who volunteer to go out, and the salvors who are employed by a ship in distress. Salvors, who volunteer to go out at their own risk for the purpose of earning a reward, and if they labour unsuccessfully, are entitled to nothing. It is the effectual performance of salvage service that gives them a title to salvage remuneration.

- The Undaunted (1860) Lush. 90, 92

6. Persons engaged by a ship in distress, whether generally or particularly, are paid according to the efforts made even though the labour and service may not prove beneficial to the ship.

- The Undaunted (1860) Lush. 90, 92

7. Every master of a ship is bound, so far as he can, without serious danger to his vessel, her crew and her passengers, to render assistance to everybody, even though an enemy, found at sea in danger of being lost. Article 11 of the Brussels Convention of 1910 and Article 98 of the Convention on the Law of the Sea, 1982 considered.

- Haynes v. Harwood (1935) 1 K.B. 146

XXVII
Legal Practitioner

1. Every litigant is entitled to defend himself or present his case either in person or by a counsel of his choice.

- *Nwambe v. State (1995) 3 NWLR (Pt. 384) 385 SC*
- *Regd. Trustees, ECWA Church v. Ijesha (1999) 13 NWLR (Pt. 635) 368 CA*

2. The State/Court has a duty to ensure that every accused person is represented by counsel of his choice.

- *Nwambe v. State (1995) 3 NWLR (Pt. 384) 385 SC*
- *Abiola v. F.R.N. (1997) 2 NWLR (Pt. 488) 439 SC*

3. Where there is a dispute between two counsel as to who has authority to represent an accused, the best person to determine the dispute is the accused person himself.

- *Abiola v. F.R.N. (1997) 2 NWLR (Pt. 488) 439 SC*

4. A legal practitioner is by virtue of section 2(3) of the Legal Practitioners Act, Cap 207, Laws of the Federation of Nigeria, 1990 entitled to and has the right to appear and have audience in any court of law or tribunal in Nigeria.

- *Olusemo v. C.O.P. (1998) 11 NWLR (Pt. 575) 547 CA*

5. There is a presumption in favour of a counsel who announces representation for a client that he has the instructions and authority of that client to do so.

- *Tukur v. Govt. of Gongola State (1988) 1 NWLR (Pt. 68) 39 SC*
- *Salim v. Ifenkwe (1996) 5 NWLR (Pt. 450) 564 CA*
- *Babajide v. Eferakeya (2001) 2 WRN 137 CA*

6. A legal practitioner adjudged of having breached any professional conduct or committed any infamous conduct may be denied the right of appearance in court and, or have his name

struck off the roll of legal practitioners in accordance with sections 10 and 12 of the Legal Practitioners Act, 1975.

- *Fawehinmi v. N.B.A. (No. 1) (1989) 2 NWLR (Pt. 105) 494 SC*

7. A counsel who announces appearance for a party in a case, whether as holding the brief of another counsel or not, is presumed to have the full mandate and, or authority to conduct the case either on behalf of a principal or his client.

- *Shyllon v. Asein (1994) 6 NWLR (Pt. 353) 670 SC*
- *Falomo v. Banigbe (1998) 7 NWLR (Pt. 559) 679 SC*

8. It is not improper for a legal practitioner to represent himself in a matter before the court.

- *Egbe v. Adefarasin (1987) 1 NWLR (Pt. 47) 1 SC*
- *Habib (Nig.) Bank Ltd. v. Oyebanji (1998) 13 NWLR (Pt. 580) 71 CA*

9. Service of court processes on a counsel is as good as service of same on his client. Although, each case will be decided on its own facts and circumstances.

- *Mohammed v. Husseini (1998) 14 NWLR (Pt. 584) 108 SC*

10. The authority of a counsel to bind his client in any matter is predicated on the existence of a counsel/client relationship.

- *Adewunmi v. Plastex Ltd. (1986) 3 NWLR (Pt. 32) 767 SC*
- *Lauwers Import-Export v. Jozebson Industries Ltd. (1988) 3 NWLR (Pt. 83) 429 SC*
- *A-G., Fed. v. A.I.C. Ltd (1995) 2 NWLR (Pt. 378) 388 SC*

11. A legal practitioner is not allowed by virtue of sections 170-173 of the Evidence Act to disclose any communication received in the course of his employment as a legal practitioner by or on behalf of his client.

- *Dawaki Gen. Ent. Ltd v. Amafco Ent. Ltd (1999) 3 NWLR (Pt. 594) 224 CA*

12. A counsel has an implied authority and power to compromise pending suit in court on behalf of his client, provided the counsel acts *bona fide* and not contrary to express negative

instruction.

> - *Obayiuwana v. Ede (1998) 1 NWLR (Pt. 535) 670 CA*

13. A counsel has the authority to settle his client's case out of court. However, where there is an express limitation to his authority and such limitation is communicated to the other side in the case, then the counsel's action in breach of the limitation becomes ineffective.

> - *Enigbokan v. Baruwa (1998) 8 NWLR (Pt. 560) 96 CA*

14. Although, a client is bound by his counsel's conduct of case, the client can however repudiate and withdraw brief from his counsel, if he does not approve the counsel's conduct of the case.

> - *Ngwu V. Ozougwu (2001) 4 WRN 26 SC*

15. The legal effect of a concession of counsel in a matter is that no further issues are joined for determination in the matter.

> - *Densa Eng. Works Ltd. v. U.B.N. Plc (1999) 1 NWLR (Pt. 585) 162 CA*

16. Counsel have a duty to eschew sharp practice in the attainment of justice.

> - *Kwaptoe v. Tsenyil (1999) 4 NWLR (Pt. 600) 571 CA*

17. Counsel are ministers in the temple of justice and as such they have a paramount duty to assist the court in arriving at a fair and just decision by protecting and fostering the course of justice.

> - *Fawehinmi v. N.B.A. (No. 1) (1989) 2 NWLR (Pt. 105) 494 SC*
> - *Carlen (Nig.) Ltd v. Unijos (1994) 1 NWLR (Pt. 323) 631 SC*
> - *Adebisi v. Odukoya (1997) 11 NWLR (Pt. 527) 83 CA*
> - *Okolo v. U.B.N. Ltd (1998) 2 NWLR (Pt. 539) 618 CA*

18. Counsel have a duty to cite all relevant authorities to court.

> - *Adio v. A-G., Oyo State (2000) 5 SC 82*
> - *Global Transport v. Free Enterprises (2001) 12 WRN 136 SC*

19. Counsel have a duty to cite authorities accurately in court.

- *Araka v. Ejeugwu (1999) 2 NWLR (Pt. 589) 107 CA*

20. Counsel owe a duty to their clients to diligently and competently handle their clients' cases.

- *Gazu v. Nyam (1998) 2 NWLR (Pt. 538) 477 CA*
- *Orizu v. Uzoegwu (1999) 6 NWLR (Pt. 605) 32 CA*

21. It is improper for a counsel to accept a brief, where it is clear that the services to be rendered flow out of or are closely connected with the previous services he had rendered to the opposing side. Rule 10 of the Rules of Professional Conduct in the Legal Profession considered.

- *Kolawole v. Alberto (1989) 1 NWLR (Pt. 98) 382 SC*
- *Anatogu v. Iweka II (1995) 8 NWLR (Pt. 415) 547 SC*
- *Onyeke v. Harriclem (Nig.) Ltd (1998) 7 NWLR (Pt. 556) 64 CA*

22. A counsel is justified to refuse to appear for a client where his fees or instructions have not been perfected.

- *Odutola v. Kayode (1994) 2 NWLR (Pt. 324) 1 SC*

23. Counsel representing an accused person in a capital offence is enjoined to give it priority over all other engagements however important or lucrative they may be.

- *Okosi v. State (1989) 1 NWLR (Pt. 100) 642 SC*
- *Okon v. State (1995) 1 NWLR (Pt. 372) 382 SC*

24. Prosecuting counsel in criminal cases have a duty to fairly and impartially present all the facts before the court.

- *Waziri v. State (1997) 3 NWLR (Pt. 496) 689 CA*

25. Where a defence counsel makes submissions to the court on behalf of an accused, such submissions must be based upon tenable facts which would assist in arriving at a just and fair decision.

- *Durwode v. The State (2001) 7 WRN 50 SC*

26. It is undesirable for a counsel to put himself in a position where he cannot properly function as a counsel.

- *Adefulu v. Okulaja (1998) 5 NWLR (Pt. 550) 435 SC*

27. It is essential for a legal practitioner to personally depose to a counter-affidavit in reply to allegations made against him in an affidavit, in the course of proceedings in which he is appearing in court.

- *Onyeke v. Harriclem (Nig.) Ltd (1998) 7 NWLR (Pt. 556) 64 CA*

28. It is improper for counsel to attend court merely to seek for adjournment to enable a more senior colleague to handle a matter. It is even unethical for counsel to appear in court without the relevant case file.

- *Madu v. Okeke (1998) 5 NWLR (Pt. 548) 159 CA*

29. Where a trial court is not willing to rely on the statement of a counsel from the Bar as to the pendency of an application at the appellate court, it behoves on the trial court to adjourn the matter to enable counsel show documentary proof thereof.

- *N.A.B. Ltd v. Comex Ltd (1999) 6 NWLR (Pt. 608) 648 CA*

30. File jacket of a counsel and the entry thereon in respect of the date of hearing of the case, is admissible in evidence as a relevant fact necessary for the determination of the issue being considered before a court. Section 223 of the Evidence Act considered.

- *Oshunrinde v. Akande (1996) 6 NWLR (Pt. 455) 383 SC*

31. A legal practitioner has the right and is entitled to conduct case as litigant speaking from the Bar and wearing his robes in civil actions.

- *Fawehinmi v. N.B.A. (No. 1) (1989) 2 NWLR (Pt. 105) 494 SC*

32. A retired judicial officer is prohibited from appearing or acting as a legal practitioner again in Nigeria.

- *Atake v. Afejuku (1994) 9 NWLR (Pt. 368) 379 SC*

33. As a rule of pleadings, counsel must not deny everything in an opponent's pleadings but should admit whatever facts can be proved against his client.

- *Meridien Trade Corpn. Ltd v. M.C. (W.A) Ltd (1998) 4 NWLR (Pt. 544) 1 SC*

34. Counsel should endeavour to learn and master the format of writing a good brief.

- *Vanderpuye v. Gbadebo (1998) 3 NWLR (Pt. 541) 271 SC*

35. A counsel has the exclusive preserve to decide on who to call as witnesses and neither the court nor the opposing counsel can influence his decision.

- *Olori Motors & Co. Ltd v. U.B.N. Ltd (1998) 6 NWLR (Pt. 554) 493 CA*

36. An admission of a counsel in a civil case is an evidence against his client, if made at the trial or during the actual progress of litigation.

- *Eboade v. Atomesin (1997) 5 NWLR (Pt. 506) 490 SC*

37. A counsel, by virtue of the apparent authority to conduct client's case, can make admissions in the course of performing his professional duty which could be ultimately binding on the client.

- *Enigbokan v. Baruwa (1998) 8 NWLR (Pt. 560) 96 CA*
- *Iso v. Eno (1999) 2 NWLR (Pt. 590) 204 CA*
- *Okegbe v. Chikere (2000) 7 SC (Pt. 1) 106*

38. An admission of facts by a counsel will not be binding on his client where there is no clear instruction from the client authorising his counsel to make admission and indeed consent to judgment.

- *Lamurde v. Adamawa State J.S.C. (1999) 12 NWLR (Pt. 629) 86 at 90-91 CA*

39. Admission by a counsel based on facts not within the knowledge of the counsel will not be binding on his client.

- *N.N.S.C. v. Sabana Ltd (1988) 2 NWLR (Pt. 74) 23 SC*

40. A counsel sending additional authority to court has a duty to send a copy of his letter to the opposing counsel who is at liberty to reply to the new authority or to request the court for further address.

- *Densa Eng. Works Ltd v. U.B.N. Plc. (1999) 1 NWLR (Pt. 585) 162 CA*

41. Counsel sending additional authorities to court have a duty to relate such additional authorities to relevant principles enunciated in their briefs, otherwise such additional authorities will not mean much to the court.

> - *Iso v. Eno (1999) 2 NWLR (Pt. 590) 204 CA*

42. Where a defence counsel rests his case on that of the plaintiff, he is understood to be saying that the plaintiff has not proved his case for the defendant to answer; or that the defendant admits the facts of the case as stated by the plaintiff; or that the defendant is relying on point of law for his answer to the plaintiff's claim. The counsel must however stand by his submission.

> - *Akanbi v. Alao (1989) 3 NWLR (Pt. 108) 118 SC*

43. A court is not bound to pronounce upon or make specific ruling on every issue raised in the address of a counsel, unless such issue comes within the issues for determination in the case before the court.

> - *N.I.D.B. v. Fembo (Nig.) Ltd. (1997) 2 NWLR (Pt. 489) 543 CA*

44. The submission of counsel cannot be substituted for evidence and no amount of brilliance shown in a counsel's address can make up for the lack of evidence needed to prove and establish or to disprove and demolish points in issue.

> - *Osuigwe v. Nwihim (1995) 3 NWLR (Pt. 386) 752 CA*
> - *Ishola v. Ajiboye (1998) 1 NWLR (Pt. 532) 71 CA*
> - *Atanze v. Attah (1999) 3 NWLR (Pt. 596) 647 CA*
> - *Edonkumoh v. Mutu (1999) 9 NWLR (Pt. 620) 633 CA*
> - *Offor v. State (1999) 12 NWLR (Pt. 632) 608 CA*

45. The court has a duty to consider relevant laws or authorities even where they are not cited or brought to the notice of the court.

> - *Hyppolite v. Egharevba (1998) 11 NWLR (Pt. 575) 598 CA*

46. Although the right to final address by counsel is constitutionally guaranteed, the right can however be expressly or impliedly waived, for it is optional at the instance of the counsel.

- Amough v. Zaki (1998) 3 NWLR (Pt. 542) 483 CA

47. Counsel must base his address on pleaded facts since litigation is made up of a combination of facts and the law.

- C.C.B. v. Onyekwelu (1999) 10 NWLR (Pt. 623) 452 CA

48. The denial of a party's counsel, where established and proved, of the opportunity of addressing the court is not a mere irregularity but a defect in proceedings which strikes at the right of the party to fair hearing, thereby rendering the proceedings a nullity.

- Ayisa v. Akanji (1995) 7 NWLR (Pt. 406) 129 SC

- Oyekan v. Akinrinwa (1996) 7 NWLR (Pt. 459) 128 SC

- Duba v. Saleh (1997) 2 NWLR (Pt. 488) 502 CA

49. An issue of fact cannot rightly be raised in the final address of a counsel. It can only be raised on pleadings in a trial where pleadings are filed.

- Kwajaffa v. B.O.N. Ltd (1999) 1 NWLR (Pt. 587) 423 CA

50. Counsel should be cautious in taking the decision to appeal because of the enormous money and time involved.

- Onwualu v. Mokwe (1999) 1 NWLR (Pt. 585) 146 CA

51. Where a counsel is not sure whether a ground of appeal is that of law or mixed law and fact, it is prudent for counsel to seek and obtain the requisite leave to obviate the unpleasant consequences of the ground being found to be incompetent.

- Irhabor v. Ogaimien (1999) 8 NWLR (Pt. 616) 517 SC

52. The courts will generally not punish a litigant for the mistake or error of his counsel when the mistake or error is in respect of procedural matters.

- Akanbi v. Alao (1989) 3 NWLR (Pt. 108) 118 SC

- Iyalabani Co. Ltd. v. Bank of Baroda (1995) 4 NWLR (Pt. 387) 20 SC

- Ohuta v. Okigbo (1995) 4 NWLR (Pt. 389) 352 CA

- F.B.N. Plc v. Ejikeme (1996) 7 NWLR (Pt. 462) 597 CA

- Agu v. Ayalogu (1999) 6 NWLR (Pt. 606) 205 CA

53. The principle that mistake or error of counsel should not be visited on litigant will not be applicable simply upon assertion of counsel only. An application for the discretionary power of the court to grant an indulgence to the applicant must therefore give reasons for the said mistake or error.

- *Williams v. Hope Rising Voluntary Funds Society (1982) 2 SC 145*
- *Nebo v. F.C.D.A. (1998) 11 NWLR (Pt. 574) 480 CA*

54. A court should not visit the negligence or inadvertence of counsel on a litigant.

- *Bello v. A-G., Oyo State (1986) 5 NWLR (Pt. 45) 828 SC*
- *Odunsi v. U.N.M.I.C. Ltd (1998) 2 NWLR (Pt. 536) 95 CA*
- *Akinriboya v. Akinsole (1998) 3 NWLR (Pt. 540) 101 CA*
- *Long-John v. Blakk (1998) 6 NWLR (Pt. 555) 524 SC*
- *Adewusi v. Popoola (1998) 12 NWLR (Pt. 579) 579 CA*

55. Counsel have a duty to operate and maintain clients' account where client's moneys are paid.

- *Anatogu v. Anatogu (1998) 6 NWLR (Pt. 552) 42 CA*

56. Counsel have a professional duty to extend professional courtesies to judges and not rude language.

- *Chukwuogor v. A-G., Cross River State (1998) 1 NWLR (Pt. 534) 375 CA*

57. A counsel who is also a director of a company is disqualified from appearing as an advocate for the said company. Rule 31(a)(i) Rules of Professional Conduct in the Legal Profession considered.

- *I.B.W.A. v. Imano (Nig.) Ltd. (1988) 3 NWLR (Pt. 85) 633 SC*

58. Any legal practitioner who satisfies the prescribed requirements of being above 10 years in practice; meeting the requisite number of appearances in the Supreme Court, Court of Appeal and State High Court or Federal High Court; and has human and material resources in his office, may be conferred with Senior Advocate of Nigeria by the Legal Practitioners

Privileges Committee.

> - *Regd. Trustees, ECWA Church v. Ijesha (1999) 13 NWLR (Pt. 635) 368 CA*

59. A Senior Advocate of Nigeria (SAN) cannot appear, apply for or issue processes in a court other than those superior courts before which he can appear in accordance with Rules 2, 3, 4 and 6 of the Senior Advocates of Nigeria (Privileges and Functions) Rules.

> - *Regd. Trustees, ECWA Church v. Ijesha (1999) 13 NWLR (Pt. 635) 368 CA*

60. In Nigeria, a barrister or a solicitor may practice as a legal practitioner; the barrister may, and quite often does, carry out the duties of a solicitor and vice versa. The two professions of barrister and solicitor are fused and as a legal practitioner, he can always sue to recover his fees.

> - *Sobodu v. Denloye (1998) 12 NWLR (Pt. 578) 341 at 346 CA*

61. By virtue of section 16(1) and (2)(a) & (b) of the Legal Practitioners Act, 1975, before a legal practitioner can recover his fees, it is mandatory for him to serve a bill of charges containing specified particulars on the client at least one month prior to commencement of action to recover same.

> - *Ocean Steamship Ltd. v. Sotuminu (1997) 2 NWLR (Pt. 487) 284 CA*
> - *Abubakar v. Manulu (1998) 10 NWLR (Pt. 568) 41 CA*
> - *Oyekanmi v. NEPA (2000) 12 SC (Pt. 1) 70*

62. Where a bill of charges is being taxed, it makes no difference that the bill is in respect of completed or uncompleted acts of a legal practitioner.

> - *Sobodu v. Denloye (1998) 12 NWLR (Pt. 578) 341 CA*

63. A legal practitioner who has rendered services up to a point before he was debriefed can claim on a *quantum meruit*.

> - *Aburime v. N.P.A. (1978) 4 SC 11*
> - *Oyo v. Mercantile Bank (Nig.) Ltd (1989) 3 NWLR (Pt. 108) 213 CA*

64. An averment of payment of fees to a legal practitioner can only be proved either by tendering the receipt of payment or by calling the legal practitioner paid to testify as a witness in court.

- *F.B.N. Ltd v. Owie (1997) 1 NWLR (Pt. 484) 744 CA*

65. The Attorney-General of a state is a creation of the Constitution and it is a legal personality capable of suing and/or being sued.

- *Ibrahim v. Judicial Service Committee (1998) 14 NWLR (Pt. 584) 1 SC*

66. An Attorney-General can brief a private legal practitioner to appear on his behalf in criminal cases.

- *State v. Aibangbee (1988) 3 NWLR (Pt. 84) 548 SC*

67. A judge is not entitled to insist on a particular counsel in a legal practitioner's chambers to conduct a case.

- *Ceekay Traders Ltd v. Gen. Motors Co. Ltd (1992) 2 NWLR (Pt. 222) 132 at 139 SC*

XXVIII
Legal System

1. Substantive laws fix duties, establish rights and responsibilities for persons, be they natural or corporate while adjectival or procedural laws prescribe the manner in which such rights and responsibilities may be exercised and enforced in a court.

- NV Scheep v. MV "S. Araz" (2001) 4 WRN 105 at 109 SC

2. The primary function of a court is to do justice between the parties in dispute and not to do abstract justice. The moment a court ceases to do justice in accordance with the law and procedure laid down for it, it ceases to be a regular court. It becomes a kangaroo court.

- Willoughby v. International Merchants Bank (Nig.) Ltd (1987) 1 NWLR (Pt. 48) 105
- Edun v. Odan Community (1980) 9-11 SC 103
- Emesim v. Nwachukwu (1999) 6 NWLR (Pt. 605) 154 CA

3. The court has a duty to do substantial justice in every case before it. The fact that an applicant relies on a wrong law to prosecute an application does not prevent the court from doing substantial justice.

- Eze v. A-G, Rivers State (1999) 9 NWLR (Pt. 619) 430 at 436 CA

4. An allegation of bias on the part of a trial judge or tribunal other than on the basis of pecuniary interest must be supported by clear, direct, positive, unequivocal and solid evidence from which real likelihood of bias could reasonably be inferred and not mere suspicion.

- Anyebe v. Adesiyun (1997) 5 NWLR (Pt. 505) 403 CA

5. If there are two routes to the truth searching or truth finding process and one of the routes is shorter than the other, a trial court is well advised to follow the shorter route, if it will result in doing the same justice to the parties, as the longer route. The administration of justice will be enhanced and that is good for society and the public.

- *Okpokpo v. Uko (1997) 11 NWLR (Pt. 527) 94 CA*

6. Pecuniary interest or favour may disqualify a judge from adjudication. The difference between the two is that proof of any pecuniary interest in the subject matter of the case however, small, on the part of a judge, disqualifies him from adjudication. On the other hand, a challenge for favour must be supported by actual evidence upon which it can be based. This may be as a result of proven personal relationship of the judge to one of the parties or to his having previously played a role whereby he cannot be expected to receive evidence in the case and decide the issue with an open mind.

- *Okpanachi v. Commissioner for Works (1997) 6 NWLR (Pt. 509) 482 CA*

7. Under the Nigerian Legal System, judges sit in a dual capacity as judges of law in matters of law and jury in matters of facts.

- *F.B.N. Plc v. Associated Motors Co. Ltd. (1998) 10 NWLR (Pt. 570) 441 at 458 CA*

8. Although an administrative panel is not bound to follow the procedure and practice of the court of law, it is bound to observe and comply with the principles of natural justice that a person who may be adversely affected by its decision is entitled to be given adequate opportunity not only to know the case against him but also to answer it.

- *Tionsha v. Judicial Service Committee Benue State (1997) 6 NWLR (Pt. 508) 307 at 311 CA*

9. The rule of *stare decisis* is that the decision of a superior court is to be binding on the lower courts. A lower court cannot pronounce a higher court's decision as given *per incuriam* in order to depart from it.

- *Global Transport v. Free Enterprises (2001) 12 WRN 136 SC*
- *Adisa v. Oyinwola (2000) 6 SC (Pt. II) 47*

10. Under the rule of *stare decisis*, where there are two conflicting decisions of the Supreme Court, the subordinate courts are entitled and bound to follow the latter decision of the Supreme Court in that the Supreme Court will depart from its previous

decision if the application of the decision to future cases will perpetuate injustice.

> - *Egboghonome v. State (1993) 7 NWLR (Pt.306) 383 at 394 SC*
> - *Akinade v. N.A.S.U. (1999) 2 NWLR (Pt.592) 570 at 572 CA*

11. The Supreme Court does not need to refer to foreign cases in construing statutes peculiar to Nigeria; its duty is to construe them in order to ascribe to the words therein their appropriate meaning and effect.

> - *A-G., Federation v. Guardian Newspapers Ltd (1999) 9 NWLR (Pt. 618) 187 at 203 SC*

12. The Supreme Court is bound by its previous decision. However, the Supreme Court will revisit its earlier decision with a view to overruling or departing from it where it is shown that the previous decision is erroneous in law; or the previous decision was given *per incuriam*; it is shown that the previous decision is contrary to public policy or is occasioning miscarriage of justice or perpetuating injustice.

> - *A.-G., Federation v. Guardian Newspaper Ltd (1999) 9 NWLR (Pt. 618) 187 at 203 SC*

13. A statute is not necessarily one of general application because it was in force in England on the 1st day of January, 1900. In order to be applicable as a statute of general application, the statute must be one, which was of general application in England 1st day of January, 1900. The tests that a court should apply to determine whether such a statute is one of general application are the general applicability of the statute; the nature of the statute; whether it was in force in England on 1st of January, 1900; the limits of local jurisdiction and the formal verbal alteration. These aforestated tests cover the provisions of section 45 of the Interpretation Act.

> - *Lawal v. Ejidike (1997) 2 NWLR (Pt. 487) 319 CA*

14. An allegation of bias against a judge merely on the basis that the instrument sought to be interpreted by such a judge was signed by her husband in his administrative capacity as a governor is remote and totally unacceptable. It cannot sustain an allegation of bias.

> - *Adio v. A.-G., Oyo State (2000) 5 SC 82 at 117*

15. By the provisions of section 5 of the Local Government and Community Boundaries Settlement Law, Cap 67, Laws of Oyo State, 1978, only the State Executive Council can refer a dispute related to settlement of boundaries to the Boundaries Settlement Commission of Oyo State.

- *Fasikun II v. Oluronke II (1999) 2 NWLR (Pt. 589) 1 at 6 SC*

16. In a case where there has been no previous precedent, the court will not fold its hands merely because the application before it has never been done. It will determine the application based on circumstances of the case and demands of justice.

- *Pelfaco v. W.A.O.S. Ltd (1997) 10 NWLR (Pt. 524) 222 at 225 CA*

17. The age-long principle of law is that law and morality are almost always poles apart. This principle is still very much alive and valid.

- *P.A.N. Ltd v. Oje (1997) 11 NWLR (Pt. 530) 625 CA*

18. Rights may be vested or contingent. A right can be said to be vested when all the investitive facts, which are necessary to create it, have occurred. It is said to be contingent when only part of the investitive facts have occurred, until the happening of the event on which the title depends.

- *Wilson v. Oshin (2000) 6 SC (Pt. III) 1*

19. A domestic legislation, which purports to repudiate the provisions of an international treaty or convention, must expressly say so. It can override provisions of international treaty only if it amends or repeals the treaty and that otherwise, a State is still under obligation to continue to recognise enforceable treaty rights and obligations.

- *Abacha v. Fawehinmi (2000) 4 SC (Pt. II) 1 at 59*

20. One point of jurisprudential interest is the relationship of the bindingness of the *ratio decidendi* contained in the leading judgment on the one hand, and the other concurring judgments on the other hand. The jurisprudence and practice of law in Nigeria is clear on the matter. It is the *ratio* or *rationes* contained

in the leading judgment that constitutes or constitute the authority for which the case stands. All other expressions contained in the concurring judgments; particularly those not addressed in the leading judgment are *obiter dicta* or *dictum*. *Obiter dicta* in the leading judgment as well as in the concurring judgments may be of persuasive effect in other occasions.

- *Abacha v. Fawehinmi (2000) 4 SC (Pt. II) 1*

21. Justice should not only be done, but should manifestly and undoubtedly be seen to be done. However, bias should connote a real likelihood of an operative prejudice, whether conscious or unconscious. There must be reasonable evidence to support a contention of real likelihood of bias. A mere vague suspicion of whimsical, capricious and unreasonable people should not be made a standard of decision.

- *Adio v. Attorney-General, Oyo State (2000) 5 SC 82 at 100*

22. Where a statute or rule having statutory effect or other binding authority, which would have affected a decision, had not been brought to the attention of court, any case decided without considering the said statute or rule is decided *per incuriam*.

- *Adisa v. Oyinwola (2000) 6 SC (Pt. II) 47*

XXIX
Medical Law

29.1 Human Fertilisation and Embryology

1. The unborn does not have legal status until it enters civil society, that is, until it is born.

> - *Paton v. British Pregnancy Advisory Service Trustees (1979) QB 276*

2. The unborn is not another "limb" of the mother. The foetus is neither a person nor an adjunct of the mother. It is a unique organism.

> - *Attorney-General's Reference (No. 3 of 1994) (1998) AC 245*

3. "Surrogacy contract" implies that for a fee, a woman agrees to be artificially inseminated with the semen of another woman's husband; she is to conceive a child, carries it to term, and after its birth surrenders it to the natural father and his wife. It is the intention of the parties to the contract that the child's natural mother will thereafter be forever separated from the child. The wife is to adopt the child, and she and the natural father are to be regarded as its parents for all purposes.

> - *R Baby M (1988) 537 A 2d 1227 (USA)*

> - *Re C (A Minor) (Wardship Surrogacy) (1985) FLR 846*

29.2 Patient's Consent

1. Every adult person of sound mind has a right to determine what shall be done with his own body; and a surgeon who performs an operation without his patient's consent commits an assault.

> - *Schloendorff v. Society of New York Hospital (1914) 105 NE 92*

2. The capacity and competence of a patient (mentally handicapped, minor) to consent has to be determined and certified before any treatment.

> - *Re C (Adult: Refusal of Treatment) (1994) 1 WLR 290*

29.3 Breach of Medical Confidence

1. It is permissible for a doctor to breach the duty of confidence owed to a patient so as to protect the welfare of third parties.

> - *W v. Egdell (1990) All ER 835*
> - *R v. Crozier (1990) 8 BMLR 128*

2. The right to privacy of an HIV patient may be waived in the public interest.

> - *Attorney-General v. Guardian Newspaper No. 2 (1988) 3 All ER 545 at 659*

3. A Health Authority is entitled to deny a patient access to his medical records on the basis that disclosure could cause serious harm to the physical and mental health of the patient or to any other individual.

> - *R v. Mid-Glamorgan Family Health Services Authority, ex parte Martin (1994) Times, 16 August*

29.4 Duty of Care

1. A doctor holding himself out as possessing special skill and knowledge owes a duty to his patient to use due caution in undertaking treatment on such patient. He is further under a duty of care to use due diligence, care, knowledge, skill and caution in administering the treatment. No contractual relation is necessary, nor is it necessary that the service be rendered for reward.

> - *R v. Bateman (1925) 94 LJ KB 791*

2. A Health Authority is under a duty to provide pregnant women with a reasonable standard of gynaecological and obstetric care, in terms of provision for the safe delivery of the baby and the health of both mother and baby.

> - *Bull v. Devon Area Health Authority (1993) 4 Med. LR 117*

3. A Health Authority owes a duty to employ competent staff in the treatment of patients.

- *Yepremian v. Scarborough General Hospital (1980) 110 DLR (3d) 513 (Canadian case)*

4. A Health Authority or a hospital is vicariously liable for the negligence of its employees including doctors and consultants.

- *Razzel v. Snowball (1954) 1 WLR 1382*

5. While the duty of medical staff is higher in the case of suicidal patients and patients who may harm themselves or others, that duty could not amount to keeping a constant vigil.

- *Thorne v. Northern Group Hospital Management Committee (1964) 108 SJ 484*

- *Selfe v. Ilford and District Hospital Management Committee (1970) 4 BMJ 754*

6. A pharmaceutical company owes a duty to keep its consumers constantly abreast with developments in the field of its products. Where subsequent research highlights dangers, there is a duty incumbent on such a pharmaceutical company to warn those who might be affected. The level of warning depends on a number of factors, viz the number of people who might be harmed by the drug, the level of the injury that might be suffered or the overall benefit the drug will have on the public as a whole.

- *Buchan v. Ortho Pharmaceuticals Ltd (Canada) (1986) 54 OR (2d) 92*

29.5 Duty to Inform of Adverse Results

1. A doctor owes a duty to tell a patient all that a prudent patient would want to know.

- *Sidaway v. Board of Governors of the Bethlem Royal Hospital (1985) 1 All ER 643 (H.L.)*

2. Doctors have a duty to warn patients of material risk inherent in a proposed treatment. A risk is material if in the circumstances of the particular case, a reasonable person in the patient's position, if warned of the risk, would likely attach significance to it.

- *Rogers v. Whitaker (1992) 67 ALJR 47 (High Court of Australia)*

29.6 Duty to Write Prescriptions Clearly

1. A handwritten prescription has to be sufficiently legible to minimize mistakes that might be made by those who will process it.

> - *Prendergast v. Sam and Dee Ltd (1988) The Times, 24 March 1988*

2. Where a prescription is of sufficient clarity that a pharmacist should suspect that it may be wrong, and the pharmacist fails to spot that error, there could be a breach of the duty of vigilance.

> - *Prendergast v. Sam and Dee Ltd (1988) The Times, 24 March 1988*
> - *Dwyer v. Rocderick (1983) 127 SJ 805*

29.7 Medical Negligence and Standard of Care

1. A doctor is not guilty of negligence if he acted in accordance with a practice accepted as proper by a responsible body of medical men skilled in that particular art.

> - *Bolam v. Friern Hospital Management Committee (1957) WLR 582*

2. The standard of care to be observed by a person with some special skill or competence is that of the ordinary skilled person exercising and professing to have that special skill.

> - *Sidaway v. Board of Governors of the Bethlem Royal Hospital (1984) QB 493*
> - *Rogers v. Whitaker (1992) 175 CLR 479 (Australian High Court)*

3. A doctor who deviates from established practice and the deviation is one, which no person of ordinary skill would have undertaken if acting with ordinary care is liable for negligence.

> - *Hunter v. Hanley (1955) SC 200*
> - *Clark v. Maclennan (1983) 1 All ER 416*

4. An error of clinical judgment may, or may not, be negligence; it depends on the nature of the error. If it is one that would not have been made by a reasonably competent professional man, then it is negligence. If, on the other hand, it is an error that such a man,

acting with ordinary care, might have made, then it is not negligence.

- *Roe v. Minister of Health (1954) 2 QB 66*
- *Whitehouse v. Jordan (1981) 1 WLR, 246*

5. The onus of proof lies on a plaintiff patient or his representative to show on the balance of probabilities that the breach of duty of care caused or materially contributed to the damage, injury or death.

- *Barnett v. Chelsea and Kensington Hospital Management Committee (1969) 1 QB 428*

6. In certain circumstances, the onus is on the defendant to establish that the breach of duty did not cause or materially contributed to the injury.

- *Wisher v. Essey Area Health Authority (1988) AC 1074*

7. A doctor is not criminally responsible for a patient's death unless his negligence or incompetence demonstrates disregard for life and safety of the patient. His negligence must be gross, not mere negligence in the eyes of the law.

- *Kim v. State (1992) 4 NWLR (Pt. 233) 17 SC*

29.8 Sterilisation and the Mentally Handicapped

1. The court has inherent jurisdiction to look after those who cannot look after themselves especially those who, although adult in years, are as incapable of making decisions as minors.

- *Re X (A Minor) (Wardship Jurisdiction) (1975) Fam 47*

2. An individual has the right to choose not to procreate and the court may or may not have jurisdiction to make that choice on behalf of an individual who is unable to do so.

- *Re Eve (1996) 31 DLR (4th) 1 (Supreme Court of Canada Judgment)*

3. Where a court has wardship jurisdiction over a mentally handicapped child, it can authorise sterilisation of the child, notwithstanding the absence of the patient's consent.

- *Re B (A Minor) Wardship: Sterilisation (1988) AC 199*

29.9 Refusal of a Patient to be Treated

1. Any treatment of "an adult person of sound mind" in the face of refusal is an assault. But, in the case of a child, the court or the parents have the right to consent on behalf of the child.

- Schloendorff v. Society of New York Hospital (1914) 105 NE 92

- Re W (A Minor) Medical Treatment: Court's Jurisdiction (1992) Fam 64

2. A minor has no right to refuse treatment.

- Re R (A Minor) (Wardship: Consent to Treatment) (1992) Fam 11

29.10 Mercy Killing/Assisted Suicide

The use of drugs to reduce pain and suffering is justified in law, notwithstanding that it may, in fact, hasten the moment of death. What is not justified in law is the use of drugs with the primary purpose of hastening the moment of death.

- R v. Adams (1957) Crim LR 365
- R v. Cox (1992) 12 BMLR 38

XXX
Military Law

30.1 The Military Man

1. A soldier, unlike an officer, is an enlisted person in the Nigerian Army not holding a commission.

> *- Chapter 01.03(k) and (o) Terms and Conditions of Service*
> *of the Nigerian Army Officers, 1984*

2. A man, who joins the Army, whether as an officer or as a soldier, does not cease to be a citizen. With a few exceptions, his position under the ordinary law of the land remains unaffected. If he commits an offence against the civil law he can be tried and punished for it by the civil courts.

> *- Burdett v. Abbott, 4 Taunt. 401*
> *- Heddon v. Evans (1919) 35 T.L.R. 1282*

3. The doctrine of compact or burden of a man, who enters the army, whether voluntarily or not, is that he will submit to military law. He must accept the Army Act, rules, regulations and orders. This "army legislation" defines his status, indicates his duties, expresses his obligations and announces his military rights. To the extent permitted by the army legislation, his person and liberty may be affected and his property touched.

> *- Heddon v. Evans (1919) 35 T.L.R 642*

4. Every citizen has a right of access to civil courts. This right cannot be ousted or taken away or restricted, unless by statute. However, service men and women, like other public servants, are expected to have exhausted all the administrative machinery available for redress before resorting to the civil courts.

> *- Major Ladejobi v. A.-G., Federation (1982) 3 N.C.L.R 563.*

30.2 Obedience to Superior Orders

1. A subordinate officer must not judge the danger, propriety, expediency or consequence of the order he receives from his superior; he must obey. Nothing can excuse him but a physical impossibility.

> - Marais (D.F) v. General Officer Commanding the Lines of Communication and Attorney General of Cape Colony (1902) AC 109

2. The law is that if an officer, or a soldier, honestly believes he is doing his duty in obeying the commands of his superior, and if the orders are not manifestly illegal that he must or ought to have known that they were unlawful, the officer or soldier would be protected by the orders of his superior officer.

> - R v. Smith (1990) Cape of Good Hope 561

3. An officer or a soldier is only bound to obey lawful orders and he is liable if he obeys an order not strictly lawful. It has thus been held that an order to eliminate a person without just or lawful cause is unlawful and obedience to it involves a violation of the law and the defence of superior orders is untenable.

> - The State v. Pius Nwaoga & Another (1970) Suit No. E/ IDC/70 of 19th November 1970, Enugu High Court (Unreported)

30.3 The Administration of Military Justice

1. A military tribunal or a commanding officer is liable for an action for damages if, when acting in excess of, or without jurisdiction, it/he does, or directs to be done to a military man, whether officer or private, an act which amounts to assault, false imprisonment or other wrong, even though the injury purported to be done is in the course of actual military discipline.

> - R v. Army Council (1917) 2 K.B 504
> - Fraser v. Hamilton (1917) 3 T.L.R 431
> - Fraser v. Balfour (1918) 34 T.L.R 502

2. It is improper for the Chief of Air Staff to arrogate to himself the powers that are statutorily vested in the Air Council unless he can show that he has the needed authority to act. Where the Air Council delegates any of its powers to the Chief of Air Staff to act, there must be a notification in the Gazette to that effect.

- Edet v. Chief of Air Staff (1994) 2 NWLR (Pt. 324) 41 CA

3. A mere report made to an Air Force Commanding Officer in respect of misconduct of an officer without more, does not amount to a charge by virtue of section 80, Air Force Act, Cap. 15 Laws of the Federation of Nigeria, 1990.

- Doukplogba v. Alamieyesigba (1999) 6 NWLR (Pt. 607) 502 at 504 CA

4. The Air Council has an unfettered power to retire an officer whose conduct is shown and proved to be capable of tarnishing the honour and integrity of the Air Force. However, the officer so affected must be given opportunity of being heard.

- Edet v. Chief of Air Staff (1994) 2 NWLR (Pt. 324) 41 CA

5. The military law requires that there should be preliminary investigation to determine whether or not an accused should be charged and tried. S.123 Armed Forces Decree, 1993

- The State v. 3 Division Provost Officer (1982) (Unreported)

6. The general principle of law is that an offence, whether committed on the Ministry of Defence premises or not, which affects the person or property of a civilian, should normally be dealt with by a civil court; but that an offence which involves only service personnel, their property or service property should normally be dealt with by the military authorities.

- R v. Kirkup, 34 Cr. App, R. 150
- R v. Hogan (1955) Cr. L.R. 181

7. It is not competent for a court martial to try a civilian where there has been no suspension of the right of trial by a civil court.

- The Head of the Federal Military Government and Commander-in-Chief of the Armed Forces of the Republic of Nigeria and the Assistant Director of Prisons, State Prison, Benin City, Ex-parte Augustine Ifeanyi Chukwu Mordi (1968) Suit No. M/35/68 (Unreported)

8. The power to convene a court martial cannot be delegated. Thus, a convening order issued by any person other than those listed in section 131 (2) of the Armed Forces Decree No. 105 of 1993, must be pronounced null and void as the power under the aforesaid section has not been expressly made delegable.

- *Ex-Squadron Leader Yakasai v. Nigeria Air Force and 2 Others Suit No. CA/L282/99. Judgment delivered by Oguntade J.C.A on 27th day of September, 2001 (Unreported)*

9. Every man is presumed to be innocent until he is proved to be guilty in a criminal case. It is always the duty of the prosecution to prove the guilt of the accused. A court martial or a commanding officer must not therefore convict unless it/he is satisfied beyond reasonable doubt by the evidence given that the offence has been committed by the accused. It is the duty of the court martial or the commanding officer to critically assess the evidence before it or him and be satisfied before passing a verdict of guilt.

- *R v. Summers 36 Cr. App. R. 14 (1952) 2 A.E.R. 1059*

30.4 Defences

1. A service person cannot excuse himself of having committed a crime by pleading that he was induced to commit it through hunger, or because of changes in his own life or property. Consequently, where A, B and C were adrift in an open boat after they were shipwrecked and A and B, to avoid starving to death, killed and ate C, they were found guilty of murder, even though they would otherwise have died themselves.

- *R v. Dudley & Stephen, 14 Q.B.D. 273, 560*

2. The defence of necessity is available only, if from an objective stand point, an accused could be said to be acting reasonably and proportionately in order to avoid a threat of death or serious injury.

- *R v. Martin 88 Cr. App. R. 18*

3. An order of a superior officer does not provide absolute

immunity. However, where the interest of justice demands, superior orders may be admitted as defence in mitigation of guilt.

> *- Article 8 of the International Military Tribunal for the Trial of German Major War Criminals (Nuremberg Charter) Cmd. 6668 (1946), p.51*

> *- Article 6 of the International Military Tribunal for the Far East (Tokyo Charter) (The occupation of Japan), 1948, p.149*

4. Where grievous and extensive crimes have been committed consciously, ruthlessly and without military excuse or justification, the defence of superior orders cannot be considered in mitigation of guilt.

> *- International Military Tribunal for the Trial of German Major War Criminals (Nuremberg Charter) Cmd. 6964 (1946), p. 92*

30.5 Command Responsibility

A commander who knew or ought to have known that offences were being committed or had been committed by officers and soldiers under his command can be held responsible for failing to prevent or punish such acts. Article 7 (3) of the Statute of International Criminal Tribunal for the former Yugoslavia considered.

> *- Nikolic and Matric (Trial) ILR 108 (1998) 21*

XXXI
Oil and Gas Law

31.1 Ownership of Mineral Oil

1. At common law, the general principle is that the owner of a parcel of land has the right to all minerals below the surface of his land and he may work them or lease them to another to work.

   - *Mitchell v. Mosley (1914) 1 Ch. 438*

2. The law is that the entire property in and control of all minerals, mineral oils and natural gas in, under or upon any land, territorial waters and Exclusive Economic Zone of Nigeria shall vest in the Federal Government of Nigeria and shall be managed in such manner as may be prescribed by the National Assembly.

   - *Section 44(3) of the 1999 Constitution of the Federal Republic of Nigeria*

31.2 Oil Spillage and Compensation

1. Crude oil spillage in the oil industry is a phenomenon that can never be completely averted.

   - *Chief G.B.A. Tiebo VII & Ors. v. Shell Petroleum Development Company (Nigeria) Limited (Unreported). Suit No. YHC/14/88 of 27/2/92. High Court, Yenagoa, Rivers State (now Bayelsa State)*

2. It is well settled that crude oil causes great havoc to fishes and crops if allowed to escape from the pipeline in which it is being carried. Therefore, where this happens, adequate compensation should be paid.

   - *San Ikpede v. Shell-BP Petroleum Development Company Nigeria Limited (1973) M.W.S.J. (Selected Judgments of the High Court of Mid-Western State) 61 at 88*

3. The State High Court has jurisdiction to adjudicate on matters relating to oil spillage particularly spillages from oil pipelines onto swampland and farmlands.

   - *Shell Petroleum Development Co. (Nig.) Ltd. v. Isaiah (1997) 6 NWLR (Pt 508) 236 CA*

4. There is a duty on a party bringing a representative action arising from oil spillage to establish a common interest or common grievance. If there is a diversity of interest, there will be no joint tort upon which the party can claim. Such a party, therefore, lacks locus to sue in a representative capacity.

   - *Chief A.D. William Jumbo v. Shell Petroleum Dev. Co. (Nig.) Ltd (SPDC) (1999) 13 NWLR (Pt. 633) 57-67 CA*

5. Holders of an oil exploration licence, oil prospecting licence or oil mining lease are liable to pay adequate compensation for the disturbance of surface or other rights to any person who owns or is in lawful occupation of the licenced or leased land. Paragraph 36 of Schedule 1 of the Petroleum Act Cap. 350 Laws of the Federation of Nigeria, 1990, considered.

   - *Shell Pet. Dev. Co. (Nig.) Ltd. v. Farrah (1995) 3 NWLR (Pt. 382) 148 CA*

6. Adequate compensation means the just value of property taken under power of eminent domain payable in money or the market value of property when taken.

   - *Shell Pet. Dev. Co. (Nig.) Ltd. v. Farrah (1995) 3 NWLR (Pt. 382) 148 CA*

7. Compensation is limited to what is fair and reasonable for diminution of the value of the land or the interests in the land. Consequently, loss of profits is too remote to be claimed as compensation. Section 20(2) of the Oil Pipelines Act Cap. 338 of the Laws of the Federation of Nigeria, 1990 considered.

   - *Amos and Others v. Shell-BP Petroleum Development Company of Nigeria Limited and Another (1974) 4 E.C.S.L.R. 486*

8. A landowner whose arable land, which generates income is damaged and rendered unproductive by oil-blow out can obtain compensation under the following heads of losses: normal

measure; consequential losses; and prospective loss.

  - *Shell Pet. Dev. Co. (Nig.) Ltd. v. Farrah (1995) 3 NWLR*
    (Pt. 382) 148 CA

9. In an award of damages for injury to land, the court will take into account not only the physical damages to the land but also inconvenience, discomfort, or even illness to the plaintiff occupier. Recovery of claims in respect of these non-pecuniary losses is, therefore, allowable and may be regarded as part of the normal measure of damages.

  - *Shell Pet. Dev. Co. (Nig.) Ltd. v. Farrah (1995) 3 NWLR*
    (Pt. 382) 148 CA

10. The Petroleum Act, Cap. 350 Laws of the Federation of Nigeria, 1990, did not prescribe any period of limitation for bringing action under it. It is, therefore, erroneous to apply the State Limitation Law to the Petroleum Act, which is Federal Act.

  - *Shell Pet. Dev. Co. (Nig.) Ltd. v. Farrah (1995) 3 NWLR*
    (Pt. 382) 148 CA

31.3 Petroleum Tax

1. "Petroleum operations" for the purpose of payment of profits tax by companies engaged in petroleum operations include not only winning or obtaining petroleum oil by drilling, mining, etc., but all activities that are incidental to such operations.

  - *Shell Pet. Dev. Co. (Nig.) Ltd. v. F.B.I.R (1996) 8 NWLR*
    (Pt. 466) 256 CA

2. The annual profits of companies engaged in petroleum operations in Nigeria are taxable. However, the payments of Central Bank commission/charges, exchange losses and scholarship awards are classified as non-taxable expenses incurred by oil companies. They are, therefore, deductible for the purpose of computing chargeable tax. Section 10(1) of the Petroleum Profits Tax Act Cap. 354 Laws of the Federation of Nigeria 1990 and regulations 26-29 of the Petroleum (Drilling and Production) Regulations, 1969, Legal Notice 69 of 1969 (now

Cap. 350 Laws of the Federation of Nigeria 1990) considered.

- *Shell Pet. Dev. Co. (Nig.) Ltd. v. F.B.I.R. (1996) 8 NWLR (Pt. 466) 256 SC*

- *Gulf Oil Co. (Nig.) Ltd v. F.B.I.R. (1997) 7 NWLR (Pt. 514) 698 at 700 CA*

3. Tenement is the freehold interest in things that are immovable. Thus, the word "tenement" includes buildings on land and all other immovable property attached to land. The 1979 Constitution limits the power of a local government to assessment of privately owned houses or tenements for the purpose of levying rates. Thus, a Local Government Council has no power to assess and levy rates on oil storage tanks or tank farm and oil pipelines, as they are not privately owned. Paragraph 1(j) of the 4th Schedule to the 1979 Constitution considered.

- *Shell Pet. Dev. Co. (Nig.) Ltd. v. Burutu L.G.C. (1998) 9 NWLR (Pt. 565) 318 CA*

4. Notice of appeal against the decision of the Federal Board of Inland Revenue must be in writing. However, once the notice of appeal is filed with a copy made available for service on the Board that automatically amounts to giving notice in writing to the Board. An appellant is at liberty to lodge his appeal within a period of 97 days from the date the decision of the Board was given. Section 39(1) and (2) of the Petroleum Profits Tax Act considered.

- *Texaco Overseas (Nig.) Petroleum Co. v. Federal Board of Inland Revenue (F.B.I.R) (1997) 4 NWLR (Pt. 501) 566 at 568-569 CA*

XXXII
Pleadings

32.1 Object and Principles of Pleadings

1. The object of pleadings is to compel parties to define accurately and precisely the issues upon which the case between them is to be contested to avoid element of surprise by either party. It also guides the parties not to give evidence outside the facts pleaded as evidence on a fact not pleaded goes to no issue.

- *Ukaegbu v. Ugoji (1991) 6 NWLR (Pt. 196) 127 SC*
- *Onwuka v. Omogui (1992) 3 NWLR (Pt. 230) 393 SC*
- *Oladunjoye v. Akinterinwa (2000) 4 SC (Part I) 19*
- *Mobil Oil (Nig.) Plc v. IAL 36 Inc. (2000) 4 SC (Part I) 85*
- *Oshodi v. Eyifunmi (2000) 7 SC (Part II) 145*

2. The main function of pleadings is to ascertain with as much certainty as possible the various matters that are in dispute between the parties and those in which there are agreement or which no issues have been joined, so as to avoid any surprise by either party.

- *Oshodi v. Eyifunmi (2000) 7 SC (Pt. II) 145*

3. Parties are strictly bound by their pleadings and they are not allowed to make a case that is at variance with their pleadings.

- *Ukaegbu v. Ugoji (1991) 6 NWLR (Pt. 196) 127 SC*
- *E.D. Tsokwa & Sons Co. Ltd v. U.B.N. Ltd (1996) 10 NWLR (Pt. 478) 281 SC*
- *Makinde v. Akinwale (2000) 1 SC 89*
- *Ito v. Ekpe (2000) 2 SC 98*
- *Musa v. Isa (2001) 13 WRN 187 CA*

4. It is trite law that what is admitted in pleadings needs no further proof.

- *Agbanelo v. Union Bank of Nigeria Ltd. (2000) 4 SC (Part 1) 233*

5. A fact contained in a pleading cannot be deemed admitted if it is either expressly or by necessary implication denied.

> - *Adegboyega v. Awe (1993) 3 NWLR (Pt. 280) 224 CA*

6. An averment in a party's pleadings is deemed to have been admitted if it is not specifically denied or traversed.

> - *British Airways v. Makanjuola (1993) 8 NWLR (Pt. 311) 276 CA*

7. It is well settled that every pleading must state facts and not law. Therefore, a party is not expected to plead conclusions of law or of mixed fact and law.

> - *Finnih v. Imade (1992) 1 NWLR (Pt. 219) 511 SC*

8. It is clearly unnecessary to plead statutes and sections thereof before reliance can be placed on them. It is sufficient to plead material facts, which will lead to the legal result sought to be relied upon.

> - *Anyanwu v. Mbara (1992) 5 NWLR (Pt. 242) 386 SC*
> - *E.D. Tsokwa & Sons Co. Ltd v. U.B.N. Ltd (1996) 10 NWLR (Pt. 478) 281 SC*

9. Evidence, which is at variance with the averments in pleadings, goes to no issue and should be disregarded or discountenanced by the court. It does not matter that such evidence, which is inconsistent with the pleadings had been received by the court.

> - *Ohiaeri v. Akabueze (1992) 2 NWLR (Pt. 221) 1 SC*
> - *Ofondu v. Niweigha (1993) 2 NWLR (Pt. 275) 253 SC*
> - *Okoromaka v. Odiri (1995) 7 NWLR (Pt. 408) 411 CA*
> - *Ogoja v. L.G.V. Offoboche (1996) 7 NWLR (Pt. 458) 48 CA*
> - *Tyum v. Atavti (1996) 8 NWLR (Pt. 469) 675 CA*
> - *Allied Bank (Nig.) Ltd v. Akubueze (1997) 6 NWLR (Pt. 509) 374 SC*

10. It is trite law that evidence led on a fact not pleaded goes to no issue. Such evidence if inadvertently admitted, will be expunged.

> - *Amobi v. Amobi (1996) 8 NWLR (Pt. 469) 638 SC*

- *Olowofoyeku v. A-G., Oyo State (1996) 10 NWLR (Pt. 477)
190 SC*

- *Ito v. Ekpe (2000) 2 SC 98*

11. An averment of a fact in pleadings is no evidence and can never be so construed. It has to be proved by evidence, subject, however to admission by the other party.

- *A.S.H.D.C. v. Emekwue (1996) 1 NWLR (Pt. 426) 505 SC*

- *Ins. Brokers of Nigeria v. A.T.M. Co. Ltd (1996) 8 NWLR (Pt. 466) 316 SC*

- *Yusuf v. Oyetunde (1998) 12 NWLR (Pt. 579) 483 SC*

- *Olorunfemi v. Asho (2000) 1 SC 15*

12. To assess the strength of a plaintiff's case, both the pleadings and evidence must be examined. If the evidence is at variance with the pleadings, such evidence will have no value. Therefore, a party who alleges a fact in his pleadings must prove such fact by adducing enough evidence.

- *Ehidimhen v. Musa (2000) 4 SC (Pt. II) 166*

- *Eze v. Atasie (2000) 6 SC (Part I) 214*

13. Documentary evidence needs not be specifically pleaded to be admissible in evidence so long as facts and not the evidence by which such a document is covered are expressly pleaded.

- *Ipinlaiye II v. Olukotun (1996) 6 NWLR (Pt. 453) 148 SC*

- *Brawal Shipping (Nigeria) Ltd v. F.I. Onwadike Co. Ltd (2000) 6 SC (Part II) 133*

14. A plaintiff who relies on a traditional history in proof of a claim for declaration of title to land must lead evidence to show the root of his title. Such evidence includes how his ancestor had come to own the land in the first place and how the land devolved over the years on the claimant's family unit until it got to the claimant.

- *Nkado v. Obiano (1997) 5 NWLR (Pt. 503) 31 SC*

15. An application for extension of time within which to file pleadings is not granted as a matter of course. There must be convincing reasons for the delay in bringing the application.

- *Chigbu v. Tonimas (Nig.) Ltd (1999) 3 NWLR (Pt. 593) 115 CA*

16. A party who intends to prove fraud must plead it expressly. Failure to plead it will preclude such a party from producing evidence to establish the case.

- *Tor Tiv v. Wombo (1996) 9 NWLR (Pt. 471) 161 CA*

17. A court can *suo motu* correct a typographical error in pleadings. However, for a court to *suo motu* correct a sum of money, which a party never applied for will no doubt prejudice the interest of the opposing party. There must be an application to that effect.

- *Eze v. Lawal (1997) 2 NWLR (Pt. 487) 333 CA*

32.2 Amendment of Pleadings

1. The main purposes of amending pleadings are to cure all discernible defects in the pleadings; to put the proposed amendment in line with evidence already adduced and to settle the real controversy between parties in a suit in order to do substantial justice between the parties.

- *Laguro v. Toku (1992) 2 NWLR (Pt. 223) 278 at 290-291 SC*
- *Diko v. Ibadan South West L.G. (1997) 2 NWLR (Pt. 486) 235 CA*
- *Alsthom S.A. v. Saraki (2000) 10-11 SC 48*

2. The aim of an amendment is usually to prevent the manifest justice of a cause from being defeated or delayed by formal slips which may arise from the inadvertence of counsel.

- *Ehidimhen v. Musa (2000) 4 SC (Pt. II) 166 at 187*

3. An amendment of pleadings takes effect not from the date when the amendment is made but from the date of the original pleadings that was amended. Therefore, once an amendment is allowed, the amended pleading is deemed to relate back to the date of the original pleadings which it amends.

- *Nwosu v. Imo State Environmental Sanitation Authority (1990) 2 NWLR (Pt. 135) 688 SC*
- *Enigbokan v. A.I.I. Co. (Nig.) Ltd (1994) 6 NWLR (Pt. 348) 1 SC*

4. The court, in granting an application for amendment of pleadings normally considers the following factors, namely: the attitude of the parties, the nature of the amendment sought in relation to the suit, the question in controversy, the time of bringing the application for amendment, the materiality of the amendment sought. The courts will not easily grant an application for amendment, which if granted will unduly delay the hearing of the suit or unfairly prejudice either party to the suit.

   - *Alsthom S.A. v. Saraki (2000) 10-11 SC 48*

5. It is well settled law that amendment of pleadings should be allowed by court except where it will entail injustice to the opposing party or where the applicant is acting *mala fide*, or that by his blunder, the applicant has done some injury to the respondent which cannot be compensated for by costs or otherwise.

   - *Ehidimhen v. Musa (2000) 4 SC (Pt. II) 166*

6. By virtue of the High Court (Civil Procedure) Rules of various States, a party can amend his pleading at any stage of the proceedings. Thus, where a motion for amendment is filed after a case has been adjourned for judgment, such motion should be heard and ruled upon.

   - *Diko v. Ibadan South West L.G. (1997) 2 NWLR (Pt. 486) 235 CA*

7. By virtue of Order 1 Rule 20(1) of the Court of Appeal Rules, 1981, the Court of Appeal can order an amendment of a writ of summons, a statement of claim or defence, such as the High Court can order. However, in the exercise of this rule, the court is slow or reluctant and would only grant such an amendment so as to bring the pleadings in line with evidence already led.

   - *Iweka v. S.C.O.A. Nigeria Ltd (2000) 3 SC 21*

8. It is the law that where leave to amend pleading within a stipulated time is granted to a party and the party fails to file an amended pleading, his case will be considered on the unamended pleading.

   - *Aunam (Nig.) Ltd v. Leventis Motors Ltd (1990) 5 NWLR (Pt. 151) 458 CA*

9. A party may, on appeal to the Court of Appeal or the Supreme Court, apply for amendment of pleadings where such application is refused by a trial court. The appellate courts are empowered to grant applications for amendment of pleadings.

- *Laguro v. Toku (1992) 2 NWLR (Pt. 223) 278 SC*
- *Diko v. Ibadan South West L.G. (1997) 2 NWLR (Pt. 486) 235 CA*

32.3 Statement of Claim

1. A statement of claim constitutes facts upon which a plaintiff is to establish his case. A statement of claim must not only contain facts, which are necessary to establish a cause of action but must also contain the relief or remedy claimed. Thus, a statement of claim, upon examination, will disclose whether the relief claimed is within the jurisdiction of the court in which the action is instituted.

- *Salami v. Chairman, L.E.D.B. (1989) 5 NWLR (Pt. 123) 539 SC*

2. It is well settled that a statement of claim supersedes the writ of summons and amends the endorsement on the writ of summons. However, for a statement of claim to supersede the writ of summons, the statement of claim must state what is being claimed and not merely claiming "as per the writ of summons".

- *Enigbokan v. A.I.I. Co. (Nig.) Ltd (1994) 6 NWLR (Pt. 348) 1 SC*
- *Ajayi v. Mil. Adm., Ondo State (1997) 5 NWLR (Pt. 504) 237 SC*
- *Buraimoh v. Karimu (1999) 9 NWLR (Pt. 618) 310 CA*
- *Agbanelo v. Union Bank of Nigeria Ltd (2000) 4 SC (Part I) 233*

3. Where a statement of claim states that the plaintiff claims "as per writ of summons", the claims in the writ of summons incorporated in the statement of claim become part of the statement of claim. Such an averment in the statement of claim constitutes an exception to the rule that the statement of claim

supersedes the writ of summons.

> - *Owena Bank (Nig.) Ltd v. N.S.C.C. Ltd (1993) 4 NWLR (Pt. 290) 698 CA*

4. Since a statement of claim supersedes a writ of summons, any claim made in the writ of summons, which is not claimed in the statement of claim is taken to have been abandoned.

> - *Enigbokan v. A.I.I. Co. (Nig.) Ltd (1994) 6 NWLR (Pt. 348) 1 SC*

5. When a statement of claim is amended by leave of court and it introduces new facts which constitute material allegations against the defendant, failure by the defendant to file an amended statement of defence to the new facts will amount to an admission of those material averments.

> - *Ojo v. Philips (1993) 5 NWLR (Pt. 296) 751 CA*

6. Where a statement of claim filed in a suit is amended, the amended claim is the relevant claim for the purposes of the suit. The original claim, which was amended drops out and ceases to have any relevance to the suit.

> - *Owena Bank (Nig.) Ltd v. N.S.C.C. Ltd (1993) 4 NWLR (Pt. 290) 698 CA*

32.4 Statement of Defence

1. A statement of defence cannot be filed before the filing of a statement of claim or in the absence of a statement of claim.

> - *Unipetrol (Nig.) Ltd. v. Bukar (1997) 2 NWLR (Pt. 488) 472 CA*

2. A statement of defence filed in contravention of the rules of court, though irregularly filed, is not a nullity but a voidable document, which remains valid until it is set aside.

> - *Nishizawa Ltd v. Jethwani (2001) 8 WRN 153 SC*

3. An averment in a statement of defence that the defendant is "not in a position to admit or deny an averment in the statement of claim and will at the trial put the plaintiff to the proof thereof"

is not a proper traverse and amounts to insufficient denial.

- *Osafile v. Odi (1994) 2 NWLR (Pt. 325) 125 SC*
- *Pabod Supplies Ltd v. Beredugo (1996) 5 NWLR (Pt. 448) 304 CA*

4. A traverse is a denial by a party to an averment by another party as to facts raised in pleadings between them. The effect of a traverse is to cast upon the plaintiff the burden of proving the allegations denied. In order to raise an issue of fact, there must be a proper traverse. A proper traverse is a complete and sufficient denial, which has the effect of joining issues between the parties.

- *Okoromaka v. Odiri (1995) 7 NWLR (Pt. 408) 411 CA*
- *U.B.N. Plc v. Scpok (Nig.) Ltd (1998) 12 NW LR (Pt. 578) 439 CA*

5. To constitute a traverse, it is not necessary that every paragraph of a statement of claim must be specifically denied. What is essential is that the defendant's case is in material particulars, in conflict with the plaintiff's case and thus put the different material averments in issue.

- *Ajao v. Alao (1986) 12 SC 193*
- *Ayansina v. Co-op. Bank Ltd (1994) 5 NWLR (Pt. 347) 742 CA*

6. A general traverse contained in a statement of defence has been recognised as convenient and permissible. In short, it is a traverse.

- *Osafile v. Odi (1994) 2 NWLR (Pt. 325) 125 SC*

7. A mere general denial of the plaintiff's claims by the defendant in his pleading is not a sufficient denial. Thus, a general traverse or denial usually contained in the first paragraph of every statement of defence, with respect to essential and material allegations in the statement of claim, is not admissible as effective denial of such essential or material allegations.

- *Balogun v. U.B.A. Ltd (1992) 6 NWLR (Pt. 247) 336 SC*

8. A paragraph in a statement of defence should not be construed in isolation but in conjunction with other paragraphs, so that the issues joined in the pleadings may be properly ascertained.

Where there is the usual general denial followed by an averment that the defendant is not in a position to admit or deny a paragraph in the statement of claim, such pleading cannot constitute an admission but a clear denial.

- *Aja v. Okoro (1991) 7 NWLR (Pt. 203) 260 SC*

- *Ugochukwu v. Co-op. & Comm. Bank (Nig.) Ltd (1996) 6 NWLR (Pt. 456) 524 SC*

9. It is necessary for a party to meet headlong the facts traversed in the lower court. Where he fails to do so, he is estopped from doing so on appeal, without the leave of the Appeal Court.

- *Musa v. Isa (2001) 13 WRN 187 CA*

10. The onus is on the defendant to specifically plead in the statement of defence that there exists a failure of a condition precedent to found the plaintiff's claim.

- *Shell Pet. Dev. Co. (Nig.) Ltd. v. Burutu L.G.C. (1998) 9 NWLR (Pt. 565) 318 CA*

11. A defendant must specifically plead in his statement of defence, facts necessary for raising special defences, and any condition precedent which are necessary to show that the plaintiff's claim is not maintainable.

- *Musa v. Isa (2001) 13 WRN 187 CA*

32.5 Reply to Statement of Defence

1. A reply is the defence of a plaintiff to the counter claim of a defendant or to new facts raised by the defendant in his defence to the plaintiff's statement of claim.

- *Oshodi v. Eyifunmi (2000) 7 SC (Pt. II) 145*

2. The function of a reply is to raise, in answer to the averments contained in a statement of defence, any matters or facts, which must be specifically pleaded or which make the defence not maintainable or which otherwise might take the defence by surprise or which raise issues of fact not arising out of the defence.

- *Akeredolu v. Akinremi (1989) 3 NWLR (Pt. 108) 164 SC*

3. Pleadings are closed when parties join issue in a case. Thus, where both the statement of claim and the statement of defence do not bring the parties to issue on all the claims, the plaintiff shall file a reply.

- *Oshodi v. Eyifunmi (2000) 7 SC (Pt. II) 145*

4. Where no counter-claim is filed, further pleadings by way of reply to the statement of defence is unnecessary, if the sole purpose is to deny the averments in the statement of defence.

- *Ishola v. S.G.B. (Nig.) Ltd (1997) 2 NWLR (Pt. 488) 405 SC*

5. A plaintiff is not entitled to introduce a different cause of action by way of a reply to a statement of defence. If, however, he wishes to raise such a new claim, he can do so by amending his statement of claim.

- *Amoo v. Aderibigbe (1994) 2 NWLR (Pt. 324) 92 CA*

32.6 Claims

1. It is settled law that a court will not award an amount, which is not claimed or pleaded by a party or which is in excess of what is claimed.

- *Ekwunife v. Wayne (W/A) Ltd (1989) 5 NWLR (Pt. 122) 422 SC*

2. Reliefs claimed by a party before a court must be clear, specific and unambiguous. This is because the court cannot grant claims, which are vague. Moreover, the court cannot award what is not claimed.

- *A.C.B. Plc v. Nwodika (1996) 4 NWLR (Pt. 443) 470 CA*

3. Where a court grants the claim of a successful party to a suit, there will be no need for the court to consider any alternative claim made by the successful party.

- *Agidigbi v. Agidigbi (1996) 6 NWLR (Pt. 454) 300 SC*

4. Where a party claims a particular amount but was able to prove a lesser amount than he claimed, the court has the power to

award the lesser amount proved.

- Simton v. Pamil (2001) 13 WRN 55 CA

5. A party who claims interest has the duty to plead and proffer credible evidence in proof thereof.

- Ishola v. S.G.B. Ltd (1997) 2 NWLR (Pt. 488) 405 SC

- Saeby v. Olaogun (2001) 11 WRN 179 SC

6. It is not proper for a court to order a foreign plaintiff to give security for a defendant's costs where such order will be oppressive or have the effect of stifling an otherwise genuine claim

- Oduba v. Houtmangracht (1997) 6 NWLR (Pt. 508) 185 SC

7. It is trite law that a court has no power to grant to a party a relief, which he has not sought or which is more than he has claimed.

- Gomwalk v. Okwosa (1999) 1 NWLR (Pt. 586) 225 CA

- Bello v. Aruwa (1999) 8 NWLR (Pt. 615) 454 CA

- WR & PC Ltd v. Onwo (1999) 12 NWLR (Pt. 630) 312 CA

- Awoniyi v. AMORC (2000) 6 SC (Pt. 1) 103

- Afrotech Technical Services (Nig.) Ltd v. MIA & Sons Ltd (2000) 12 SC (Part II) 1

- Simton v. Pamil (2001) 13 WRN 55 CA

32.7 Counter-Claim

1. A counter-claim is, for all intents and purposes, a separate and independent action in its own right. Although, a defendant, for convenience and speed may join it with his defence.

- Ogbonna v. A.-G., Imo State (1992) 1 NWLR (Pt. 220) 647 SC

- Ogbonda v. Eke (1998) 10 NWLR (Pt. 568) 73 CA

2. A counter-claim is an independent action, which enables a defendant to enforce a claim against a plaintiff. It is by nature a 'sword' and not a 'shield'. Thus, the rules of pleadings apply

with the same force and potency to a counter-claim and a defence to a counter claim as if they are respectively, a statement of claim and a statement of defence.

- *Amata v. Omofuma (1997) 2 NWLR (Pt. 485) 93 CA*
- *Okonkwo v. C.C.B. (Nig.) Plc (1997) 6 NWLR (Pt. 507) 48 CA*

3. A counter-claim is a cross-action, which must be proved at the hearing of a case.

- *Obmiami Brick & Stone (Nig.) Ltd v. A.C.B. Ltd (1992) 3 NWLR (Pt. 229) 260 SC*

4. Where a defendant counter-claims against a plaintiff, the plaintiff is duty bound to file a reply in defence to the counter-claim. Failure to do so, the court is entitled, in fact obliged, to assume that the plaintiff has no defence to the counter-claim and may enter judgment accordingly for the defendant.

- *Ogbonna v. A.-G., Imo State (1992) 1 NWLR (Pt. 220) 647 SC*

5. The fate of a counter-claim, being an independent action, does not depend upon the outcome of the plaintiff's claim. Therefore, where the plaintiff's claim is dismissed, stayed or discontinued, the court may proceed with the counter-claim.

- *Hassan v. Reg. Trustees, Baptist Conv. (1993) 7 NWLR (Pt. 308) 679 CA*
- *Ogbonda v. Eke (1998) 10 NWLR (Pt. 568) 73 CA*

32.8 Damages

1. General damages are damages, which the law implies or presumes to have accrued from the wrong complained of. General damages are presumed to flow from the immediate, direct and proximate result of the wrong complained of. The court, in exercising its discretion in awarding general damages, has the responsibility to calculate what sum of money will be reasonable in the circumstances of the case.

- *Osuji v. Isiocha (1989) 3 NWLR (Pt. III) 623 SC*

- *Ijebu-Ode Local Govt. v. Adedeji Balogun & Co. (1991) 1 NWLR (Pt. 166) 136 SC*

- *Akanmu v. Olugbode (2001) 13 WRN 132 at 139 CA*

2. General damages cannot be properly substituted for special damages which a plaintiff fails to prove or claim, even where evidence is led on it.

- *Badmus v. Abegunde (2001) 3 WRN 40 SC*

3. In personal injury cases, once there is evidence of injury, pain, discomfort and permanent scarring, even though these are not quantified in monetary terms, the plaintiff will be entitled to reasonable general damages.

- *Eseigbe v. Agholor (1993) 9 NWLR (Pt. 316) 128 SC*

4. Special damages are damages, which the law does not infer from the nature of an act, but which are exceptional in character. Special damages denote those pecuniary losses, which have crystallised in terms of cash and value before trial.

- *Ijebu-Ode Local Govt. v. Adedeji Balogun & Co. (1991) 1 NWLR (Pt. 166) 136 SC*

5. Special damages must be specifically pleaded and strictly proved. Consequently, any evidence of special damages, which are not specifically pleaded and claimed in the statement of claim, goes to no issue.

- *British Airways v. Makanjuola (1993) 8 NWLR (Pt. 311) 276 CA*

6. Special damages have to be strictly proved. Where various items are claimed under special damages, the plaintiff is entitled to be awarded any of those items, which he can prove with sufficient evidence, even if he is not able to prove all the items.

- *Badmus v. Abegunde (2001) 3 WRN 40 SC*

7. It is a settled principle that special damages must not only be specifically pleaded with relevant particulars, but must also be strictly proved with credible evidence. Without such proof, no special damages can be awarded.

- *Osuji v. Isiocha (1989) 3 NWLR (Pt. 111) 623 SC*

- *Alhaji Otaru & Sons Ltd v. Idris (1999) 6 NWLR (Pt. 606) 330 SC*

8. Exemplary damages are usually awarded whenever a defendant's conduct is sufficiently outrageous to merit punishment, as when it discloses malice, fraud, cruelty, insolence, flagrant disregard of the law and the like.

> - *Eliochin (Nig.) Ltd v. Mbadiwe (1986) 1 NWLR (Pt. 14) 47 SC*
> - *Odogu v. A.-G., Fed. (1996) 6 NWLR (Pt. 456) 508 SC*

9. There is need to specifically claim and plead exemplary damages before it can be awarded.

> - *Odogu v. A.-G., Fed. (1996) 6 NWLR (Pt. 456) 508 SC*

10. Except in cases of breach of promise of marriage, exemplary damages are not recoverable in actions for breach of contract.

> - *Allied Bank (Nig.) Ltd v. Akubueze (1997) 6 NWLR (Pt. 509) 374 SC*

11. In cases of breach of contract, assessment of damages is calculated on the loss sustained by the injured party which loss was either in the contemplation of the parties or is an unavoidable consequence of the breach.

> - *Ijebu-Ode Local Govt. v. Adedeji Balogun & Co. (1991) 1 NWLR (Pt. 166) 136 SC*

12. In awarding damages, courts are expected to keep up with the times and economic trend in the country. In particular, the courts are to consider the prevailing decline in the purchasing power of the Naira over the past years.

> - *Onwu v. Nka (1996) 7 NWLR (Pt. 458) 1 SC*
> - *Allied Bank (Nig.) Ltd v. Akubueze (1997) 6 NWLR (Pt. 509) 374 SC*

13. It is trite that an appellate court will not normally alter or interfere with an award of damages by a trial court, on the ground that the appellate court would have awarded a different amount if it had tried the case at first instance. However, an appellate court may alter an award of damages where it is satisfied that the trial court acted upon a wrong principle of law or where the damages awarded was based on an entirely erroneous estimate, or that the award is either manifestly too

high or manifestly too low.

- *Eseigbe v. Agholor (1993) 9 NWLR (Pt. 316) 128 SC*
- *Okonkwo v. Ogbogu (1996) 5 NWLR (Pt. 449) 420 SC*
- *Odogu v. A.-G., Fed. (1996) 6 NWLR (Pt. 456) 508 SC*
- *Onwu v. Nka (1996) 7 NWLR (Pt. 458) 1 SC*
- *Concord Press (Nig.) Ltd v. Asaolu (1999) 10 NWLR (Pt. 621) 123 CA*
- *Savanah Bank (Nig.) Plc. v. P.M.S. Ltd (1999) 10 NWLR (Pt. 621) 160 CA*
- *Ya'u v. Dikwa (2001) 5 WRN 40 CA*
- *A.C.B. v. Apugo (2001) 10 WRN 124 SC*

14. Any trespass to the person by another, however slight, gives a right of action to recover nominal damages. Even, where there is no physical injury, substantial damages may be awarded for the man's dignity or for discomfort or inconvenience.

- *Okonkwo v. Ogbogu (1996) 5 NWLR (Pt. 449) 420 SC*

15. A plaintiff is required to take all reasonable steps to mitigate the loss resulting from the defendant's wrong, as no damages will be awarded in respect of any part of the loss which the plaintiff could have averted if he has taken reasonable steps.

- *Kosile v. Folarin (1989) 3 NWLR (Pt. 107) 1 SC*

16. A claim for anticipated profit is a special one, which must be strictly established by evidence. The onus of establishing anticipated profit is on the plaintiff, as he who asserts must prove.

- *A.-G., Oyo State v. Fairlakes Hotels Ltd (No. 2) (1989) 5 NWLR (Pt. 121) 255 SC*

17. In fatal accident cases, damages are to be based on a reasonable expectation of pecuniary benefit or benefit reducible to money value. The plaintiff must show that he has lost a reasonable probability of pecuniary advantage. A mere speculative possibility of benefit will not suffice.

- *Jenyo v. Akinreti (1990) 2 NWLR (Pt. 135) 663 SC*
- *N.B.C. Plc v. Ogundele (1997) 9 NWLR (Pt. 521) 446 CA*

XXXIII
Process

1. Service of process is vital under due process of law.

    - Guda v. Kitta (1999) 12 NWLR (Pt. 629) 21 CA

2. A defect in the service of a court process is voidable only if the complainant has not taken any step that can be regarded as a waiver of the defect.

    - B.B.N. v. Olayiwola (2001) 6 WRN 141 CA

3. Leave of the State High Court must be obtained before a writ of summons can be issued for service outside jurisdiction. If no such leave was obtained the issuance and service of the said writ of summons will be a nullity, invalid and void.

    - Miti v. N.N.B. Plc (1997) 3 NWLR (Pt. 496) 737 CA

    - B.B.N. v. Olayiwola (2001) 6 WRN 141 CA

4. Any judgment based on a process, which is not served, is liable to be set aside.

    - Hyppolite v. Egharevba (1998) 11 NWLR (Pt. 575) 598 CA

5. Failure to give notice of proceedings to an opposing party in a case where service of process is required is a fundamental omission which renders such proceedings void because the court has no jurisdiction to entertain it.

    - Wema Bank Nigeria Ltd v. Odulaja (2000) 3 SC 83

6. Where the requirement of a notice is that it should be served on a particular person, service on a person other than the person stipulated is a non-compliance with the provision.

    - Amadi v. NNPC (2000) 6 SC (Part I) 66

7. There are three modes of service of court process on a limited liability company within a State. They are service by registered post addressed to its principal officer in the State; service by delivery to the principal officer wherever he may be found in the State; and service by delivery at the company's office in the State to anyone apparently in charge of such office. However,

for service outside a State, the mode is by registered post. Order 7 Rule 4(1) & (2) of the High Court of Anambra State (Civil Procedure) Rules, 1988, considered.

> - *Daily Times (Nig.) Plc. v. Amaizu (1999) 12 NWLR (Pt. 630) 242 CA*

8. The concept of abuse of judicial process is very wide and the category cannot be closed. However, the general principle is that an abuse of the process of the court is constituted when more than one suit is instituted by a plaintiff against a defendant in respect of the same subject matter to the harassment, irritation and annoyance of the defendant, and in such a manner as to interfere with the administration of justice.

> - *Okafor v. A-G., Anambra State (1991) 6 NWLR (Pt. 200) 659 SC*
> - *Saraki v. Kotoye (1992) 9 NWLR (Pt. 264) 156 SC*
> - *Mohammed v. Husseini (1998) 14 NWLR (Pt. 584) 108 SC*
> - *Messr. NV Scheep v. The MV. "S. Araz" (2000) 12 SC (Part I) 164*

9. Multiplicity of suits is not desirable and the courts have constantly held that a party should not be allowed to institute proceedings in any court if the circumstances are such that to do so would really be vexatious.

> - *Registered Trustees of the Living Christ Mission v. Aduba (2000) 2 SC 1*

10. Consolidation of suits makes it possible for a trial court to treat the suits together. The purpose of consolidation is to save time and cost.

> - *Delta Steel Co. Ltd v. Owners of Ship "Aditya Prabha" (1991) 3 NWLR (Pt. 179) 369 CA*
> - *Alaribe v. Nwankpa (1999) 4 NWLR (Pt. 600) 551 CA*

11. An affidavit used in previous proceedings could be relied upon in current proceedings for the purpose of showing that a particular person had once deposed to that affidavit. It could also be used to impeach the credibility of the deponent in subsequent judicial proceedings. A party relying on a process used in earlier judicial proceedings needs to show that the earlier process is readily available for use in the current proceedings, and that the process is still relevant to the issues in the current

proceedings.

> - *Afribank Nig. Plc v. Geneva (1999)12 NWLR (Pt. 632) 567 CA*

12. The fact that a process was filed in a previous suit, which has been struck out or dismissed, does not render such process useless for the purpose of all judicial proceedings.

> - *Afribank (Nig.) Plc v. Geneva (1999) 12 NWLR (Pt. 632) 567 CA*

13. The procedure governing the transfer of a suit from the undefended list to the general cause list is that a party served with a writ of summons and an affidavit shall deliver to the Registrar a notice in writing that he intends to defend the suit, together with an affidavit disclosing a defence on the merit. The court may then give leave to defend. It is only when such leave is obtained that the case can be transferred from the undefended list to the general cause list. Order 23 Rule 3(1) and (2) of the High Court of Kano State (Civil Procedure) Rules 1988, considered.

> - *Taiwo v. Danbare Agency Ltd (2001) 14 WRN 52 CA*

14. The undefended list procedure is not intended to shut out a defendant from contesting the suit brought thereunder. Where a defendant can show in his affidavit that he has a defence on the merit, he will be granted leave to defend the suit. The defendant at this stage need not show a complete defence. It suffices if the defence set up shows that there is a triable issue or that for some other reasons there ought to be a trial.

> - *Fesco (Nig.) Ltd v. N.R. & C.P. Co. Ltd (1998) 11 NWLR (Pt. 573) 227 CA*

15. A trial court has the discretion to grant or refuse the adjournment of a matter but the discretion is to be exercised judicially and judiciously. Where an application for adjournment is refused, the procedure to be adopted is for the trial judge to call on the party to continue with the case and where he is unable to proceed, especially a plaintiff, to dismiss the case for want of prosecution.

> - *Ceekay Traders Ltd v. Gen. Motors Co. Ltd (1992) 2 NWLR (Pt. 222) 132 SC*

- *Chiedozie v. Omosowan (1999) 1 NWLR (Pt. 586) 317 CA*
- *Offor v. State (1999) 12 NWLR (Pt. 632) 608 CA*

16. It is a basic principle of law that a Limitation Law or Act removes the right of action, the right of enforcement and the right to judicial relief and leaves the plaintiff with a bare and empty cause of action which he cannot enforce if such cause of action is statute-barred. Accordingly, the court lacks jurisdiction to entertain the suit.

- *Araka v. Ejeagwu (2000) 12 SC (Part I) 99*

17. By virtue of section 15(2)(a) of the Interpretation Act, a reference in an enactment to a period of days shall be construed, where the period is reckoned from a particular event as excluding·the day on which the event occurs.

- *Atikpekpe v. Joe (1999) 6 NWLR (Pt. 607) 428 CA*

18. A writ of summons being an originating process cannot be deemed as having been duly filed and served because it is a document which by definition commences proceedings. The documents which a court can 'deem' are those which parties exchange between themselves during the course of proceedings, such as statement of claim or defence and briefs of argument, and not those which require the signature of the Registrar for their validity.

- *Miti v. N.N.B. Plc (1997) 3 NWLR (Pt. 496) 737 CA*

19. Where a person registers his name in a professional register sanctioned by law, such a person cannot at random rearrange his initials or the order in which his names have been registered. This is to ensure consistency and easy identification of a member of a professional body.

- *Esenowo v. Ukpong (1999) 6 NWLR (Pt. 608) 611 at 613 SC*

20. By virtue of section 15(5) of the Interpretation Act and section 1 of the Public Holidays Act, Saturday, as a day of the week, does not qualify as a public holiday.

- *Balogun v. Odumosu (1999) 2 NWLR (Pt. 592) 590 at 593 CA*

XXXIV
Stay of Proceedings/Stay of Execution Pending Appeal

34.1 *Stay of Proceedings*

1. An appeal does not operate as a stay of proceedings. Thus, any party appealing against an interlocutory decision of a court is under a duty to apply for stay of further proceedings pending appeal, if he believes the result of his appeal will affect further proceedings in the matter.

> - *J.C. Ltd v. Ezenwa (1996) 4 NWLR (Pt. 443) 391 SC*

2. An application for stay of proceedings may only be made by a party who has appealed against an interlocutory ruling of a court and seeks a stay of proceedings in the matter before the court, pending the outcome of the appeal on the interlocutory decision.

> - *Akilu v. Fawehinmi (No. 2) (1989) 2 NWLR (Pt. 102) 122 SC*

3. An application for stay of proceedings may also be made by a defendant or a plaintiff against whom final judgment was given. The defendant or plaintiff must have appealed against the final judgment, seeking for an order of stay of proceedings in respect of execution of the judgment pending the determination of the appeal.

> - *Akilu v. Fawehinmi (No. 2) (1989) 2 NWLR (Pt. 102) 122 SC*

4. It is trite that all applications for stay of proceedings, whether in civil or criminal matters, are always brought under inherent powers or inherent jurisdiction of the court. This is because there is no statutory provision under any Nigerian statute that grants the right to apply for stay of proceedings in clear terms.

> - *State v. Ajayi (1996) 1 NWLR (Pt. 423) 169 CA*

5. The courts, in criminal cases, have the power to grant a stay of proceedings pending an interlocutory appeal. However, before granting stay of proceedings, the court, whether in a civil or a criminal case, must satisfy itself that there are arguable grounds of appeal to be canvassed at the appellate court, and not just something fanciful that is calculated to waste judicial time.

> - *State v. Ajayi (1996) 1 NWLR (Pt. 423) 169 CA*

6. A court has a duty to stay or adjourn a case before it, pending the determination of an appeal against its ruling or decision where the continuing hearing of the case could work injustice to a party or constitute an exercise in futility.

> - *Nalsa and Team Ass. v. N.N.P.C (1996) 3 NWLR (Pt. 439) 621 SC*

7. The law is that both stay of proceedings and stay of execution are equitable remedies which depend entirely on the discretion of the courts.

> - *State v. Ajayi (1996) 1 NWLR (Pt. 423) 169 CA*

34.2 *Stay of Execution*

1. An order of stay of execution pending appeal is made to prevent the successful party from reaping the fruits of his success at the trial. Thus, a stay of execution being a grave interruption of the interest of the successful party in a legal duel, any person who seeks such equitable remedy to deny even temporarily the right of enjoyment by the successful party of the fruits of the judgment must have strong facts. The court will be hesitant to grant an order for stay pending appeal where such an order will put an end to the proceedings in the main case.

> - *Jadesimi v. Akele (1998) 11 NWLR (Pt. 572) 133 CA*

2. Having regard to section 24 of the Supreme Court Act, and Order VII Rule 37 of the Rules of the Supreme Court, an appeal does not operate as a stay of execution. An applicant is bound to apply for an order for stay of execution of the judgment of the lower court at the lower court in the first instance and upon

refusal to grant the application, the application may be brought to the appellate court for determination.

- *Cheshe v. Nicon Hotels Ltd (1998) 12 NWLR (Pt. 576) 82 CA*

- *Pavex International Co. (Nig.) Ltd. v. I.B.W.A. Ltd (2000) 4 SC (Pt. II) 196*

3. The grant of stay of execution pending appeal is undoubtedly and clearly at the discretion of the court. However, such discretion must be exercised judiciously.

- *Ifeadi v. Atedze (1995) 5 NWLR (Pt. 394) 196 CA*

4. Stay of execution is a discretionary remedy. An appellate court, in considering an appeal against the refusal of a court to order for stay of execution should ensure that the successful litigants are not unduly deprived of the fruits of the judgment, which they obtained at the lower court even though that judgment is the subject of a pending appeal.

- *Franchal Nigeria Ltd v. Nigeria Arab Bank Ltd (2000) 6 SC (Pt. I) 1*

5. An applicant seeking for an order of stay of execution must show special or exceptional circumstances why the order should be made because the court will not make an order depriving a successful litigant of the fruits of his success.

- *Josien Holdings Ltd v. Lornamead Ltd (1995) 1 NWLR (Pt. 371) 254 SC*

6. In deciding whether or not to grant a stay of execution pending an appeal, the court must consider the chances of the applicant on appeal; where such chances are non-existent, then, a stay must necessarily be refused. The court must also consider the nature of the subject matter of the appeal. In doing this, it ascertains whether the sustenance of the *status quo* pending the determination of the appeal is tantamount to the justice of the case. Other factors to be considered are whether the applicant will be able to reap the fruits of his judgment on appeal, should the appeal succeed and, whether there are any special grounds necessitating a grant of the application. For instance, poverty *per se* is not a special ground for grant of an application for stay. However, where it is established that poverty will deprive the appellant of the means to prosecute his appeal, it will constitute

a ground for the grant of a stay.

- *U.B.N. Plc v. Olori Motors Co. Ltd (1998) 5 NWLR (Pt. 551) 652 CA*
- *Olaseinde v. F.H.A. (1999) 9 NWLR (619) 448 CA*

7. Poverty *per se* is not a valid ground for the grant of stay of execution of judgment. The applicant has to go beyond mere allegation of poverty by supplying the court with all the facts about his income and the source of his income. He must establish that he has indeed no resources before his claim to poverty can amount to a special circumstance warranting a grant of an order of stay.

- *Abdulkadiri v. Ali (1999) 1 NWLR (Pt. 588) 613 CA*
- *Franchal Nigeria Ltd v. Nigeria Arab Bank Ltd (2000) 6 SC (Pt. I) 1*

8. In an application for stay of execution, the special circumstances which have received approval include, where execution would destroy the subject-matter of the proceeding; or foist upon the court, especially the Court of Appeal, a situation of complete helplessness; or render nugatory any orders of the Court of Appeal; or generally provide a situation in which whatever happens to the case even if the appellant succeeds in the Court of Appeal there would be no return to the *status quo*.

- *Wema Bank Plc v. Balogun (1999) 7 NWLR (Pt. 610) 242 CA*
- *Oyelami v. Mil. Administrator, Osun State (1999) 8 NWLR (Pt. 613) 45 CA*
- *Agro-Allied Dev. Ent. Ltd. v. U.S.T.C. Inc. (1999) 13 NWLR (Pt. 633) 127 CA*

9. In an application for stay of execution pending appeal, the guiding principle is that a victorious party must not lightly be deprived of the fruit of his victory unless a special circumstance is advanced to justify stay of execution. Special circumstance is very wide and its category is not closed. However, it may include strong and substantial ground of appeal, which threatens the *res*. In cases where the *res* is at the risk of destruction, if a stay is not granted, or the *res* may be altered as to make it irreversible to its original state; or if it is monetary, and the victorious party

is poor, and may not be able to redeem the money should the substantive appeal be decided against him, the court in its discretion will grant a stay of execution pending the determination of the appeal.

- *Vaswani Trading Co. v. Savalakh & Co. (1972) 1 All NLR 483*

- *Agro-Allied Dev. Ent. Ltd v. U.S.T.C. Inc. (1999) 13 NWLR (Pt. 633) 127 CA*

- *Odedeyi v. Odedeyi (2000) 2 SC 93*

10. It is not in every case where an issue is labelled with the word 'jurisdiction' without more that it will create an exceptional circumstance for the grant of stay of execution. Whether or not an issue of jurisdiction will amount to special circumstance will depend on the particular case.

- *Adedoyin v. Sonuga (1999) 13 NWLR (Pt. 635) 355 CA*

11. An application for stay of execution pending appeal shall be brought in the first instance before the High Court except there are special circumstances which makes it impossible or impracticable to apply to the High Court. Such special circumstances include where the High Court has shown a bent towards a certain matter, which is likely or probable to be dismissed or struck out because of its negative antecedents.

- *Ifeadi v. Atedze (1995) 5 NWLR (Pt. 394) 196 CA*
- *Compt. Nigerian Prisons Service v. Adekanye (1999) 6 NWLR (Pt. 607) 381 CA*

12. Where the ground of appeal raises substantial issue of law in an area that is recondite and where either party could have judgment in his favour, a stay must be granted. However, it is not in all cases that an applicant who has raised substantial or recondite issue of law in his ground of appeal will *ipso facto* be entitled to stay of execution. Each case must be viewed from its own peculiar or surrounding circumstances.

- *Odunsi v. Abeke (1999) 12 NWLR (Pt. 632) 601 CA*

13. An order of stay of execution of an injunction in restraint of business will be granted where it appears that considerable damage will be done pending appeal to an applicant by way of stoppage of his business which stoppage cannot be compensated

by damages.

> - *Josien Holdings Ltd v. Lornamead Ltd (1995) 1 NWLR (Pt. 371) 254 SC*
>
> - *Shell Pet. Dev. Co. (Nig.) Ltd v. Omu (1998) 9 NWLR (Pt. 567) 672 CA*

14. Where the *res* of an action is a quantified amount, an applicant may obtain a stay of execution pending appeal if he can show that the respondent will be unable to re-pay the money if the appeal succeeded.

> - *Fawehinmi v. Akilu (1990) 1 NWLR (Pt. 127) 450 CA*

15. A court cannot make an order of stay of execution in a case where execution had already been lawfully carried out. Therefore, an executed or completed judgment cannot be stayed, as the court does not make an order in vain.

> - *The Regency Council of Olota v. Sodeinde (1998) 6 NWLR (Pt. 552) 72 CA*

16. A stay of execution will only prevent a plaintiff or beneficiary of a judgment or an order from putting into motion the machinery of the law. An order of stay of execution pending appeal can only be made in respect of executory judgment or order and not otherwise. Accordingly, stay of execution cannot be ordered in respect of declaratory judgment.

> - *Yaro v. Arewa Construction Ltd (1998) 7 NWLR (Pt. 558) 368 SC*

17. Where a party is appealing against a matter to which he had suffered a defeat and asked for a stay of execution pending the determination of the appeal, he cannot be held liable for contempt merely because he had not obeyed the order which he is appealing against or which he wants to be stayed pending the appeal.

> - *Globestar Eng. (Nig.) Ltd v. Malle Holdings Ltd. (1999) 10 NWLR (Pt. 622) 270 CA*

18. It is settled law that a party who had earlier been granted a stay of execution in the lower court and who is not satisfied with the conditions attached to the order for stay of execution of a judgment granted him can apply to a higher court for the variation of that order without lodging an appeal against the earlier order itself.

> - *R.E.A.N. v. Aswani Textile Ltd (1992) 3 NWLR (Pt. 227) 1 SC*
> - *Tidex (Nig.) Ltd. v. Maskew (1997) 1 NWLR (Pt. 482) 453 CA*

19. Where an applicant is urging an appellate court to modify the conditions for stay granted by the lower court, the onus is on the applicant to swear to an affidavit spelling out the present conditions and why the conditions are onerous or unfair to him.

> - *Ladipo v. Aminike Invest. Co. Ltd (1998) 4 NWLR (Pt. 546) 496 CA*

20. Where a bank or financial institution is a judgment debtor and, in an application for stay of execution of the judgment pending appeal, it is conceded by the judgment creditor or it appears to the court that the bank or financial institution is reputable or financially buoyant, there will be no basis for ordering that the amount involved be deposited in an account in another bank pending the determination of the appeal lodged by the bank or financial institution.

> - *Owena Bank (Nig.) Plc v. O.B.C. Ltd (1998) 9 NWLR (Pt. 564) 129 CA*

XXXV
The Law and Practice of Banking

35.1 Meaning of Bank and Customer

1. At common law, there is no exhaustive definition of a bank. The usual characteristics of the business of bank are: the acceptance of money from, and collection of cheques for customers and the placing of them to the customers' credit; the honouring of cheques or orders drawn on the bank by their customers when presented for payment; and the keeping of some form of current or running accounts in their books in which credits and debits are entered. In addition to these three usual characteristics, there are, of course, others, for example, lending of money.

> - *United Dominions Trust Ltd v. Kirkwood (1966) 2 QB 431, (1966) 1 All ER 968 CA*

2. The word "bank" in its ordinary grammatical meaning means an organisation or place that provides financial services.

> - *FMBN v. NDIC (1999) 2 NWLR (Pt. 591) 333 at 339 SC*

3. There is no statutory definition of a bank's customer. The general rule is that a person must have some sort of account, either a deposit account or a current account or some similar relation, to make a person a customer of a bank. This general rule is qualified to the extent that a person who is about to open an account may sometimes be regarded as a customer.

> - *Great Western Railway Co. v. London and Country Banking Co. Ltd (1901) AC 414 at 420-1*
> - *Woods v. Martins Bank Ltd and Another (1959) 1 QB 55*

4. If a person has no account with a bank and is not about to open an account, the fact that a bank renders some casual services to him will not make him a customer.

> - *Great Western Railway Co. v. London and Country Banking Co. Ltd (1901) AC 414*

35.2 Relationship between Banker and Customer

1. The relationship between a banker and his customer who pays money into the bank is the ordinary relation of debtor and creditor, with a super-added obligation arising out of the custom of banking to honour the customer's cheques.

- *Foley v. Hill and Others (1848) 2 HLC 28 at 36-37*
- *F.B.N. Plc v. Nagarfi (1998) 6 NWLR (Pt. 555) 692 CA*

2. The relationship of debtor and creditor or between a banker and customer does not exist until the money or other instruments to be deposited by the customer have been checked and the bank has signified its acceptance thereof.

- *Balmoral Supermarket Ltd v. Bank of New Zealand (1974) 2 NZLR 155 (Supreme Court of New Zealand Judgment)*

35.3 Accounts of Customers

1. Proof of payment of money paid into an account may be by oral evidence of the person who actually made the payment personally to the bank or by the production of a bank teller or acknowledgment showing on the face of it that the bank had received the money.

- *Aeroflot v. U.B.A. (1986) 3 NWLR (Pt. 27) 188 SC*
- *Ishola v. S.G.B. (Nig.) Ltd (1997) 2 NWLR (Pt. 488) 405 SC*

2. The general principle of law is that where a customer has several accounts with a banker, these accounts must be kept distinct and separate. The banker has no right to combine them or to transfer assets or liabilities from one account to another without the assent of the customer or without reasonable notice to the customer of the intention so to do.

- *Allied Bank (Nig.) Ltd. v. Akubueze (1997) 6 NWLR (Pt. 509) 374 SC*
- *Bank of the North Ltd v. Akintoye (1999) 12 NWLR (Pt. 631) 392 CA*

3. It is permissible for a customer of a bank to close his account

through an oral instruction but he cannot take out any outstanding credit therein until a proper discharge of obligations on both sides is carried out.

> - *D. Stephens Ind. Ltd v. B.C.C.I. (Nig.) Ltd (1999) 11 NWLR (Pt. 625) 29 SC*

4. A banker who freezes a customer's account, even without publishing to the whole world or in the press that the customer was fraudulent can be sued for the tort of defamation.

> - *Royal Petroleum Co. Ltd. v. F.B.N. Ltd (1997) 6 NWLR (Pt. 510) 584 CA*

5. The police have no authority or power to order the transfer of a person's funds from one bank account to another regardless of the fact that the police is investigating the person.

> - *Societe Generale Bank (Nig.) Ltd v. Afekoro (1999) 11 NWLR (Pt. 628) 521 SC*

6. One of the terms of the contract between banker and customer is that the banker will not cease to do business with a customer except upon reasonable notice. Thus, where a banker decides to close the account of a customer, he must give the customer reasonable notice.

> - *Buckingham & Co. v. London and Midland Bank Ltd (1895) 12 TLR 70*
> - *Joachinson v. Swiss Bank Corporation (1921) 3 KB 110*
> - *D. Stephens Ind. Ltd v. B.C.C.I. (Nig.) Ltd (1999) 11 NWLR (Pt. 625) 29 SC*

7. When a customer's account has been closed, either by the customer or by the bank, the relationship of banker and customer is at an end, and neither party is under any contractual obligation to the other, save only in one respect, namely that the banker's duty of secrecy still subsists.

> - *Tournier v. National Provincial and Union Bank of England (1924) 1 KB 461 at 473*

8. The relationship between banker and customer may, like any other contractual relationship, be terminated by mutual agreement; by notice given by the customer or the banker; by death of the customer; by mental disorder of the customer; and

by bankruptcy or winding up of either party.

> - *D. Stephens Ind. Ltd. v. B.C.C.I. (Nig.) Ltd (1999) 11 NWLR (Pt. 625) 29 SC*

9. In banking business, certificate of deposit, tellers and passbooks can be used as proof for monetary deposits. A letter on the letterhead paper is not suficient proof for monetary deposits.

> - *Owners (Home Savings and Loans) v. Tojuomo (Nig.) Ltd (1998) 5 NWLR (Pt. 549) 326 CA*

35.4 Banker's Right to Set-Off

Where a customer has more than one account at the same branch of a bank, or at two or more branches of the same bank, the bank has the right to set off what is due to the customer on one account against what is due from him on another account. Thus, the bank can use the money of a customer in a deposit account to set off a debt owed to it by the customer.

> - *Garneft v. M'Kewan (1872) LR 8 Ex 10*
> - *Barclays Bank Ltd v. Okenarche (1966) 2 Lloyd's Rep 87*
> - *F.B.N. (Nig.) Ltd v. Osunsedo (1997) 11 NWLR (Pt. 527) 132 CA*

35.5 Banker's Duties to his Customer

1. It is an established principle of law that a bank is under a legal obligation to keep its customer's affairs secret. However, a banker is justified in making disclosure concerning its customer's affairs where disclosure is under compulsion by law; or where there is a duty to the public to disclose; or where the interests of the bank require disclosure; or where the disclosure is made by the express or implied consent of the customer.

> - *Tournier v. National Provincial and Union Bank of England (1924) 1 KB 461 at 473*

2. A bank has a duty to exercise reasonable care and skill in carrying out banking business in relation to its customer. The duty applies to interpreting, ascertaining and acting in accordance with the instructions of the customer.

- *Agbanelo v. Union Bank of Nigeria (2000) 4 SC (Pt. I) 243*

35.6 Customer's Duties to his Banker

1. The customer must exercise reasonable care in drawing his cheques so as not to mislead his banker or to facilitate forgery. If he draws the cheque in a manner which facilitates fraud, he is guilty of a breach of duty as between himself and the banker, and he will be responsible to the banker for any loss sustained by the banker as a natural and direct consequence of this breach of duty.

- *London Joint Stock Bank Ltd v. Macmillian and Arthur (1918) AC 777*

- *Kulatilleke v. Mercantile Bank of India (1958) 59 Ceylon NLR 190 (Supreme Court of Ceylon Judgment)*

2. If a customer discovers that cheques purporting to have been signed by him have been forged, he must inform his bank promptly.

- *Greenwood v. Martins Bank Ltd (1932) 1 KB 371*

35.7 Breach of Contract under Banker and Customer Relationship

1. Where a customer brings an action against his bank for wrongfully debiting his account, he is entitled to recover damages, which will flow as natural or probable consequence of the breach.

- *A.C.B. Plc v. Haston (Nig.) Ltd. (1997) 8 NWLR (Pt. 515) 110 CA*

2. Where a banker fails to effect a customer's instruction to transfer funds for overseas transactions without any justifiable

reason, he will be liable for breach of contract.

> - *F.B.N. Plc v. Associated Motors Co. Ltd (1998) 10 NWLR (Pt. 570) 441 CA*

35.8 Cheque and Bank Draft

1. A cheque is not money until it is presented to a bank and paid. It is a Bill of Exchange drawn on a banker and payable on demand. Section 73 of the Bills of Exchange Act Cap 35 Laws of the Federation of Nigeria 1990 considered.

> - *G.S. & F.C. Ltd v. Obiekezie (1997) 10 NWLR (Pt. 526) 577 CA*

2. A cheque which has been cleared, where clearance is necessary, puts the account of a customer in funds.

> - *Union Bank of Nigeria Ltd v. Nwoye (1996) 3 NWLR (Pt. 435) 135 SC*

3. A bank is under an obligation to pay cheques drawn on it by its customer provided that the customer has sufficient fund to satisfy the amount payable on the cheque and there are no legal bars to payment. A customer whose cheque has been wrongfully dishonoured is entitled to claim damages against his banker. The claim may be for breach of contract and/or for libel.

> - *Gibbons v. Westminster Bank Ltd (1939) 2 KB 882*
> - *Allied Bank (Nig.) Ltd v. Akubueze (1997) 6 NWLR (Pt. 509) 374 SC*
> - *UBA Ltd v. Ademuyiwa (1999) 11 NWLR (Pt. 628) 570 CA*

4. A customer must exercise reasonable care in drawing his cheques so as not to facilitate forgery. Where a customer's signature on a cheque is, however, forged, then the cheque is not valid. Indeed, there is no bill at all. Therefore, a banker is not entitled to debit the account of the customer. If he does, he is liable to pay the customer the amount that was paid away on the face of the forged cheque.

> - *Bank of the North v. Maidamisa (1997) 10 NWLR (Pt. 525) 408 CA*

5. The combined effect of crossing a bank draft "not negotiable", "account payee only" is to ensure that the proceeds of that particular draft are lodged only in the account endorsed on the draft and also to make it non-transferable. Thus, it puts the collecting bank on notice that if it collects the draft for someone other than the payee and that person is not entitled to it, the banker may be liable in damages to the person who is entitled to it.

> - *U.B.A. Plc v. Ekene Dili Chukwu (Nig.) Ltd. (1999) 12 NWLR (Pt. 629) 128 CA*

6. Under Section 2(1)(c) of the Bills of Exchange Act Cap 35 Laws of the Federation of Nigeria 1990, a bank draft means a draft drawn by a banker upon himself and payable on demand at an office of his bank. The distinction between a bank draft and a cheque is that while a banker may refuse to honour a cheque because the drawer has no money in his account to cover the amount contained in the cheque; a bank draft, on the other hand, is payable on presentation regardless of the fact as to whether the person on whose behalf the draft was issued has money in his account at the material time or not.

> - *U.B.N. Plc v. Scpok (Nig.) Ltd (1998) 12 NWLR (Pt. 578) 439 CA*

7. The measure of or category of damages arising out of dishonoured bill is covered by the provision of section 57 of the Bills of Exchange Act. The damages are deemed to be liquidated damages and they consist of the amount of the bill, the interest thereon from the time of presentation for payment and the expenses of noting or expenses of protest where protest is necessary

> - *U.B.N. Plc v. Scpok (Nig.) Ltd (1998) 12 NWLR (Pt. 578) 439 at 449 CA*

8. It is a well-established rule that in an action for breach of contract against a bank for wrongfully dishonouring a trader's cheque, the plaintiff is entitled to recover substantial, though temperate and reasonable damages for injury to his commercial credit without the necessity of alleging and proving any actual damage.

> - *Rolin v. Steward (1854) 14 CB 595*
> - *Wilson v. United Countries Bank Ltd (1920) AC 102 at 112*

& 133

- Salami v. Savannah Bank of Nigeria Ltd (1990) 2 NWLR
(Pt. 130) 106 CA

9. A customer who is not a trader is entitled to recover substantial damages for breach of contract in respect of wrongful dishonour of his cheque if, and only if, he alleges and proves special damage.

- Gibbons v. Westminister Bank Ltd (1939) 2 KB 882

10. Where a bank wrongfully dishonoured the cheque of a customer who is a non-trader and the bank writes such words as "Refer to drawer" or "Not sufficient" or "Present again" the customer is entitled to claim damages for breach of contract and for libel.

- Davidson v. Barclays Bank Ltd (1940) 1 AII ER 316

- Baker v. Australia and New Zealand Bank (1958) NZLR
907 (Supreme Court of New Zealand)

35.9 Bank Interest

1. In banking business, "interest" is the money payable by a banker to a customer for money deposited or money payable by a customer to the bank for money received from the bank, by way of loan, overdraft, and advance or in any related business. Banks are empowered to charge interests on loans or other advances granted to a customer even where there is no express agreement on the rate of interest to be charged because it is implied that the customer must have consented to an interest to be charged on his account. However, the determination of interest rate is not done arbitrarily by banks. The Central Bank of Nigeria is empowered under section 15 of the Banking Act, Cap. 28 Laws of the Federation of Nigeria 1990 to regulate from time to time, by way of guidelines, the interest rates to be charged by banks.

- U.B.N. Ltd v. Salami (1998) 3 NWLR (Pt. 543) 538 CA

- U.B.N. Ltd v. Ayoola (1998) 11 NWLR (Pt. 573) 338 CA

2. A banker is under a duty to bring to the attention of his customer any change in the rate of interest as a condition for the banker to change the agreed rate of interest.

   - *Okolo v. U.B.N. Ltd (1998) 2 NWLR (Pt. 539) 618 CA*
   - *Ayanlere v. F.M.B. (Nig.) Ltd (1998)11 NWLR (Pt 575) 621 CA*

3. The burden of proof is on a bank which asserts that there is an agreement between it and its customer to charge interest on loan and advances by adducing sufficient evidence to show that the rate of interest which it is charging is within the terms of the agreement and in accordance with banking practice.

   - *First Bank of Nigeria Plc v. Mamman (Nig.) Ltd (2001) 3 WRN 58 CA*

35.10 Letters of Credit

1. In modern banking practice, a confirmed letter of credit is effected so as to assure a seller of goods in advance that the buyer is serious and also to assure the buyer that the seller shall deliver the goods upon payment. In practice a buyer will request his banker to open a credit in favour of the seller and in pursuance of that request, the banker or his foreign agent, issues a confirmed credit in favour of the seller.

   - *U.B.N. Plc v. Sparkling Breweries Ltd (1997) 5 NWLR (Pt. 505) 344 CA*

2. In international trade involving irrevocable letters of credit, four autonomous but inter-related contractual relations are involved namely: a contract for sale of goods between the buyer and the seller; a contract between the buyer and the issuing bank for the opening of a letter of credit; a contract between the issuing bank and the confirming bank for making payment to the seller; and a contract between the confirming bank and the seller for the payment to the seller on presentation of the documents stated in the letter.

   - *I.B.W.A. Ltd v. Unakalamba (1998) 9 NWLR (Pt. 565) 245 CA*

3. A confirmed letter of credit is an irrevocable one. Thus, an irrevocable or confirmed letter of credit which has been communicated to the beneficiary cannot be cancelled or amended by the buyer without the beneficiary's consent. Also, the issuing banker cannot at the instigation of the buyer force an amendment.

- *U.B.N. Ltd v. Osezuah (1997) 2 NWLR (Pt. 485) 28 CA*

4. A letter of credit can be validly cancelled at the processing stage, that is, when it is still in the possession of the issuing bank.

- *U.B.N. Ltd v. Okwara (1998) 1 NWLR (Pt. 532) 118 CA*

35.11 Recovery of Loans

1. In an action for recovery of loan advanced by a banker to his customer, the court is required to firstly establish whether the banker granted the customer a loan. If so, how much; the interest agreed upon and how much, if any, has the customer paid out of the loan.

- *F.B.N. Plc v. Obeya (1998) 2 NWLR (Pt. 537) 205 CA*

2. A debt is repayable either on demand or on notice given or upon any other condition agreed upon by the parties. Thus, before a banker can successfully institute an action for recovery of loan from his customer he must first of all make a demand or give notice to the customer concerned.

- *Ishola v. S.G.B. Ltd (1997) 2 NWLR (Pt. 488) 405 SC*
- *U.B.N. Ltd v. Oki (1999) 8 NWLR (Pt. 614) 244 CA*

3. Where there is a dispute between two banks, the forum for the resolution of the dispute is not exclusive to the jurisdiction of the Federal High Court. The nature of the transaction and the capacity in which one of the banks related with the other shall determine the proper forum.

- *F.M.B.N. v. N.D.I.C. (1999) 2 NWLR (Pt. 591) 333 SC*

4. A person may deposit his title deed with his bank for two primary purposes namely, for safe custody and as collateral to

obtain a loan from the bank. Where he deposits it as collateral and the bank refuses to grant him the loan, the bank is under an obligation to return the title deed. If the bank retains it, it shall be liable to pay damages to the customer for wrongful detention.

> - *Royal Petroleum Co. Ltd v. F.B.N. Ltd (1997) 6 NWLR (Pt. 510) 584 CA*

5. A bank is vicariously liable where any of its servants fails to strictly adhere to the banking regulations and rules in force.

> - *U.B.N. Plc. v. Eskol Paints (Nig.) Ltd (1997) 8 NWLR (Pt. 515) 157 CA*

35.12 Effect of Revoking a Bank's Licence

A revocation of a bank's licence by the Central Bank does not rob the bank concerned of its legal personality. The bank is still capable of suing or being sued.

> - *C.C.B. (Nig.) Plc v. O'Silvawax Int. Ltd (1999) 7 NWLR (Pt. 609) 97 CA*

XXXVI
Tort

36.1 Libel and Slander

1. A "tort" is an act which gives rise to a right of action, being a wrongful act or injury consisting in the infringement of a right created otherwise than by a contract.

> - *Utih v. Oroboko (1996) 3 NWLR (Pt. 434) 36 CA*

2. An action for libel is a purely personal action as the proper person to sue as plaintiff is the person directly defamed, and the proper person to be sued as defendant is the person who published the defamatory words or caused them to be so published.

> - *C.R.S.N Corp. v. Oni (1995) 1 NWLR (Pt. 371) 270 at 276 SC*

3. The material part of a cause of action in libel is not the writing of the libellous matter complained of, but the publication of the libel. Thus, an action for libel must fail if publication of the defamatory matter is not proved.

> - *Nsirim v. Nsirim (1990) 3 NWLR (Pt. 138) 285 SC*

4. "Publication" of a libellous matter means the making known of the defamatory matter to some persons other than the person of whom it is written.

> - *Nsirim v. Nsirim (1990) 3 NWLR (Pt. 138) 285 SC*
> - *Ugo v. Okafor (1996) 3 NWLR. (Pt. 438) 542 at 545 CA*

5. If a plaintiff can prove that a libel has been published of him without justification, his cause of action is complete and he need not prove that he has suffered any resulting actual damage or injury to his reputation for such damage is presumed.

> - *C.R.S.N. Corp v. Oni (1995) 1 NWLR (Pt. 371) 270 SC*

6. The law is that a plaintiff's general character or reputation need not be transparently stainless, unimpeachable and without any blemish before he can successfully maintain an action in defamation.

> - *C.R.S.N Corp v. Oni (1995) 1 NWLR (Pt. 371) 270 SC*

7. For the defence of justification to succeed, it would suffice if the defendant establishes that the main substance of the libellous statement is true and justified.

> - *Registered Trustees of Amorc v. Awoniyi (1994) 7 NWLR (Pt. 355) 154 SC*
> - *A.C.B. Ltd. v. Apugo (1995) 6 NWLR (Pt. 399) 65 at 72 CA*
> - *Ojeme v. Punch (Nig.) Ltd. (1996) 1 NWLR (Pt. 427) 701 at 703 CA*
> - *Ugo v. Okafor (1996) 3 NWLR (Pt. 438) 542 at 547 CA*

8. The law requires that in an action for libel, a plaintiff must set out in his statement of claim the exact words, which he alleges to be defamatory of him to enable the court to determine whether the words constitute a ground of action.

> - *Ningi v. F.B.N Plc. (1996) 3 NWLR (Pt. 435) 220 at 225 CA*

9. As a matter of law, the words "dishonest", "liar" and "thief" are defamatory in their natural and ordinary meanings and they are capable of bearing defamatory meanings in the minds of reasonable men.

> - *N.T.B. Lawson v. Kevin Mahor & Anor (1975) N.N.L.R. 154, High Court of North-Central State. Suit No. NCH/45/75*

10. A defamatory statement is a statement which, if published of and concerning a person, is calculated to lower him in the estimation of right-thinking men or cause him to be shunned or avoided or to expose him to hatred, contempt or ridicule, or to convey an imputation on him disparaging or injurious to him in his office, profession, calling, trade or business.

> - *Sketch v. Ajagbemokeferi (1989) 1 NWLR (Pt. 100) 678 SC*
> - *Ningi v. F.B.N Plc. (1996) 3 NWLR (Pt. 435) 220 CA*
> - *Ciroma v. Ali (1999) 2 NWLR (Pt. 590) 317 CA*

11. In an action for libel, the questions whether the words complained of are in fact defamatory and whether they are capable of conveying a defamatory meaning in the minds of reasonable persons in a particular case are to be determined by the court.

- *Sketch v. Ajagbemokeferi (1989) 1 NWLR (Pt. 100) 678 SC*
- *Ciroma v. Ali (1999) 2 NWLR (Pt. 590) 317 CA*

12. In an action for defamation, the plaintiff must prove the six co-terminus ingredients, viz, publication of the offending words; that the words refer to the plaintiff; that the words are defamatory of the plaintiff; publication of the words to third parties; falsity of the words; and that there is no legal justification for the publication of the words complained of.

- *Concord Press (Nig.) Ltd. v. Olutola (1999) 9 NWLR (Pt. 620) 578 CA*

13. Malice in an action for libel is defined as the intentional doing of a wrongful act without just cause or excuse, with an intent to inflict an injury or under circumstances that the law will imply an evil intent.

- *Ciroma v. Ali (1999) 2 NWLR (Pt. 590) 317 CA*

14. Where the defendant rebuts the inference of malice by relying on the plea of fair comment or qualified privilege, the burden is thrown upon the plaintiff to show and prove, through a reply, express malice against the defendant.

- *Akamagwunna v. S.B.N. Ltd (1995) 3 NWLR (Pt. 383) 343 at 344 CA*

15. It is not every annoying, vulgar statement or mere abuse or insult that is *ipso facto* defamatory.

- *Sketch v. Ajagbemokeferi (1989) 1 NWLR (Pt. 100) 678 SC*

16. Where a particular word or expression or statement complained of has a local connotation and can be defamatory only in a particular locality or region or within a sect, the onus is on the plaintiff to prove that a defamatory meaning will be placed on that word, expression or statement by those to whom it was published, as the meaning of such word or expression vary from locality to locality.

- Sketch v. Ajagbemokeferi (1989) 1 NWLR (Pt. 100) 678 SC

17. An utterer of defamation is not liable, without more, for the individual or collective responsibility of those who choose to repeat whatever the utterer may have said.

- Acka v. Akure (1987) 1 NWLR (Pt. 47) 74 CA

18. Slander is actionable without proof of special damage.

- Egbe v. Adefarasin (1987) 1 NWLR (Pt. 47) 1 SC

19. For the purposes of the Limitation Law, time in a slander actionable per se, starts to run on the publication of the words complained of.

- Egbe v. Adefarasin (1987) 1 NWLR (Pt. 47) 1 SC

20. For the defence of qualified privilege to succeed in an action for libel, the defendant must establish that the person who made the communication complained about had an interest or duty to make it to the person to whom it was made, and the person to whom it was so made, had a corresponding interest or duty to receive it.

- Akamagwunna v. S.B.N. Ltd (1995) 3 NWLR (Pt. 383) 343 CA

- African Newspapers Ltd v. Ciroma (1996) 1 NWLR (Pt. 423) 156 at 159 CA

- Ugo v. Okafor (1996) 3 NWLR (Pt. 438) 542 CA

36.2 Trespass to the Person

1. Ordinarily, an improper arrest of a person is a trespass to the person, which unless it can otherwise be justified will attract liability against the tortfeasor.

- Ikonne v. C.O.P. (1986) 4 NWLR (Pt. 36) 473 SC

2. The law is that every person's body is inviolate. Thus, an intentional interference, however slight, with the elementary civil right to security of a person, and self-determination in relation to his own body, constitutes trespass to the person. Tresspass to the person may take three forms, namely: battery, assault and false imprisonment.

- *Collins v. Wilcock (1984) 3 All E.R. 374*

3. Any trespass to the person of another, however slight, gives a right of action to recover nominal damages. Even where there has been no physical injury, substantial damages may be awarded for the injury to a person's dignity or for discomfort or inconvenience.

- *Okonkwo v. Ogbogu (1996) 5 NWLR (Pt. 449) 420 SC*

36.3 Assault and Battery

1. Assault is any wilful attempt or threat to inflict injury upon the person of another, when coupled with an apparent present ability to do so, and any intentional display of force such as would give the victim reason to fear or expect immediate bodily harm.

- *Collins v. Wilcock (1984) 3 All E.R. 374*

2. A medical practitioner will be liable for assault or other forms of trespass to the person where he proceeds to administer medical measure or treatment on a patient without obtaining the informed consent of such patient.

- *Okonkwo v. M.D.P.D.T. (1999) 9 NWLR (Pt. 617) 1 at 8 CA*

3. Battery is the direct and intentional application of any physical force to the plaintiff.

- *Collins v. Wilcock (1984) 3 All E.R. 374*
- *Wilson v. Pringle (1986) 2 All E.R. 440 CA*

4. A defendant in an action for assault or battery may escape liability by raising the plea of reasonable self-defence. The self-defence must however, be reasonably commensurate with the attack.

- *Turner v. M.G.M. Pictures Ltd (1950) 1 All E.R. 449*

36.4 False Imprisonment

1. False imprisonment is an intentional instigation of the arrest and detention of a person without reasonable or probable cause. The tort of false imprisonment also consists of the act of continuing a lawful imprisonment longer than is justifiable.

> - *Barau v. Chaba (1995) 1 NWLR (Pt. 371) 357 at 361 CA*
> - *Okonkwo v. Ogbogu (1996) 5 NWLR (Pt. 449) 420 SC*

2. To succeed in an action for false imprisonment, the plaintiff must show that it was the defendant who was actively instrumental in setting the law in motion against him.

> - *Okonkwo v. Ogbogu (1996) 5 NWLR (Pt. 449) 420 SC*

3. Every restraint of the liberty of a free man is an imprisonment, even if he was not restrained within the walls of any common prison. Thus, where a customer of a bank was not allowed to leave the bank premises by the bank's gateman, the tort of false imprisonment was said to have been committed.

> - *Union Bank (Nig.) Ltd v. Ajagu (1990) 1 NWLR (Pt. 126) 328 CA*

36.5 Malicious Prosecution

1. Malicious prosecution is an action for damages brought by a plaintiff, against whom a criminal proceedings was initiated without reasonable and probable cause, which was however, terminated in his favour.

> - *Barau v. Chaba (1995) 1 NWLR (Pt. 371) 357 CA*
> - *Bayol v. Ahemba (1999) 10 NWLR (Pt. 623) 381 SC*

2. For a plaintiff to succeed in an action for malicious prosecution, he must plead and successfully establish in evidence that the prosecution was commenced at the instance of the defendant who set the law in motion against him on a criminal charge; that he was prosecuted and the criminal prosecution was determined in his favour; that the prosecution was without reasonable and probable cause; and that the

prosecution was instituted maliciously.

- *Garba v. Maigoro (1992) 5 NWLR (Pt. 243) 588 CA*
- *Barau v. Chaba (1995) 1 NWLR (Pt. 371) 357 at 359, 361 CA*
- *Bayol v. Ahemba (1999) 10 NWLR (Pt. 623) 381 SC*

3. In an action for malicious prosecution, the requirement that the prosecution must have terminated in favour of the plaintiff does not mean that the plaintiff has to be discharged on the merits. It suffices if the plaintiff is discharged or where a *nolle prosequi* is entered by the Attorney General staying further proceedings on the indictment.

- *Yeboah v. Boateng (1963) 1 G.L.R. 182*
- *Barau v. Chaba (1995) 1 NWLR (Pt. 371) 357 CA*

4. Malicious prosecution will also lie against a defendant where the plaintiff was acquitted of the charge in question but convicted of a lesser offence.

- *Boaler v. Holder (1887) 3 T.L.R. 546*

5. A defendant, who maliciously makes a false statement against a plaintiff and causes a judicial act, like the issue of arrest warrant to the prejudice of the plaintiff, will be liable for malicious prosecution even though he may not technically have been the prosecutor in the strict sense.

- *Balogun v. Amubikahun (1989) 3 NWLR (Pt. 107) 18 SC*

6. When a complainant makes a report to the police and strenuously pursues it through mischievous lying, and the police not only makes an arrest of the incriminated person, but proffers a charge against him and takes him to court for prosecution, the complainant has set the law in motion for a person clothed with authority to arrest and charge the incriminated person.

- *Balogun v. Amubikahun (1989) 3 NWLR (Pt. 107) 18 SC*

7. Where a person makes a charge to the police and an arrest is made, the person making the charge, if liable at all will be liable for false imprisonment but if he goes before a Magistrate who thereupon issues a warrant or summons, then his liability, if any, is for malicious prosecution.

- *Iwunze v. Edoka (1995) 5 NWLR (Pt. 394) 174 CA*

36.6 Tresspass to Land

1. Trespass to land means any unjustifiable interference with land in the possession of a party. It constitutes the slightest disturbance to the possession of land by a person who cannot show a better right to possession.

- *Imona-Russel v. Niger Construction Ltd. (1987) 3 NWLR (Pt. 60) 298 SC*
- *Bamgbade v. Balogun (1994) 1 NWLR (Pt. 323) 718 CA*
- *Queen v. Uche (1994) 6 NWLR (Pt. 350) 329 CA*
- *NITEL Plc. v. Rockonoh Prop. Co. Ltd. (1995) 2 NWLR (Pt. 378) 473 at 480 CA*
- *Eze v. Obiefuna (1995) 6 NWLR (Pt. 404) 639 SC*

2. It is settled law that every person in exclusive possession of land can bring an action for trespass against any person other than the true owner or a person with a better title in respect of any interference with his possession. Therefore, for a plaintiff to succeed in an action for trespass, he must establish exclusive possession of the land at the material time.

- *Adelaja v. Fanoiki (1990) 2 NWLR (Pt. 131) 137 SC*
- *Obi v. Ozor (1991) 9 NWLR (Pt. 213) 94 at 98 CA*
- *Tewogbade v. Obadina (1994) 4 NWLR (Pt. 338) 326 SC*
- *NITEL Plc. v. Rockonoh Prop. Co. Ltd. (1995) 2 NWLR (Pt. 378) 473 CA*

3. Where a person who initially entered upon land lawfully or pursuant to an authority given by the true owner or person in possession, subsequently abuses his position or that authority, he becomes a trespasser *ab initio* and his misconduct will relate back to make his initial entry trespass.

- *Ajibade v. Pedro (1992) 5 NWLR (Pt. 241) 257 SC*

4. Liability under the rule in *Ryland v. Fletcher* is proved when the plaintiff shows that the defendant brings on his land and collects and keeps there anything likely to do mischief if it escaped.

- *Israel Wuraola v. Arewa Textiles Ltd (1975) N.N.L.R. 74, High Court of North-Central State. Suit No. NCH/18/73*

5. A customary tenant can maintain an action in trespass against his landlord so far as he is in possession. But this is always subject to the condition that the landlord's title to reversionary interest is not placed in jeopardy.

- *Olugbode v. Sangodeyi (1996) 4 NWLR (Pt. 444) 500 SC*

36.7 Detinue and Conversion

1. Detinue is an action which lies for the recovery of a chattel wrongfully detained by a defendant, coupled with an unqualified and unjustifiable refusal to deliver it up following a demand by the plaintiff, or in the alternative, payment of its value, together with damages for its detention.

- *Rosenthal v. Alderton & Sons (1946) K.B. 374*

2. In an action for detinue, a successful plaintiff is entitled to an order of specific restitution of the chattel, or in default, its value and also damages for its detention up to the date of judgment.

- *Kosile v. Folarin (1989) 3 NWLR (Pt. 107) 1 SC*
- *Oluwa Glass Co. v. Ehinlanwo (1990) 7 NWLR (Pt. 160) 14 CA*

3. For an action in detinue to succeed, the plaintiff must have made a demand to the defendant for the return of the chattel. If the defendant, on receipt of this notice of demand, persists in keeping the chattel, he will be liable in an action for detinue.

- *Kosile v. Folarin (1989) 3 NWLR (Pt. 107) 1 SC*

4. For a plaintiff to succeed in an action for detinue, he must establish by pleading the wrongful detention of his chattel by the defendant and the refusal by the defendant to return the chattel after demand.

- *Yisau v. Wema Bank (2001) 11 WRN 91 CA*

5. Detinue differs from conversion. Detinue is in the form of an action in *rem* whereby the plaintiff seeks specific restitution of his chattel resulting in judgment for the delivery up of the chattel or payment of its value as assessed at the time of judgment and for damages for its detention; while an action for

conversion is a purely personal action which entitles the plaintiff to a single sum which is the value of the chattel at the date of the conversion.

  - *Kosile v. Folarin (1989) 3 NWLR (Pt. 107) 1 SC*
  - *Ajikawo v. Ansaldo (Nig.) Ltd (1991) 2 NWLR (Pt. 173) 359 CA*
  - *Ordia v. Piedmont (Nig.) Ltd (1995) 2 NWLR (Pt. 379) 516 SC*

6. Conversion is an act of deliberate dealing with a chattel in a manner inconsistent with the plaintiff's right whereby the plaintiff is deprived of the use and possession of it.

  - *Owena Bank (Nig.) Ltd v. N.S.C.C. Ltd (1993) 4 NWLR (Pt. 290) 698 CA*

7. A claim in conversion is a claim for value of the chattel, be it goods or document. The claim is in the nature of special damages, which must be specifically pleaded and the particulars given.

  - *Owena Bank (Nig.) Ltd v. N.S.C.C. Ltd (1993) 4 NWLR (Pt. 290) 698 CA*

36.8 Nuisance

1. Nuisance is an act or omission which is an interference with, a disturbance of or an annoyance to a person in the exercise or enjoyment of his right as a member of the public, when it is a public nuisance, or his right of ownership or occupation of land or of some easement, profit or other right used or enjoyed in connection with land, when it is a private nuisance.

  - *Eholor v. Idahosa (1992) 2 NWLR (Pt. 223) 323 CA*

2. For a plaintiff to succeed in an action for nuisance, he must show and establish a substantial injury to himself arising from the nuisance. The existence of the nuisance *per se* does not provide a remedy.

  - *Adediran v. Interland Transport Ltd (1991) 9 NWLR (Pt. 214) 155 SC*

3. In Nigeria, the distinction between public and private nuisance has been abolished by the 1979 Constitution and therefore the exercise of the right of action for nuisance is no longer based on or determined by the distinction.

> - *Adediran v. Interland Transport Ltd (1991) 9 NWLR (Pt. 214) 155 at 163 SC*

36.9 Negligence

1. Negligence is the failure to take reasonable care where there is a duty, and it is attributable to the person whose failure to take reasonable care has resulted in damage to another. In other words, it is the omission or failure to do something which a reasonable man under similar circumstance would do or the doing of something which a reasonable and prudent man would not do.

> - *U.B.A Ltd v. Achoru (1990)6 NWLR (Pt. 156) 254 SC*
> - *Odinaka v. Moghalu (1992) 4 NWLR (Pt. 233) 1 SC*
> - *N.A.B Ltd. V Felly Keme (Nig.) Ltd. (1995) 4 NWLR (Pt. 387) 100 at 106 CA*
> - *Progress Bank (Nig.) Ltd. V. Ugonna (Nig.) Ltd. (1996) 3 NWLR (Pt. 435) 202 at 206 CA*
> - *N.B.C. Plc V Borgundu (1999) 2 NWLR (Pt. 591) 408 at 412 CA*

2. Duty of care in negligence exists where there is a sufficient relationship of proximity or neighbourhood, as between a wrongdoer and the person who has suffered damage, such that in the reasonable contemplation of the wrongdoer, carelessness on his part may likely cause damage to the injured person.

> - *Donoghue v. Stevenson (1932) A.C. 562 at 597*
> - *Abusomwan v. Mercantile Bank Ltd. (1987) 3 NWLR (Pt. 60) 196 SC*
> - *Enyika v. Shell B.P. Pet. Dev. Co. (1997) 10 NWLR (Pt. 526) 638 CA*
> - *Aliyu v. Aturu (1999) 7 NWLR (Pt. 612) 536 CA*

3. A medical doctor owes his patient a duty of care, which the

law regards as reasonable. Thus, failure on the part of a medical doctor to administer medical treatment, which he ought to have administered to a patient admitted in his hospital and who eventually died, is a breach of such duty and amounts to a criminal offence.

- *Okonkwo v. M.D.P.D.T. (1999) 9 NWLR (Pt. 617) 1 at 5 CA*

4. Owing a duty of care, without more, and without the court deciding correctly that the duty of care has been breached would not make a defendant liable to the plaintiff.

- *S.G.S. v. Rastico (Nig.) Ltd (1992) 6 NWLR (Pt. 245) 93 CA*

5. The heads of claim for damages for 'pain and suffering' and 'loss of amenities of life', in personal injury cases are two distinct and separate claims arising from the same damage and injury. Unlike claim for damages for pain and suffering which is a head of claim used to describe the pain associated with the injury resulting from the damage suffered, claim for damages for loss of amenities of life is a head of claim based on the loss resulting from the extent of disability, that is, impairment of the enjoyment of facilities of life.

- *U.B.A Ltd. v. Achoru (1990) 6 NWLR (Pt. 156) 254 SC*

6. If an owner or his servant is driving a vehicle, the fact that the vehicle overturns on the highway, that a wheel comes off, that a tyre bursts or that any part of the vehicle breaks and causes a collision is an evidence on which, in the absence of a satisfactory explanation, negligence on the part of the owner can be found.

- *N.B.C. Plc V Borgundu (1999) 2 NWLR (Pt. 591) 408 at 415 CA*

7. The burden of proof of negligence falls upon the plaintiff who alleges negligence. This is because, negligence is a question of fact, not law, and it is the duty of the person who asserts it to prove it. Failure to prove particulars of negligence pleaded is fatal to the plaintiff's case.

- *Alhaji Otaru & Sons Ltd. v. Idris (1999) 6 NWLR (Pt. 606) 330 SC*

8. The fact that two motor vehicles collided on the highway raises

a presumption that one or other or both drivers was or were negligent. The onus is on the defendant to rebut the presumption of negligence by showing that he or she was not negligent. In the absence of evidence that one driver was more to blame than the other, the blame should be apportioned equally between the two drivers.

> - M. Ibrahim Abba v. Mrs. Margret A. Mohammed & Anor (1975) N.N.L.R. 208, High Court of North-Central State. Suit No. NCH/26/74

9. The maxim *res ipsa loquitur* literally means, "the thing speaks for itself", and is applicable to actions for injury by negligence where no proof of such negligence is required beyond the accident itself. Where the maxim is pleaded and applied, it shifts the onus of proof from the plaintiff to the defendant.

> - Management Enterprises Ltd. v. Otusanya (1987) 2 NWLR (Pt. 55) 179 SC

10. "Contributory negligence" means the failure by a plaintiff to use reasonable care for the safety of himself or his property, so that he becomes 'the author of his own wrong'.

> - N.B.C. Plc V Borgundu (1999) 2 NWLR (Pt. 591) 408 CA

11. Where a careful, reasonable and law abiding user of the public highway successfully avoids collision with a negligent or reckless user, but suffers damage from a collision with another object as a result of the avoidance with the reckless user, the damage so subsequently suffered is the direct result of the negligence or recklessness of the other road user.

> - U.B.A Ltd. v. Achoru (1990) 6 NWLR (Pt. 156) 254 SC
> - N.B.C. Plc v. Borgundu (1999) 2 NWLR (Pt. 591) 408 CA

12. Electricity, being a very dangerous thing, if it should escape, the "owner" thereof owes a duty to the consumers to exercise reasonable care and skill to ensure that the consumers should not suffer damages and the rule in *Rylands v. Fletcher* will apply.

> - NEPA v. Alli (1992) 8 NWLR (Pt. 259) 279 SC

13. A hotel or its management is not liable without more, for the theft of a car parked by a hotel lodger on its premises. There is no duty of care on the part of the hotel to safeguard the car of

an hotel lodger from being stolen, and security arrangement at the hotel is merely an inducement to attract customers and cannot *per se* constitute a contract of bailment between customers or visitors and the owners of the hotel.

- *Imo Concorde Hotel Ltd v. Anya (1992) 4 NWLR (Pt. 234) 210 CA*

14. For a master to be vicariously liable for the act of his servant, it must be established that the servant was at the material time in the employment of the master; and that the negligence occurred whilst the servant was acting in the course of his employment.

- *Union Bank (Nig.) Ltd. v. Ajagu (1990) 1 NWLR (Pt. 126) 328 CA*
- *Eseigbe v. Agholor (1990) 7 NWLR (Pt. 161) 234 CA*

15. A person sued in a vicarious capacity cannot be liable where the liability of the principal tortfeasor cannot be established.

- *Management Enterprises Ltd. v. Otusanya (1987) 2 NWLR (Pt. 55) 179 SC*

16. An employer is, in general, and subject to exceptions, not liable for the negligent act of an independent contractor.

- *Shell Dev. Co. Ltd. v. Otoko (1990) 6 NWLR (Pt. 159) 693 CA*
- *N.B.C. Plc. v. Borgundu (1999) 2 NWLR (Pt. 591) 408 CA*

17. It is well settled that a negligent mis-statement, whether spoken or written, which causes financial loss, may give rise to an action in damages for negligence, despite the absence of any fiduciary or contractual relationship between the parties.

- *Hedley Byrne & Co. Ltd. v. Heller & Partners Ltd. (1964) A.C. 465*

18. It is trite law that a party claiming special damages in cases of tort, must strictly prove by way of credible evidence that he did suffer such special damages as he claimed.

- *Okunzua v. Amosu (1992) 6 NWLR (Pt. 248) 416 SC*

Index

examination malpractice 20
exceptional circumstances 397
Exchange Control Act 314
exclusion clause 312
exclusion of evidence 220
exclusion of other children 137
Exclusive Economic Zone 335, 371
exclusive jurisdiction
73, 148, 234, 235, 277
exclusive possession 255, 422
execution 107, 147, 396
executory judgment 215
exemption clause 313
exercise of jurisdiction 17, 233
expenses 56
extension of time 377
extension of time to appeal 48
extensive crimes 369
extradition proceedings 148

F

fact not pleaded 376
failure to plead 378
fair hearing 71, 72, 148, 231
false imprisonment 421
family head 259
family land 259, 260
family status 137
Fatal Accident Law 177
female witnesses 206, 207
Femi Falana V
fiduciary duties 61
final order 222
financial statement 63
findings of the trial court 39
first information report 88
first instance courts 203
flag 187, 336
foetus 359
forbearances 295
forced resignation 240
foreclosure 264
foreign arbitration proceedings 27
forest 207
fraud 219
fraudulent trading 54
free and voluntary confession of
guilt 94
freedom of association 75

freedom of movement 75, 148
freedom of speech 149
freehold interest 374
fresh plea 87
frustration 324
full disclosure 175
functus officio 213, 214, 222
fundamental human rights 71
fundamental right 75, 112, 152
fundamental right to life 147
Fundamental Rights (Enforcement
Procedure) Rules 73

G

Gani Fawehinmi V
general meeting 64
grant of land 249
ground for the grant of stay of
execution 398
ground of action 416
ground of appeal 40
ground of insanity 99
grounds of appeal 38, 42
guilty 368

H

habeas corpus17, 26
handwritten prescription 362
harassment 392
Harris V
Hauzi 208, 210
head of the family 137
hearsay evidence 120, 121
heir 210
hereditary chief 112
high seas 336
hire purchase agreement 311
Holden V
holding company 54
honour and dignity of the court 80
human rights 152
humanitarian law 285
husband and wife 303

V

valid marriage 139
vested 356
vicarious liability 63, 239
void act 22
voidable 304
voluntary confession 131
voyage policy 181

W

wakf 210
war 283
war crimes 185, 189, 289
wardship jurisdiction 363
Warsaw Convention 7
warship 292
ways of removing public officers 22
welfare of every child 144

widow 209
wife 178
Will 116
winding up 68, 69
witchcraft 102
withdraw a citizen's passport 75
witnesses 87
worker 237
working hours 239
writ of certiorari 17
writ of prohibition 25
writ of quo warranto 26
writ of summons 173, 230, 232, 379, 380, 381, 391
wrongful dismissal 152, 243, 244
wrongful repudiation 324

Y

Yoruba customary law 138, 254
Yoruba native law 269

Printed in the United Kingdom by
Lightning Source UK Ltd., Milton Keynes
136719UK00001B/7/A